T0334628

ELECTRICITY COST MODELING CALCULATIONS

ELECTRICITY COST MODELING CALCULATIONS

MONICA GREER

AMSTERDAM • BOSTON • HEIDELBERG • LONDON
NEW YORK • OXFORD • PARIS • SAN DIEGO
SAN FRANCISCO • SINGAPORE • SYDNEY • TOKYO

Academic Press is an imprint of Elsevier

Academic Press is an imprint of Elsevier
30 Corporate Drive, Suite 400, Burlington, MA 01803, USA
The Boulevard, Langford Lane, Kidlington, Oxford, OX5 1GB, UK

Notices
Knowledge and best practice in this field are constantly changing. As new research and
experience broaden our understanding, changes in research methods, professional practices,
or medical treatment may become necessary.

Practitioners and researchers must always rely on their own experience and knowledge
in evaluating and using any information, methods, compounds, or experiments described
herein. In using such information or methods they should be mindful of their own safety
and the safety of others, including parties for whom they have a professional responsibility.

To the fullest extent of the law, neither the Publisher nor the authors, contributors,
or editors, assume any liability for any injury and/or damage to persons or property as a
matter of products liability, negligence or otherwise, or from any use or operation of any
methods, products, instructions, or ideas contained in the material herein.

Library of Congress Cataloging-in-Publication Data
Greer, Monica.
    Electricity cost modeling calculations / Monica Greer.
       p. cm.
    Includes bibliographical references and index.
    ISBN 978-0-12-810217-6
    1. Electric utilities–United States–Costs–Mathematical models. 2. Electric
utilities–Rates–Estimates–United States. 3. Electric power consumption–United
States–Forecasting–Mathematics. 4. Electric power plants–Load–Mathematical
models. I. Title.
    HD9685.U5G755 2011
    333.79–dc22

                                                                    2010012954

British Library Cataloguing-in-Publication Data
A catalogue record for this book is available from the British Library.

For information on all Academic Press publications,
visit our website: www.elsevierdirect.com

Printed in the United States of America
10   11   12   13   14   15   9   8   7   6   5   4   3   2   1

Working together to grow
libraries in developing countries

www.elsevier.com | www.bookaid.org | www.sabre.org

ELSEVIER   BOOK AID
             International   Sabre Foundation

CONTENTS

I decided to work toward my doctorate in economics because I was fascinated by the subject of economics and had a professor who truly inspired me. I especially enjoyed the theory of market structure, in particular monopoly theory and natural monopolies.

While working on my master's degree at Indiana University, I was intrigued by the attempt of the Indianapolis Power and Light Company's (IPL's) attempt to takeover the then Public Service of Indiana (PSI, which became Cinergy and is now Duke). IPL was sort of the "donut hole," serving the metropolis of Indianapolis, while PSI served the surrounding area (the "donut"). My thinking was that it would be more efficient if one entity served the entire service territory rather than the two separate entities (in other words, one served the entire "donut"). Subsequently, my master's thesis examined cases in which horizontal mergers between utilities could be welfare enhancing, which essentially boiled down to cost modeling and the savings that could be realized from such mergers.

In 1996, the Federal Energy Regulatory Commission (FERC) Orders 888 and 889 were passed. FERC Orders 888 and 889 were implemented to facilitate wholesale competition in the bulk power supply market. More specifically, Order 888 addresses the issues of open access to the transmission network, giving FERC the jurisdiction over all transmission issues, especially pricing. Order 889 requires utilities to establish electronic systems to share information about available transmission capacity. These are discussed in more detail in the chapter on regulation (Chapter 3).

While thinking about a dissertation topic, I began to study the cost models that supported the electric industry, which were typically under some sort of price regulation (since electric utilities were deemed "natural monopolies," as discussed in Chapter 2 of this book). What I found was that these cost models were lacking, not only did they inappropriately assume that distributed electricity was a single output but they also were not true cost models in the sense that they did not conform to the properties to which a true cost model should conform (this is discussed in subsequent chapters). As a result, in my dissertation, I developed an appropriately specified cost model, which is quadratic in output and detailed in Chapter 4 and in the case studies presented in Chapters 7 and 8.

More recently, I began thinking about the structure of prices and the appropriate specification of the cost functions employed to model the production (and distribution) of electricity; that is, a total cost function should be cubic in output, experiencing regions of increasing, constant, and decreasing returns to scale. Only in this form can appropriately shaped average and marginal cost curves result, the latter of which could then be used to price electricity efficiently, which means that price reflects the marginal cost of supplying power at a given time. As such, only under these conditions can the true variable (i.e., marginal) cost of supplying electricity be estimated, a cost that increases with output, since higher-cost generating units come online to provide service. Figure P.1 displays such a cost function. This cubic form yields the average and marginal cost curves depicted in Figure P.2.

Only the proper specification of costs facilitates the appropriate pricing of electricity that truly incentivizes producers to invest in new generating technologies and demand-side management and consumers to invest in energy efficiency and become more conservative, so that a real reduction in greenhouse gases can occur and real climate change is possible. To date, this is the missing link: This problem is not just a supply-side or demand-side issue; it is a fundamental issue, which essentially has been ignored thus far. And that is the purpose of this book: effecting a real change in the methodology by which rates are set and costs are modeled so as to precipitate the changes that need to be made to combat global warming of the planet on which we live.

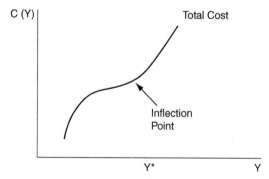

Figure P.1 An appropriately shaped total cost function. A cost function that is cubic in output (Y). Y* denotes the inflection point, which is the point at which returns to scale go from increasing to decreasing.

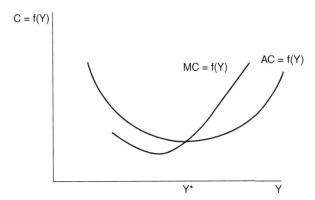

Figure P.2 Average and marginal cost curves. At output levels $Y < Y^*$, increasing returns to scale are indicated by declining average costs, $AC = f(Y)$. At $Y = Y^*$, returns to scale are constant (and average cost = marginal cost). Beyond this level of output, $Y > Y^*$, diminishing returns to production set in (i.e., marginal cost increases with output) and decreasing returns to scale are experienced.

With all this said, the motivation of this book emanates from my desire to effect a change in the way that rates are set in the United States (and possibly in other places that have similarly set rate structures or regulations). Having worked for a public utility commission (and a regulated, investor-owned utility), it frustrates me as an economist to see that the true cost of service is not the mechanism by which rates are set; rather, other forces (such as politics, demand elasticities, and the ability to hire attorneys to argue on behalf of their customers, namely industrial users) influence the rate-making process.

SOME BASIC ECONOMIC THEORY

Fundamentally, it has been ingrained in me that consumers (and producers) respond to prices, which should reflect the cost of providing a particular service, in this case electricity. To wit, Figure P.3 depicts the equilibrium price (P^*) and output (Y^*), which are set by the interaction of supply (or marginal cost, MC) and demand.

Granted, we are not discussing a perfectly competitive market. That being said, this paradigm should not be dismissed outright, as there are lessons to be learned here. First and foremost, price should always be a function of cost, which is not necessarily the case. It has been my experience in the electric industry that the price (or the rate charged to end users) has

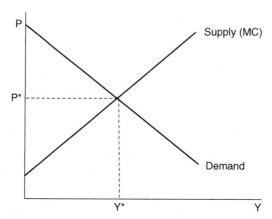

Figure P.3 Market equilibrium. My apologies. Basic in nature, this figure merely represents the laws of supply and demand.

little to do with the cost of providing such service but rather tends to be a function of other factors, politics among them.

Several years ago, I had the first flavor of the politics of regulation for electric utilities. As the economist at a state regulatory commission (in a state with predominately coal-fired generation), I struggled to understand the logic behind the methodology of how rates were set and how costs were allocated among the various customer classes. I still struggle with this today, which is expounded on in this manuscript.

The bottom line is that the antiquated methodology under which rates have been set in the United States (and possibly other countries using the same rate-making processes) are archaic; they do little (if anything) to provide the proper incentives to end users to use energy wisely.

A NEW REGULATORY PARADIGM

With all of this said, I recently attended a conference on climate change sponsored by the National Association of Regulatory Utility Commissioners. There, I was pleased to hear talk of a new "regulatory paradigm," which includes a departure from the traditional methodology by which rates have been set in this country. Needless to say, I was very pleased to hear this. If we are to achieve a reduction in the amount of greenhouse gases being emitted into the atmosphere, such a new paradigm must transpire; both producers and consumers must be incentivized to pursue energy efficiency, demand-side management, and conservation, in general.

Renewable resources must be a part of the generation mix and the way that investor-owned utilities provide returns to shareholders be changed. Utility investment in renewables (or avoided costs) should allow a higher return to investors, while those in the fossil-fuel-fired generation return a lower return, since the latter produce the very greenhouse gas emissions that wreak havoc on the environment. Finally, it is time to pay the piper, and this is everyone's responsibility.

ACKNOWLEDGMENTS

This book has been quite an endeavor and would not have been possible without the loving support of my family: my husband David and "daughter" Ali Anne; my parents, David and Helen, who instilled in me the value of an education and a strong work ethic; and my Graduate school Professors, who believed in me and encouraged me when times were tough. They are: Subir Chakrabarti, Partha Deb, David Freshwater, Roy Gardner, and Frank Scott.

CHAPTER 1

Introduction

The issue of global climate change and its consequences has become one of growing concern in recent years. As a result, there has been an increased focus on energy efficiency and the development of alternative sources of energy, particularly renewable resources but also nuclear and clean coal technologies, such as carbon capture and storage (CCS).[1] "Going green" has become the buzzword of the early 21st century.

As a result, much of the work being performed at utilities is focused on the potential impacts of conservation and energy efficiency on load forecasts, resource planning that includes renewable resources and, in the case of investor-owned utilities, shareholder value. What seems to be missing are well-designed rate-setting mechanisms that provide the proper incentives to consumers to make the appropriate choices in energy efficiency; in other words, the majority of the methodologies by which electric rates are set in the United States (and some other countries that regulate the rates paid by end users) provide neither the proper incentive to consumers nor the reward for "doing what is right." The bottom line is that rates are not based on economic efficiency, which occurs when fixed costs are recovered via fixed charges (i.e., customer- or demand-related costs) and variable costs via the energy charge. Instead, other motivations tend to guide the rate-making process, politics being among them (these are detailed later and in Chapter 10, "Pricing").

In the Preface, Figure P.3 displays a market in equilibrium in which the market clearing price (P^*) and output (Y^*) are set by the interaction of the demand and supply (or marginal cost) curves. In this situation, it is clearly the case that

$$P^* = \text{marginal cost}$$

which, as the introductory economics text books tell us, is both allocatively and productively efficient. In addition, marginal cost pricing yields a welfare-maximizing outcome in which both the consumer and producer

---

[1] Renewable technologies have the added benefit of not being subject to the price volatility of fossil fuels but may have drawbacks that include intermittent availability and high initial capital costs.

Electricity Cost Modeling Calculations
DOI: 10.1016/B978-1-85617-726-9.00001-7

receive the maximum benefit possible. This is discussed in much more detail in the chapters on pricing and regulation. But for now, an excerpt from the section "The Marginal Cost Pricing Doctrine" of *Marginal Cost Pricing for Utilities: A Digest of the California Experience* makes this point well.

1.1 THE MARGINAL COST PRICING DOCTRINE

The "marginal cost pricing doctrine" is shorthand for the proposition that utility rates should be predicated upon marginal costs for the purpose of attaining economic efficiency by means of accurate price signals. The doctrine stems from Professor Alfred E. Kahn's hugely influential two-volume book, *The Economics of Regulation* (1970 and 1971). Kahn espoused marginal cost pricing as a means of bringing "economic efficiency" to regulated utilities. This pricing would result in "price signals" to consumers of sufficient accuracy that they could evaluate the appropriate economic level and timing of their use of utility services. Thus, the buying decisions of consumers is the means by which the end purpose of economic efficiency would be reached.

Quoting Professor Kahn, normative/welfare microeconomics concludes that "under pure competition, price will be set at marginal cost" (the price will equal the marginal cost of production), and this results in "the use of society's limited resources in such a way as to maximize consumer satisfactions" (economic efficiency) (vol. I, pp. 16–17).

The basis for the theory is clearcut: Since productive resources are limited, making the most effective use of these limited resources is a logical goal. In a competitive economy, consumers direct the use of resources by their buying choices. When they buy any given product or buy more of that product, they direct the economy to produce less of other products. The production of other products must be sacrificed in favor of the chosen product.

From this point, marginal cost theory takes a giant step. In essence, it states that, if consumers are to choose rationally whether to buy more or less of any product, the price they pay should equate to the cost of supplying more or less of that product. This cost is the marginal cost of the product. If consumers are charged this cost, optimum quantities are purchased, maximizing consumer satisfaction. If they are charged more, less than optimum quantities are purchased: The sacrifice of other, foregone products has been overstated. If they are charged less, the production of the product is greater than optimum: The sacrifice of other, foregone products has been understated. A price based on marginal costs is presumed to convey "price signals" that lead to the efficient allocation of resources. This is the theory, drawn from the microeconomic model of pricing under perfect competition, upon which the doctrine rests (Conkling, 1999).

To be fair, the reticence to adopt marginal cost pricing is due in large part to the thus far inability to accurately estimate or calculate the marginal cost of distributing electricity to various types of end users. And this aspect of the puzzle has been ignored thus far and is the primary motivation of this book: How do we accurately estimate the true cost of providing electric service so that rates can be set in an efficient manner, which provides the proper incentives to both producers and consumers to make the appropriate investments in energy efficiency, demand-side management, and conservation in general. (This is discussed in more detail in Chapter 10, "The Efficiency of Pricing Electricity.") Note: I am not ignoring the "naturally monopolistic" nature of the electric industry, which is discussed in detail in Chapter 2.

But first, I would like to provide a brief overview of the U.S. electric power industry, including the types of players (i.e., suppliers) and a general overview of the regulatory environment and its relationship to greenhouse gases.

1.2 A BRIEF OVERVIEW OF THE U.S. ELECTRIC MARKET
The structure of the U.S. electricity industry

The majority of the electricity that is distributed in the United States is by investor-owned utilities, which tend to be vertically integrated, which means that the same entity generates, transmits, and distributes electricity to the end users in its service territory. In the case of such investor-owned firms, traditional rate making is that a return to investors is earned on every kilowatt-hour sold, thus providing the incentive to sell as much as possible. Figure 1.1 displays the structure of the electric industry in the United States in 2006.

The players and their incentives

To assess the impact of various policies and rate-making schemes that are intended to affect climate change, it is necessary to distinguish each type of electric supplier and examine the incentives that each type faces. Unlike investor-owned utilities, whose objective is profit maximization, publicly and cooperatively owned utilities face their own set of circumstances and have their own objectives. Nonetheless, the ability to accurately estimate

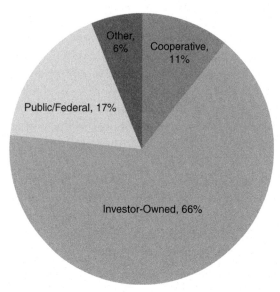

Figure 1.1 The structure of the electric industry in the United States, breakdown of 2006 sales by type of supplier

the true cost of providing service to various types of customers is tantamount to designing effective legislation despite the different objective functions faced by each, which are described here.

First and foremost, all utilities in the United States have an obligation to serve that is part of their franchise agreement, which means that they have been given an exclusive right to supply utility service to the customers that reside within that service territory. Whether a supplier is subject to certain types of regulation depends on the type of supplier, the state in which it operates, and whether it is vertically integrated or not. Each has its own objective function, which is discussed in the next section.

Objective functions: The players
Investor-owned utilities: Profit maximization
All investor-owned utilities in the United States are subject to some type of regulation, typically price and performance (for example, an obligation to serve native load and reliability in providing service). The objective function of the *regulated* investor-owned utility is to maximize profit (π), which is equal to total revenue (TR) less total cost (TC), subject to a

break-even constraint under a regulated price, P_r, while procuring (or generating) enough electricity to satisfy market demand, Y_m. That is,

$$\text{Maximize } \pi = \text{TR}(P_r, Y_m) - \text{TC}(p_i, Y_m) \qquad (1.1)$$

subject to

$$\text{TR} \geq \text{TC}$$

and

$$Y \geq Y_m$$

where Y = total output and p_i = the prices of inputs.

Under the type of regulation to which the utility is subject, which is discussed in more detail later (and in subsequent chapters), the price allowed by the regulator (P_r) includes an appropriate rate of return to investors. The intent here is to compensate the shareholders for the risks involved in holding the stock issued by the utility.

Publicly owned firms

Under the umbrella of publicly owned utilities are nonprofit organizations established to serve their communities at cost. While some generate their own electricity, many others serve to transmit and distribute power purchased from other wholesale generators, which are mostly federally owned entities such as the Tennessee Valley Authority (TVA) and the Bonneville Power Administration (BPA). (Some other power administrations include the Southeastern Power Administration, SEPA, and the Southwestern Power Administration, SWPA). This being said, some publicly owned entities do purchase from investor-owned or cooperatively owned entities. To best serve the public interest, the objective function is cost minimization subject to a break-even constraint (i.e., that total revenues cover total costs). This is given by equation (1.2):

$$\text{Minimize } C = f(Y, p_i) \qquad (1.2)$$

subject to

$$\text{Total Revenue} \geq \text{Total Cost}$$

where Y = output and p_i = price of inputs.

Organizational types include municipals, public power districts, and state authorities. Publicly owned utilities are exempt from certain taxes and typically can obtain new financing at lower rates than investor-owned utilities. In addition, they are given priority in the purchase of the less-expensive power produced by federally owned generators. These are discussed in much more detail in Chapter 3, "The U.S. Electric Markets, Structure, and Regulation."

Cooperatively owned firms

Rural electric cooperatives (RECs) are owned by the members of the cooperative and established to provide electricity to their members, which reside in rural areas deemed too costly to be served by investor-owned entities. (This is discussed in more detail in the case studies of Chapters 7 and 8.) Like publicly owned utilities, cooperatives enjoy benefits that the investor-owned utilities do not: They are able to borrow directly from various federal agencies created especially to serve them, predominantly the Rural Utilities Service (RUS), which allows them to obtain financing at a lower interest rate than the market. In addition, they enjoy certain tax exemptions and are given preference in the purchasing of lower-cost federally produced power.

Presumably, the cooperatives' incentives are welfare maximization (W), which is equal to consumer surplus (CS) plus producer surplus (PS), due to the coincidence of sellers and buyers. The objective function is displayed in equation (1.3). (They are also subject to satisfying market demand, Y_m.)

$$\text{Maximize } W = \text{PS} + \text{CS} \qquad (1.3)$$

subject to

$$Y \geq Y_m$$

where

PS = the area below P^* and above the supply curve in Figure P.3 in the Preface.

CS = the area above P^* and below the demand curve.

Cooperatively owned utilities are interesting in that they are not subject to price regulation in all states. In fact, fewer than 20 states regulate the rates charged by rural electric cooperatives, which are organized as either generation and transmission (G&T) or distribution only (also known as *member coops*). While not truly vertically integrated, member coops are typically contractually bound to a G&T coop to supply its power needs. While this is not always the case, it is far more common than not. This particular organizational structure was the impetus for the paper entitled "A Test of Vertical Economies for Non-Vertically Integrated Firms: The Case of Rural Electric Cooperatives" (Greer, 2008). This paper is presented as a case study in Chapter 8.

Other suppliers

Other types of suppliers include power marketers, independent power producers, public power agencies, power pools, and energy service providers. These are discussed in more detail in Chapter 3.

1.3 REDUCING CARBON EMISSIONS

Regulation and rate making

There is little doubt that any meaningful limit or reduction of carbon dioxide emissions will have a significant impact on the electric supply industry. For example, in the United States, the electric power sector accounted for about 40% of the total carbon dioxide emissions in 2006, which increased by 2.3% in 2007 (U.S. Department of Energy. Energy Information Administration, 2009). Also, these emissions have increased by over 14% from 1996 to 2006, as the demand of electricity has increased. Over 97% of carbon dioxide emissions come from burning coal and natural gas to generate electricity. This is not surprising, since together these fuels account for 69% of the fuel used to generate electricity in 2006.[2]

The U.S. electric power industry, regulation

In addition to the scale of the emissions and importance of fossil fuel in generating electricity, a complicating factor is that electric generation in the United States is regulated by a complex mix of federal and state laws and regulations. These laws and regulations have an influence on the generation resource choices that suppliers make. At the federal level, generation is subject to oversight by the Federal Energy Regulatory Commission (FERC). Since the mid-1990s, the FERC has increasingly relied on market mechanisms to determine prices and generation resources for the wholesale regions they regulate. Also, at the state level, 20 states modified or "restructured" their regulation of their electric utilities and permitted some or all utility customers the opportunity to choose their own supplier. However, 30 states remain regulated in the "traditional" or cost based/rate of return manner that has been used for over a century. And, while the mix of federal and state regulation may be unique to the United States, many features of markets and regulations apply to other countries as well.

---

[2] Based on data from the U.S. Department of Energy, Energy Information Administration, "Emissions of Greenhouse Gases Report" and "Electric Power Annual" 2007.

Regulation of investor-owned electric utilities in the United States

Average-cost pricing is the typical regulatory mechanism employed by the states that are price regulated in the United States, which is displayed in Figure 1.2. Not only does this permit the utility to recover its prudent costs but also compensates shareholders for the risk that they bear by holding the stock of the utility. Typically initiated by the utility when rates fall below average cost, a rate case is the formal procedure for determining the price of electricity sold to various types of end users (i.e., residential, commercial, industrial, or other). More specifically, this process involves the establishment of the utility's *revenue requirement*, which is the amount of dollars that must be collected from ratepayers to recover the utility's expenses (and required return, in the case of investor-owned utilities) for the period during which such rates would be in effect. Once the revenue requirement is determined, it is multiplied by the allowed rate of return (i.e., return on equity, ROE) set by the public regulatory commission. From here, allocations ("base rates") are made among the various rate or revenue classes served by the utility based on cost of service, price elasticity of demand, and politics. This is described in much more detail in Chapter 10, "Efficient Pricing of Electricity."

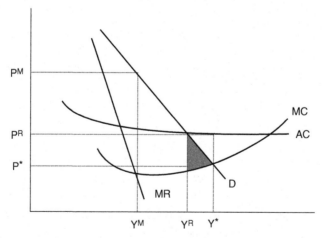

Figure 1.2 Average-cost pricing. Rate-of-return regulation creates a deadweight loss since price (P^R) is set above marginal cost, which yields a price of P^*. (The deadweight loss is approximated by the shaded triangle.) However, this loss is de minimis when compared to the lost consumer surplus from monopoly pricing without regulation, which is given by P^M

Aside: Issues with rate-of-return regulation, the Averch-Johnson effect

Despite its prevalence in the United States, rate-of-return regulation creates an inefficient use of resources, since it provides an incentive for the utility to overinvest in capital (and hence increase its rate base, which is one component of its revenue requirement), thus earning higher returns for the shareholders of investor-owned firms.

To show this, I appeal to Averch and Johnson (1962), which is reproduced in Rothwell and Gomez (2003) as Exercise 4.4. Averch and Johnson assume that the utility maximizes profit subject to the rate-of-return constraint:

$$\text{Max } \pi = P \times Q(L, K) - w \times L - r \times K \tag{1.4}$$

subject to

$$s = [P \times Q(L, K) - w \times L]/K \tag{1.5}$$

where

$P = $ Price.

$Q(L, K) = $ output, a function of capital (K) and labor (L).

$r = $ utility's cost of capital.

$s = $ allowed rate of return.

It is further assumed that $s > r$; that is, its rate of return is higher than its cost of capital.

Using the Lagrangian multiplier technique, equations (1.4) and (1.5) become

$$\text{Max } \pi = P \times Q(L, K) - w \times L - r \times K + \lambda \\ \times [s \times K + w \times L - P \times Q(L, K)] \tag{1.6}$$

where $\lambda = $ the Lagrangian multiplier.

The profit-maximizing levels of capital (K^*) and labor (L^*) are obtained by setting the derivative of profit with respect to each input and λ equal to zero then solving for that level of input. That is,

$$\partial \pi / \partial K = P \times Q_K - r + \lambda \times (s - P \times Q_K) = 0 \tag{1.7}$$

$$\partial \pi / \partial L = P \times Q_L - w + \lambda \times (w - P \times Q_L) = 0 \tag{1.8}$$

$$\partial \pi / \partial \lambda = s \times K + w \times L - P \times Q = 0 \tag{1.9}$$

where $Q_K = $ the marginal product of capital and $Q_L = $ the marginal product of labor. If the constraint is binding, then $s \times K + w \times L - P \times Q = 0$.

Since $\partial\pi/\partial\lambda = 0$, the rate-of-return constraint is satisfied at maximum profit. Averch and Johnson show that the marginal rate of technical substitution (MRTS) of labor for capital is given by

$$\text{MRTS} = \{r - [(s - r) \times \lambda/(1 - \lambda)]\}/w = (r - \alpha)/w \qquad (1.10)$$

If the allowed rate of return is equal to the cost of capital (i.e., $s - r = 0$), then $\text{MRTS} = r/w$; that is, the profit-maximizing level of capital and labor to be employed occurs where the ratio of input prices equals the marginal rate of technical substitution.

However, if $s > r$, then the higher return on capital motivates the firm to increase investment in capital beyond K^* (the efficient level of capital) so that

$$K > K^*,$$

a nonoptimal outcome.

In addition, and also from an investor-owned utility's perspective, the nature of rate-of-return regulation is such that the more electricity sold, the more money (i.e., profit) is earned. According to a recent "National Action Plan for Energy Efficiency" (U.S. Environmental Protection Agency, 2007) report, "Between rate cases utilities have a financial incentive to increase retail sales of electricity (relative to forecast or historical levels, which set 'base' rates) and to maximize the 'throughput' across their wires since there is often a significant incremental profit margin on such sales."

Furthermore, this report indicates three impediments to the pursuit of energy efficiency under traditional regulation:

1. Negative impact on cash flow and earnings if expenditures on energy efficiency and demand-side management are not recovered in a timely fashion.
2. Reduction in sales and revenues could lead to under-recovery of fixed costs.
3. Unlike supply-side investments (i.e., new generation), investments in energy efficiency do not earn a return.

Addressing the concerns raised by suppliers without causing harm to ratepayers requires compromises among regulators, utilities, and consumers. This is a global issue that transcends regulatory structure, whether one is an electric customer in a deregulated European market or in the United States. The result will be the same: Decarbonizing electricity entails extra costs that will be reflected in rates. But what is important here is *how* those rates are structured; unlike traditional rate making, which does not necessarily differentiate rates by the actual cost to serve (meaning the per kilowatt-hour charge vs. the demand charge) but rather are based on the elasticity of demand, politics, and so forth. In other words, rates are not set efficiently, which means that energy charges should be based on the marginal cost of providing electricity and demand charges based on fixed costs. This is discussed in more detail in the chapter on pricing.

1.4 INTERNALIZING THE COST OF REDUCING CARBON EMISSIONS

To effect a reduction in the amount of carbon emitted into the atmosphere, at least two events must occur. First, from an economic efficiency perspective, those who are causing the problem should pay for it. In the case of electricity, we can identify two sources:

1. Producers of electricity, since carbon emissions and greenhouse gases (GHGs) are the result of using fossil fuels to generate electricity.
2. Consumers of electricity, since without them there would be no need to produce electricity, which generates GHGs.

Subsequently, prices must rise, which could result in two things:

1. Conservation and investment in energy efficiency (on the part of consumers).
2. Seeking, investing in, and obtaining regulatory approval for energy efficiency programs, including demand-side management, renewable sources of power supply, clean coal and nuclear, and in generating technologies such as carbon capture and storage.

As stated previously, this entails a compromise between the utility, the state regulatory commission, and the ratepayers.

Current policy

Currently, policy measures being used or discussed to internalize the costs of carbon emissions include a carbon tax, cap and trade, and mandates including renewable portfolio standards and incentives for energy efficiency investments. With a tax, a specific carbon "price" is imposed directly on the producer, typically on a per-ton basis, while a cap-and-trade system sets a price indirectly by establishing an emissions limit that allows trading rights to emit so that the forces of supply and demand determine the price (at least theoretically). Both result in an increase in costs, which is borne by producers and passed onto consumers, as allowed by state regulatory commissions.

Clearly, rates will rise. How much depends on the relative price elasticities (producer vs. consumer) and on how much the state regulatory commission allows the utility to pass on to ratepayers and in what fashion.[3] The bottom line is that both producers and consumers are affected; as rates rise, consumers will likely reduce their consumption and begin to invest in energy efficiency (appliances, home weatherization, and other improvements), especially given the tax credits made available by both federal and state governments. The subsequent reduction in utility sales will affect shareholder returns, thus necessitating a rate case filing and an additional increase in rates.[4]

Before long, a vicious cycle emerges, which could be obviated by simply charging the marginal cost of the power that is consumed at the time that it is consumed. This is expounded on in subsequent chapters. A recent article by Kevin Bullis ("Pricing Carbon Emissions," 2009) provides a nice overview of the American Clean Energy and Security Act of 2009 which is also referred to as the Waxman-Markey bill, after its sponsors, Henry Waxman (D-Ca.) and Edward Markey (D-Mass.). This bill, which passed the House in June 2009, "would establish a cap and trade system to reduce greenhouse gases, an approach favored by most economists over conventional regulatory approaches because it provides a great deal of flexibility in how emissions targets are met. But it also contains mandates that could significantly reduce the cost savings that the cap and trade approach is supposed to provide." This bill is described in more detail in Chapter 3.

1.5 OPTIMAL RATE OR TARIFF DESIGN AND TAX CREDITS TO PROMOTE EFFICIENT USE OF ENERGY AND A REDUCTION IN CARBON EMISSIONS

The bottom line is that any policy implemented to encourage energy efficiency must be carefully crafted to protect both shareholders and consumers and not one at the other's expense. On the other hand,

---

[3] For example, will it be incorporated into the base rate or be a "below-the-line," item like environmental cost recovery (ECR) or demand-side management mechanisms? In states like Kentucky where construction work in process (CWIP) is allowed, such items are recovered "below the line" until a rate proceeding in which they become part of the base rate.

[4] Also known as *decoupling*, it is a method by which utility revenues are not tied to throughput, so that a reduction in sales of electricity may not affect the bottom line.

rates should be structured to encourage consumers to use energy wisely.[5]

Economic theory dictates that, as rates rise, consumers' incentives to increase investments in energy efficiency also rise. As a result, not only does the quantity demanded of electricity decline but so does the demand for it (ceteris paribus). The result is that, not only do emissions fall (a good thing), but also the utility's need for additional generating capacity is obviated (or at least delayed), a move that typically results in the utility's filing a rate case that subsequently ends in an upward adjustment in rates. However, investments in energy efficiency on the part of the consumer allow the utility to recover only (and earn a return on) its current (and possibly shrinking) rate base, which may diminish the utilities' ability to attract and retain appropriate levels of capital and provide safe, reliable service at a reasonable cost. As a result, it is likely that a series of rate increases will ensue. And this is the crux of the matter for regulators to consider in this critical matter. The regulators, after all, hold the key to the success of this endeavor by structuring rates and tariffs in such a way as to motivate consumers to use energy wisely and producers to make prudent investment choices that earn appropriate returns, either supply side or demand side.

Up to this point, much of the focus has been on appropriate policies that encourage producers to invest in energy efficiency and DSM. But, as noted, given the type of regulation that utilities face, there is clearly an inclination to *not* make such investments under the current regulatory scheme, as they may impede the utilities' fiduciary duty to its shareholders. One solution offered has been that of decoupling of revenues from throughput, which likely means that rates simply adjust (upward) so that the utility is held harmless. But this raises several questions. For example, how can behavior be altered to reduce usage during peak hours when

---

[5] Sovacool and Brown (2010) show that cities in Ohio (Toledo), Indiana (Indianapolis), and Kentucky (Lexington) have the highest carbon footprints in the United States, averaging 3.4 metric tons per person in 2005. This is not surprising, given that the generating plants serving the areas are coal fired and customers pay some of the lowest rates in the nation. In 2006, Kentucky ranked fourth and Indiana sixth in terms of lowest average retail price paid by all sectors. Toledo Edison's industrial customers' average retail price was actually lower than that paid by industrial customers of Kentucky Utilities, which serves Lexington Kentucky (4.42 vs. 4.50 cents/kWh); Kentucky ranked fifth and Indiana ranked seventh in terms of lowest average price paid by industrial customers. Kentucky also ranked fourth in terms of average retail price paid by residential customers in 2006. (Source: EIA, Office of Coal, Nuclear, Electric and Alternative fuels, www.eia.doe.gov/cneaf/electricity/esr/.)

power is the most expensive? Is it possible to devise a pricing mechanism to accomplish the objectives set forth in this chapter?

From the consumer's perspective, one could argue that the pricing signal is adequate to motivate investments in energy efficiency and conservation. However, it has been argued that, in relatively low-cost areas, electric rates are not sufficiently high to promote any real change in behavior. This is because the price is in the inelastic portion of the demand curve, so that a small price change has little impact on the quantity demanded. However, incorporating the effects of carbon legislation for controlling emissions of greenhouse gases, developing alternative technologies and fuel sources (renewable, even nuclear), and investing in more efficient appliances and equipment could be enough to precipitate some of the changes required to make a difference in the amount of carbon dioxide emitted into the atmosphere. But some fundamental issues are not addressed by uniform increases in rates (i.e., rates that change by a certain percentage without regard to the amount of electricity distributed).

Tariff design and rate-making issues

Earlier it was stated that effecting any real changes and minimizing losses to both consumers and producers requires compromise among consumers, producers, and public regulatory commissions. This means that tariffs must be designed to motivate investments in energy efficiency on the parts of both producers and consumers. Economic theory suggests that setting price equal to marginal cost maximizes total welfare, which is equal to consumer plus producer surplus. However, given the nature of the industry (a natural monopoly), this first best outcome is often deemed infeasible, since all costs may not be recovered (see Figure 1.2), which gives rise to the use of a second-best pricing scheme. Also known as *Ramsey prices*, this set of uniform prices serves to maximize total surplus (and minimize deadweight loss) subject to a break-even constraint. (This will be described more in chapter on pricing). To provide this in the electric utility industry, a modification must be made: Rather than a schedule of uniform prices, a nonuniform pricing scheme, in which prices *increase* with usage, could be used to approximate marginal cost and promote more efficient behavior and energy usage.

Marginal cost pricing for electric utilities

With this all said, pricing at marginal cost is not new. An excerpt from "Marginal Cost Pricing for Utilities: A Digest of the California Experience" (Conkling, 1999) informs us that this methodology was in place until 1996, when California became the first state to embark on the restructuring of its electric market (this, also known as the *California debacle*, is discussed in detail in Chapter 11). More specifically, Conkling advises that

> *California was not the first state to consider marginal costs. That distinction goes to the Wisconsin PUC. Its August 8, 1974 decision re Madison Gas and Electric Company is recognized as the first to hold that marginal costs, together with peak load pricing, were appropriate rate design considerations. The New York PUC was only five months behind California's March 16, 1976 adoption of marginal costs. The New York PUC's Opinion 76-15, of August 10, 1976, issued when Professor Kahn was chairman, held that marginal costs, as distinguished from average costs, are the most relevant costs for rote-setting [sic] and should be utilized to the greatest extent practicable. Other early states were Florida, North Carolina, and Connecticut.*

1.6 CONCLUSION

This book is divided into 11 chapters, including this introductory chapter. The second chapter encompasses the theories of natural monopoly and the related topics of scale and scope economies, network economies, and vertical integration. Also included is a review of the literature pertaining to the electric industry and these topics. In the third chapter, I offer a review of the types of regulation that have transpired and the problems therewith, along with a discussion of market structure. Currently proposed legislation is included, along with suggestions as to the direction that rate design should go in terms of the efficient pricing of electricity. Chapters 4 and 6 are similar, in that they introduce cost models and provide examples and exercises, so that the user may have hands-on experience with estimating the various models used to estimate economies of scale, scope, and vertical integration in the electric industry. Chapters 5, 7, and 8 include case studies, which are provided to illustrate the importance of the concepts introduced in Chapters 4 and 6. Chapter 5 has a study on the breaking up of the Bell System, a landmark decision based on faulty econometrics and model specification. In Chapters 7 and 8, I reproduce two previously published papers. Both include data on rural electric cooperatives and employ a properly specified quadratic cost function to estimate economies of scale, scope, and vertical integration for rural coops in 1997. Chapter 9 is a bit of a departure, in that the demand side is the focus. Load forecasting is an integral part of every electric utility's business and, given what has transpired over the past few decades, has come under increasing scrutiny by regulatory agencies. More sophisticated techniques have been developed and are discussed to some degree in this chapter. Chapter 10 is all about pricing electricity efficiently, which is a key element in promoting the efficient use of energy and in the subsequent reduction of greenhouse gas emissions into the atmosphere. This chapter provides an overview of how rates are designed (and their flaws) in the United States, along with a series of examples and exercises designed to illustrate various rate-making mechanisms and the shortcomings of each. The final chapter presents another case study, which details the pecuniary nature of the electric industry and the reasons that deregulation failed so abysmally in California.

CHAPTER 2

The Theory of Natural Monopoly

2.1 THE NATURAL MONOPOLY CONUNDRUM

Historically, conventional wisdom has held that certain markets were "naturally monopolistic," which means that, due to the presence of high fixed costs whose average declines with increases in output, efficiency is best obtained when there is only one supplier. According to Kahn (Kahn, p. 15), "the public utility industries are preeminently characterized in important respects by decreasing unit costs with increasing levels of output. That is indeed one important reason why they are organized as regulated monopolies: a 'natural monopoly' is an industry in which the economies of scale are such that one company supplies the entire demand. It is a reason, also, why competition is not supposed to work well in these industries." Included here are the markets for electricity, natural gas, telephone, and water services. It has often been argued that this phenomenon is driven by the irreversibility of the initial investment required to produce a particular good or service in a naturally monopolistic industry. More specifically, the underlying production technology of this product is such that there exists a level of output for which average cost is minimized; at levels of output below this level, average costs decline, and at levels above it, they rise. This, known as *economies of scale*, is investigated further in context to its relationship with the theory of natural monopoly.

Economists have spent many years attempting to assess that level of output at which the minimum efficient scale occurs. In some industries, such as the generation of electricity, consensus has been reached that, at least in 1970, most firms were producing in and around this level, given a particular production technology (Christensen and Greene, 1976). In other words, economies of scale in the generation of electricity had been exhausted.

Until recently, no one questioned that the production of electricity was in fact a natural monopoly, since, like telephony, what is required here is a network, a complex, interactive, interdependent connection of wires (by which individuals gain access to the local distribution company, which is connected to the transmission grid at various nodes). This network

Electricity Cost Modeling Calculations
DOI: 10.1016/B978-1-85617-726-9.00002-9

represents an irreversible investment, which is characterized by both economies of scale and those of network planning, and as such yields a natural monopoly. Because this network leads to externalities, vertical integration has traditionally yielded the most efficient organization of the industry, especially for larger firms. But, due to the vertical nature of electricity production, questions have arisen concerning whether any aspect of the production process may not be a natural monopoly. And, if this is the case, the questions then become: Would the market be better served by allowing competition into that component and would the gains from competition exceed the lost economies that would result? This is the critical element that needs to be explored.

But things are not always so clear. While little work has been done in the areas of testing whether the transmission and distribution processes are natural monopolies, they are usually assumed to be so, since both are characterized by what is known as *network economies*. Network economies arise due to the interconnectedness of the national transmission grid, so that significant saving in inputs and direct routing yield both economies of scale and economies of scope. These are defined later in this chapter, along with a review of the relevant literature.

Defining natural monopoly

Older industrial organization theory cited that the presence of scale economies determines whether an industry is a natural monopoly. It is important to note that much of the *theory* of natural monopoly is concerned with the precise meaning of *increasing returns* or, equivalently, *decreasing average costs*. Scale economies exist when a proportionate increase in output leads to a less-than-proportionate increase in cost. Mathematically, a cost function (one output) is said to exhibit global (local) economies of scale if

$$C(\lambda q) < \lambda C(q) \qquad (2.1)$$

for $\lambda > 1$, $q \geq 0$.

According to Marshall (1927), increasing returns can be either internal or external to the firm and, similarly, internal or external to the industry. A natural monopoly tends to arise due to high fixed costs, which tend to be asset specific and, as such, are largely sunk. As a result, average cost tends to decline as output is expanded over a large range, thus rendering a single provider socially optimal. In addition, economies of scale can be either technical (relating to the production process) or pecuniary, related to the prices paid for inputs.

One of the difficulties in testing for natural monopoly is the practical application of testing for the subadditivity of a firm's cost function, which is critical, since local (global) subadditivity is a necessary and sufficient condition for local (global) natural monopoly (Evans, 1983). In addition, it is necessary to distinguish between single-output and multiple-output natural monopolies, which I do in the following sections.

2.2 FOR A SINGLE-OUTPUT MARKET

An industry is said to be a natural monopoly if one firm can produce the desired market demand at a lower cost than two (or more) firms. More specifically, it is defined in terms of a single-firm's efficiency relative to the efficiency of other firms in the industry (as opposed to a firm's being the controller of an essential resource or having a patent on a particular product). In other words, economies of scale may exist in the production of a particular product. Some characteristics of a natural monopoly attributable to economies of scale include

1. Decreasing long-run average cost.
2. High fixed costs.
3. Subadditivity of its cost function.

Although interrelated, the most important of these is subadditivity of the firm's cost function, which means that it is cheaper for one firm to produce the total output demanded than it would be for several firms to produce proportions of it. This can be expressed as

$$C(Y) < \Sigma C(y^i) \qquad (2.2)$$

where $\Sigma y^i = Y$.

If this holds, then the cost function is strictly subadditive at output level Y (Sharkey, 1982). For a single-output firm, subadditivity is both necessary and sufficient for a natural monopoly, since subadditivity implies that it is more efficient for a single firm to produce all the output in the market. It is important to note that subadditivity is a local concept; that is, just because the cost is subadditive at one level of output does not necessarily mean that it is subadditive at all output levels, or globally subadditive. This implies that the total cost of production must be evaluated at all levels of output up to the level that satisfies market demand.

Average cost

Certainly, declining average cost throughout the relevant range of outputs is an indicator that the cost function is subadditive and it is more efficient for one firm to supply the entire industry output; that is, a natural monopoly. What this requires, however, is that the marginal cost also declines throughout a subset of this range of outputs. And necessary for this is a twice-differentiable cost function, which yields the appropriately shaped average and marginal cost curves. Such a cost function is displayed in Figure 2.1.

A cubic cost function yields the appropriately shaped average and marginal cost curves. For $Y < Y^*$, cost increases at a decreasing rate. In this range, both marginal and average cost decline. However, once diminishing returns set in, costs begin to increase at an increasing rate; it is in this range that marginal costs begin to rise and total cost increases at an increasing rate, which causes average cost to begin rising and yields the U-shaped average cost curve displayed in Figure 2.2.

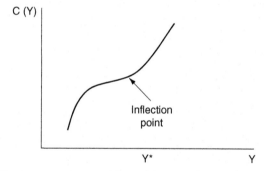

Figure 2.1 Total cost curve generated by a cubic cost function

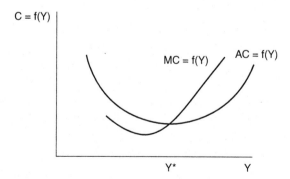

Figure 2.2 Average and marginal cost curves generated by cubic total cost function

A cubic cost function generates this particular shape and is of the general form

$$C(Y) = a + bY + cY^2 + dY^3 \qquad (2.3)$$

so that average cost is given by

$$AC(Y) = a/Y + b + cY + dY^2 \qquad (2.4)$$

where $AC(Y) = C(Y)/Y$. And marginal cost is given by

$$\partial C(Y)/\partial Y = b + 2cY + 3dY^2 \qquad (2.5)$$

Note: As long as a, b, and $d > 0$, and $c < 0$, the total cost curve is as displayed in Figure 2.1, which yields appropriately shaped (U-shaped, due to diminishing returns) average and marginal cost curves; that is, as displayed in Figure 2.2.

The cubic cost function just described generates the average (AC) and marginal (MC) cost curves displayed in Figure 2.2. For $Y < Y^*$, marginal cost declines and pulls average cost down with it; this is the region of the total cost curve in which cost rises at a decreasing rate. Once diminishing returns set in, marginal costs rise and eventually cause average cost to rise as well, which occurs at Y^*, when total costs begin to increase at an increasing rate.

Economies of scale

Of the three cost concepts just described, average cost is the most important in the determination of the most efficient industry structure (i.e., number of firms supplying the market demand).

Appealing to Baumol, Panzar, and Willig (1982), scale economies are said to be present when a k-fold *proportionate* increase in every input results in a k'-fold increase in output where $k' > k > 1$. This is even stronger than declining average cost, since it implies that average costs are declining but the converse is not necessarily true. The reason is that it may be even less costly to increase output by non-proportional increases in inputs (see Baumol et al., 1982, p. 21 for more details). With this said the following propositions are offered:

> Proposition 2.1. Locally, economies of scale are sufficient but not necessary for declining average cost.
> Proposition 2.2. Globally, economies of scale are sufficient but not necessary for subadditivity of costs (i.e., natural monopoly).

Aside: Necessary versus sufficient conditions

In logic, the words *necessity* and *sufficiency* refer to the implicational relationships between statements. The assertion that one statement is a *necessary and sufficient* condition of another means that the former statement is
true *if and only if* the latter is true. In other words,

- A *necessary* condition of a statement must be satisfied for the statement
  to be true. Formally, a statement P is a necessary condition of a statement Q if Q implies P.
- A *sufficient* condition is one that, if satisfied, assures the statement's
  truth. Formally, a statement P is a sufficient condition of a statement
  Q if P implies Q.

Examples

1. Given the average cost curve displayed in Figure 2.2, a necessary condition for cost minimization is that its derivative, which is equal to

$$\partial AC(Y)/\partial Y \tag{2.6}$$

is equal to zero.

Does this guarantee that costs are minimized? No. There is also a sufficient
condition that must be satisfied: the second derivative, which is given by

$$\partial^2 AC(Y)/\partial Y^2 > 0 \tag{2.7}$$

Otherwise, a strictly negative second derivative guarantees a maximum,
not a minimum as required.

2. A total revenue function of the following form:

$$PY = AY - BY^2 \tag{2.8}$$

where $P =$ price and $Y =$ output, so that $P \times Y =$ total revenue, yields a
marginal revenue curve that is given by

$$\partial TR(Y)/\partial Y = A - 2BY \tag{2.9}$$

A necessary condition for profit maximization is that marginal revenue
equal marginal cost (thus implying that the slope of the total cost curve is
equal to the slope of the total revenue curve). Solving equations (2.5) and
(2.9) for Y^*, the profit maximizing level of output, we have

$$3dY^2 + 2(B - c)Y + b - A = 0 \tag{2.10}$$

(recall, $c < 0$). This requires the quadratic formula to solve and yields two
distinct (and feasible) values for Y^* as long as

$$(B - c)^2 > 3d(b - A) \qquad (2.11)$$

so that

$$[(B - c)^2 > 3d(b - A)]^{1/2} \qquad (2.12)$$

is defined.

Given that there are two possible solutions, which are displayed in Figure 2.3, a sufficient condition must be established.

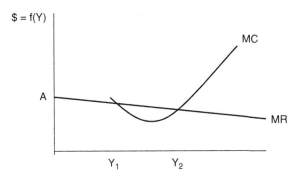

Figure 2.3 Profit maximizing level of output (Y_2 not Y_1)

Marginal cost equals marginal revenue at Y_1 and Y_2. Clearly, at output level Y_1, marginal cost exceeds marginal revenue, which results in a loss to the firm. At any Y such that $Y_1 < Y < Y_2$, marginal revenue exceeds marginal cost, so that profit is being earned. And, at Y_2, the entire profit is captured by the firm. What is the sufficient condition? Marginal cost must rise faster than marginal revenue, as displayed in Figure 2.3. In other words, the derivative of marginal cost with respect to output is higher than the derivative of marginal revenue, which is expressed as

$$\partial MC(Y)/\partial Y > \partial MR(Y)/\partial Y \qquad (2.13)$$

That is,

$$Y > (c - B)/3d \qquad (2.14)$$

These cost concepts are used extensively throughout the economics literature and are revisited in subsequent chapters. As such, it would be instructive to work through a numerical example here.

Numerical example 2.1

Let the demand and cost curves be given by

$$P = 20 - 0.5Y \qquad (2.15)$$

and

$$C = 0.04Y^3 - 1.94Y^2 + 32.96Y \tag{2.16}$$

In the absence of regulation, the monopolist's profit maximizing levels of output are determined by setting marginal revenue equal to marginal cost. In this case, marginal revenue and marginal cost are given by

$$\partial \text{TR}(Y)/\partial Y = 20 - Y \tag{2.17}$$

and

$$\partial \text{TC}(Y)/\partial Y = 0.12Y^2 - 3.88Y + 32.96 \tag{2.18}$$

Using the quadratic formula to solve for Y^*, the profit maximizing level of output, yields two solutions:

$$Y^* = (18, 6)$$

Which solution is correct? A check of the second-order (or sufficient) conditions is now required, which involves evaluating the second derivatives of the cost and revenue functions. This yields

$$\partial \text{MC}(Y)/\partial Y = 0.24Y - 3.88 \tag{2.19}$$

Evaluating at Y^* yields two solutions:

$$\partial \text{MC}(Y)/\partial Y = (0.44, -2.44)$$

and

$$\partial \text{MR}(Y)/\partial Y = -1$$

Only one solution ($Y^* = 18$) satisfies the sufficient condition for profit maximization; that is, that marginal cost rises faster than marginal revenue (i.e., $\partial \text{MC}(Y)/\partial Y > \partial \text{MR}(Y)/\partial Y$).

Efficient industry structure

For now, let us move on to the fundamental concept in determining the most efficient industry structure in single-output markets.

Degree of scale economies

The degree of scale economies (SCE) at output Y, is the elasticity of output at Y with respect to the cost to produce it. Formally, it is defined as

$$\text{SCE}(Y) = C(Y)/YC'(Y) \tag{2.20}$$

where

$$C'(Y) = \partial C(Y)/\partial Y \qquad (2.21)$$

Equation (2.20) is equivalent to the ratio of average cost to marginal cost. Returns to scale are said to be increasing, constant, or decreasing as SCE is greater than, equal to, or less than unity.

Economies of scale applied to the electric utility industry

Due to the nature of electricity, which is not storable and flows along the path of least resistance; the high, largely sunk required capital investment (which yields declining long-run average costs over the relevant range of output); and the well-established presence of economies of scale and vertical integration (see the literature review later in this chapter for details), for many years, conventional wisdom held that competition was infeasible and price regulation was necessary to ensure that consumers pay a fair price and producers and owners are appropriately compensated for any risks associated with supplying the electricity. Clearly characterized as natural monopolies, Figure 2.4 displays the theoretical construct of a naturally monopolistic market and the reason that utilities have historically been subjected to price regulation.

Without price regulation, the consumer would pay the monopoly price (denoted P^M) and the output in the market would be Y^M. Although allocative efficiency would dictate that price equal marginal cost (denoted P^C in Figure 2.4), which would yield an industry output of Y^C, this is not

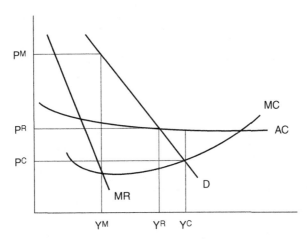

Figure 2.4 Traditional price regulation in the United States

feasible since the firm cannot cover its costs. Thus, the regulator would set the price equal to average cost, which yields a higher level of output (Y^R) than the monopoly output and a lower price would prevail in the marketplace (denoted by P^R). In addition, the regulated price allows the firm to recover its prudent costs and earn an acceptable return on equity (in the case of investor-owned utilities, which supply 66% of the U.S. market as indicated in the introductory chapter to this book).

2.3 LITERATURE REVIEW—ECONOMIES OF SCALE IN GENERATION: SINGLE-OUTPUT MODELS

In the electric utility industry, several papers in the literature treat electricity as a single (homogeneous) output. However, they pertain mostly to the generation of electricity only, the cost of which has been estimated using increasingly sophisticated econometric techniques, which typically employ either production functions or cost functions to reach their findings. Among those studies that estimate economies of scale in generation are Nerlove (1963), who used 1955 data on 145 utilities and found that the cost function was characterized by increasing returns to scale but that returns to scale tended to decline with the size of the firm. His study is discussed in more detail in Chapter 4.

Concerning the generating stage, it is necessary to distinguish between studies that use the plant as the sample unit and those that use the firm itself. In their seminal paper, Christensen and Greene (1976), used both Nerlove's 1955 data and also 1970 data on the same firms and found that, by 1970, most firms were generating electricity at a point on the average cost curve in which economies of scale had been exhausted. Using a different cost specification than Nerlove, they found that the minimum efficient scale was attained at 3800 MW and some firms were producing even beyond this level of output (i.e., in the diseconomies of scale region of the long-run average cost curve). This implied that the generation of electricity was not a natural monopoly and led to the realization that competition in the generation component was not only feasible but may also be more efficient. This realization precipitated the eventual deregulation of the generation component of the industry, which is discussed in a subsequent chapter (Chapter 3). In addition, the translogarithmic cost function employed in this particular study is the subject of further analysis in Chapters 4, 5, and 6.

Joskow and Schmalensee (1983) present a summary of studies carried out in the United States based on econometric estimations and engineering methods. At the time, the minimum efficient scale (MES) for conventional electricity generation was around 800 MW and around 2000 MW for nuclear energy. In a later study, Huettner and Landon (1978), using yet another cost specification and 1971 data on 74 electric utilities, confirmed the Christensen and Greene results, although they found that scale economies were exhausted at an even lower level of output. As they pointed out, the relationships observed at plant level, particularly scale economies, are often modified by interrelationships at higher levels of decision making, such as the firm level. Greene (1983) studied economies of scale using panel data on investor-owned utilities from 1955 to 1975 and found that scale economies actually declined over that period of time. Technical change, he argues, was a significant factor in the decreasing average costs that firms were experiencing throughout the majority of the study period. Thermal efficiencies were being exhausted while the demand for electricity was rising, thanks to declining power prices. Atkinson and Halvorsen (1984) employed yet a different cost model and found that, using 1970 data on 123 privately owned firms, most of the firms in the sample were operating in the downward sloping portion of the long-run average cost curve.

For the most part, these studies consider cost functions in which the output is the kilowatt-hours of electricity generated. (Christensen and Greene, 1976; Huettner and Landon, 1978; Atkinson and Halvorsen, 1984). But others, namely, Kamerschen and Thompson (1993) and Thompson and Wolf (1993), studied possible cost differences between conventional electricity generating technology (fossil-fuel generation) and nuclear electricity generation.

This was not the case, however, in the years (and decades) that followed, which were extremely turbulent ones for the industry. Rapidly rising fuel prices, double-digit inflation, and rising capital prices led to a decline in the demand for electricity, causing financial distress for a number of utilities, which were saddled with excess capacity. (Thompson, 1995).

Later studies include Maloney (2001), who estimated the MES at 321 MW and 260 MW for coal- and gas-fired plants, respectively, but found that the average cost curve is flat at this level. Kleit and Terrell (2001) and Hiebert (2002) found increasing scale economies for most observations. Hiebert found that the degree of scale economies was 20% in coal-fired plants and 12% for natural-gas-fired plants for average sample values (780 MW and 284 MW, respectively). This work also found that major economies can be attained by producing with more than one plant for each kind of generation. This latter aspect highlights the importance of distinguishing between plant and company in generation.

Whereas these studies focus on the generation component, a few studies focus on either transmission or distribution alone, two of the three components, and all three components. Of those that focus on some combination of the components, most do so to study the economies associated with vertical integration, which is discussed later in this chapter. In virtually all these studies, the consensus is that distributed electricity is not a homogenous good. This is discussed further in Chapter 4, but for now suffice it to say that different end users have different elasticities of demand and some users are more costly to serve than others.

Economies of scale and density in transmission and distribution

Some studies estimated the economies of scale for the transmission and distribution elements, like Huettner and Landon (1978), who found that the minimum efficient scale occurred at around 2600 MW capacity. Kaserman and Mayo (1991) also found specific economies of scale for these phases, and they situate the minimum efficient scale at around 5 GWh. And Greer (2003) found that none of the rural electric cooperatives distributed anywhere near the minimum efficient scale in 1996.

The network elements and the costs involved in these activities can be studied in greater depth by studying economies of density. This concept explains the evolution of average costs when production is increased and some of the characteristics that define the product are maintained constant, for example, the size of the service area or the number of consumers.

Network economies

For electricity, a quintessential element is the transmission network grid by which electricity, once generated, is transmitted to local distribution companies then to end users. Because of economies of scale, the per mile cost of transmitting electricity along a longer, interconnected grid is much less than doing so along a series of shorter grids (assuming, of course, that line losses are minimal). Furthermore, because some electricity is sold in bulk while the rest is sold to various classes of end users, both economies of scale and of scope arise as these multiple outputs jointly utilize this interconnected transmission grid. Furthermore, the very nature of this grid yields additional savings due to the network economies or economies of density, which play a critical role in such an industry. According to Salvanes and Tjotta (1994), who examined the distribution function in Norway, "the characteristics of the network affect all costs and should be included by a measure of the number of nodes supplied." They asserted that, "In industries where output is delivered via a network to spatially distributed points with distinct demand characteristics and thus a continuum of outputs exists, a traditional approach with a single output to represent firm size to facilitate econometric estimation may have serious implication for measuring productivity differences."

Hence, no longer is it sufficient to measure only returns to scale; returns to density must also be considered if one is to obtain precise and relevant measures of industry structure and form appropriate public policy. Employing the definition of Caves, Christensen, and Tretheway (1984), returns to density (for the translogarithmic cost specification) are given by

$$\text{RTD} = 1/(\partial \ln C / \partial \ln Y) \qquad (2.22)$$

where $\partial \ln C / \partial \ln Y$ is the cost elasticity with respect to output.

Returns to density are increasing, constant, or decreasing for RTD greater than, equal to, or less than unity. Therefore, returns to density measure the economies of increasing the number of kilowatt-hours produced where the size of the network is fixed.

While only a few studies attempted to measure economies in the transmission and distribution functions, few dispute that they exist. Schmalensee (1978) asserted that: "Total distribution cost depends on the cost of transmitting services and on the spatial pattern of demand. Everywhere-decreasing average cost of transmission is found to be sufficient, but not necessary, for natural monopoly."

Nonetheless, Schmalensee developed a model to show that economies in transmission at all service flows are sufficient, but not necessary, for distribution to be a natural monopoly. Furthermore, pricing at marginal cost fails to cover total cost, and even in the presence of economies of scale in transmission, average distribution cost may rise with total demand. Of those (few) studies that attempt to quantify such economies, Huettner and Landon (1978) employed nonconventional (in that some variables are in natural logarithms while others enter as quadratics) cost functions for both transmission and distribution. They found that, for transmission, both the long-run and the short-run average variable cost curves (oddly, they do not include the fixed costs of transmitting electricity) were inverted U-shaped with the maximum occurring at a capacity of

4000 trillion MW (long-run curve) and utilization rate of 94% (short-run curve). Neither the capacity nor the utilization variables' coefficients were significant, however. For distribution, another nonconventional cost function was utilized, with the finding that the coefficients of the capacity variables were statistically significant and of the appropriate sign, generating the appropriate U-shaped long-run average variable cost curve with the minimum point occurring at a firm size of 2600 MW. However, they go on to indicate that "this U-shaped curve is somewhat L-shaped over the range of observed firm sizes." On examining the short-run average variable cost curve for distribution, they again found an inverted U-shaped curve with its maximum occurring at a 54% utilization rate. Finally, they included a measure for the density of the distribution network and found higher unit costs for more densely populated areas (this is not what they expected to find). They concluded that higher congestion costs associated with higher density overwhelm any economies that may have been present. What is interesting is that they included fixed costs in the generation component but not in either the transmission or distribution function. As previously stated, economies of scale, scope, and density are primarily the result of the highly sunk capital investments required in both transmission and distribution.

Another study that sought to measure scale economies in the distribution of electricity is that of Giles and Wyatt (1989), who examined the presence of economies of density in New Zealand. They found that the number of firms operating in the industry at the time was greater than that which was consistent with average cost minimization. They found that the cost minimizing level of output was 2315 GWh, which could have been produced efficiently by about 20 firms, 40 fewer than there actually were at the time of this study.

2.4 FOR A MULTIPLE-OUTPUT NATURAL MONOPOLY

It is well-established that distributed electricity is not a homogeneous good; that is, the electricity distributed to different types of end users can be differentiated by voltage level. For example, many industrial customers can accept electricity at much higher voltage levels than either commercial or residential customers, which is one reason why rates are set in the fashion that they are; that is, different rate and revenue classes pay different base rates (i.e., energy charges) and often residential customers do not pay demand charges. The structure of rates is discussed in more detail in the chapters on pricing and regulation. Given this, numerous studies recognize that distributed electricity should be modeled as a multiproduct industry, which motivates the concepts described in the following section.

Multiproduct natural monopoly

While single-output scale economies imply single-output natural monopoly, this is not necessarily the case for multiple-output (or multiproduct) firms. The subadditivity conditions for a multiple-output natural monopoly are far more complex than are those of a single-output monopolist. In this case, economies of scale are not equivalent to decreasing average cost, since the firm may not operate along a linear expansion path. For a multiproduct firm, cost analysis requires the examination of not one but several concepts.

Ray average costs

Ray average costs (RAC) describe the behavior of the cost function as output is expanded proportionally along a ray emanating from the origin. Baumol et al. (1982) offer the following definition: In the two-product case, one considers the behavior of costs along a cross-section of the total cost surface. Defining a *composite* good, this measure allows a calculation of the average cost of this particular bundle and is given by

$$\text{RAC} = C(tY^0)/t \qquad (2.23)$$

where Y^0 is the unit bundle for a particular mix of outputs and t is the number of units in the bundle such that $Y = tY^0$ (Baumol et al., 1982, p. 49). This is displayed in Figure 2.5.

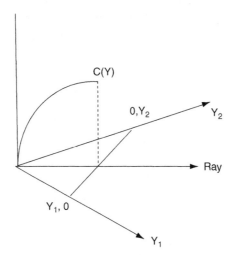

Figure 2.5 Ray average (*Source: Baumol et al., 1982, Figure 3A1. It is reproduced here with the consent of the authors.*)

Consider the behavior of costs along a cross-section of the total cost surface obtained by dropping a perpendicular plane along a ray that emanates from the origin. The ray average cost at any point on $C(Y)$ is equal to the slope of the cost function at that point. Note: In the case of Figure 2.5, *as drawn,* the slope of the cost function $C(Y)$ at $C(Y_1, Y_2) = 0$.

Degree of scale economies

As the analog to the single-output concept of economies of scale, the degree of scale economies, S_N, is equal to the ratio of average cost to marginal cost. In the multiple-output case, we have

$$S_N(Y) = C(Y)/Y_i C_i(Y), \quad \text{for } i = 1, \ldots, n \tag{2.24}$$

where $C_i(Y)$ is the marginal cost with respect to Y_i. Baumol et al. (1982, p. 51) show that

$$S_N = 1/(1 + e) \tag{2.25}$$

where e is the elasticity of RAC (tY) with respect to t at a point Y (t is a scalar).

Corollary: Returns to scale at the output point y are increasing, decreasing, or locally constant ($S_N > 1$, $S_N < 1$, $S_N = 1$, respectively) as the elasticity of RAC at y is negative, positive, or 0, respectively. Moreover, increasing or decreasing returns at y imply that RAC is decreasing or increasing at Y, respectively.

As such, S_N (the degree of scale economies) may be interpreted as a measure of the percentage rate of decline or increase in ray average cost with respect to output (Baumol et al., 1982).

Cost concepts applicable to multiproduct cases for nonproportionate changes in output

As said, ray average costs are relevant when outputs move in fixed proportions, which is quite often not the case in the distribution of electricity. For this, several concepts are required to establish subadditivity of the cost function, which are discussed here in more detail.

Product-specific economies of scale

Because output is not always expanded proportionally for a multiproduct firm, the concept of product–specific economies of scale must be examined. That is, to assess the impact on cost of a change in one output, holding other outputs constant, one must examine the average incremental cost (AIC) of the product of which output is being varied. This is defined as

$$\text{AIC}(y_i) = [C(Y_N) - C(Y_{N-i})]/Y_i \tag{2.26}$$

where $C(Y_{N-i})$ is the cost of producing all N of the multiproduct firm outputs except product i.

This specification allows the identification of returns to scale that are specific to a particular output. Hence, product-specific returns to scale are given by

$$S_i(y) = \text{AIC}(y_i)/(\partial C/\partial y_i) \tag{2.27}$$

where $\partial C/\partial y_i$ is the marginal cost with respect to product i.

Returns to scale of product i at y are said to be increasing, decreasing, or constant as $S_i(y)$ is greater than, less than, or equal to unity, respectively.

If product $2(Y_2)$, as shown in Figure 2.6, has no output-specific fixed costs, then the total cost surface rises continuously above ST (curve AE). However, if there exists some special fixed cost that must be incurred to begin production of Y_2 as an addition to the firm's line of other products,

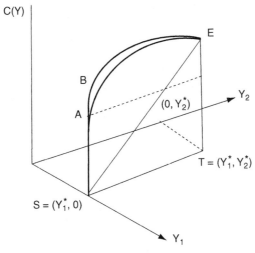

Figure 2.6 Product-specific returns to scale *(Source: Baumol et al., 1982, Figure 4A2. It is reproduced here with the consent of the authors.)*

then the cross-section of the cost surface contains a vertical fixed cost segment, AB, which results in a jump discontinuity of $C(Y)$ above the Y_1 axis. Thus, the height CE in Figure 2.6 measures the total incremental cost of Y_2 at output vector **T,** which is the addition to the firm's total cost resulting from the decision to add Y_2 to the firm's product mix. The average incremental cost of Y_2, $AIC_2(Y_1^*, Y_2^*)$, is clearly given by the slope of the line from A to E. What is also clear from Figure 2.6 is that the average incremental costs of product 2 decline with Y_2, at least between 0 and Y_2^*. This suggests, by analogy to the single-output case, the novel and useful concept of product-specific scale economies.

Economies of scope

The multiproduct cost concepts discussed prior to this relate to the behavior of cost along a cross-section of the cost-output space. In addition to economies that result from the size or scale of a firm's operations, other cost savings can result from the production of several outputs at the same time; that is, in many cases and certainly in the case of electricity, there are fixed costs that are jointly utilized in the production of the firm's outputs. These common costs, as they are also known, give rise to the concept of economies of scope (or economies of horizontal integration) and provide a basis for determining whether an industry is a multiproduct natural monopoly.

Mayo (1984) argues that: "In addition to measures of scale, efficient industry structure is determined by the behavior of costs as the scope of the firm is altered. The cost savings or dissavings that result from multiproduct versus specialized firm operations are given by the notion of economies and diseconomies of scope."

Therefore, economies of scope (also known as *economies of joint production*) are said to exist if a given quantity of each of two or more goods can be produced by one firm at a lower cost than if each good were produced by two different firms or even two different production processes. That is, for a two-product case, weak economies of scope are given by

$$C(Y_1, Y_2) \leq [C(Y_1, 0) + C(0, Y_2)] \tag{2.28}$$

for all $Y_1, Y_2 > 0$. If not, then there are diseconomies of scope, and separate production of outputs is more efficient.

As in the single-output case, we define the degree of economies of scope, which is given by

$$S_c = [C(Y_1, 0) + C(0, Y_2) - C(Y_1, Y_2)]/C(Y_1, Y_2) \tag{2.29}$$

The importance of economies of scope cannot be overstated: Economies of scope are a necessary condition for natural monopoly in a multiple output firm.

Both economies of scale and of scope tend to occur due to specialization. As stated previously, the latter can arise from the sharing or joint utilization of inputs. According to Panzar and Willig (1977), if a given input is imperfectly divisible, production of a small set of goods may leave excess capacity in the utilization of that input. Another way that economies of scope can arise is that the input may have some properties of a public good, so that when it is purchased for one production process, it can then be freely available to another. A third way is that economies of scope can arise due to the economies of networking (recall the discussion of network economies and returns to density).

Subadditivity of the cost function

However, even if a cost function exhibits both economies of scale and economies of scope, it is not necessarily subadditive. A sufficient condition must now be established for natural monopoly in a multiproduct industry. Cost complementarity, which requires that marginal or incremental costs of any output decline when that output or any other outputs increase, provides such a condition. Mathematically, cost complementarity for a twice differential multiproduct cost function exists if

$$\partial^2 C(Y)/\partial Y_i \partial Y_j < 0, \text{for } i \neq j \tag{2.30}$$

and for all Y_i, $Y_j > 0$.

If this is satisfied, then the cost function exhibits cost complementarity, which is a sufficient condition for subadditivity in a multiproduct cost function. An industry is said to be a natural monopoly if, over the entire relevant range of outputs, the firm's cost function is subadditive.

2.5 ELECTRICITY AS A MULTIPLE-OUTPUT INDUSTRY AND ECONOMIES OF SCOPE AND SUBADDITIVITY

While treating generated electricity as a homogeneous good may seem appropriate, it is certainly not appropriate treatment for distributed electricity. A quote from Joskow and Schmalensee (1983, pp. 54–55) summarizes this principle nicely: "treating diverse power systems as single-product firms is likely to produce error. The cost of an optimally designed power system depends in complex ways on the distribution of demand over time and space. No two power systems produce the same mix of products and product mix differences affect the magnitude and form of optimal investments in transmission and in distribution."

Among the first to actually model electricity as a multiple-output function was Neuberg (1977), who examined the market for distribution employing four interdependent outputs. The predominant output in his analysis was the number of customers served; the other outputs were the number of megawatt-hours sold, the size of distribution territory, and the miles of overhead distribution line. Karlson (1986) tested for and found that the multiproduct characterization of electricity was appropriate, having treated residential and commercial electricity as distinct outputs. He found that the marginal cost of any one output depended on the levels of all other outputs and all other inputs. Furthermore, he rejected the hypothesis of separability between inputs and outputs, which implies that the marginal rate of substitution between any two inputs is not independent of the quantities of outputs nor is the marginal rate of transformation between any two outputs independent of the quantities of inputs.

Some studies attempted to identify the existence of scope economies in this industry. Mayo (1984) employed a multiproduct quadratic cost function to estimate the cost of producing both electricity and gas for 200 public utilities. Using 1979 data, he confirmed the presence of economies of scope for smaller firms. However, as output is expanded, the absence of competitive pressure leads to cost inefficiencies and eventual diseconomies of scope. His finding led to the realization that the regulated utilities in his sample were characterized by interproduct discomplementarities, since his empirical results confirmed that

$$\partial^2 C(Y)/\partial Y_1 \partial Y_2 > 0 \qquad (2.31)$$

This particular result, which was anticipated by Kahn, can be attributed (at least in part) to the *type* of regulation imposed on these firms; that is, average cost pricing in which firms are certainly not incentivized to minimize costs. Furthermore, the Averch-Johnson effect,[1] which is also a result of

---

[1] Traditional rate making provides an incentive to overinvest in capital (i.e., the rate base). For an investor-owned utility, this is a large component of the revenue requirement on which the utility is allowed to earn a return to its investors. Known as the *Averch-Johnson effect*, this is the tendency of companies to engage in excessive amounts of capital accumulation to expand the volume of their profits. If a firm's profits-to-capital ratio is regulated at a certain percentage, then there is a strong incentive for companies to overinvest to increase profits overall. This goes against any optimal efficiency point for capital that the company may have calculated as higher profit is almost always desired over and above efficiency.

rate-of-return regulation, is still at play, since firms have an incentive to overinvest in capital as a mechanism to increase rates and hence profits.

Like Mayo's 1984 study, Sing (1987) employed a different cost specification (a generalized translog cost function) to estimate whether a sample of U.S. electric and gas utilities were natural monopolies. He found that the average combination utility exhibited diseconomies of scope, but other output combinations were associated with economies of scope.

Roberts (1986) and Thompson (1997) differentiated output according to voltage level. Their results suggest that there are economies of density; that is, for a given network size and a fixed number of customers, average costs fall when the quantity of power supplied increases. Roberts defined a measure of economies of output density as

$$R_D = 1/(\partial \ln C / \partial \ln Y_L + \partial \ln C / \partial \ln Y_H) \qquad (2.32)$$

where Y_L and Y_H denote low-voltage and high-voltage output, respectively.

He rejected the hypothesis of separability of the generation and transmission functions from distribution. This was predominantly due to the lack of separability between the inputs required to perform all three functions, which is the reason that a majority of the utilities in the United States are vertically integrated. (This confirms Karlson's finding.) The concept of economies of vertical integration is explored later in this chapter and throughout this book, since it is integral to the appropriate cost modeling and public policy making for electric utilities. In addition, it provides the subject of a case study presented in Chapter 8.

As previously stated, most of the studies of this nature focus on investor-owned utilities. However, and as stated in the introductory chapter, other types of entities are worthy of such analysis. Yatchew (2000) estimated the costs of distributing electricity using data on municipal electric utilities in Ontario, Canada, for the period 1993–1995. The data reveal substantial evidence of increasing returns to scale with minimum efficient scale being achieved by firms with about 20,000 customers. Larger firms exhibit constant or decreasing returns. Utilities that deliver additional services (such as water and sewage), have significantly lower costs, indicating the presence of economies of scope.

Greer (2003) estimated economies of scale and scope for U.S. distribution cooperatives. Distributed electricity (i.e., output) was differentiated by voltage level, with 1000 kVA being the distinction between "small" users and "large" users. She found that the cost function exhibits product-specific economies as well as economies of scope, and substantial cost savings could be realized via mergers between distribution coops. This study and the cost model used in the analysis are the subject of much more detail as well as the case studies examined in Chapters 7 and 8.

Fraquaelli, Piancenza, and Vannoni (2004) studied Italian public utilities that provided the combination of gas, water, and electricity. They confirmed the presence of global scope and scale economies only for multiutilities, with output levels lower than the ones characterizing the "median" firm. This indicates that relatively small specialized firms would benefit from cost reductions by evolving into multiutilities, providing similar network services such as gas, water, and electricity. However, for larger-scale utilities, the hypothesis of null cost advantages is not rejected. Therefore, it is possible that the recent diversification waves of leading companies are explained by factors other than cost synergies, so that the welfare gains that can be reasonably expected from such examples of horizontal integration, if any, are likely to be very low.

2.6 ECONOMIES OF VERTICAL INTEGRATION AND SEPARABILITY

The issue with which we are dealing is the appropriate modeling of costs to formulate public policy that maximizes the total welfare of the players (both consumers and producers) involved. Thus far, we have been concerned with the separate stages (or processes) required to supply electricity to end users and whether each stage (or process) may be a natural monopoly. What has been established is that the generation component, due mostly to technological change, is no longer a natural monopoly and there could be societal gains from allowing competition into that component of the process, which is what the deregulation of the industry was all about. Unfortunately, what was essentially ignored was the *network* (or wires) aspect of the business; that is, unlike telephony (voice, data, fax—more on this in Chapter 5, a case study on deregulation and the breaking up of the Bell System), water, and natural gas, electricity cannot be economically stored and, once generated, flows according to Kirchoff's law (i.e., the path of least resistance).[2]

---

[2] This is a critical point that needs to be kept in mind. In my opinion, it is the reason that deregulation of the industry was such an abject failure.

Given this, what now needs to be established is the relationship between these three functional components. After all, part of the notion of deregulation was that generation could be separated (lack of scale economies, so competition was deemed feasible) from the transmission and distribution functions (irrefutably natural monopolies). More specifically, what is necessary is to establish the existence (or lack thereof) of economies of vertical integration, which are another critical and distinguishing aspect of this industry?

Vertical integration of electric utilities

Landon (1983) argued that "the electricity industry has special characteristics such as close coordination of each process, transaction costs, and idiosyncratic capital requirements, which all favour vertical integration."

Vertical integration makes sense when a product is produced sequentially, such that the output from the first stage of production is employed as an input in successive stages, which is the case of electricity. When a firm is vertically integrated, it owns the entire production process, controlling both the upstream (input) supply and the downstream (output) production processes. Needless to say, the electric utility industry in the United States was organized in this fashion for a number of years by investor-owned firms, who were willing to supply power to the larger, more densely populated areas of the country. Vertical integration makes sense since it provides an alternative to market transactions, which tend to be costly given the nature of the industry, which requires specialized assets and sunk costs. It would have been extremely difficult to foresee the input-price increases experienced since the mid-1970s; were the industry not vertically integrated but rather contractually related, the financial difficulties experienced by utilities in the late 1970s–1990s would have been far greater, since it is unlikely that these price increases were foreseen and could be written into the contracts, which were typically of longer duration.

Vertical integration is especially appealing in industries characterized by bottlenecks, which tend to occur with exclusive ownership of a resource necessary to the production of the good but whose cost is prohibitive, so that it is not economically feasible for separate firms to invest. This type of investment yields a market that approximates a natural monopoly in the sense that its cost is sunk and its duplication would be wasteful. In the case of electricity, the bottleneck is that which yields access to the transmission mechanism that delivers electricity from generation to the local distribution system.

Additional benefits are attributable to vertical integration as well:

1. The elimination of the "wedge" that results when the upstream firm sells its product to the downstream firm at a price above economic cost.
2. The mitigation of certain problems that arise due to the separation of ownership of the firm from whoever actually controls it, which is also known as a *principal-agent problem*.

For the presence of economies of vertical integration in the supply of electricity, it must be the case that successive stages of production (generation, transmission, and distribution) are less costly for a single firm to perform than for these functions to be performed by separate producers. Both issues are relevant in the production of electricity, whose underlying production technology not only lends itself to economies of scale but also to economies of vertical integration.

Defining vertical integration

Mathematically, economies of vertical integration exist if the following is satisfied:

$$C(G, D) < C(G, 0) + C(0, D) \qquad (2.33)$$

where $G > 0$ represents the first stage of production (upstream production) and $D > 0$ represents the latter stage (downstream production), so that $C(G, D)$ is the cost of production for a vertically integrated firm. If this is less than the sum of the cost of separate production by separate entities, given by $C(G, 0) + C(0, D)$, then it is said that there exist economies of vertical integration. Or, expressed in percentage terms,

$$S_v = [C(G, 0) + C(0, D) - C(G, D)]/C(G, D) \qquad (2.34)$$

where

$S_v > 0$, there are economies of vertical integration.

$S_v < 0$, there are no economies of vertical integration.

Separability

Because the marginal cost of any one output depends on the levels of all other outputs and all other inputs, the issue of separability must be considered on the formation of appropriate policy. Karlson (1986, p. 78) states that: "Separability between inputs and outputs requires that the marginal rate of substitution between any two inputs is independent of the quantities of outputs, and the marginal rate of transformation between any two outputs is independent of the quantities of inputs ... The rejection of the hypothesis of separability between inputs and outputs implies that the relative marginal costs of electricity sold to different consumer classes depend on the product and input mixes; furthermore, it is impossible to construct some homogeneous aggregate output called 'electricity' to be sold to consumers."

Karlson rejects the hypothesis of such separability, as do Henderson (1985), Roberts (1986), and Lee (1995). These are discussed in more detail next.

2.7 RELEVANT LITERATURE REVIEW—VERTICAL INTEGRATION AND SEPARABILITY

Several studies tested for the presence of vertical economies in the supply of electricity. Virtually all of them test for and reject the separability of the functional components. In fact, it has been empirically demonstrated that there exist economies of vertical integration in the production of electricity. Such studies include Henderson (1985), who finds downstream costs are dependent on input usage at the generation stage, hence the cost function (which is translogarithmic) fails the test for separability between generation and distribution. Roberts (1986) concurs, as do Hayashi, Yeoung-Jia Goo, and Chamberlain (1997) and Thompson (1995). Other studies include those by Kaserman and Mayo (1991) and Gilsdorf (1994, 1995). As an extension to their testing for vertical economies, both Kaserman and Mayo (1991) and Gilsdorf (1994, 1995) employ a multiproduct cost function to determine whether vertical integration and economies of scale together constitute a natural monopoly. In fact, Kaserman and Mayo also test for multistage economies between generation and transmission/distribution. They too reject the separability of inputs and outputs (what is generated is an input to what is transmitted or distributed) in the cost function. It is important to note that separability is not the same thing as economies of vertical integration, where output-output interactions matter. Byung-Joo Lee (1995) estimated a production function and performed more direct tests for vertical integration and economies of scale. All reject separability of all three functional components of electricity production. Kwoka (1996) employed the Kaserman and Mayo approach to test for multistage economies between generation and distribution. He too rejects separability (especially for "larger" systems) and argues that these vertical economies are precisely the reason that most investor-owned utilities are vertically integrated, while most "smaller" systems (i.e., publicly owned utilities and rural electric cooperatives) are not. In addition he found that vertical integration achieves significant cost efficiencies, in some cases, sufficient to offset diseconomies of scale in generation and distribution separately.

More recent studies include Goto and Nemoto (2004), who test the technological externality effects of generation assets on the costs of transmission and distribution stages in their study of vertically integrated Japanese utilities. Their results show that downstream costs depend on the generation capital, suggesting significant economies of vertical integration. Fraquaelli, Piancenza, and Vannoni's (2005) analysis of Italian municipal electric utilities finds significant vertical economies for average size and large utilities while failing to find any significant effects for smaller than average size utilities. Efficiencies associated with vertical integration are largest for fully integrated utilities, confirming results found in most other studies. Greer (2008) estimated the lost economies of vertical integration due to the rural electric cooperatives' choice of market structure. As indicated in the introductory chapter, cooperatives are organized as either generation and transmission or member coops (distribution only). Greer found that cost savings of close to 40% could be realized had they adopted a truly vertically integrated structure. This paper and the cost models used to generate these results are the basis for the case study presented in Chapter 8.

2.8 CONCLUSION

This chapter provides an overview of electric utility industry structure and some relevant cost concepts as well as a brief survey of the literature pertaining to this industry. In subsequent chapters, these concepts are expounded on and examined in much more detail.

CHAPTER 3

The U.S. Electric Markets, Structure, and Regulations

Chris Blazek

Over the past 20 years, the U.S. electric utility industry has gone through sweeping changes associated with deregulation, regulations, reregulation, and the rate-making process. Due to the largely sunk capital investment and the well-established presence of economies of scale, economies of scope, and vertical integration, conventional wisdom has held that competition is infeasible (at least in the transmission and distribution segments). This same wisdom holds that price regulation is necessary to ensure that consumers pay a fair price and producers and shareholders are appropriately compensated for the risk associated with holding the stock of the utility (in the case of investor-owned utilities, which supply approximately two thirds of the power to end users in the United States). This chapter discusses the electric market structure, how utilities recover their costs, the different recovery mechanisms, both federal and state regulations, and how the regulatory process can affect rates.

3.1 THE U.S. ELECTRIC INDUSTRY STRUCTURE

In recent years, the industry has been evolving from vertically integrated monopolies that provide generation, transmission, and distribution service at cost-based rates (regulated model) to an industry where the operation of generation, transmission, and distribution assets have been increasingly unbundled and even divested (in the case of generating assets, a deregulated model). In certain markets, the wholesale and retail price of electricity is determined competitively under a regulatory framework that promotes competition. Although transmission and distribution markets are still monopolistic and follow traditional cost-based rates, the Federal Energy Regulatory Commission (FERC) and a number of states have implemented rate-making approaches that give regulated utilities financial incentives to cost-effectively and reliably expand their transmission and distribution systems. Fourteen states (Maine, New Hampshire, Massachusetts, Rhode Island, Connecticut, New York, New Jersey, Pennsylvania, Delaware,

Electricity Cost Modeling Calculations
DOI: 10.1016/B978-1-85617-726-9.00003-0

Maryland, Ohio, Michigan, Illinois, and Texas) and the District of Columbia have retail markets where customers can access alternative power suppliers or continue to purchase power from their historic supplier. In these markets, competitive bidding is used to determine a portion or the entire retail price for electricity. However, a number of states have either suspended deregulation or amended laws and regulations governing competition due to the lack of competition and resulting increases in price. States that suspended retail competition include Virginia, Arkansas, New Mexico, Arizona, Nevada, California, Oregon, and Montana. In 2008, Delaware, Illinois, and Ohio enacted legislation allowing utilities to once again build their own generation capacity based on a formalized competitive procurement process. Illinois went one step further and created a new government entity that can build new capacity and procure power.

In the most basic sense, the electric industry is divided into generation, transmission, and distribution functions. Prior to deregulation, the term *electric utility* traditionally denoted an investor-owned company or government agency that produced, transmitted, distributed, and sold electricity to the end user. Also prior to deregulation, vertically integrated utilities that served all four market segments were granted a monopoly franchise by the state or local government, which gave them the right to produce and sell electricity in that service territory. In return for this monopoly position, the utility accepted the obligation to serve all customers in that territory regardless of profitability or ease of access and were subjected to regulatory oversight regarding their operations and pricing. Under regulation, profits were constrained. However, utilities used regulated tariffs to pass costs onto customers, and incentives to minimize costs or take on unrecoverable risk were largely absent. (Recall the earlier discussions on the Averch-Johnson effect.)

In addition to traditional vertically integrated utilities, generation and transmission cooperatives (G&Ts) produced electricity in bulk and transmitted and sold it in bulk (wholesale) to other utilities. Often G&Ts provide bulk power within a region to local distribution companies and municipal utilities. Local distribution companies (LDCs) owned and operated only the local distribution network and sold power to the end user. They also provided retail sales and service to local customers, who often viewed these entities as the "utility company." LDCs were investor-owned, operated by the local municipality, or were part of a rural cooperative.

The Public Utility Regulatory Policies Act of 1978 (PURPA) created two other types of organizations: the independent power producer (IPP) and the nonutility generator (NUG). Both IPPs and NUGs are privately owned firms that own, operate, and sell power into the market. IPPs typically sell power to local LDCs whereas NUGs are usually industrial companies that use much of the power they generate internally but sell excess power back into the market. PURPA requires traditional utilities to buy power from these entities if the power is priced less than the utility's own cost of generation.

Deregulation

This vertically integrated model changed over the years through the introduction of deregulation. Today regulated, unregulated, and partially regulated markets exist, with a host of different entities serving various market elements. Utilities can be viewed by the segment of the electric market they serve (generation, transmission, distribution, or sales) or by their ownership type (investor owned, government agency, or cooperative) in either a regulated or unregulated market. As part of deregulation and industry restructuring, the vertically integrated company concept has effectively been unbundled in some markets. In theory, deregulation promotes the interaction of many sellers and buyers to create economically efficient market pricing that is equal to the cost of producing the last unit sold (i.e., the marginal cost). It should be noted that transmission and distribution are still considered natural monopolies that require regulation to ensure fair access for all market participants and to take advantage of the inherent economies of scale, scope, and vertical integration.

The intent of deregulation and the resulting industry restructuring was to protect the short- and long-term interests of consumers by creating an efficient market through the introduction of competition. Reasons often cited for deregulation include advances in combined-cycle gas turbines (CCGT) that produced economies of scale at low capital costs (lower generation market entry price), global competition, the ability of private sector companies to respond more quickly to economic and technology changes, and improved information and communication systems that could better manage the markets. Although many of these reasons have a certain degree of merit, they have not been enough to support universal deregulation. For example, although advanced CCGT plants are considerably less expensive to build than comparably sized coal-fired plants, the fact that fuel costs (natural gas) contribute to a greater extent to the cost of electricity production is ignored. Yes, the lower entry price created by this technology allowed new unregulated competition into the market, but this

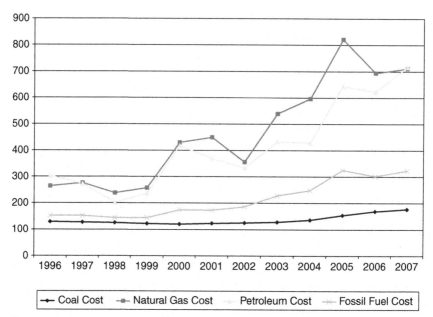

Figure 3.1 Energy price trends *(Source: U.S. Energy Information Administration, www.eia.doe.gov/cneaf/electricity/epa/figes4.pdf)*

also introduced additional risk in the market associated with volatile fuel prices. As a result, when natural gas prices increased significantly in 2005 (as displayed in Figure 3.1, in cents per MMBTU), some of these assets became stranded and the production cost of electricity increased in local markets dominated by natural gas turbine generation. In the case of information and communication systems, these technologies facilitate day-ahead and online electricity markets between market participants and different transaction types. Real-time metering, billing, load management, and quality control are also being offered under deregulation and are an integral part of the smart grid process.

Market participants

As previously stated, entities within the electric utility industry can be classified by ownership, and this is an important distinction, as different types of ownership classes can be regulated somewhat differently. In addition to ownership classes, entities can be viewed in either a regulated or unregulated context. In 2007, there were 3273 investor-owned, cooperative, publicly owned, and federal electric utilities, as well as retail and wholesale power marketers, as shown in Figure 3.2.

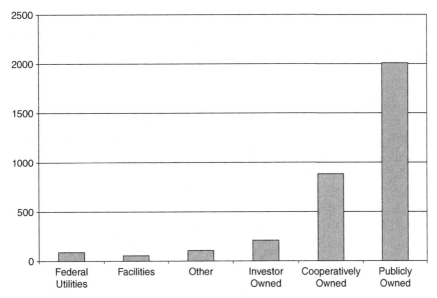

Figure 3.2 Ownership types

The vertically integrated model

The vertically integrated market model is represented by a monopoly that controls the different functions of generation, transmission, or distribution needed to serve the end user. There are a number of monopoly ownership types in the United States, including investor owned, federal, cooperative, municipal, public power agencies, power pools, energy service providers, and independent power producers. Each is discussed in some detail next.

Investor-owned utilities

Investor-owned utilities (IOUs) are owned by stockholders that typically seek to maximize profits within the framework of regulations governing these types of utilities. These entities tend to be large organizations that try to take advantage of economies of scale, as exemplified by recent mergers such as Duke/Cinergy, Great Plains Energy/Kansas City Power & Light/Aquila/Black Hills, Dynegy/LS Power, MidAmerican Energy/Scottish Power/PacifiCorp., and the recently announced merger between PP&L and EOn US. Investor-owned utilities can exist as individual corporations or holding companies as part of a parent company that owns one or more operating utility. Most IOUs sell power at retail rates to various classes of customers and at wholesale rates to other utilities, including federal, state, and local government utilities, public utility districts, rural electric cooperatives, and even other investor-owned utilities. They can also be characterized as having high-density service territories. As monopolies, IOUs are regulated and required to provide service to all customers in their franchised territory, charge reasonable and comparable prices to similar classifications of consumers, and provide consumers access to services under similar conditions. Most IOUs that operate in regulated retail states operate on a vertically integrated basis, providing generation, transmission, and delivery service at a bundled price to retail customers.

The 211 IOUs in the United States represent roughly 6% of the total number of electric utilities and approximately 38% of installed capacity, as shown later. They generate approximately 42% of the power produced and generate 66% of the sales and 67% of the revenue. Investor-owned utilities serve about 100 million consumers, representing about 71% of the total U.S. market, and operate in all states except Nebraska. Also referred to as *privately owned utilities*, they typically earn a return for their investors that is either distributed to stockholders as dividends or reinvested in the company. Because of their for-profit nature, they are regulated by the state's utility regulatory commission to ensure that the interest of the customer is taken into consideration.

Independent power producers
In a vertically integrated market the role of an independent power producer is to generate power and sell the output under long-term contracts, which can offer an alternative to the utility's building and financing the construction of a new facility. As such, they are nonutility, for-profit companies with no assigned service territories. In addition, IPPs are not allowed to own transmission facilities and must contract for this service to deliver power to their customers, which they sell at market-based rates that are subject to receiving FERC authorization. Finally, IPPs are not "qualified facilities" and some are exempt wholesale generators (EWGs), which means that they are exempt from certain FERC financial reporting and ownership restrictions.

Municipal utilities and other publicly owned utilities
Municipal utilities (Munis) and other publicly owned utilities are nonprofit government entities that serve at either the local or state level. There are 2009 publicly owned electric utilities in the United States, representing approximately 61% of the players in the power industry, 9% of the

generating capability, 8% generation, 15% of retail sales, and 13% of the industry's revenue in 2007. This group of utilities consists of municipal, public utility, and power districts; state authorities; irrigation districts; and joint municipal action agencies. Publicly owned utilities have certain advantages, such as access to tax-free financing (municipal treasuries), ability to issue low-cost tax-exempt debt to finance construction, and generally are not subject to state and federal taxes. Often they are financed by general obligation bonds and revenue bonds secured by the sale of electricity. This can result in lower retail rates than IOUs.

Municipal utilities are owned and operated by local communities and often operate within the local municipal public works department. They can also be characterized as having a concentrated service territory similar to many IOUs. Munis are concentrated largely in the Midwest and Southeast and are located in every state except Hawaii. According to the 2007 Energy Information Administration (EIA) records, there are nearly 1950 municipally owned utilities in the United States. Municipal utilities can own and operate their own generation and distribution system, such as those in Austin, Texas; Jacksonville, Florida; and Colorado Springs, Colorado. However, more than half the municipal utilities own and operate only the local distribution system and purchase their power wholesale, from either federal agencies, IOUs, or other entities. This class of utility is often not regulated by state or federal agencies, and municipalities may operate the utility as a tool to promote local economic expansion or lower local tax burdens. Municipal utilities can range in size from one customer to over a million customers (e.g., the city of Los Angeles).

In some regions of the country, municipal utilities are run by a number of cities or a county, and are called public utility districts (PUDs). Public utility districts and projects are more prevalent in Nebraska, Washington, Oregon, Arizona, and California, where voters elect commissioners or directors to govern the district independent of any local government. Smaller municipal utilities frequently band together to create public utility districts that share ownership in generation and transmission assets.

Other publicly owned utilities include municipal authorities, state authorities, and irrigation districts. State authorities, such as the New York State Power Authority and Santee Cooper (South Carolina Public Service) are utilities that function under a state charter and can generate or purchase electricity from other utilities, sell power into the wholesale market or to groups of other utilities within their states, as well as distribute power to local customers. The New York State Power Authority supplies wholesale power to municipal and cooperative utilities but also provides power to certain industrial customers. Santee Cooper provides both retail and wholesale electric service. Irrigation districts, such as the Salt River Agricultural and Improvement District, are controlled by a board of directors apportioned according to the size of landholdings. The Salt River Project provides both retail electric and water services. Irrigation districts are primarily located in the western United States and were initially formed for agricultural purposes by local farmers to manage water resources. Some states created entities, called *joint municipal action agencies*, for the purpose of constructing power plants and purchasing wholesale power for resale to municipal distribution utilities. Some of these entities include the Massachusetts Municipal Wholesale Electric Company, the Indiana Municipal Power Agency, and the Municipal Electric Authority of Georgia.

Federal power agencies

Federal power agencies were initially established by the federal government to market the power from federal hydropower projects. There are nine federal power agencies controlled by various government agencies that operate in all areas except the Northeast, the upper Midwest, and Hawaii. These include

- The U.S. Army Corps of Engineers.
- The Bureau of Indian Affairs and the Bureau of Reclamation in the Department of the Interior.
- The International Boundary and Water Commission in the Department of State.
- The power marketing administrations (PMAs) in the Department of Energy—Bonneville Power Administration (BPA), Southwestern Power Administration (SWPA), Southeastern Power Administration (SEPA), Western Area Power Administration (WAPA).
- The Tennessee Valley Authority (TVA).

The TVA, the U.S. Army Corps of Engineers, and the U.S. Bureau of Reclamation are the only federal agencies that own and operate generating facilities. These federal power agencies were largely established based on the premise that publicly supported electricity was essential to provide electricity to large parts of rural America. The primary purpose of the TVA, the BPA, and the other PMAs was to market the surplus output of hydroelectric facilities generated as part of riverway navigation, flood control, and irrigation requirements.

The federal role in providing electric power dates back to the beginning of electrification. In the United States, federal involvement in the electric market began with the Reclamation Act of 1902 and the Town Sites and Power Development Act of 1906. With the Reclamation Act of 1902, the federal government became involved in the reclamation of arid lands largely through the development of irrigation projects, which generated electricity as a by-product. At the turn of the last century, hydroelectric power was the dominant source of electricity. At that time, the sale of surplus power, preferentially to local communities as defined in the 1906 act, was viewed as a way of repaying the costs associated with reclamation. In the 1930s the role of the federal government in marketing electricity from federally owned facilities grew rapidly, largely due to the Great Depression and the need to create jobs to stimulate the economy. At the time, the power produced by these entities was sold primarily to municipals and cooperatives. During the Great Depression, some of the world's largest hydroelectric power plants were constructed, including the Hoover Dam in 1936, the Bonneville Dam in 1938, and the Grand Coulee Dam in 1941. In the years leading up to the Second World War, nearly half of all new generating capacity was built by the federal government, which mitigated the effects of the depression to some degree through electrification and jobs. Due to the federal dam projects during this era, federal utilities today produce more hydroelectric power than other types of utilities, which makes the power they produce relatively inexpensive. With the exception of parts of the Midwest and Northeast, federal power is sold throughout the nation. States in the Pacific Northwest and the Tennessee River Valley receive the largest share of federal power.

Federal electric utilities primarily generate power from federally owned facilities and transmit and sell their power to statutorily defined preferential customers, including municipal utilities, cooperatives, Indian tribes, state utilities, irrigation districts, state governments, and federal agencies. As required by law, they operate as not-for-profit entities and are required to recover the cost of operation and repay the U.S. Treasury for funds borrowed to construct generation and transmission facilities. After meeting these statutory customer commitments, federal power agencies can and do sell surplus electricity to IOUs or directly to large, power-intensive industries (i.e., aluminum industry) in wholesale markets. The federal agencies do not directly sell to residential or commercial customers. These agencies also own transmission lines from their power generation facilities to other utility-owned grids.

The Tennessee Valley Authority, which is the largest federal power producer, operates its own power plants and sells both wholesale and retail power into the Tennessee Valley region markets. Power generated by the Bureau of Reclamation and the U.S. Army Corps of Engineers (except for the North Central Division in areas such as Saint Mary's Falls at Sault Ste. Marie, Michigan) is marketed by the various federal power marketing administrations. These administrations also purchase energy from other electric utilities for resale into wholesale markets. Federal power authorities represent less than 1% of all electric utilities in the United States, yet they provide approximately 7% of all generating capability and about 4% of the generated electricity. Federal utilities are not subject to rate regulation, but they must submit their rates to the FERC to demonstrate that they are at a level sufficient to repay debt owed the federal government.

The Tennessee Valley Authority

The TVA was established during the Great Depression on May 18, 1933, under the Tennessee Valley Act, as an "experiment" in social planning as part of Franklin Delano Roosevelt's (FDR) "First New Deal." (The First New Deal occurred during the first 100 days of FDR's administration and resulted in the passage of dozens of congressional acts and executive orders.) During that period of the Great Depression, the nations' economic peril was so severe (nearly 25% unemployment, bank closings, mortgage defaults, and 50% drop in farm crop prices) that Congress felt it did not have the time to seriously debate FDR's various acts before voting.

Supporting the creation of the TVA was the belief by many at the time that privately held power companies were charging too much, as directed by their owners, the utility's holding company. These private utility holding companies controlled 94% of generation by 1921 and were largely unregulated (Public Utility Reports, Inc., 1988). The eight largest utility holding companies controlled 73% of the investor-owned electric industry by 1932 (Hyman, 1994), which led to the Public Utility Holding Act of 1935, enacted during the "Second New Deal" era of 1934–1935. As a result of the creation of TVA, many private companies in the valley were purchased by the federal government.

The TVA was largely formed to promote economic development in the Tennessee Valley, improve navigation, aid in flood control, and provide fertilizer manufacturing. In the early years, the TVA was financed through federal appropriations. The 1959 TVA Act authorized the TVA to "self-finance," giving the TVA more freedom in making investment decisions. The TVA Act limited how much power the TVA could sell outside its jurisdiction, which was defined as the geographic area of the distributors served by the TVA in 1957. Direct appropriations for the TVA power program ended in 1959; and appropriations for TVA's stewardship, economic development, and multipurpose activities ended in 1999. Since 1999, TVA has funded all its operations almost entirely from the sale of electricity and power system financings. The Energy Policy Act of 1992 provided the TVA with an exemption from the Federal Power Act[1] and FERC authority to order utilities to provide transmission service. This exemption, referred to as the "anti-cherry picking" advantage, limits competition to the TVA by limiting access by others to its transmission lines and customers within the TVA's defined service territory. TVA's rates are not subject to state or FERC regulation but are set by the TVA's board of directors.

Like other federal entities, the TVA sells power to municipalities and cooperatives, which resell the power to their customers at a retail rate. The TVA also sells power to federal agencies, customers with large or unusual loads, and exchange power customers (systems that border the TVA's service area). It is the largest federal power agency and supplies power to most of Tennessee, northern Alabama, northeastern Mississippi, and southwestern Kentucky as well as sections of northern Georgia, western North Carolina, and southwestern Virginia. In 2008, the TVA's revenues were $10.4 billion, virtually all from its power programs including wholesale power contracts with 159 municipalities and cooperatives,

---

[1] From Wikipedia, the free encyclopedia:

"The Federal Power Act is a law appearing in chapter 12 of Title 16 of the United States Code, 'Federal regulation and development of power.' Enacted as the Federal Water Power Act in 1920, its original purpose was coordinating hydroelectric projects in the United States. Representative John J. Esch (R-Wisconsin) was the sponsor.

The act created the Federal Power Commission (FPC) (now the Federal Energy Regulatory Commission) as the licensing authority for these plants. The FPC regulated the interstate activities of the electric power and natural gas industries, and coordinated national hydroelectric power activities. The Commission's mandate called for it to maintain reasonable, nondiscriminatory and just rates to the consumer. It was ensured that 37.5% of the income derived from hydroelectric power leases given out under the Water Power Act of 1920 went to the state in which the dam was established.

In 1935 the law was renamed the Federal Power Act, and the FPC's regulatory jurisdiction was expanded to include all interstate electricity transmission.

Subsequent amendments to the law include the following statutes:

Public Utility Regulatory Policies Act (PURPA) (Public Law 95-617)

Energy Security Act (P.L. 96-294)

Electric Consumers Protection Act of 1986 (PL 99-495)

Energy Policy Act of 1992 (PL 102-486)"

which represented nearly 83.4% of total operating revenues in 2008 (SEC 2008 10-K filing). All these contracts require customers to purchase all their electric power and energy requirements from the TVA under a 5, 10, or 15 year notice of termination agreement, which provides for stability in the TVA's revenue from electricity generation.

Today, the TVA operates 3 nuclear, 11 fossil-fuel-fired, 29 hydroelectric, 6 combustion-turbine, and one pumped-storage plants. The TVA's Green Power Switch renewable program includes 16 solar sites, 1 wind-energy site, 1 methane gas facility, and 1 biomass/coal cofiring program. Fossil-fuel plants produce about 60% of TVA's power, nuclear another 30%, and hydropower dams about 10%. Green power contributes less than 1% to the generation mix.

The power marketing administrations

The Bonneville Project Act of 1937 created the Bonneville Power Administration (BPA) for the purpose of generating hydropower from the Columbia River system and promoting regional economic development. The BPA is the largest PMA and second largest federal utility in terms of assets after the TVA. The Western Area Power Administration (WAPA) is the second largest PMA and was created in 1977 by the Department of Energy Organization Act of 1977. The WAPA markets hydropower in the western United States, including power from the Hoover Dam (built in 1935). Both the Southwestern Power Administration and the Southeastern Power Administration were created by the Pick-Sloan Flood Control Act of 1944. According to Section 5 of this act:

> Electric power and energy generated at reservoir projects under the control of the War Department and in the opinion of the Secretary of War not required in the operation of such projects shall be delivered to the Secretary of the Interior, who shall transmit and dispose of such power and energy in such manner as to encourage the most widespread use thereof at the lowest possible rates to consumers consistent with sound business principles, the rate schedules to become effective upon confirmation and approval of the Federal Power Commission. Rate schedules shall be drawn having regard to the recovery (upon the basis of the application of such rate schedules to the capacity of the electric facilities of the projects) of the cost of producing and transmitting such electric energy, including the amortization of the capital investment allocated to power over a reasonable period of years. Preference in the sale of such power and energy shall be given to public bodies and cooperatives.

The federal government provides federal utilities, such as the power marketing administrations (and cooperatives) that participate in the rural utility services (RUS) electric program, access to capital at reduced interest rates. The PMAs sell about 5% of the nation's electricity into the wholesale electric markets, including the sale of power to municipalities and cooperatives, state agencies, IOUs, public utility districts, federal agencies, and industrial customers. The service territory of the Bonneville Power Administration covers Washington, Oregon, and small pieces of western Montana and western Wyoming. The SWPA serves part of Kansas and Texas, Missouri, Oklahoma, Arkansas, and Louisiana. The SEPA serves Illinois, West Virginia, Kentucky, Tennessee, Mississippi, Alabama, Georgia, the Florida Panhandle, North and South Carolina, and Virginia. The WAPA covers California, Nevada, Utah, Arizona, New Mexico, Utah, most of Montana and Wyoming, parts of Texas, North and South Dakota, Nebraska, western and southern Kansas, and the western edges of Minnesota and Iowa.

Based on the 1944 Flood Control Act, PMA electricity is sold "at the lowest possible rates consistent with sound business principles," which are generally less than the price power would be under competitive market conditions. Essentially, PMAs pass lower prices on to statutorily defined preference customers in lieu of profits to particular groups of preferred customers, representing a level of price supports. An exception to this is the TVA, which was estimated by the Energy Information Administration to have had higher wholesale prices than neighboring utilities in 2006.

Rural electric cooperatives

In the 1920s and 1930s, as the electric grid evolved in the United States, it became readily apparent that investor-owned utilities had little interest in building distribution systems in sparsely populated rural areas. To promote agriculture and quality of life in these rural areas, the federal government created the Rural Electrification Administration in 1936, which provided for the creation of the rural electric cooperatives. Rural electric cooperatives are customer-owned electric utilities that provide electricity to end users in their service territories. They are largely in rural areas and cooperatives are organized under state law and subject to the following:

- Cost-based operations (i.e., no profit incentive).
- Members (owner-customers) are entitled to receive a return of, but not a return on, capital they contribute to the organization.
- Governance is based on one-member/one-vote. (The board of directors is elected by the membership.)

In addition to customer-owned cooperatives, some coops may be owned by a number of other coops. Three types of cooperatives exist: (1) distribution only, (2) distribution with power supply, and (3) generation and transmission. Some distribution cooperatives resemble municipal utilities, in that they often do not generate electricity but purchase it from other utilities and federal generation agencies. In the event there is not enough federally provided electricity, groups of coops have come together regionally to create generation-and-transmission cooperatives that own facilities on behalf of the distribution coops. These generating and transmission cooperatives are usually referred to as *power supply cooperatives*.

Generation and transmission coops were largely brought about by regulations in 1970s that made it more difficult for distribution coops to purchase electricity from entities other than the federal government. Currently, total nameplate capacity for G&Ts is 38,604 MW, and they supply approximately 5% of the nation's power needs (U.S. Department of Agriculture, Rural Utilities Service, 2008). There are 864 distribution cooperatives and 66 generation and transmission cooperatives operating in 47 states.

Many cooperatives qualify as tax-exempt organizations under Section 501(c)(12) of the Internal Revenue Code. Under this tax-exempt status, cooperatives must receive at least 85% of their revenue from business conducted with members. Cooperatives that meet Rural Utilities Service eligibility requirements have access to low-cost federal government loans and loan guarantees. Cooperatives account for roughly 10% of electricity sales to ultimate consumers, 12% of the customers, 10% of the revenue, and nearly 43% of the miles of distribution lines in the United States.

An important facet of rural electric cooperatives is their ability to obtain financing through the Rural Utilities Service (RUS) loan program, which was established under the Federal Crop Insurance Reform and Department of Agriculture Reorganization Act of 1994 to provide financial and technical assistance and facilitate electrification of rural America. The RUS is the successor to the Rural Electrification Administration, which was created under the Rural Electrification Act of 1936. This act provided for direct loans and loan guarantees to electric utilities serving customers in rural areas and also provided low-interest, long-term loans from the federal government, which were made at a 2% interest rate until 1973 and increased to 5% between 1973 and 1993 with up to 35 years to maturity.

Today, the RUS program loans and guarantees are used to finance the construction and improvement of electric generation, transmission, and distribution facilities in rural areas. In addition to cooperatives, entities eligible to apply for loan and loan guarantees include states, territories, public power districts, and agencies, such as municipalities that provide retail electric service to rural areas or supply the power needs of distribution borrowers in rural areas. To qualify for loans and loan guarantees, borrowers must show that the loans will be repaid in accordance with their terms and provide adequate security pursuant to the RUS mortgage and loan contract. In 2008, the RUS loan program was redirected in recognition of the deregulation of the wholesale markets, so that the focus of the RUS became the provision of financial assistance for transmission and distribution facilities and so that G&Ts were to consider commercial capital markets for funding new generation (although upgrades to existing generation would still be provided).[2]

Although the RUS loan program supports the coops' need for capital, it is interesting to note that many coops face competitive challenges they find difficult to overcome due to lack of scale economies. As an example of these competitive pressures, in late 2009 American Electric Power's subsidiary AEP Southwestern Electric Power Co. (SWEPCO) offered to purchase the Valley Electric Membership Corporation (VEMCO, a coop), and the VEMCO board unanimously approved a voluntary dissolution of the cooperative, which serves 30,000 member customers in eight Louisiana parishes with 7000 miles of distribution and 90 miles of transmission lines. As a result, VEMCO's members are expected to save nearly 20% on their retail rates from this change of ownership, and in addition, SWEPCO provides payment for the VEMCO patronage capital (return of equity to the membership) at closing subject to approval of this transaction by the Louisiana Public Service Commission, the Arkansas Public Service Commission, the Rural Utilities Service, and the National Rural Utilities Cooperative Finance Corporation.

Nonutility power producers

Nonutility power producers are also referred to as *qualifying facilities* (QFs). Qualifying facilities were established under the Public Utility Regulatory Policies Act of 1978 (PURPA) and include combined heat and power (CHP) plants and small power producers. Combined heat and power plants cogenerate (produce process/district heat and electricity) for primarily

---

[2] Office of Management and Budget, Department of Agriculture, *Budget of the United States Government, Fiscal Year 2008—Appendix*, p. 146 (see www.whitehouse.gov/omb/budget/fy2008/appendix.html.)

business purposes, but also produce electricity for sale into the market. Other nonutility power producers include entities that use renewable resources to generate electricity. These entities have been a small but growing segment of the overall power market.

Power pools

Prior to the creation of independent system operators (ISOs) and regional transmission organizations (RTOs), power pools were created by groups of utilities to merge the scheduling and dispatch function for their generation assets. Multiple utilities within a region could then share their assets, producing higher reliability and lower costs for the pool. This allowed higher cost utilities access to lower priced power and lower cost utilities to receive additional revenue. By pooling scheduling and resources, utilities relied on the pool to minimize costs as opposed to power trading. Prior to deregulation, power pools were used extensively in the Northeast with the largest being PJM (New England and New York), prior to being replaced by ISOs.

Industry restructuring and the competitive electric market

As mentioned earlier, the electric market in the United States has evolved into a hybrid regulated, unregulated, and partially regulated landscape. This restructuring allowed competition in the generation and retail sales sides of the business in unregulated and partially regulated markets, providing opportunities for new players. As noted earlier, the restructuring first took place in the generation market, but other activities, such as system operations and retail sales to end-use customers, moved away from the monopoly (regulated utility) in the restructured power industry. This created distribution and transmission organizations that provide only a service: They do not trade or sell power but distribute power on behalf of other market players. In the evolving competitive markets, these new players include merchant generators, transmission companies, independent system operators, regional transmission organizations, transmission owners, distribution companies (DISTCOs), electric power marketers, and energy service companies (ESCOs).

Merchant generators

In a deregulated market, the role of the IPP to generate and sell power has evolved to that of a merchant generator. In a restructured market, merchant generators are independent for-profit organizations that own and operate generation assets outside the regulated utility. As opposed to IPPs,

who sell their power output under long-term contracts, merchant generators are more likely to sell to a variety of market participants and are generally more at risk to market prices. The markets for merchant generators
include utilities, marketers, ISOs, or directly to end-use customers. Many
merchant generators were formed through the acquisition of the existing
generation's assets of traditional, vertically integrated, regulated utilities
during a state's restructuring process. Other merchant generators were
formed as unregulated subsidiaries of utility holding companies. Examples
of merchant generators include Mirant (MIR), NRG Energy (NRG),
Reliant (RRI), and Dynegy (DYN).

Transmission companies

Transmission companies (transcos) are investor-owned and operate as for-
profit companies. FERC Order 2000 explicitly allows for transcos to own
and operate their transmission facilities (unlike ISOs, which only operate
the system), allowing for a profit structure subject to some regulatory constraints. As competition is generally limited, they are regulated by FERC.
Again, as with merchant generators, transcos typically acquire their transmission lines from formerly vertically integrated utilities or are required
to build their own new transmission lines. An example of a transco is
ITC Transmission, the nation's first and currently largest fully independent
transmission business, which was established in 2003. ITC Transmission
consists of three operating companies: ITC Transmission; Michigan Electric Transmission Company, LLC (METC); and ITC Midwest serving
nearly 80,000 square miles in five states with approximately 15,000 miles
of overhead and underground transmission lines. Through a subsidiary,
ITC Great Plains, new transmission lines are being built in Kansas and
Oklahoma to support the development of the growing wind industry in
the region.

In late 2009, the American Electric Power Company (AEP) announced
the formation of a new transco to cover at least 11 states as part of a
three-part national transmission strategy. According to AEP, "Pursuing
these activities in a Transco, with formula rates adjusted annually by the
Federal Energy Regulatory Commission (FERC), benefits customers
by enhancing AEP's access to capital. This enables the company to under-
take substantial new investment while relieving our operating company
balance sheets of the burden of meeting those capital demands, thereby
allowing them to put capital to work on distribution and generation
needs."

Independent system operators and regional transmission organizations

The FERC proposed the creation of ISOs in 1996, in response to the Energy Policy Act of 1992. FERC's Order 888 in 1996 provided for the creation of ISOs to consolidate and manage the operation of transmission facilities in order to provide nondiscriminatory open transmission service for all generators and transmission customers. FERC Order 2000 supported the role of RTOs to oversee electric transmission and operate wholesale markets across a broad territory (multiple states). Both ISOs and RTOs are independent entities, not affiliated with other market players, and the functions of each include day-to-day grid operations, long-term regional planning, billing and settlements, and other wholesale electric market services. ISOs tend to be smaller in geographic size, and some are not subject to FERC jurisdiction (for example, Canada and central Texas).

The 10 ISOs/RTOs in North America serve two thirds of electricity consumers in the United States and more than 50% in Canada. They include the following:

- Alberta Electric System Operator (AESO, an ISO).
- California Independent System Operator (California, an ISO).
- Electric Reliability Council of Texas (ERCOT, an ISO).
- Ontario's Independent Electricity System Operator (IESO, an ISO).
- ISO New England (ISO-NE, an RTO).
- Midwest Independent Transmission System Operator (Midwest ISO, an RTO).
- New York Independent System Operator (NYISO).
- PJM Interconnection (PJM, an RTO).
- Southwest Power Pool (SPP, an RTO).
- New Brunswick System Operator (NBSO, an ISO).

These are displayed in Figure 3.3.

ISOs/RTOs coordinate generation and transmission across a wide geographic area, matching generation instantaneously to the market demand for electricity. Maintaining an optimal transmission grid requires management of the flow of power across the power grid, an understanding of the capabilities of the system, and the management of payments between producers, marketers, transmission owners, buyers, and others. In ISO and RTO regions, the owner of the transmission assets is referred to as the *transmission owner* (TO), which can be a transco or utility distribution company. The TOs own, maintain, and can expand the transmission system when

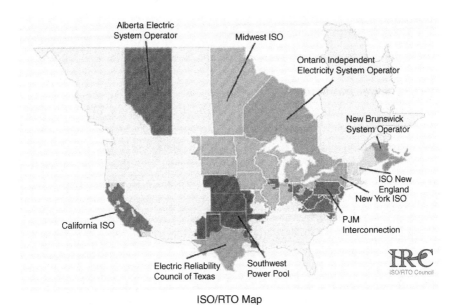

Figure 3.3 North American regions serviced by ISOs and RTOs *(Source: ISO/RTO Council (IRC), 2009 State of the Market Report)*

appropriate. ISOs/RTOs control the operation of the system and provide the TOs compensation for ownership and operation of the transmission lines.

ISOs/RTOs are more than transmission operators, as they provide more extensive grid reliability and transaction support services than previously offered in the market. In addition to nondiscriminatory transmission access, ISOs/RTOs facilitate competition among wholesale suppliers and provide regional planning, energy, or capacity market operation; outage coordination; transactions settlement; billing and collections; risk management; credit risk management; and other ancillary services. Across large regions, they schedule the use of transmission lines, manage the interconnection of new generation, and provide market monitoring services to ensure fair market operations for all participants.

The ISOs/RTOs also play a large role in grid reliability to avoid the types of blackouts experienced in the eastern United States in the past (for example, the northeastern blackouts of 1965 and 2003). In addition, they forecast load and schedule the order that generation is dispatched to assure sufficient power is available in the event that demand rises or a system failure occurs. Regional planning is another important function, in that it takes a broad view of the market to plan intra- and interregional infrastructure expansion for reliability and economic improvement. The ISOs/RTOs play a pivotal role in planning for transmission lines associated with new generation, especially from renewable sources such as wind, geothermal, and solar.

Electric power marketers

Electric power marketers support a competitive market by purchasing electricity from generators and selling the power to utilities, end users, and other market players. As with the stock market, electric power marketers add value by bringing buyers and sellers together, arranging for transmission and other services, and (at times) accepting market risk. Frequently generators have an electric marketing arm that not only sells their own generated power but also buys and trades power in the open market.

Electric power marketers can be divided into two broad categories; those that sell wholesale power to utilities, the grid, or large industrial customers; and the retail electric marketers that focus solely on sales to end-use customers. Retail electric markets tend to focus much of their effort in sales, customer service, billing, collection, product development, and brand awareness, due to large number of potential customers they are trying to reach. Electric power marketers have also created new products, such as the availability of renewable energy to customers in diverse markets, as well as unique services in response to rapidly changing market needs. The following is an example of a customer "carbon footprint" service provided by Constellation New Energy: "The service provides a structured platform that helps prepare customers for participation in GHG emissions reporting programs, including the U.S. EPA Climate Leaders® program, the Carbon Disclosure Project, Global Reporting Initiative (GRI), and other emerging regulatory initiatives. Both scalable and flexible, the offering is easily customized for specific reporting needs, including Corporate Social Responsibility (CSR) reporting, and it provides a web-based, enterprise-level system to manage GHG emissions and broader sustainability program metrics" (www.newenergy.com).

In essence, electric power marketers replicate many of the services previously provided by traditional vertically integrated utilities prior to restructuring.

Utility distribution company

The utility distribution company (UDC) is the monopoly provider of distribution services in a restructured market. Unlike the traditional regulated market distribution company, the UDC may be prohibited by law from selling power (and be allowed only to collect a distribution charge) or may be able to supply power to select customers (typically those not serviced by electric marketers or those who elect not to be serviced by electric marketers).

The distribution of electric power is an intrastate function under the jurisdiction of state public utility commissions (PUCs). Under the traditional regulatory system, the PUCs set the retail rates for electricity, based on the cost of service, which includes the costs of distribution. Retail rates are set by the PUC in ratemaking rulings. The rates include the cost to the utility for generated and purchased power; the capital costs of power, transmission, and distribution plants; all operations and maintenance expenses; and the costs to provide programs often mandated by the PUC for consumer protection and energy efficiency, as well as taxes. As the industry restructures, in some states the PUC will eventually no longer regulate the retail rates for generated or purchased power. Retail electricity prices will be open to the market forces of competition. The PUCs will continue to regulate the rates for distribution of power to the consumer. They also have a say in the siting of distribution lines, substations, and generators. Metering and billing are under the jurisdiction of the PUC and, in some states, are becoming competitive functions. As the industry restructures, the PUCs' responsibilities are changing. The goal of each state PUC remains to provide its state's consumers with reliable, reasonably and fairly priced electric power. More recently, states have taken on the task of promoting renewable energy, which will affect the utility market both in sources of generation and costs. Figure 3.4 shows the current status of state restructuring.

Energy service companies

Energy services companies (ESCOs) actually came about in the regulated market to provide services beyond those provided by the regulated provider, such as appliance maintenance, appliance sales, and demand-side management or energy audits. ESCOs are for-profit entities and, in a restructured market, continue their traditional roles as well as other new roles associated with the restructured market. This can include assisting customers in evaluating energy needs and determining the best solutions to meet those needs based on supplies and services from the various market participants.

Thus far, this chapter has examined the structure of the electric industry, expounding on that which was presented in the introductory chapter.

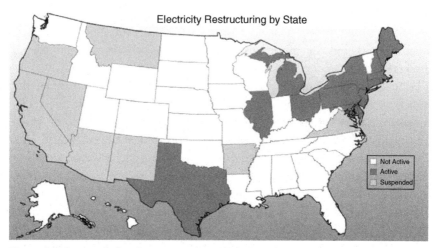

Figure 3.4 Status of electric restructuring, May 2009 *(Source: www.eia.doe.gov/cneaf/ electricity/page/restructuring/restructure_elect.html)*

Next, a comprehensive time line of industry regulation is presented. It should be duly noted that, at the time of this writing, both the regulatory paradigm and the structure of this industry continue to unfold.

3.2 REGULATION OF THE ELECTRIC UTILITY INDUSTRY

A history of regulation in the U.S. electric utility industry

The modern electric utility industry began in the 1880s in New York City with Thomas Edison's Pearl Street generating station. A novelty of its time, it provided reliable central generation, distribution, and a competitive price of 24 cents per kilowatt-hour, compared to the 2009 national average of 9.89 cents per kilowatt-hour (The U.S. Energy Information Administration, 2010). Electric utilities spread rapidly through the rest of the decade, as demand grew from nighttime only, to one that required electricity on demand 24 hours a day, every day of the week. The rapid spread of electric utilities characterized the remainder of that century, with most of the electricity supplied by multiservice privately-owned utilities, which competed aggressively for central city markets, because of the population density that characterized such areas.

In the early part of the 20th century, it became apparent that the supply of electricity was characterized by growing economies of scale. In addition, technological change precipitated the growth and consolidation of the industry, as private suppliers merged into utility holding companies. Even smaller private and municipally owned suppliers were forced to merge with or be acquired by these privately owned multiservice firms. At their peak in the late 1920s, the 16 largest electric power holding companies controlled over 75% of all U.S. generation. And with this came the inevitable: Regulation.

The rise of regulation

The holding companies that evolved in the 1920s had significant monopolistic powers over the market. These "natural monopolies" came about due to the need for large capital investment (high entry hurdle) and economies of scale and scope that produced a lower cost of goods and services compared to many smaller firms serving the same market. The potential for excess profits and nondiscriminatory service to all was real, and the government felt a need to control these powers. The solution to these natural monopolies was the creation of a regulatory structure that granted exclusive service territories and, in exchange, set rates at what was deemed "fair" to the investors (IOUs) and to the customer.[3] This paradigm still exists.

Throughout the 1880s and 1890s, there was fierce competition among the various utilities in existence at that time. However, by the early 1900s, many local governments perceived a need for change in the market or regulation. Reacting to the need to control these natural monopolies, many local governments created municipal utility systems, which effectively eliminated investor-owned utilities. The number of municipally owned utilities tripled between 1896 and 1906, sending a strong signal to IOUs that they could lose their market to government entities. In 1907, the largest utility associations (such as the National Electric Light Association) and business advocacy groups (for example, the National Civic Federation) started to promote regulation of utilities by the state. States quickly adopted regulation, and by 1916, 33 states had created regulatory agencies. At this time, the vertically integrated natural monopoly model was already well established; therefore, state and local governments oversaw all aspects of this market.

Regulation by the federal government was also evolving during this time period. Prior to 1905, utilities were allowed to build and operate

---

[3] Within the boundaries of allowing a fair return on the investment in a utility's stock, regulators also seek to minimize costs to consumers, ensure reliable service, and provide relatively stable rates and an efficient use of resources. Furthermore, ensuring safe practices by utilities is paramount.

dams with little or no government oversight. However, in 1905, the federal government began to license dams and charge fees for their construction. In 1920, the Federal Water Power Act and the Federal Power Commission were created to regulate rates, financing, and services of utilities with licensed dams. As a result of the Great Depression, the government started to compete with investor-owned utilities through the creation of federal utility agencies, such as the TVA (1933) and numerous dam projects.

During the 1920s holding companies incurred increasing amounts of debt, and the economics of generating and transmitting electricity were rapidly changing. A classic monopoly situation was unfolding, in that economies of scale had not been taken advantage of when the marginal costs of adding new generation were less than the average cost of new generation. During the prosperous 1920s, these highly leveraged holding companies managed to remain solvent, but after the stock market crash in 1929 and the resulting lower demand (and hence revenue), these entities could no longer service their debt. As more holding companies went bankrupt, service deteriorated, and investors lost millions of dollars. From 1929 to 1936, 53 holding companies went into bankruptcy or receivership and 23 others were forced to default on interest payments.

In 1928, the Federal Trade Commission issued a report warning that the holding company structure was unsound and "frequently a menace to the investor or the consumer or both." As the Great Depression dragged on, the federal government decided regulatory action was required. The Federal Power Act, which established a federal utility regulatory system, was enacted at the same time as the Public Utility Act of 1935; these two acts were intended to work in tandem. Title I of the Public Utility Act of 1935 is known as the Public Utilities Holding Company Act of 1935 (PUHCA). PUHCA ultimately broke up interstate holding companies, and between 1935 and 1958, 759 utilities were separated and the number of holding companies dropped from 216 to 18.

The Public Utility Holding Company Act

The Public Utility Holding Company Act, enacted in 1935, was aimed at breaking up the unconstrained and excessively large trusts that then controlled the nation's electric and gas distribution networks. Before PUHCA, almost half of all electricity generated in the United States was controlled by three huge holding companies and more than 100 other holding companies existed. The size and complexity of these huge trusts made industry regulation and oversight control by the states impossible. Many of these holding companies were looked at as either pyramid schemes (investing a small amount at the top and reaping big rewards) or complex organizations formed solely to avoid state regulations and hide true service costs to the customer. PUHCA was passed in an era when financial pyramid schemes were extensive through the country and Congress felt a need to act. These pyramids were sometimes 10 organizational layers deep, illustrating the difficulty in regulation as shown in the following discussion (Hyman, 1994):

> The Insull[4] interests (which operated in 32 states and owned electric companies, textile mills, ice houses, a paper mill, and a hotel) controlled 69% of the stock of Corporation Securities and 64% of the stock of Insull Utility Investments. Those two companies together owned 28% of the voting stock of Middle West Utilities. Middle West Utilities owned 8 holding companies, 5 investment companies, 2 service companies, 2 securities companies, and 14 operating companies. It also owned 99% of the voting stock of National Electric Power. National, in turn, owned one holding company, one Service company, one paper mill, and two operating companies. It also owned 93% of the voting stock of National Public Service. National Public Service owned three building companies, three miscellaneous firms, and four operating utilities. It also owned 100% of the voting stock of Seaboard Public Service. Seaboard Public Service owned the voting stock of five utility operating companies and one Ice Company. The utilities, in turn, owned 18 subsidiaries.

As a result of the Great Depression and collapse of several large holding companies, the ensuing Federal Trade Commission (FTC) investigations criticized these holding company structures for their many abuses, including higher-cost electricity to consumers. In 1932, presidential hopeful Franklin D. Roosevelt criticized the "Insull monstrosity" for inflating the value of its holdings and selling worthless bonds when Middle West Utilities and many of its 284 affiliates were placed in receivership. Under PUHCA, the Securities Exchange Commission (SEC) was charged with the administration of the act and the regulation of the holding companies. One of the most important features of the act was that the SEC was given the power to break up the massive interstate holding companies by requiring them to divest their holdings until each became a single consolidated system serving a circumscribed geographic area. Another feature of the

---

[4] Samuel Insull worked for Thomas Edison and later became the vice-president of the Edison General Electric Company. In 1887, Insull established the Chicago Edison Company, and in 1897, Commonwealth Electric was formed. In 1907, Insull consolidated Chicago Edison and Commonwealth Electric to form Commonwealth Edison Company.

law permitted holding companies to engage only in business that was essential and appropriate for the operation of a single integrated utility. This latter restriction practically eliminated the participation of nonutilities in wholesale electric power sales. The law contained a provision that all holding companies had to register with the SEC, which was authorized to supervise and regulate the holding company system. Through the registration process, the SEC decided whether the holding company would need to be regulated under or exempted from the requirements of the act. The SEC also was charged with regulating the issuance and acquisition of securities by holding companies. Strict limitations on intrasystem transactions and political activities were also imposed.

Aside

PUHCA effectively reorganized the electric and gas industries and facilitated greater federal and state regulation of both wholesale and retail prices. However, over the years, there have been movements to repeal PUHCA and allow holding companies to buy utilities in different parts of the country to provide economies of scale and corresponding lower rates. In 1992, PUHCA was amended by the Energy Policy Act to exempt firms engaged exclusively in wholesale sale of electricity. However, during the Enron corporate scandal, there was a sense of déjà vu back to the formative years before PUHCA, when investors lost confidence in the basic institutions of capitalism. The many parallels between Enron and Insull Investments include the years it took the FTC to unravel both firms, financial structures and corruption of the chief executives (Insull and Lay) and the ability of both firms to successfully keep the government out of their business dealings. Both firms were even groundbreaking: Enron with EnronOnline, its Internet-based energy-trading system; and Insull, which pioneered "massing production" (later shortened to "mass production") and keeping power plants running 24/7 to defray its high fixed costs. And like Enron, Insull's empire pushed its financial dealings to the brink of manipulating the nation's energy markets. As a result of the Energy Policy Act of 2005, repeal of PUHCA became effective in 2006, marking the beginning of a new era of holding company regulation, which is discussed further in the following section.

The era after PUHCA

Through the 1940s, 1950s, and 1960s, the electric industry continued to grow and electric prices dropped significantly due in part to the economies of scale, regulation, and technological advancements. In the early 1960s, the electricity industry created the North American Power Systems Interconnection Committee (NAPSIC), an informal voluntary organization, to coordinate the bulk power system in the United States and Canada, resulting in the formation of the largest electricity grid in the world. However, unrecognized weaknesses were developing in the system that were revealed in the northeast blackout in 1965. The blackout started with the failure of one line and interrupted electric service across 80,000 square miles (eight states), affecting 30 million customers in the Northeastern United States and large parts of Canada. In response to this situation, Congress established a regional coordinating body to ensure electricity supply reliability. The North American Electric Reliability Council (NERC) was formed in 1968 as part of the Electric Power Reliability Act of 1967.

Focus on reliability: The North America Reliability Council

In 1968, nine regional reliability organizations were formalized under the North American Reliability Council, along with regional planning coordination guides, as a replacement to the previous voluntary organization, the North American Power Systems Interconnection Committee. NERC was responsible for promoting reliability efforts and assisting the regional councils by developing common operating policies and procedures. NERC developed a complex committee structure to bring together volunteer industry experts to consider power integration issues and provide education to support its mission to improve system reliability.

After the northeast blackout of 2003 and passage of the Energy Policy Act of 2005, FERC was authorized to designate a national electric reliability organization (ERO) to develop and enforce compliance with mandatory reliability standards in the United States. As a nongovernment body, it was designated a "self-regulatory organization," recognizing the interconnected and international nature of the electric grid. In 2006, FERC certified NERC as the ERO for the United States. The North American Electric Reliability Corporation, a nonprofit corporation was then formed as the successor to the North American Electric Reliability Council.

Prior to becoming the national ERO, NERC's guidelines for power system operation and accreditation were referred to as *policies* and, although strongly encouraged, were ultimately only voluntary. As an ERO, NERC worked with all stakeholders to revise its policies into standards and now has authority to enforce those standards under financial penalties in the United States as well as several provinces in Canada.

U.S. organizations violating the standards can be fined up to $1 million per day per violation. Efforts are currently underway with Canadian and Mexican governments to obtain comparable authority for NERC.

NERC currently oversees eight regional reliability entities that control all the interconnected power systems in the contiguous United States, Canada, and a portion of Baja California in Mexico. NERC's new responsibilities include working with stakeholders to develop standards, monitoring and enforcing compliance, assessing resource adequacy, and providing accredited education and training programs to operators. NERC also investigates and analyzes the causes of significant power system disturbances to better prevent others from occurring in the future.

There are three major and two minor NERC interconnections and nine regional reliability councils. The reliability councils within the eastern interconnection are

- Florida Reliability Coordinating Council (FRCC).
- Midwest Reliability Organization (MRO).
- Northeast Power Coordinating Council (NPCC).
- Reliability First Corporation (RFC).
- SERC Reliability Corporation (SERC).
- Southwest Power Pool, Inc. (SPP).

The western interconnection consists of the Western Electricity Coordinating Council (WECC), and the Texas council is the Electric Reliability Council of Texas (ERCOT).

The Northeast Power Coordinating Council (NPCC) covers portions of Canada and is often considered to be part of the eastern interconnection. The Alaska interconnection, Alaska Systems Coordinating Council (ASCC), is not tied to any of the other interconnections, is not generally counted among North America's interconnections, and is an affiliate member of NERC.

NERC develops and maintains reliability standards, including regional reliability standards that must approved by FERC and applicable authorities in Canada and Mexico. These are displayed in Figure 3.5.

NERC relies on the regional councils to enforce the NERC standards with bulk power system owners, operators, and users through approved delegation agreements. Regional councils are also responsible for monitoring compliance of the registered entities within their regional boundaries, assuring correction of all violations, and assessing penalties for failure to comply. U.S. law requires that NERC's enforcement actions be filed publicly with the FERC.

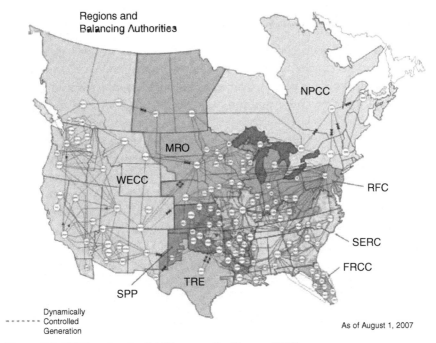

Figure 3.5 NERC regional reliability councils *(Source: NERC)*

The 1970s, a time of change

The electric power industry was buffeted by change throughout the 1970s, almost a perfect storm of unforeseen and uncontrollable events. In 1970, Congress passed the Clean Air Act as a response to acid rain caused by power plants as well as other environmental issues. This act significantly reduced allowable emissions from power plants, signaling the beginning of massive investments in non-generating emission control equipment, cleaner technologies, and "compliance" fuels. The Clean Air Act was soon followed by the Water Pollution Control Act of 1972, regulating water emissions and how a power plant uses water for importing functions, such as cooling and thermal emissions. The year 1973 can been seen as the beginning of the nation's energy crisis, when the Organization of Petroleum Exporting Countries' (OPEC) oil embargo hit, resulting in substantial fuel and electric price increases. Congress reacted to the oil embargo and energy shortages by focusing on conservation and energy efficiency through the passage of the Energy Supply and Environmental Coordination Act of 1974, requiring utilities to stop using natural gas or other petroleum-based products to generate electricity. Even residential use of natural gas was affected by the curtailment of gas used for residential lighting. The Resource Conservation and Recovery Act (RCRA) of 1976 and the Federal Hazardous Waste Amendment in 1984 gave EPA the authority to control hazardous waste from "cradle to grave" and established a framework for the management of nonhazardous solid wastes. This included a focus on waste minimization and phasing out land disposal of hazardous waste.

Prior to the 1970s, energy regulation development was controlled by a number of federal agencies, including such cabinet-level departments as the Department of Interior and the Department of Agriculture, as well as independent regulatory agencies, such as the Federal Power Commission and the Atomic Energy Commission. In 1977, a number of government institutions were established to address the energy crisis more centrally, including the Department of Energy (DOE) and the Western and the Federal Energy Regulatory Commissions. The Department of Energy Organization Act in 1977 placed a number of federal energy agencies under the direction of the DOE, including the Federal Energy Administration, the Energy Research and Development Administration, the Federal Power Commission, and parts of several other agencies and programs including the nuclear weapons program (with the exception of nuclear energy, which is controlled by the Nuclear Regulatory Commission). The act requires the DOE to work with other agencies, including the Environmental Protection Agency (EPA), the Bureau of Mines, and the Nuclear Regulatory Commission (NRC) in regard to standards and regulations as they pertain to the utility industry. The 1977 act directs the DOE to conduct research and development to support the development of new technologies within the energy field and requires the DOE to submit a National Energy Policy Plan biennially.

The Federal Energy Regulatory Commission

The Federal Energy Regulatory Commission was established within the DOE and is an independent agency that regulates the interstate transmission of electricity, natural gas, and oil. The Federal Power Commission (FPC), founded in 1920, was the predecessor to FERC created to coordinate federal hydropower development. In 1935, the FPC was transformed into an independent agency to regulate both hydropower and interstate electricity. All FERC decisions are reviewable by the federal courts. In 1983, Congress ended federal regulation of wellhead natural gas prices, and in response, FERC sought greater competition to both the natural gas and electric industries. The Energy Policy Act (EPAct) of 2005 expanded FERC's authority to impose mandatory reliability standards on the bulk transmission system and impose penalties for the manipulation of electricity and natural gas markets. These additional FERC responsibilities as they pertain to the electric industry include

- Regulation of transmission and wholesale electricity in interstate commerce.
- Review of certain mergers and acquisitions and corporate transactions by electricity companies.
- Review of siting application for electric transmission projects under limited circumstances.
- Licensing and inspection of private, municipal, and state hydroelectric projects.
- Protecting the reliability of the high-voltage interstate transmission system through mandatory reliability standards.
- Monitoring and investigating energy markets.
- Enforcing FERC regulatory requirements through imposition of civil penalties and other means.
- Overseeing environmental matters related to natural gas and hydroelectricity projects and other matters.
- Administering accounting and financial reporting regulations and conduct of regulated companies.

The FERC regulates approximately 1600 hydroelectric projects in the United States and oversees new mergers and antimarket manipulation regulations. FERC was heavily involved in the California electricity crisis and has collected over $6.3 billion from California electric market participants by facilitating settlements. It also investigated allegations of electricity market manipulation by Enron and others in the electric markets. More recently, it promoted the voluntary formation of the RTOs and ISOs to facilitate access to the grid and supported the repeal of PUHCA and enactment of the Public Utility Holding Company Act of 2005.

The National Energy Conservation Policy Act of 1978

The National Energy Conservation Policy Act of 1978 was a comprehensive energy statute comprising five separate but intertwined public laws dealing with energy conservation (National Energy Conservation Policy Act), coal conversion (The Power Plant and Industrial Fuel Use Act), public utility rates (Public Utility Regulatory Policies Act), natural gas pricing (Natural Gas Policy Act), and a series of taxes (Energy Tax Act) designed to discourage energy consumption and accelerate the transition to alternative fuels. The main purpose of the National Energy Conservation Policy Act was to reduce oil imports and promote more efficient use of energy. The Power Plant and Industrial Fuel Use Act specifically restricted the construction of power plants fueled by natural gas or petroleum and promoted the use of coal and alternative fuels, supporting the need for greater energy security. However, the most significant of these acts was the Public Utility Regulatory Policies Act.

The Public Utility Regulatory Policies Act of 1978

Restructuring of the electric utility industry began with the passage of the Public Utility Regulatory Policies Act. In 1978, President Carter suggested changes to electric pricing structures, as he felt that the typical "rate structure" encouraged the use of electricity by charging higher prices for the first increments of electricity used by customers with subsequent increments costing less per unit. As an example, the first 50 kWh of use might cost 5.0 cents/kWh, the next 50 kWh 4.0 cents/kWh, and the next 100 kWh 3.5 cents/kWh, and anything greater than 200 kWh only 3.0 cents/kWh. (This is known as a decliningblock rate structure.) In an era when utilities were trying to reach an economy of scale and costs were decreasing, this "promotional rate structure" made sense. But in an era of increasing energy costs, when the country was more concerned about conservation, this declining block rate structure did not support public policy. PURPA supported the elimination of these declining block rate structures and required state commissions to order utilities to develop new rate structures. However, the most significant part of PURPA was the requirement of electric utilities to interconnect with and buy whatever amount of capacity and energy was offered from any facility meeting the criteria for a qualifying facility. This was a significant departure from traditional regulation, which generally sets the price of electricity on the basis of the cost of production. The utilities were then required to pay for that power at the utility's own incremental or avoided cost of production. An initial interpretation of *avoided* was the cost of additional electricity produced by the utility itself. However, under PURPA's requirements, some utilities that already had sufficient supply available to meet demand, either through their own generation or through purchases from other sources, also had to purchase generation from a qualifying facility.

To facilitate the entry of the nonutility companies into the market, Congress exempted most qualifying facilities from rate and accounting regulation by the FERC under the Federal Power Act; from regulation by the Securities and Exchange Commission under PUHCA; and from the state rate, financial, and organizational regulation of the regulated utilities. In addition, by simplifying contracts and the power sales process, it provided increased financial certainty for creditors and equity sponsors and eliminated several barriers into the marketplace for smaller energy producers. Another significant provision of PURPA was the encouragement of independent power producers and wheeling so that large, industrial firms could contract with other nonutility sources rather than be forced to purchase from the local utility (in fact, PURPA required that electric utilities contract with certain independent power suppliers for their power).

At the time of PURPA, energy conservation and the concept of demand-side management were critical components of energy policy but not the only elements. The Carter administration at the time also sought greater production of coal and oil as well as nuclear energy (President Carter had a nuclear background) with the hope of not adversely affecting the environment. Federal funding through agencies such as the DOE also promoted alternative energy technologies. PURPA also facilitated the further development of gas-turbine technology and cogeneration. During the military buildup of the 1980s, manufacturers of jet engines received government funding for research and development to advance the efficiency and reliability of this technology. The market responded to these increases in efficiency and reliability by creating aero-derivative jet engines (nominal 10 MW) for use in electric power production (previous to this, industrial turbines dominated the electric generation market). These aero-derivative gas turbine cogeneration units could be installed at much lower capital costs and obtain thermal efficiencies in the 50% range, which made them much more attractive than central station plants. The technological advances were then extended to industrial turbines and included the concept of combining cycles (gas combustion cycle with a steam heat recovery cycle) to produce more efficient gas turbine technology and reduce the cost-minimizing level of capacity to 400 MW. The reduced cost also made it easier for new players to enter the market, and for existing players, the lower cost reduced the risk of investment should market conditions change. PURPA also supported development in renewable energy technologies, and in states such as California, new alternative energy producers flourished. This situation created a new fledgling industry that would advance the technology to where we are today.

As mentioned earlier, PURPA also started the movement for the deregulation of the power industry and the breakup of the traditional vertically integrated electric utility firms. With the new entrants into the electric market, regulators started to question the need for monopolies and the vertically integrated structure. This act broke the stranglehold that traditional power companies had on the generation function, since any unregulated qualifying facility could now sell electricity to the power grid. However, it should be recognized that PURPA did not create a competitive market, in that qualifying facilities sold and generated power at a premium and not at rates competitive with existing utility generation rates. Rather, PURPA brought into question the need for the traditional vertically integrated monopoly to supply future new generation needs, as qualifying facilities demonstrated that they could bring new capacity online at the same cost as the monopolies. Prior to the 1970s, utilities could still exploit economies of scale and the increasing thermal efficiencies of steam turbines, generators, and boiler technology. In the 1970s and 1980s, the cost of new generation was now driven more by the economics of cogeneration (the ability to sell both steam and electricity) and later by the lower cost and efficiency of combined cycle gas turbines, as well as reduced natural gas prices and greater gas availability (recall earlier that the use of natural gas for electricity generation was actually banned four years earlier in the Energy Supply and Environmental Coordination Act of 1974). In addition to questioning the concept of utilities as natural monopolies, the justification for regulations was even brought into question. As qualifying facilities demonstrated that many generators in a market could exist, the seed for a competitive generation market was planted. Interestingly, there are many similarities between PURPA andcurrent state renewable portfolio standards, including the fact that many cogenerators sold power into the market not at the control of the utility or regional dispatch but when it just happened to be available, similar to the situation today with wind and solar energy.

The 1970s and passage of PURPA represented difficult times for the electric utility industry, marked by environmental legislation and concerns, a poor economy, inflation that adversely affected the construction of new plants, occupational safety, and low load growth. However, the 1970s also marked a time when many power plants were still being constructed to supply the forecasted load growth. These primarily coal and nuclear power plants took years to construct and represented significant capital outlays by the industry. Despite the robust regulatory climate and well-intentioned natural monopolies, rapid inflation made the cost of new power plants unpredictable, financing more costly, risks associated with safety concerns and regulation more apparent, and most important, the diminished load growth meant that the industry now had excess generation and reserve margins. These regulatory-approved costs were then passed on to consumers, which resulted in the near tripling of electric energy costs between 1969 and 1985. In 1983, the president of Virginia Electric and Power Company, William Berry, made the profound statement that "[a]s in so many other regulated monopolies, technological developments have overtaken and destroyed the rationale for regulation. Electricity generation is no longer a natural monopoly."

It seemed only fitting, given all the changes and turmoil of the 1970s, that the end of the decade was marked by additional energy turmoil. In January 1979, the Shah of Iran was removed from power and the resulting oil embargo created worldwide shortages and significantly disrupted the U.S. economy. This was followed by the accident at Three Mile Island in 1979, which significantly increased the cost of nuclear power, initiated regulatory delays, and certainly brought into question the future of nuclear power in this country. In April 1979, responding to growing energy shortages, President Carter announced gradual price controls on oil and proposed a windfall profit tax on oil companies. This was quickly followed by government programs to increase research and development funding of renewable energy and promote commercialization of these technologies through solar development banks. In July 1979, President Carter proposed an $88 billion decade-long effort to support U.S. energy independence through the development of synthetic fuel from the nation's coal and oil shale reserves. In 1980, Congress passed the Energy Security Act to support the creation of a synthetic fuel industry producing 2 million barrels of oil per day by 1992. This act created the United States Synthetic Fuels Corporation to provide financial assistance and encourage private investment in this new industry.

Industry restructuring in the 1980s and 1990s

The 1980s represented an era of deregulation for a number of industries in the United States. In 1978, the airline industry was deregulated followed by the telecommunications industry in 1984. In many areas of the country, electric utilities also distributed natural gas (known as combination utilities), and the movement for deregulation hit this segment of the market first, when deregulation opened access to transmission pipelines and created a spot market in 1987 (the gas industry has a similar vertical structure to the electric industry, in that there are producers, transmission pipelines, and distribution pipelines). Based on the discussions surrounding the deregulation of other industries at the time, Congress, the FERC, and many state regulators believed that electric industry deregulation would lower costs to consumers while increasing supply and improving reliability.

From its inception, the FERC has encouraged and approved the use of market-based electric rates to support the development of an efficient and competitive market. Between 1985 and 1991, the FERC addressed 31 requests to sell wholesale electric power at market-based rates, although only a few were approved (Notice of Public Conference and Request for Comments on Electricity Issues, Docket No. PL91-1-000, April 1991). The pace of market-based rate requests picked up substantially after the passage of the Natural Gas Utilization Act.

The promotion of market-based rates was a significant step by FERC in industry restructuring and deregulation. In the traditional regulated culture, wholesale and retail electricity rates are calculated based on a utility's costs plus a negotiated rate of return on the utility's (prudent) investments. This approach ensures investors that the utility will cover its costs of operation but does not encourage that full evaluation of all risks associated with that investment. Should the project be uneconomical (cost overruns, changes in demand, etc.), the utility could still recover its costs plus the return on the investment by passing along the costs to the customer in the form of higher electric prices.[5] This may shelter the investor from risk and facilitate financing, but it does not necessarily promote competitive wholesale power markets. By the mid-1990s, the FERC had approved the use of market-based rates for more than 100 power suppliers and a competitive electric power market was emerging.

Other federal legislation in the 1980s that affected the electric power industry included the Pacific Northwest Electric Power Planning and Conservation Act of 1980. This act, in addition to creating the Pacific Northwest Electric Power and Conservation Council, provided for the Bonneville Power Administration to purchase and exchange electric

---

[5] However, it is more likely the case that some of these costs will be not be recoverable in the utility's rate base. This occurred with the Louisville Gas and Electric Company's Trimble County Unit Number 1 in which 25% of the cost was not allowed to be recovered in the rate base since anticipated load growth did not materialize. In addition, a $2.5 million refund and an $8.5 million rate reduction was ordered as part of the settlement agreement.

power with Northwest utilities at the "average system cost" and gave the agency authority to plan for and acquire additional power to meet its growing load requirements.

The Economic Recovery Tax Act of 1981 introduced a new formula for determining allowable tax depreciation deductions. The accelerated cost recovery system (ACRS) enabled taxpayers to claim generous depreciation deductions based on the system's permitted depreciable life, method, and salvage value assumptions. The generation, transmission, and distribution assets of regulated electric utilities were categorized as public utility property and, under ACRS, were assigned relatively long depreciable lives, which influenced new capital investments toward lower-cost technologies.

The Electric Consumers Protection Act of 1986 (ECPA) was the first significant change to the hydropower licensing provisions of the Federal Power Act (FPA) since 1935. The changes included elimination of preferences on relicensing and the importance of environmental considerations in the licensing process associated with an increased role of the state and federal fish and wildlife agencies in reviewing licenses. The act also eliminated PURPA benefits for hydroelectric projects at new dams and diversions, unless the projects satisfy stringent environmental conditions. Under this act, FERC's enforcement powers were also substantially increased.

Another important law of the 1980s was the Tax Reform Act of 1986. In this legislation the ACRS method for determining asset depreciation (Economic Recovery Act of 1981) was replaced with the modified accelerated cost recovery system (MACRS). The MACRS corrected the disparity in treatment of property between regulated and non-regulated utilities. As part of the act, investment tax credits were repealed. (The investment credit of the federal income tax law was a dollar-to-dollar offset, available for regulated and non-regulated utilities such as taxpayers, and intended to encourage capital investment.)

Natural Gas Utilization Act of 1987

As it affected the electric industry, the Natural Gas Utilization Act (NGUA) amended the Power Plant and Industrial Fuel Use Act of 1978 to repeal the prohibitions on the use of natural gas and petroleum as a primary energy source in new power plants and new major fuel-burning installations. This act gave the secretary of the DOE authority to prohibit the use of natural gas in certain boilers and restricted increased use of petroleum by existing power plants. The act also required power plants to have sufficient inherent design characteristics to permit the addition of equipment, such as pollution control devices, necessary to allow the plant to be capable of using coal or another alternate fuel as the primary energy source. In addition, this act stipulated that no new power plant could be constructed or operated as a base-load power plant without the inherent design capability of being able to be converted to coal from natural gas or oil in the event market conditions warranted. Exempt from this requirement were peak-load and intermediate-load power plants, which opened the door for IPPs, as often such plants were constructed to meet peak or intermediate loads using integrated gasification combined cycle (IGCC) gas turbines fueled by natural gas. Supporting the use of natural gas to generate power was the act's repeal of the incremental natural gas pricing provisions in the Natural Gas Policy Act of 1978.

The 1990s—The pace of industry restructuring accelerates

In January 1990, energy prices were relatively stable. However, this changed dramatically in August 1990, when Iraq invaded Kuwait, marking the beginning of the Gulf War and another era of energy concern. Another important event affecting the electric utility industry was the passage of the Clean Air Act Amendments of 1990 (CAAA). These amendments significantly affected the industry, both in the need to reduce emissions and changes to fuel buying practices. A major objective of the CAAA was to reduce annual sulfur dioxide emissions by 10 million tons and annual nitrogen oxide emissions by 2 million tons from 1980 levels, understanding that electric generators were responsible for a large portion of the proposed reductions. The program instituted under the CAAA established a market-based approach to sulfur dioxide emission reductions (cap and trade), while relying on more traditional technological methods for nitrogen oxide reductions.

Despite PURPA's objective of providing market access to qualifying facilities, many new players in the market accused vertically integrated electric utilities of favoring their own generation and control area operators giving preference to their company's resources. Both the FERC and Congress believed that, without open access to the transmission system, the end-use customer would not realize all the benefits of market-based rates and new generation technologies. The primary intent of the Energy Policy Act of 1992 was to create open access to the transmission system for qualifying facilities, other utility generating companies, and independent power producers.

The Energy Policy Act of 1992

The Energy Policy Act of 1992 (EPACT) created a structure of competition in the wholesale electric generation market and defined a new category of electric generator, the exempt wholesale generator (EWG). EWGs were not constrained by PUHCA imposed limitations, which made it easier for them to enter the wholesale electricity market. EWGs differ from PURPA qualifying facilities in that they were not required to meet PURPA's cogeneration or renewable fuels provisions, and utilities were not required to purchase power from EWGs. Like qualifying facilities, EWGs did not sell to retail customers nor did they own transmission facilities. But, unlike qualifying facilities, EWGs were not regulated and were able to charge market-based rates. EPACT also mandated that FERC provide transmission system access to wholesale suppliers on a case-by-case basis. This access provision eliminated a major barrier for utility-affiliated and nonaffiliated power producers to compete for new non–rate-based power plants. At the time of EPACT, many of the new non–rate-based generating units were expected to be gas turbines, due to the lower capital costs compared relative to coal-fired plants.

EPACT has been considered one of the most significant pieces of legislation in the history of the industry. The act had a significant impact on municipal and rural cooperatives, in that it provided access to new generators (EWGs and qualifying facilities) in distant wholesale markets, freeing them from their dependency on surrounding investor-owned utilities for their wholesale power requirements. This led to a nationwide open-access electric power transmission grid supporting the wholesale market (EPACT prohibits FERC from ordering retail wheeling to end-use customers). Anyone selling power at wholesale now has the ability to gain access to transmission at "just and reasonable" rates as defined by the FERC. EPACT directs FERC when it issues a transmission order to approve rates that permit the utility to recover all legitimate, verifiable economic costs incurred in connection with the transmission services. Such costs include "an appropriate share, if any, [of] necessary associated services, including, but not limited to, an appropriate share of any enlargement of transmission facilities." The language also says that FERC "shall ensure, to the extent practicable," that costs incurred by the wheeling utility are recovered from the transmission customer rather than "from a transmitting utility's existing wholesale, retail, and transmission customers."

EPACT also provided reforms to PUHCA, including the expansion of FERC's authority and the creation of players in the market now exempt from SEC regulation. PUHCA reform was seen as critical by many of the market players. Nonutility groups argued that revising PUHCA without revising transmission-access rules would reinforce the utility monopolistic structure, while regulated public utilities expressed concern that the increased access to transmission would jeopardize the reliability of the grid. Prior to EPACT, utilities had no obligation to provide access to their transmission lines, except under PURPA, they were required to interconnect with and purchase power from qualifying facilities. Under the Federal Power Act, as amended by PURPA, FERC also appeared to have authority to require wheeling under limited circumstances. *Wheeling* is defined when a transmission utility owner allows another utility or independent power producer to move (or wheel) power over its transmission lines. However, FERC and the federal courts later ruled that PURPA authority was limited and did not allow FERC to require a utility to wheel power to its wholesale customers or to encourage competition in bulk power markets. It should be noted that, in addition to FERC, the federal courts can also require wheeling, but only when the Sherman Antitrust Act has been violated. This would include circumstances where a regulated public utility refuses to wheel power in an attempt to monopolize a particular market. The Atomic Energy Act of 1954, the Nuclear Regulatory Commission, and the U.S. Attorney General may require wheeling access as a condition for issuing a construction permit for a nuclear plant. EPACT broadened available exceptions substantially by giving FERC new authority to order utilities to provide wheeling over their transmission systems to utilities and nonutilities alike.

In addition to granting greater access to the transmission grid and defining EWGs, EPACT also encouraged utilities to make investments in conservation and energy efficiency as amendments to PURPA. Utilities are now required on a regular basis to perform integrated resource planning, file those plans with state regulatory authority, allow for public participation and comment, and implement the plan. The law also stipulated that state-regulated utilities invest in energy conservation, energy efficiency, and demand-side management programs and be allowed a rate of return to be "at least as profitable, giving appropriate consideration to income lost from reduced sales due to investments in and expenditures for conservation and efficiency, as its investments in and expenditures for the construction of new generation, transmission, and distribution equipment."

Energy efficiency under EPACT also extended to the utilities, own assets. The act provided for rate charges to be sufficient to encourage energy efficiency investments in cost-effective improvements associated with power generation, transmission, and distribution. State regulatory authorities and non-regulated electric utilities under EPACT were "required to consider the disincentives caused by existing ratemaking policies, and practices, and consider incentives that would encourage better maintenance, and investment in more efficient power generation, transmission and distribution equipment."

EPACT also repealed the alternative minimum tax for some smaller producers. In addition to other regulatory measures, such as the Natural Gas Utilization Act of 1987, EPACT was intended in part to expand the use of natural gas and contributed to the rise of gas-fired nonutility generators as the fastest growing source of electric generation capacity. Electric generation from natural gas grew from 17% of the market in 1996 to 22% of the market in 2003.

It quickly became clear, after the passage of EPACT, that additional work was still needed to support industry restructuring. In 1993, the FERC issued a policy statement regarding regional transmission groups (RTGs) to clarify the provision of transmission services and facilitate the resolution of disputes. The FERC believed that RTGs would encourage negotiated agreements between transmission providers and minimize litigation before FERC (U.S. Federal Energy Commission, 1993).

During the mid-1990s, FERC also established guidelines for "comparable transmission access" for third parties. The concept of comparable access is based on the assumption that owners of the transmission grid should offer third parties access to the grid on the same or comparable basis and under the same or comparable terms and conditions as the transmission owner's use of the system. Comparable access is one of the key provisions in the open access transmission tariff specified in Order 888 (67FERC61, 168). The FERC also issued, in 1995, its *Transmission Pricing Policy Statement*, expanding the prior "postage-stamp" and contract path pricing mechanisms to a variety of other pricing methods more suitable for competitive wholesale power markets (U.S. Federal Energy Commission, 1994, 1995).

Despite the FERC's authority and rulings regarding wheeling, disparities still existed in the comprehensiveness and quality of transmission services provided by transmission owners to other users. To further encourage open access to transmission grids, the FERC applied the comparability standard when a utility requested as a condition for approval for market-based rates or approval to merge with another utility. Despite these FERC efforts, open, nondiscriminatory transmission access still did not exist universally at the end of 1995. In 1996, FERC issued Order 888 to correct the lack of universal access, which was considered at the time to be the most ambitious and far-reaching ruling by FERC to eliminate impediments to competition in the electric power industry.

FERC Orders 888 and 889 (1996)

FERC Order 888 required all public utilities that own, control, or operate transmission facilities to have on file an open-access, nondiscriminatory transmission tariff. The order also allows public utilities to seek recovery of stranded costs associated with providing open access (U.S. Federal Energy Commission, 1996). The FERC issued Order 889 establishing the open-access, same-time information system (OASIS). By eliminating anticompetitive practices through a universally applied open-access transmission tariff, the FERC also recognized that regulated utilities could have stranded costs and provided for the recovery of those costs as part of the transition to competitive markets. The FERC nondiscriminatory transmission tariff specified that, by July 9, 1996, utilities that own or control transmission must have filed a single pro forma open-access tariff specifying minimum conditions that offer load-based and point-to-point network services, contract-based services, and ancillary services to eligible customers comparable to the service they provide themselves at the wholesale level. The universal transmission tariff eliminated FERC's time-consuming case-by-case evaluation of wheeling requests. Including the rights, terms, and conditions to wheel power in the tariff meant that a company could respond immediately to opportunities in short-term markets that were previously not available in a timely manner and facilitated the proper function of a competitive short-term power market. FERC Order 888 also required transmission owners to unbundle their activities, which meant that they were now under the same tariff as other transmission users (comparability standard) and had to rely on the same electronic information network that its customers relied on to obtain information about prices and the available capacity of the transmission system. Transmission owners were also required to separate their rates for wholesale generation and ancillary services. Functional unbundling essentially eliminated the vertically integrated utility by separating its transmission services functions from other business activities in the company. Six ancillary services were defined in Order 888 as part of the open access tariff:

- Scheduling, system control, and dispatch.
- Reactive supply and voltage control from generation sources.

- Regulation and frequency response.
- Energy imbalance.
- Operating reserve—spinning reserve.
- Operating reserve—supplemental reserve.

The transmission customer must purchase the first two services from the transmission provider.

As mentioned earlier, Order 888 included the provision enabling electric utilities to recover their stranded costs in the new competitive marketplace. These transition costs (stranded costs) represent a utility's capital investments that are unrecoverable due to the transition to competition. Since regulations allowed the cost recovery of prudent investments and potentially billions of dollars in the industry could be affected, the recovery of these stranded costs was critical to the restructuring process and creation of a competitive market as well as to gain support and cooperation from industry participants. The FERC also acknowledged that the recovery of these stranded costs could delay some of the benefits of competition. FERC Order 888 specified that cost recovery was limited to the loss of wholesale power customers and FERC's required open-access transmission tariff and required that wholesale stranded costs should be assigned to the departing wholesale customer (typically, the regulated utility). At the retail level, states still retained primary jurisdiction over cost recovery resulting from retail competition, although FERC indicated that it would entertain requests to recover costs resulting from retail competition when a state did not have the authority. Since Order 888 was issued, FERC has had relatively few stranded costs cases, with most being in states that implemented retail competition.

FERC Order 889 also required all IOUs to participate in the open-access, same-time information system, which provides unrestricted timely and accurate day-to-day information about transmission and is accessible to all transmission users.

The OASIS is an interactive Internet-based database containing information on available transmission capacity, capacity reservations, ancillary services, and transmission prices. The underlying idea of the OASIS is to create an interactive computerized market for transmission-related products and services that is accessible by all qualified users of the transmission system. In that role, the OASIS facilitates the functioning of competitive power markets. OASIS "nodes" are Internet-based interfaces to each transmission system's market offerings and transmission availability announcements. Power marketers that sign an open-access tariff agreement are allowed complete access to view existing transmission and service availability as well as existing service requests made by other parties.

Transmission facilities have power transfer limits, which must be maintained to allow for reliable operation of the power grid. Transmission operators perform system studies in various future time frames to determine how much transfer capacity is required to serve their own "native load" and how much capacity must remain as a buffer to prevent unscheduled or accidental overflows, which can damage high-voltage equipment. The difference between the capacity needed to serve load and to maintain safe flow margins can be made available for purchase on the OASIS node. OASIS also provides for "firm" and "nonfirm" transmission rates to allow for unplanned outages and other conditions limiting capacity. These different transmission rates carry different cost structures.

Open access has caused much higher loads on the transmission systems. In reality, power flows along the paths of least resistance, resulting in "loop flows" of energy flowing on alternate paths creating overload stress on the system, requiring curtailments. To address this issue, NERC developed a tagging method designed to capture the entire transaction from beginning to end, which could then be used to determine scheduling and possible curtailments. NERC also assumed control of the transmission system information network (TSIN) database, a comprehensive listing of generation points, transmission facilities, and delivery points as well as transmission and generation priority definitions that support the various OASIS nodes and NERC tagging applications.

FERC Order 888 also encouraged the formation of the independent system operators. Although FERC in 1993 issued a policy statement recommending that transmission owners, transmission customers, and other interested parties form regional transmission groups to coordinate transmission planning and expansion on a regional and interregional basis, few RTGs were established. Order 888 now encouraged the formation of ISOs to facilitate the transfer of a utility operating control of their transmission assets to the ISO. Ownership would remain with the utility and participation in an ISO was voluntary. An unbundled utility and control of the grid by an ISO with no economic interest in marketing and selling power now ensured fair and open-access transmission tariffs and eliminated discriminatory practices while achieving an efficient marketplace and regional control of the grid. By the end of 1998, the FERC had conditionally approved five independent system operators: California ISO;

ISO-New England; New York ISO; Pennsylvania, New Jersey, Maryland (PJM Interconnect) ISO; and the Midwest ISO.

Despite the creation of these ISOs, the development of wholesale power markets after FERC Order 888/889 was slow, and obstacles to competition still remained. Four major obstacles were identified, including continued complaints of transmission owners' discriminating against independent power companies. The increased number of market participants and transactions made detecting the discriminatory behavior more difficult to identify. The second issue was that the functional unbundling under the new orders did not produce sufficient separation between operating the transmission system and marketing and selling power, further contributing to discriminatory behavior. The third element was the fact that voluntary ISO formation had yet to occur in some areas of the country, despite the expectation that more regions would seek grid regionalization to support a competitive market. Finally, the increase in trading and movement of electricity in new directions within the grids made it more difficult to manage the grids, and the concern about grid reliability and its capacity to deal with these new loads was brought into question.

Because transmission congestion increased, the existing procedures at the time were found to be inadequate. As the FERC itself pointed out, "current transmission loading relief (TLR) procedures [for relieving congestion] are cumbersome, inefficient, and disruptive to power markets because they rely exclusively on physical measures of [electricity] flows with no attempt to assess the relative costs and benefits of alternative congestion management techniques." Furthermore, due to the uncertainties in predicting load growth, responsibility for transmission expansion was not always clear and financial motivations for the construction of new facilities appeared to carry greater risk. Pancake pricing, the additive charge customers paid every time the power crosses the boundary of a transmission owner, had the effect of increasing transmission costs and reducing the geographic size of competitive power markets. Shortly after FERC Order 888/889, it became clear that additional changes were needed.

FERC Order 2000 and grid regionalization

FERC Order 2000, issued in December 1999, asked all transmission-owning utilities, including nonpublic utilities, to voluntarily place their transmission facilities under the control of a regional transmission organization and defined the characteristics and minimum functions required by the RTO. Order 2000 was designed to take the transmission system from one that was owned and controlled mostly by vertically integrated electric utilities to a system owned or controlled by unaffiliated RTOs. The FERC believed that a voluntary approach would be successful, as many vertically integrated utilities would recognize the benefits, and clear rules and guidance were established for the function of the RTO. Furthermore, the FERC established a collaborative process for RTO formation and provided rate-making incentives for utilities that assume the risks of a transition to a new corporate structure.

FERC Order 2000 required that each public utility that owns, operates, or controls interstate transmission facilities (except those already participating in an approved regional transmission entity) file a proposal to participate in a regional transmission organization or file a description of efforts to participate in an RTO, obstacles to participation, and plans and a timetable for future efforts. Each public utility that was already a member of an existing transmission entity that conformed with the ISO principles contained in Order 888 was required to file a description that explained the extent to which the transmission entity in which it participates meets the minimum characteristics and functions of an RTO, how it proposes to modify the entity to become an RTO, or a description of efforts, obstacles, and plans to conform to an RTO's minimum characteristics and functions. All RTOs were given a timetable to implement their minimum functions, including congestion management, parallel path flow coordination, and transmission planning and expansion.

FERC Order 2000 also requires that the RTO be independent of market participants. Independence was defined as a set of conditions that included that the RTO, its employees, and any nonstakeholder director not have any financial interest in any market participants; the RTO must have a decision-making process independent of control by any market participant; and the RTO must have exclusive authority under Section 205 of the Federal Power Act to file changes to its transmission tariff. The RTOs were also required to be of sufficient scope and configuration to perform effectively the required function and support efficient and nondiscriminatory power markets. FERC provided guidance on the term *sufficient scope* through the following nine criteria:

- Facilitates performing essential RTO functions.
- Encompasses one contiguous geographic area.
- Encompasses a highly interconnected portion of the grid.
- Deters the exercise of market power.
- Recognizes existing trading patterns.

- Takes into account existing regional boundaries (e.g., NERC regions).
- Encompasses existing regional transmission entities.
- Encompasses existing control areas.
- Takes into account international boundaries.

In addition, the RTOs must have operational authority for all transmission facilities under its control including security aspects to ensure real-time operating reliability. The RTO was also tasked with the exclusive authority for maintaining the short-term reliability of the transmission grid. Additional RTO minimum functions include

- Tariff administration and design.
- Congestion management.
- Parallel path flow management.
- Promotion or provision of ancillary services.
- Provision of an open-access, same-time information system and capability calculations.
- Market monitoring.
- Planning and expansion.
- Interregional coordination.

FERC Order 2000 was designed to create effective transmission rates to promote economic efficiency in the generation and transmission sectors and support the success of the RTOs as stand-alone transmission businesses. Under Order 2000, FERC is responsible for an RTO's transmission rate schedule and rates were required to address the following issues:

- Eliminating pancake pricing.
- Reciprocal waiving of access charges between RTOs.
- Uniform access charges.
- Congestion pricing.
- Servicing transmission-owning utilities that do not participate in an RTO.
- Performance-based regulation.
- Other RTO transmission rate reforms.
- Additional rate-making issues.
- Filing procedures for innovative rate proposals.

In Order 2000, FERC identified eight issues, other than the ones just discussed that may have an impact on the structure, completeness, regulation, and design of RTOs:

1. **Public power and cooperative participation in RTOs.** FERC expects public power entities to participate in the formation of RTOs, but it is aware that public power entities face several obstacles. Internal

Revenue Service codes may prevent facilities financed by tax-exempt debt from wheeling privately owned power, or they may prevent transfer of operational control of transmission facilities financed by tax-exempt debt to a for-profit transmission company. State and local government laws may prevent public power entities from participating in RTOs. The lack of participation of public power entities may negate some of the effectiveness and expected benefits of RTOs.

2. **Participation by Canadian and Mexican entities.** FERC opined that Mexican and Canadian participation in an RTO would be beneficial.

3. **Existing transmission contracts.** FERC indicated that it would examine, case by case, how to handle existing contractual arrangements when forming an RTO. For example, one issue may involve how to handle pancaked rates in existing contracts for others when transmission-owning utilities design a nonpancaked rate for their own transactions.

4. **Power exchanges.** FERC leaves it to each region to determine a need for a power exchange, and whether the RTO should operate the exchange should there be a need.

5. **Effects on retail markets and retail access.** FERC opined that formation of an RTO would not affect the ability of states to implement retail markets and competition. In Order 2000, FERC noted that experience with the independent system operators indicates that an RTO could be a benefit to states implementing retail competition.

6. **Effects on states with low-cost generation.** Some states are concerned that an RTO would result in local utilities selling their low-cost power to other states. FERC asserted that an RTO would provide access to future low-cost generation plants and new low-cost generation plants would be attracted to regions with an RTO because of dependable and nondiscriminatory access to the transmission system.

7. **States' role with regard to RTOs.** FERC believes that states have an important role to play, but they chose not to specify what role in Order 2000.

8. **Accounting issues.** FERC would require that RTOs conform to the Uniform System of Accounts, but they also indicated that changes in the industry require them to reexamine existing accounting and related reporting requirements.

The FERC envisions that bid-based markets for wholesale electric power would be a central feature in many RTO proposals. Although bid-based markets for electric power do not now represent the dominant method for buying and selling electricity, this method is expected to grow. In Order 2000, FERC summarizes lessons learned from its analysis and approval of bid-based markets for four independent system operators. As these and other power markets mature, additional information on how to design and operate power markets would develop. The lessons learned include

- **Multiple product markets.** Efficiency of a multiproduct market operating in the same time period is maximized when arbitrage opportunities reflected in the bids are exhausted. That is, it is efficient when, after the RTO's market has cleared, no market participant would have preferred to be in another of the RTO's markets.
- **Physical feasibility.** Transaction in the market should be physically feasible.
- **Access to a real-time balancing market.** *Real-time balancing* refers to the moment-to-moment matching of loads and generation on a systemwide basis. A real-time balancing market should be available to all grid users for purposes of settling their individual imbalances.
- **Market participation.** Markets are more efficient with a broad participation.
- **Demand-side bidding.** The current wholesale power markets do not offer customer demand-side bidding, only power suppliers bid into the markets. However, demand-side bidding, to the extent it is practical, is desirable to make electricity supply and prices more responsive to competitive markets.
- **Bidding rules.** The market should allow generators to make bids that approximate their costs.
- **Transaction costs and risks.** Transaction costs should be low and participation in the market should involve no unnecessary risk.
- **Price recalculations.** Market clearing prices should minimize electricity price recalculations.
- **Multisettlement markets.** Multisettlement markets may involve a day-ahead market and a real-time market. If the day-ahead market bids are needed for reliability, these bids need to be physically binding and may be subject to penalties for failing to adhere to the bid.
- **Preventing abusive market power.** FERC highlights three items that help lessen the potential for market power: (1) having fewer restrictions on importing power into the region, (2) having less segmentation of geographic markets for the same product, and (3) stop

allowing market participants to change bids before they complete the financial settlement. Bid changing can be used as signaling to facilitate collusive behavior.

- **Market information and marketing monitoring.** Market clearing prices and quantities should be transparent, so market participants can assess the market and plan their business efficiently.

One significant issue not addressed in FERC Order 2000 is that of federally owned and other public power and cooperative utilities, defined as FERC nonjurisdictional utilities. In essence, they have no filing requirements under Order 2000, and FERC has no leverage in obtaining their participation. Because these utilities own approximately 30% of the nation's power grid, the potential exists for substantial gaps in regional coverage. In Order 2000, FERC encourages nonjurisdictional utility participation but also recognizes that municipally owned utilities face numerous regulatory and legal obstacles. The Internal Revenue Code has private use restrictions on the transmission facilities of municipally owned utilities financed by tax-exempt bonds. State and local government limitations, such as prohibitions on participating in stock-owning entities and other restrictions, may also impede full participation.

The new millennium

The Energy Policy Act of 2005

The Energy Policy Act (EPACT) of 2005 contains several provisions affecting the electric industry structure. EPACT required the secretary of the Department of Energy to identify critically constrained transmission corridors that cross the borders of two or more states. Proposed transmission projects in these corridors may petition the FERC, under certain conditions, to exercise federal eminent domain authority to allow acquisition of rights of way to construct new transmission facilities. Historically, transmission siting and eminent domain authority have been left to state government authorities. The FERC was granted this authority to resolve impediments to construction of multistate transmission. The act also authorizes FERC to approve incentive rates for the construction of transmission facilities to enhance reliability and expand the system to increase the efficiency of the supply of generation in wholesale power markets. This was quickly followed by FERC Order No. 679, which sets forth the criteria for new transmission infrastructure to qualify for incentive rate treatment. The act also resulted in the establishment of a loan guarantee program within the DOE for advanced generation technologies, including nuclear, coal, and renewables, as well as other technologies enhancing the efficient delivery and use of electricity.

Regarding renewables, EPACT extends and modifies the renewable electricity production tax credit (PTC), which is a per-kilowatt-hour tax credit for electricity generated by qualified energy sources. Originally part of the Energy Policy Act of 1992, it is a corporate tax credit to owners or operators of electric generation facilities that produce electricity from qualified energy resources, including wind, biomass, geothermal, solar, and hydropower over the first 10 years of operation. The renewable energy production incentive (REPI) also originated with the Energy Policy Act of 1992 but expired and appropriations were reauthorized by EPACT 2005 to extend through 2026. An interesting twist to this is that it is intended for the following:

- Not-for-profit electric cooperatives.
- Public utilities.
- State governments, commonwealths, and U.S. possessions.
- Indian tribal governments and native corporations.

In essence, this applies to non-vertically integrated, non-investor-owned utilities since the production payment applies only to the electricity sold to another entity.

As mentioned earlier, EPACT 2005 repeals PUHCA, which significantly limited the merger of electric utilities, subjected holding companies to SEC regulation, and allowed holding companies to acquire or merge only with interconnected utilities that would operate as a single integrated system. Under EPACT, utilities no longer need to apply to the SEC to determine their compliance with PUHCA or find "transmission paths" by which to connect their utility with others they wish to acquire or with which to merge. In exchange, the new act requires utilities to provide additional data from their "books and records" so that the states and U.S. Federal Energy Regulatory Commission can mitigate a utility's potential to exercise undue market power or to cross-subsidize between utility and nonutility activities. Also, the FERC is given responsibility for reviewing the loans and other utility encumbrances to assess financial risks that utilities or their holding companies may assume by virtue of an acquisition.

The Energy Independence and Security Act of 2007

In December 2007, the Energy Independence and Security Act of 2007 (EISA) provided a legislative framework for transmission system modernization, including initiating "smart grid" expansion, providing tax incentives for investment, creating federal "smart grid" committees, and assigning federal funding for research and development. "Smart grids" would present consumers with real-time electricity prices, thereby encouraging efficient consumption and possibly reducing demand.

EISA also established four standards under Section 111(d) of the Public Utility Regulatory Policies Act. The EISA requires that each state regulatory authority and non-regulated electric utility must consider adopting the new PURPA standards. This includes consideration by the Tennessee Valley Authority as a non-regulated electric utility with respect to its own operations and retail sales to directly served customers and in its separate capacity as the designated state regulatory authority under PURPA for the distributors of TVA power. EISA further requires that consideration of the new PURPA standards be addressed in proceedings to be concluded by December 19, 2009.

Also in 2007, FERC issued an advance notice of proposed rulemaking (ANOPR), identifying four specific issues in organized market regions that were not being adequately addressed. These included the greater use of market prices to elicit demand response during periods of operating reserve shortage, increasing opportunities for long-term power contracting, stronger market monitoring, and enhancing the responsiveness of RTOs and ISOs to customers and other stakeholders. (Based on comments received from the ANOPR, FERC issued Order 719.)

FERC Order No. 719

Order 719, issued in October 2008, addressed reforms to improve the operation and competitiveness of organized wholesale electric power markets. These reforms represented an incremental improvement to the operation of organized wholesale electric markets in the areas of demand response, long-term power contracting, market monitoring policies, and RTO and ISO responsiveness. Regarding demand response, FERC ordered the use of market prices to elicit demand response and required RTOs and ISOs to

1. Accept bids from demand response resources on a basis comparable to other resources.
2. During a system emergency, the elimination of a charge to a buyer that takes less electric energy in the real-time market than they purchased in the day-ahead market.
3. In select situations, permit an aggregator of retail customers to bid demand response on behalf of retail customers directly into the organized energy market.

4. As necessary, modify market rules to allow the market-clearing price to reach a level that rebalances supply and demand, so as to maintain reliability while providing sufficient provisions for mitigating market power during periods of operating reserve shortage.

Order 719 also required that qualifying demand response resources in the RTOs and ISOs be eligible to bid to supply energy imbalance, spinning reserves, supplemental reserves, reactive and voltage control, and regulation and frequency response. FERC also required that RTOs and ISOs establish Web sites to allow market participants to place bids to buy or sell power on a long-term basis to promote long-term contracts and transparency among market participants. The market monitoring units (MMUs) of the RTOs and ISOs were also required to identify ineffective market rules, reporting, and notification of market participant's behavior that may require investigation.

The Consolidated Appropriations Act of 2008

The Consolidated Appropriations Act of 2008, passed in December 2007, directed the U.S. EPA to develop a mandatory reporting rule for greenhouse gases. The rule requires that emitters of GHGs from 31 source categories report their emissions to the EPA. Approximately 80–85% of total U.S. GHG emissions from 10,000 facilities are covered by the rule, with reporting and monitoring begun by January 1, 2010, and the first annual emissions reports due in 2011.

FERC Order 890

In March 2009, FERC Order No. 890 was issued to prevent undue discrimination and preference in transmission service. This included strengthening the open-access transmission tariff (OATT) pro forma to reduce undue discrimination, provide greater details in the tariff to facilitate enforcement efforts, and increase transparency in the rules applicable to the planning and use of the transmission system. Order 890 also included changes to the terms and conditions of point-to-point and network transmission services and the information required to be posted on OASIS. To address pricing, Order 890 provides for changes to the pricing of energy and generator imbalances and requirements to provide conditional firm service and planning redispatch associated with point-to-point service. Transmission providers were also required to implement an open and transparent transmission planning process.

The American Recovery and Reinvestment Act of 2009

The American Recovery and Reinvestment Act of 2009 (ARRA) is an economic stimulus package intended to mitigate the effects of the U.S. recession and followed other such emergency acts passed by Congress in 2008. Regarding the electric industry, the act allocated funding for a number of initiatives affecting the industry in the areas of renewable energy, energy efficiency, modernization of the nation's electrical grid, smart metering, energy research and development, green-job training, and carbon capture demonstrations. The act also extends tax credits for renewable energy production (until 2014) and provides for renewable energy and electric transmission technology loan guarantees and grants. The long-term impact of these stimulus measures has yet to be seen in the industry.

The American Energy and Security Act of 2009

Also known as H.R. 2454, the American Energy and Security Act of 2009 (ACESA) passed the House of Representatives in June 2009. A nice summary is provided by the Congressional Budget Office (www.cbo.gov/ftpdocs/102xx/doc10262/hr2454.pdf):

> H.R. 2454 would make a number of changes in energy and environmental policies largely aimed at reducing emissions of gases that contribute to global warming. The bill would limit or cap the quantity of certain greenhouse gases (GHGs) emitted from facilities that generate electricity and from other industrial activities over the 2012–2050 period. The Environmental Protection Agency (EPA) would establish two separate regulatory initiatives known as cap-and-trade programs—one covering emissions of most types of GHGs and one covering hydrofluorocarbons (HFCs). EPA would issue allowances to emit those gases under the cap-and-trade programs. Some of those allowances would be auctioned by the federal government, and the remainder would be distributed at no charge.
>
> Other major provisions of the legislation would:
> - Provide energy tax credits or energy rebates to certain low-income families to offset the impact of higher energy-related prices from the cap-and-trade programs;
> - Require certain retail electricity suppliers to satisfy a minimum percentage of their electricity sales with electricity generated by facilities that use qualifying renewable fuels or energy sources;
> - Establish a Carbon Storage Research Corporation to support research and development of technologies related to carbon capture and sequestration;
> - Increase, by $25 billion, the aggregate amount of loans DOE is authorized to make to automobile manufacturers and component suppliers under the existing Advanced Technology Vehicle Manufacturing Loan Program;
> - Establish a Clean Energy Deployment Administration (CEDA) within the Department of Energy (DOE), which would be authorized to provide direct loans, loan guarantees, and letters of credit for clean energy projects;

- *Authorize the Department of Transportation (DOT) to provide individuals with vouchers to acquire new vehicles that achieve greater fuel efficiency than the existing qualifying vehicles owned by the individuals; and*
- *Authorize appropriations for various programs under EPA, DOE, and other agencies.*

CBO and the Joint Committee on Taxation (JCT) estimate that over the 2010–2019 period enacting this legislation would:

- *Increase federal revenues by about $846 billion; and*
- *Increase direct spending by about $821 billion.*

In total, those changes would reduce budget deficits (or increase future surpluses) by about $24 billion over the 2010–2019 period. In addition, assuming appropriation of the necessary amounts, CBO estimates that implementing H.R. 2454 would increase discretionary spending by about $50 billion over the 2010–2019 period. Most of that funding would stem from spending auction proceeds from various funds established under this legislation.

CBO has determined that the non-tax provisions of H.R. 2454 contain intergovernmental and private-sector mandates as defined in the Unfunded Mandates Reform Act (UMRA). Several of those mandates would require utilities, manufacturers, and other entities to reduce greenhouse gas emissions through cap-and-trade programs and performance standards. CBO estimates that the cost of mandates in the bill would well exceed the annual thresholds established in UMRA for intergovernmental and private-sector mandates (in 2009, $69 million and $139 million respectively, adjusted annually for inflation).

The American Clean Energy Leadership Act of 2009

The U.S. senate had its own bill, which is known as the American Clean Energy Leadership Act of 2009 (see http://energy.senate.gov/public/_files/TheAmericanCleanEnergyLeadershipActof2009.pdf). The provisions of this bill are as follows:

On June 17, 2009, the Senate Committee on Energy and Natural Resources voted 15 to 8 to report a new original bill, the American Clean Energy Leadership Act of 2009. This balanced, comprehensive, and bipartisan energy legislation will—

- *Accelerate the introduction of new clean energy technologies in the United States, creating new jobs and helping businesses grow through clean energy project financing, a renewable electricity standard, and a robust and secure national electricity transmission highway;*
- *Increase energy efficiency in buildings, major equipment, and appliances, saving consumers and businesses billions of dollars on their energy bills;*
- *Enhance America's energy independence by increasing clean energy supplies and energy security, including new access to over 20 trillion cubic feet of clean natural gas resources;*
- *Strengthen America as the world leader in energy innovation, by doubling our national investment in energy research and technology;*
- *Build a new energy workforce for the future;*

- *Protect consumers by making energy markets more transparent and fair, and by providing new tools to fight market manipulation; and*
- *Tackle future energy and climate challenges with smarter, more integrated planning.*

Key provisions

Key provisions in the American Clean Energy Leadership Act:
- *Set up a new Clean Energy Deployment Administration to facilitate tens of billions of dollars in new financing to get breakthrough clean energy technologies introduced into U.S. markets and expanded as quickly as possible;*
- *Require electric utilities nationwide to meet 15% of their electricity sales through renewable sources of energy (e.g., the sun, the wind, biomass, geothermal energy, hydropower) or energy efficiency by 2021;*
- *Establish an "interstate highway system" for electricity by creating a new bottoms-up planning system for a national transmission grid—based on regional, State, and local planning and input; allowing States to take the initial lead in deciding where to build high-priority national transmission projects; ensuring that if an impasse develops over high-priority projects that have been identified in the consensus planning process, that they can proceed with Federal authority as a backstop; and making sure that the costs of "interstate highway system" transmission projects are shared fairly;*
- *Promote distributed generation by harmonizing and streamlining the current patchwork of interconnection standards and processes. It directs the Federal Energy Regulatory Commission to establish a national interconnection standard for small power production facilities (15 kW or less) which would cover nearly all residential-sized distributed generation.*
- *Revitalize America's manufacturing industries by boosting their use of clean energy and energy efficiency, so that they remain competitive—and we prevent American jobs from being lost overseas as energy costs rise in the future.*
- *Improve efficiency in buildings, homes, equipment, appliances, and the Federal government, to cut costs to consumers and stop energy waste.*
- *Ensure that the U.S. electrical grid is protected from cyber vulnerabilities, threats, and attacks, by giving the Secretary of Energy and the Federal Energy Regulatory Commission the authority and responsibility to respond quickly to threats and attacks that might emerge;*
- *Modernize the Strategic Petroleum Reserve through the creation of a 30-million barrel petroleum product reserve, so that U.S. supplies of gasoline and diesel fuel will not face sudden shortfalls and price spikes due to the shutdown of refineries by hurricanes and other natural disasters, as occurred in 2008;*
- *Open the Eastern Gulf of Mexico to leasing and exploration for oil and gas, making over 3.8 billion barrels of new oil resources and 21.5 trillion cubic feet of new natural gas resources available;*
- *Lay out a 4-year integrated plan to double the U.S. investment in energy innovation and technology, to a total of almost $6.6 billion, with a*

complementary set of programs to enhance energy jobs training and workforce development. The bill also facilitates the large-scale demonstration and early deployment of carbon dioxide capture and storage technologies, by providing a legal and regulatory framework for the first 10 "early-mover" projects;

- *Protect U.S. energy consumers and businesses from energy price manipulation and volatility by increasing the transparency of what is happening in oil markets in the United States and around the world—including the role of financial markets in driving oil prices—and by giving U.S. energy regulators the same strong enforcement authorities against market tampering and manipulation that are now available in financial markets;*
- *Reform the Federal energy planning process by requiring a new comprehensive energy plan one year into each new Presidential term, and by providing a baseline of specific studies of resources and international climate and energy policies.*

An Open and Bipartisan Process

The American Clean Energy Leadership Act is based on six major bills, all with bipartisan sponsorship, and five other bills with either Republican or Democratic sponsorship, that were introduced in the Senate in this Congress. Key provisions of the bill were developed through over 39 bipartisan staff briefings, 20 formal hearings, and 11 open business meetings of the Committee on Energy and Natural Resources. During the Committee's process of writing the bill, 100 amendments were considered and adopted, most on a bipartisan basis and many unanimously. The result is a significant bipartisan achievement that will serve as a foundation for advancing this key energy legislation through the full Senate.

At the time of this writing, no consensus has been reached nor has any national energy policy bill been passed. A bill by Kerry, Graham, and Lieberman is expected to be unveiled soon. This is discussed in more detail later but first, let us turn to what is transpiring at the state level.

3.3 STATE REGULATIONS

Thus far, the focus has been at the federal level. But the states play an integral role in developing and implementing energy policy as well. As previously stated, the distribution of electric power is an intrastate function under the jurisdiction of state public utility commissions. Under the traditional regulatory system, the PUCs set the retail rates for electricity, based on the cost of service, which includes the costs of distribution. Retail rates are set by the PUC in rate-making rulings. The rates include the cost to the utility for generated and purchasing power; the capital costs of power, transmission, and distribution plants; all operations and maintenance expenses; and the costs to provide programs often mandated by the

PUC for consumer protection and energy efficiency. Prior to 1992, essentially all vertically integrated IOUs were regulated but much has transpired since then.

Despite whether retail choice is offered, many states have generally chosen to restructure by transitioning existing power pools to ISOs and RTOs, creating new state or regional RTOs and ISOs, or implementing restructuring without establishing new competitive wholesale markets. In reality, no two states have implemented restructuring in the same way and each state is a unique example. In terms of unbundling vertically structured utilities, states have taken a number of approaches, including requiring utilities to create new and separate departments, moving of assets into separate subsidiary companies, or divesting generation and, in some cases, transmission assets as well. Clearly, federal Acts and FERC Rulings, as discussed earlier, have played a role in how state PUCs regulate.

Allowing retail access has meant allowing all customers to choose, no customer choice, or defining classes of customers granted choices. To maintain the competitiveness of local business, the most accepted approach has been to allow commercial and industrial customers choices. Less popular is to allow the customer choices but still regulate the default supply service from the utility to provide competition and a regulated price point.

As the industry restructures, in some states, the PUC will eventually no longer regulate the retail rates for generated or purchased power. Retail electricity prices will be open to the market forces of competition. The PUCs will continue to regulate the rates for distribution of power to the consumer and have a say in the siting of distribution lines, substations, and generators. Metering and billing are under jurisdiction of the PUC and, in some states, are becoming competitive functions. As the industry restructures, the PUCs' responsibilities are changing. The goal of each state PUC remains to provide its state's consumers with reliable, reasonably, and fairly priced electric power.

Renewable portfolio standards

More recently, states have taken on the task of promoting renewable energy, which will affect the utility market both in sources of generation and costs. Figure 3.6 displays the 29 states that have adopted a renewable portfolio standard as of January 2010. Another six states have renewable portfolio goals, including the Dakotas, Utah, Vermont, Virginia, and West Virginia.

Renewable Portfolio Standards

WWW.dsireusa.org / January 2010

Figure 3.6 States with renewable portfolio standards *(Source: Database of State Incentives for Renewables and Efficiency, www.dsireusa.org/summarymaps/index.cfm? ee=1&RE=1)*

A renewable portfolio standard (RPS) requires utilities to own or acquire renewable energy or renewable energy certificates corresponding to percentage goals of sales or generating capacity within certain time frames as set forth by the state. Renewable portfolio goals differ only in that they are not legally binding. In addition to broad percentage goals, many state RPSs have set-asides that are renewable-resource specific, calling for a certain percentage of retail sales or a certain amount of generating capacity from these specific resources. Renewable portfolio standards may have the most sweeping impact on the utility industry, as goals and time frames are relatively aggressive given the historical evolution of the industry. Renewable energy targets differ by state but generally range from 10% to as much as 27% of a state's retail generation sales, and most programs require that these goals be met within the 2015–2025 time frame.

States also offer incentives (grant programs) to support the development of renewable energy technologies. Renewable technologies supported by state grants often focus on the local renewable sources. These grants are generally available only to nonresidential customers.

The following discussions briefly cover the various types of state initiatives and their impact on the utility industry.

Green power purchasing and aggregation policies

In 2009, nine states (primarily in the Midwest and Northeast) implemented programs to purchase electricity from renewable sources or purchase renewable energy credits. These programs are designed to support the growth of renewable-energy-based electrical generation through voluntary means, as frequently the cost of green power is more expensive than that from fossil fuels. These programs include commitments and percentage targets by state and local governments. Some states even allow local governments to aggregate the electric load of an entire community (community choice programs) to purchase green power. Green power is typically purchased directly from project developers or power marketers and facilitates the development of renewable projects that may not otherwise compete in the market.

Interconnection standards

As of July 2009, 39 states implemented interconnection standards. These standards specify the technical, contractual, rate, and metering rules regarding the connection of a customer's electric-generating system to the grid (see Network for New Energy Choices, 2008). Interconnection standards for local distribution standards have typically been adopted by state PUCs, while FERC adopted standards for systems interconnected at the transmission level. These interconnection standards clearly introduced competition to incumbent generation utilities, even in states with regulated IOUs. Furthermore, these interconnection standards support the robustness of the RTO and ISO regions by providing access to the grid and increasing the number of participants, which is critical to an effective marketplace.

Utility green power consumer option

By mid-2009, nine states required specific classes of electric utilities to offer their customers the option of buying electricity generated from renewable resources either by the utility or purchased elsewhere under contract. Some states also allow for the purchase of renewable energy credits from renewable energy providers certified by a state PUC (www.dsireusa.org/).

Net metering

As shown in Figure 3.7, by mid-2009, 42 states and the District of Columbia adopted net metering practices. Net metering allows electric customers who generate their own electricity to meter the flow of electricity both to and

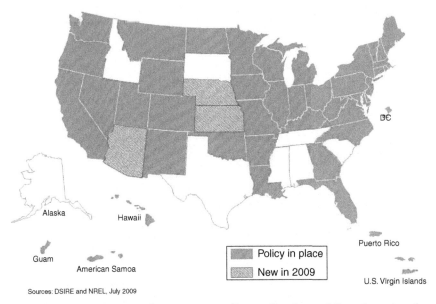

Figure 3.7 State adoption of net metering *(Source: Database of State Incentives for Renewables and Efficiency, National Renewable Energy Laboratory)*

from the customer's premises. When a customer is generating electricity in excess of the customer's needs, excess electricity can flow back into the distribution system, offsetting electricity consumed by the customer from the grid. Indirectly, the customer "stores" excess power on the grid and uses it later when needed to avoid buying power at the full retail price.

Public benefit funds and system benefit charges

Public benefit funds (PBFs), or system benefit charges, represent programs run by the state typically used to support renewable energy generation, energy efficiency programs, and low-income energy support. Most often funds are raised as a surcharge tied to electricity consumption but other models, such as Maine's voluntary funding program and Pennsylvania's self-sustaining program, are supported by load repayments and other returns on investments. PBFs typically support rebate programs for renewable energy systems, loan programs, grants, and energy education programs. Loans and equity have been used by some states to support the development of clean energy projects, while business development grants, marketing support, research and development grants, and other forms of technical assistance have been used to promote clean energy industry development. By mid-2009, 17 states and the District of Columbia had implemented PBFs.

Rebate programs

At the time of this writing, 18 states offer rebate programs to promote the installation of renewable energy systems, such as solar water heaters and photovoltaic systems, primarily at the residential and commercial level. The bulk of these programs are administered by states, municipal utilities, and electric cooperatives. Rebate amounts can vary considerably, depending on the technology and size of investment.

Renewable energy access laws

Nearly 35 states recognized that, in addition to financial issues, many barriers exist to the installation of renewable energy technologies, such as solar and wind. Wind and solar access laws protect a consumer's right to install and operate these types of energy system at a home or business. In some states, laws exist to protect an owner's access to sunlight and prohibit homeowners associations, neighborhood covenants, or local ordinances from restricting a homeowner's right to use solar or wind energy. The most prevalent type of access law is the granting of easements to allow for access to a renewable resource and prevent adjoining property owners from restricting that resource.

Renewable energy production incentives

This type of program typically provides cash payments based on renewable energy generated to support the creation of new energy projects. Many states found that payments based on actual production (performance) are more effective in generating actual kilowatt-hours than payments based on project capacity ratings. By mid-2009, six states enacted renewable energy production incentives.

Tax incentives

In addition to the numerous federal tax incentives enacted as part of energy legislation and other acts, states created multiple types of tax incentives to promote renewable energy. These include corporate, industry recruitment and support, personal, property, and sales tax incentives. Generally, state tax incentives are not renewable-energy-resource specific, to provide developers the opportunity to select the technology best suited for their needs and locally available renewable resources. Corporate tax incentives offered by states include credits, deductions, and exemptions. Twenty-four states provide a corporate tax incentive to promote renewable energy. In addition to electrical generation technology, these corporate tax incentives may pertain to energy efficiency equipment or green building construction. For production technologies, incentives may be a function of the energy produced. Minimum investment amounts in an eligible project are also called for by some states, and typically, there is a maximum limit on the dollar amount of the credit or deduction.

To create new jobs, many states offer financial incentives to promote the manufacturing and development of renewable energy resources and technologies. In 2009, 15 states had industry recruitment and support incentives. These tax credits, tax exemptions, and grants may be based on the quantity of electricity produced or the resources used. In most cases, these tax incentives are established as temporary measures to encourage growth in their early years and are reduced or eliminated as the industry becomes self-sufficient.

Personal tax incentives include personal income tax credits and deductions to reduce the expense of installing renewable energy systems. Although credit and deductions vary by state, in most cases there is a maximum limit on the dollar amount of the credit or deduction. Twenty-two states provided a personal tax incentive in 2009.

Property tax incentives are also used by states to promote renewable resources, and these can include exemptions, exclusions, and credits and generally pertain to only the added value of the renewable technology and not the entire property value. As property taxes are collected locally, some states granted local taxing authorities the option of allowing a property tax incentive for renewable energy systems. Thirty-five states in 2009 provided a property tax incentive to promote renewable energy development.

State sales taxes are also being used to promote renewable energy sources and technologies. Sales tax incentives may include exemptions from the sales tax, or sales and use tax, for the acquisition of renewable energy technology. Thirty states in 2009 provided a sales tax incentive to promote renewable energy development.

Feed-in tariffs

A feed-in tariff generally requires a utility to purchase electricity from an eligible renewable energy generator. The tariff provides a guarantee of payment associated with each unit of energy produced for the full capacity output of the system over a guaranteed period of time, usually spanning 15–20 years. This payment guarantee often includes access to the grid, and payments are frequently structured as a function of the technology type, project size, quality of renewable resources, and other local variables that may affect project economics. Feed-in tariff payments can be based on the levelized cost of service plus a specified return or the value of generation to the utility or society. The advantage of the levelized cost-of-service approach is that feed-in tariff payments can be designed to be more conducive to market growth by setting favorable returns. In the second approach, value to the utility or society, the value can be defined by the utility's avoided costs or by attempting to internalize the "externality" costs associated with fossil-fuel-powered generation. These externality costs can include the value of climate mitigation, health and air quality impacts, and effects on energy security to name a few. Value-based approaches must be tested to ensure that value is set higher than the actual generation cost to ensure payments are sufficient to promote market development. Based on European feed-in tariff policies, payments structured to cover the renewable project costs plus an estimated profit have proven to be the most successful (Klein et al., 2008). However, U.S. states typically use value-based cost approaches, which have so far been unsuccessful (Grace, Rickerson, and Corfee, 2008; Jacobsson and Lauber, 2005).

Feed-in tariff and RPS policies differ, as RPS mandates prescribe how much customer demand must be met with renewable energy by a utility, while properly structured feed-in tariff policies support new renewable energy supply projects by providing investor certainty in regard to rates of return and long-term contract structures. As of early 2009, only a few states passed feed-in tariff policies, including California and Washington. Several utilities in the United States also created fixed-price production-based incentive policies that can be considered feed-in tariffs. At the time of this writing, approximately 14 states are currently considering feed-in tariff legislation and a federal feed-in tariff has been proposed.

3.4 THE FUTURE OF THE ELECTRIC INDUSTRY

Both federal and state regulations and initiatives continue to shape the future of the electric utility industry at an ever-increasing rate. Today, no one business model can describe the structure of the industry and regulated vertically integrated utilities, traditional government, municipal and cooperative utilities, and unregulated utility and service organizations exist in various areas of the United States. Even in regulated states with RTOs, the true sense of a vertically integrated utility has been broken as the transmission grid is open to competition and controlled by an unrelated third party.

Rate-making mechanisms are also being tested, as utilities increasingly are asked to address and account for externalities, such as global warming and national energy security, with no clear path to investment recovery. Historically, a utility's rates are a function of the estimated costs of providing service (including an allowed rate of return) divided by a forecasted amount of unit sales over a given period. The allowed rate of return is achieved when sales equals forecasts. If forecasts are exceeded, the utility earns additional profits, and conversely, not meeting forecast sales reduces profit. To increase profits the utility must increase demand, which is contrary to conservation, emission reductions, and national security goals. To change this approach to rate making, the concept of decoupling profits from electrical demand is gaining acceptance. In the simplest form, *decoupling* refers to rate adjustment mechanisms that "decouple" the utilities' ability to recover its agreed-on fixed costs and earnings from electrical consumption. Various rate adjustment mechanisms exist but essentially most are based on a "true-up" mechanism once actual sales levels are known. The "true-up" mechanism accounts for both lower and higher than forecast sales, compensating the utility when demand decreases and penalizing the utility for higher demand with the "true-up" mechanism incentivizing the utility to meet the stated objectives (externalities). Typically these "adjustments" are small and "caps" are established to limit risk both from the ratepayer's and utility's viewpoints. By reducing cost-recovery risks to the utility and its investors, society benefits by encouraging energy efficiency programs. This has been proven in California and Oregon, where decoupling has produced some of the highest levels of utility funding for energy efficiency.

In addition to changes in rate making, a number of legislative, environmental, and energy conservation initiates are being debated that may dramatically change the structure of the industry. In 2009, the House of Representatives passed the American Clean Energy and Security Act of 2009 (pending Senate approval, which has not occurred at the time of this writing) with provisions regarding clean energy, energy efficiency, global warming pollution, and transitioning to a clean energy economy. The bill (H.R. 2454) establishes a renewable electricity standard (RES) requiring utilities to produce 6% of electricity from renewables by 2012, gradually increasing to 20% by 2020. At least 75% of the RES must be met by renewable energy with the remainder from efficiency savings. H.R. 2454 also mandates the gradual reduction of global warming emissions to 97% of 2005 levels by 2012, 83% by 2020, 58% by 2030, and 17% of 2005 levels by 2050.

The House's American Clean Energy and Security Act proposes to establish an "emission allowances" program, creating tradable greenhouse gas pollution permits fashioned after existing programs to prevent acid rain. Greenhouse gases consisting primarily of carbon dioxide (CO_2), methane (CH_4), and nitrous oxides (NO_x) are cited as the primary cause of global warming. Carbon dioxide emissions from the combustion of fossil fuels (petroleum, coal, and natural gas) represented approximately 81% of the total U.S. human-caused (anthropogenic) greenhouse gas emissions in 2008. Methane (natural gas) emanating from landfills, coal mines, oil and natural gas operations, and agriculture contributed another 11% of total emissions. Nitrous oxide emitted from nitrogen fertilizer production, fossil-fuel combustion, and other industrial processes accounted for another 4% of total emissions, with the remainder from other human-made gases. In 2008, the United States generated roughly 5,814.4 million metric tons equivalent of CO_2 with nearly 2,359.1 million metric tons (40.6%) coming from the electric power industry. Of this, 1,945.9 million metric tons represent carbon dioxide equivalent emissions from the use of coal to generate electric power (U.S. Department of Energy, Energy Information Administration, 2009).

The total value of the allowances that would be created by ACESA has been estimated by the EPA to range from approximately $70–80 billion in 2015 to $90–120 billion in 2030 with approximately 80% of allowances given away for free until 2025, after which an increasing percentage would be auctioned. Revenue from the sale of these allowances would be used to protect consumers from increases in energy prices, support clean energy and efficiency programs, assist in the transition to a clean energy economy, and create training and worker assistance programs. The bill also proposes to create emission offsets, allowing capped sources to increase their carbon emissions by investing in projects that offset their target emissions reduction.

Building on the Energy Independence and Security Act of 2007, H.R. 2454 also proposes to legislate carbon capture and storage technology (CCS) at all new coal plants permitted after 2020, and coal plants permitted between 2009 and 2020 must be retrofitted with CCS by 2025. No CCS requirements were placed on coal plants permitted before 2009. These CCS proposed requirements are significant in that large scale carbon capture technologies have yet to be demonstrated, costs appear to be substantial, and new plant permits would require siting of these stations in areas with favorable underground storage geologic structures to store the carbon dioxide. These siting restrictions would limit placement of new coal plants to certain parts of the country and raise additional liability issues regarding the integrity of storage and possible future releases.

Subsequent to ACESA, the EPA in December 2009 formally declared that carbon dioxide from the burning of fossil fuels poses a threat to human health and welfare. This designation establishes the path for the federal government to regulate greenhouse gas emissions from power plants and other major sources. This action was anticipated based on the 2007 Supreme Court decision that declared carbon dioxide and five other greenhouse gases pollutants covered by the Clean Air Act. However, in January 2010, a Senate "disapproval resolution" was filed. This is a rarely used procedural move that prohibits rules written by executive branch agencies from taking effect. The disapproval resolution would essentially throw out the process by which the EPA found that greenhouse gases endanger public health.

In addition to federal initiatives such as ACESA, states and regions of the country have become involved with greenhouse emission issues and cap-and-trade programs. The Regional Greenhouse Gas Initiative (RGGI), comprising 10 northeastern and mid-Atlantic states, is the first mandatory, market-based effort in the United States to reduce greenhouse gas emissions with the goal of reducing CO_2 emissions from the electric utility sector by 10% by 2018. In RGGI, states sell emission allowances through auctions and use the proceeds to invest in energy efficiency, renewable energy, and other clean energy technologies. The states of Connecticut, Delaware, Maine, Maryland, Massachusetts, New Hampshire, New Jersey, New York, Rhode Island, and Vermont are signatory states to the RGGI agreement. RGGI conducts individual CO_2 budget trading for each of the 10 participating states. State regulations, based on an RGGI model rule, govern activities and are linked across the states through CO_2 allowance reciprocity. Regulated power plants (>25 MWe) can use allowances issued by any of the participating states to show compliance with their own state programs. In effect, the 10 state programs function as a single regional compliance market.

The RGGI market-based cap-and-trade approach establishes a multi-state CO_2 emissions budget (cap) that decreases gradually over time. Electric generating utilities are required to acquire allowances equal to their CO_2 emissions over a specified period. Allowances are purchased through a market-based emissions auction and trading system, where CO_2 allowances can be bought and sold. RGGI also employs offsets, which are greenhouse gas emissions reduction projects outside the power generation sector, to further facilitate compliance. To minimize dramatic changes in electricity prices, RGGI uses a gradual phased-in approach, which is more conducive to generation planning and provides a certain degree of regulatory certainty. However, it should be noted that H.R. 2454, if enacted, would prohibit state and regional cap-and-trade programs from operating between 2012 and 2017. The first three of four auctions conducted by RGGI in 2009 involved approximately $90 million in allowances, generating more than $432.8 million. As of the time of this writing, this bill has not been passed by the Senate.

Another important trend influencing the electric industry is energy conservation and the concept of demand management. Reducing energy consumption has been demonstrated in states such as California, where annual per-capita electric consumption has remained relatively flat since 1980 (about 7200 kWh), while the rest of the nation's per-capita electrical consumption increased by 50% over that period (California Energy Commission, 2007). Increases in per-capita electrical consumption have historically been encouraged through rate models charging customers a flat rate per kilowatt-hour of electricity consumed.

This "average-cost pricing" structure does not accurately reflect the true cost of producing, transmitting, and delivery of power, especially during peak demand periods. Average-cost pricing encourages electrical consumption, makes markets inefficient, increases wholesale price volatility, and underutilizes utility assets during nonpeak periods. This is discussed in more detail in the chapter on pricing.

Average-cost pricing has been set to make energy seem more affordable and thus provides the customer with no incentive to reduce energy consumption. In addition to average-cost pricing, some utilities use pricing structures that actually encourage more energy consumption, such as declining block rates (the price per unit of energy decreases as consumption increases). Higher consumption encourages more capital investment, resulting in more revenue and profits (i.e., the Averch-Johnson effect). This inefficient model has been replaced in some areas of the country by decoupling mechanisms that have separate utility revenues from the sale of electricity. Due to this lack of incentive to change ratepayer consumption behavior, utilities have been forced to overinvest in generation and transmission capacity to meet peak demand. Average-cost pricing and certainly declining block rates therefore created an inefficient market with poorly utilized assets, volatile wholesale prices, and reduced grid reliability.

Demand-side management and the concept of dynamic pricing are designed to send the consumer price signals to support appropriate consumer response, such as during peak demand hours. Instead of a flat rate and a monthly bill showing total energy consumed, dynamic pricing incentivizes customers to shift their load from peak to off-peak hours and exposes customers to more realistic energy prices based on generation costs and overall market supply and demand.

In addition, dynamic pricing enables customers to gain a better understanding of how they use energy and how the cost of energy changes during the day. The Energy Independence and Security Act of 2007 took the first step in this direction by supporting the need for a "smart grid" and advanced meters that allow utilities to monitor energy consumption in real time. In addition to smart meters, the "smart grid" must also include enabling elements, such as two-way communication networks, data storage systems, automated device control, and advanced billing and cost modeling to make dynamic pricing possible. Nearly 60 utilities in the United States participated in voluntary real-time pricing tariffs, through either pilot or permanent programs (see Barbose and Goldman, 2004).

A number of dynamic pricing models exist. Time-of-use (TOU) rates are the most widely implemented and differentiate between peak and off-peak periods throughout the day. The day is typically divided into sections such as off-peak, mid-peak, and peak time periods. Predetermined prices are assigned to those periods with peak demand consumption, producing a higher energy bill, which should provide incentives to reduce energy consumption. Conversely, customers shifting their load to off-peak times experience lower energy bills. Pricing reflects the utility's cost of generating electricity or purchasing power in the wholesale markets to meet customer demand. Clearly, cost models play an important role in determining pricing under dynamic conditions.

Time-of-use rates demonstrated their effectiveness in bringing down ratepayer energy bills, and by exposing customers to price signals for marginal demand costs, the utility can improve its economic efficiency. These rates also encourage conservation and eliminate cross-subsidies between customer classes that produce "fairer" rate structures. Customers feel empowered, as they now have choices regarding their management of energy consumption and costs.

Other forms of dynamic pricing include critical peak pricing (CPP), which is a form of time-of-use pricing except that very high electric prices are set for critical peak times during the year to discourage consumption during these limited numbers of hours per year. These critical peak periods are typically identified the day before, allowing price signals to be set to traditional peak-use customers. Critical peak pricing can be based on a maximum number of days with defined time and duration (fixed-period CPP), no predetermined duration or time with little advance warning (variable-period CPP), off-peak and mid-peak period prices set in advance for a designated length of time (variable-peak CPP), and critical peak rebates, where customers remain on fixed rates but receive rebates for load reductions during critical peak periods. By making customers more responsive to increases in energy demand and market prices as well as supply shortages, CPP programs provide several benefits, including reducing the use of peak power and stress on the transmission and distribution systems. By curtailing peak demand, utilities also avoid the use of expensive generation assets and avoid high transmission marginal costs to produce overall lower costs to the ratepayer.

Real-time pricing (RTP) programs are another form of dynamic pricing that provides the ratepayer with hourly retail prices that reflect hourly changes in the cost of production or purchases from the grid. Unlike time-of-use and critical peak pricing, real-time pricing is not based on preset prices for specified periods. Real-time pricing sends actual market prices to customers, exposing them to sudden and sometimes unexpected changes in the price of electricity caused by events such as unexpected high demand, supply interruptions, weather, and other factors. In RTP programs, the cost per kilowatt-hour changes hourly and is based on either the marginal cost to produce electricity or the current market price. Variations in RTP also include two-part pricing, which will be discussed in some detail in the chapter on pricing. In this model, a base usage level is priced at fixed rates and real-time prices are used for demand above the base usage level. The advantage of this approach is that low-usage customers see no change in rates and high-usage customers are encouraged to reduce usage.

Since real-time prices more accurately reflect the real-time marginal costs of producing electricity, they tend to be of more benefit than time-of-use rates. Dynamic pricing and the use of robust cost modeling can provide numerous benefits to both the customer and utility. By reducing peak demand, utilities can defer the construction of new transmission or distribution systems and offer new programs, such as giving the customers the option to purchase risk management tools, including caps and other hedging contracts. Dynamic pricing also enables utilities to implement demand response, conservation, and energy efficiency programs that can positively affect the grid. Utilities involved in dynamic pricing programs experienced improved operational efficiency, lower capital costs, and greater quality and reliability of service.

From a utility standpoint, dynamic pricing and demand-side management can reduce or eliminate in the near term the construction of more generation assets. Utilities that implemented dynamic pricing programs experienced improved operation efficiency, lower capital costs, and greater power quality and reliability. Dynamic pricing also lowers the cost of service over time and allocates resources more efficiently. By eliminating cross-subsidies that occur with average-cost pricing or in the implementation of distributed generation and net metering programs without dynamic pricing, distributed generators that reduce grid and distribution load can purchase electricity when prices are lower than their cost of generation, and the distributed generation can then be used to more cost-effectively meet peak loads.

Customers who adjust their demand behavior receive the most direct benefits in reduced energy costs. For those ratepayers who either choose not to or cannot adjust their demand behavior, dynamic pricing can still have benefits since the reduction of the peak demand of other customers reduces the transmission and distribution losses so that more expensive generation will not be called upon as frequently. Dynamic pricing also shifts market power to the customers, when they actively respond to price signals, limiting the ability to increase prices. Over time, dynamic pricing has been shown to decrease wholesale prices. Changes in electric pricing structures and the use of dynamic pricing also encourages innovation such as the development of energy use monitors, remote device control, Internet-connected appliances, and certainly more robust cost models as presented in this book.

CHAPTER 4

The Economics (and Econometrics) of Cost Modeling

4.1 THE GENERAL COST MODEL

In general, a cost function describes the relationship between inputs, outputs, and other factors on total cost. That is,

$$C = f(\mathbf{Y}, \mathbf{P}, \mathbf{O}) + e, \tag{4.1}$$

where

C = total cost, which is equal to total operating expenses plus the cost of capital.

$\mathbf{Y}$ = a vector of total outputs.

$\mathbf{P}$ = a vector of input prices.

$\mathbf{O}$ = a vector of other factors.

It is critical to note that not every such relationship describes a proper cost function, which follows from the hypothesis of cost minimization. Therefore, a proper cost function is characterized by the following:

1. **Monotonicity in Y.** Given a cost function of the preceding general form, an increase (decrease) in output should always increase (decrease) total cost. Mathematically, this is given by

    $$\partial C / \partial Y > 0 \tag{4.2}$$

    where $\partial C / \partial Y$ = marginal cost. A second-order condition would be that cost increases with output at a decreasing rate. That is,

    $$\partial^2 C / \partial Y^2 < 0 \tag{4.3}$$

    which yields the cost curve displayed in Figure 2.1.

2. **Homogeneity of degree 1 in input prices** (also known as *linear homogeneity*). Formally, this implies that, for $t > 0$,

    $$C(t\mathbf{p}, Y) = tC(\mathbf{p}, Y) \tag{4.4}$$

    Simply put, if $t = 2$, then a doubling of input prices will double the total cost. Furthermore, the derivatives of this cost function, the factor demands (or inputs), are homogeneous of degree 0.

Electricity Cost Modeling Calculations
DOI: 10.1016/B978-1-85617-726-9.00004-2

3. **Nondecreasing in input prices.** Let $\mathbf{p}$ and $\mathbf{p}'$ denote vectors of input prices such that $\mathbf{p}' \geq \mathbf{p}$. Nondecreasing in input prices implies that

$$C(\mathbf{p}', Y) \geq C(\mathbf{p}, Y) \qquad (4.5)$$

That is, an increase in the price of an input cannot cause total production cost to fall. In addition, since the derivatives of this cost function result in the optimal factor demands, this restriction is further warranted. That is, it is the result of Shephard's lemma (see note 10), which states that the optimal factor demands, x_i, are derived from:

$$\partial C(\mathbf{p}, Y)/\partial p_i = x_i(p, Y) \geq 0 \qquad (4.6)$$

4. **Concavity in input prices.** This is not an obvious outcome of cost minimization and has several implications: First, the cross-price effects are symmetric. That is, by Young's theorem,

$$\partial x_i(\mathbf{p}, \mathbf{Y})/\partial \mathbf{p}_j = \partial^2 C(\mathbf{p}, \mathbf{Y})/\partial \mathbf{p}_j \partial \mathbf{p}_i = \partial^2 C(\mathbf{p}, \mathbf{Y})/\partial \mathbf{p}_i \partial \mathbf{p}_j$$
$$= \partial x_j(\mathbf{p}, \mathbf{Y})/\partial p_i \qquad (4.7)$$

Second, own price effects are nonpositive:

$$\partial x_i(\mathbf{p}, Y)/\partial \mathbf{p}_i = \partial^2 C(\mathbf{p}, Y)/\partial \mathbf{p}_i^2 \leq 0 \qquad (4.8)$$

That is, cost minimization requires that the matrix of first derivatives of the factor demand equations be negative semidefinite, which requires that the diagonal terms of the Hessian matrix to be nonpositive (these are the own-price coefficients). (See the chapter appendix for details.)

5. **Multiproduct firm cost function.** For multiproduct firms, the cost function should be able to accommodate output vectors in which some goods take on a value of 0, which is certainly the case throughout the cost function literature for electric utilities. As we will see, two of the more commonly used specifications in the literature that violate these criteria are the Cobb-Douglas and the translogarithmic functional form. Each is explored in more detail, but for now, it suffices to review the general form of each as well as its salient properties.

The (two output) Cobb-Douglas cost function (input prices are omitted for simplicity) is

$$C(\mathbf{Y}, p) = A(Y_1)^{\alpha 1}(Y_2)^{\alpha 2} \qquad (4.9)$$

Where

A = a technology parameter.

Y_1, Y_2 = outputs.

α_1, α_2 = parameters to be estimated.

It is easy to see that, if one of the outputs is 0, then total cost equals 0, which is not likely the case for a firm producing positive amounts of the other output. Note: Because the parameters to be estimated enter nonlinearly in the equation, ordinary least squares cannot be used.

The (two output) translogarithmic cost function (with input prices, p_k) is

$$\ln C(Y, p) = \alpha_0 + \sum_i \alpha_i \ln Y_i + \sum_i \sum_j \alpha_{ij} \ln Y_i Y_j$$
$$+ \sum_k \beta_k \ln p_k, \text{ for } i, j = 1, 2 \tag{4.10}$$

Since the natural log of zero is undefined, any output vector in which **Y** takes on a value of 0 renders the total cost of production undefined. Despite its popularity, this form is simply not appropriate for modeling cost in multiple output industries.

6. **Form of cost function.** The functional form of the cost function should not influence the analysis and resulting conclusions. Cost functions are often used to determine the optimal industry structure (i.e., number of firms, etc.) via concepts like economies of scale and scope, horizontal and vertical integration, and subadditivity of the cost function, which is a sufficient condition for natural monopoly (from Chapter 2). That is, the form itself must be flexible enough to allow for the emergence of these important cost concepts, which can then be used to shape industry structure and optimal policy making.

Again, despite its popularity, the translogarithmic functional form precludes a finding of economies of scope or subadditivity of the cost function due to its inability to deal with outputs that take on a value of 0. The Cobb-Douglas form is also excluded. Recall from Chapter 2, cost complementarity, which is a sufficient condition for subadditivity, is given by

$$\partial^2 C(Y)/\partial Y_i \partial Y_j < 0 \tag{4.11}$$

where $\mathbf{Y} = \sum_i y_i$ for $i, j = 1, \ldots, n$ and $i \neq j$.

In the case of the Cobb-Douglas functional form, this is equivalent to

$$\partial^2 C(Y)/\partial Y_i \partial Y_j = \alpha_i \alpha_j C / Y_i Y_j \tag{4.12}$$

where

$$C = A(Y_i)^{\alpha i}(Y_j)^{\alpha j}$$

and $i \neq j$. Clearly, as long as marginal costs are positive and all outputs are positive,

$$\partial^2 C(Y)/\partial Y_i \partial Y_j > 0 \qquad (4.13)$$

which precludes a finding of cost complementarity and, hence, subadditivity of the cost function. Thus, it should be the data, not the functional form, that determine the findings and support the conclusions reached.

7. Finally, whenever possible, parsimony is key. Include only the variables that are theoretically relevant and for which accurate data can be obtained. Be certain to review the data carefully, looking for outliers and other oddities.

4.2 THE ECONOMETRICS OF COST MODELING: AN OVERVIEW

Ordinary least squares estimation

You may recall that certain assumptions must be met for ordinary least squares (OLS) estimators to be the "best" (aka BLUE, best linear unbiased estimators). Known as the *classical assumptions*, when met, OLS estimators are unbiased, efficient (i.e., minimum variance), consistent, and normally distributed. These assumptions follow:

- The model is linear in coefficients, correctly specified, and the error term (ε_i) is additive. That is,

$$Y = \beta \mathbf{X} + \varepsilon_i \qquad (4.14)$$

- The error term has a population mean $= 0$.
- The explanatory variables are not correlated with the error term.
- The error terms are not serially correlated (i.e., no autocorrelation).
- The error term has a constant variance (i.e., no heteroscedasticity).
- No explanatory variable is a perfect linear function of another explanatory variable (i.e., no multicollinearity).
- The error term, ε_i, is normally distributed; that is, $\varepsilon_i \sim N(0, \sigma^2)$, or

$$E(\varepsilon_i) = 0 \text{ and } \text{Var}(\varepsilon_i) = \sigma^2 \qquad (4.15)$$

Regression analysis and cost modeling

Basically put, regression analysis is a statistical technique that attempts to quantify the effect of a change in an independent variable on a dependent variable. In the case of cost modeling, the dependent variable, cost, is a function of other explanatory variables, such as the prices of inputs and, of course, output. That is, at the very least, a cost function is of the general form

$$C = f(Y, \mathbf{p}) \qquad (4.16)$$

where

C = cost.

Y = output.

$\mathbf{p}$ = (a vector of) input prices.

In its simplest form, a single output linear cost model is of the form

$$C = \alpha_0 + \alpha_y Y + \sum_i \beta_i p_i \qquad (4.17)$$

In this case, the parameters to be estimated via regression are the coefficients on output (α_y), input prices (β_i), and the constant (α_0).

On the surface, this particular specification appears to conform to the classical assumptions mentioned previously, which indicates that the parameters can be estimated via OLS. In upcoming chapters, we see much more complex models that cannot be estimated via this technique, but for now, we continue along this vein. At this juncture, some examples are probably in order.

Examples: Examining data—An illustration of salient points

The data set RUS97_Basic contains data on the cost of distributing electricity for 707 rural electric cooperatives that distributed electricity in 1997. To get familiar with this data (we use it extensively in upcoming chapters), the variables of which are defined in Table 4.1, a review of the summary statistics and variable plots can prove to be helpful in the determination of outliers and other data irregularities. Table 4.2 contains the summary statistics of the relevant variables. Note in particular the composition of the load: mostly residential customers and low density, which has implications in terms of optimal industry structure and public policy.

Example 4.1. Check for outliers

One of the first things that one should always do is review the data. Plots of the variables can yield important clues as to appropriate specification and whether there are errors in the data. Since purchased power is one of the largest costs faced by a distribution utility, it is informative to plot this variable, which is displayed in Figure 4.1.

Figure 4.1 displays the frequency distribution of the price of purchased power (in $/MWh) for the coops in the sample. Note the wide range of

Table 4.1 Variables Included in RUS97_Basic Dataset

Variable	Definition
State FIPS	State indicator
Coop	Coop indicator
Borrower	RUS borrower (distribution coop)
Supplier	Type of supplier: G&T cooperative, IOU, federal, other
Cost	The total cost of distributing electricity (thousands $)
RES	Electricity distributed to residential customers (MWh)
CISmall	Electricity distributed to small commercial/industrial customers (MWh)
Y_1	Electricity distributed to "small" (i.e., low-voltage) customers (MWh)
Y_2	Electricity distributed to "large" (i.e., high-voltage) customers (MWh)
Y	Total electricity distributed ($Y_1 + Y_2$) in MWh
Pk	Price of capital (interest on LTD/LTD)
Pp	Price of purchased power (cost of purchased power/MWh purchased)
Pl	Price of labor (total payroll expense/number hours worked)
TR	Miles of transmission lines
DensAll	Customer density (customers/mile distribution line)

Table 4.2 Summary Statistics—RUS97_Basic Dataset: 1997 Rural Electric Cooperatives

Variable	Mean	Std dev	Minimum	Maximum
Cost (000)	19,397	23,255	429	186,796
RES	172	214	2	1677
CISmall	53	77	0	694
Y_1	225	280	2	2371
Y_2	63	230	0	4040
Y	288	400	2	4573
Pk	5	1	0	7
Pp	43	10	18	90
Pl	16	4	0	59
TR	28	58	0	348
DensAll	6	3	0	24
ResCust	13,422	15,621	282	132,780
CISmallCust	1365	1788	0	12,327
CILargeCust	11	57	0	1336

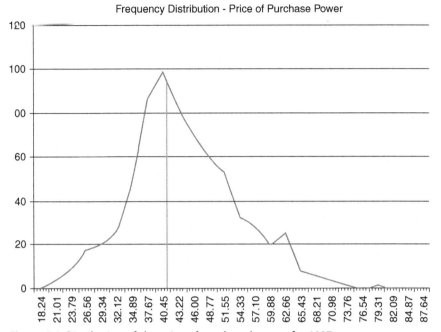

Figure 4.1 Distribution of the price of purchased power for 1997 coops

values and that it does not appear to be normally distributed. This is not surprising; in the case of electricity, power prices tend to vary with more observations at higher levels, especially given the types of suppliers and the various sources of generation fuel sources.

Example 4.2. Suppliers—Cost of purchased power by supplier type

Even though many distribution coops are members of generation and transmission (G&T) cooperatives, some are not. In fact, 46 members purchase power from an investor-owned utility and over 10% ($n = 72$) purchase power from a federal power supplier. As an exercise, you are asked to review the descriptive statistics associated with the distribution coops that purchase power from each of these types of suppliers.

Example 4.3. Estimating a basic cost function

Using the data contained in RUS97_Basic, estimate the parameters of a single-output, three-input regression equation of the form

$$C = \alpha_0 + \alpha_y Y + \beta_k p_k + \beta_l p_l + \beta_p p_p \qquad (4.18)$$

where p_k = price of capital, p_l = price of labor, and p_p = price of purchased power.

Using OLS, the estimated equation is (*t*-statistics in parentheses)

$$C = -17{,}635 + 53.11 \times Y + 938.80 \times p_k + 123.30 \times p_l + 351.07 \times p_p$$
$$\quad\ (-6.86)\ \ (68.14)\qquad (2.46)\qquad\qquad (1.51)\qquad\qquad (11.52)$$

$$(4.18')$$

Estimation results: Basic cost model

An adjusted R^2 of 0.88 indicates that the independent variables explain 88% of the variation in the cost of distributing electricity. A check for serial correlation (also known as *autocorrelation*) reveals that this is not an issue; the Durbin-Watson statistic of 1.827 is very close to 2.0, which are the criteria indicated by the Durbin-Watson test statistic, and given the nature of the data (cross-sectional) this is not surprising (serial correlation typically occurs with time-series data). What is a possible concern, however, is that the errors do not have a constant variance. That is, they are heteroscedastic in nature, which is one of the criteria that obviates the use of OLS to estimate the parameters of the regression model, since the distribution of the error term is not of constant variance. That is, rather than

$Var(\varepsilon_i) = \sigma^2$ from equation (4.2)

The variance is equal to

$$Var(\varepsilon_i) = \sigma^2 Z_i^2 \qquad\qquad (4.2')$$

where Z_i may or may not be one of the regressors in the equation. The variable Z is called a proportionality factor, because the variance of the error term changes in proportion to the square of Z_i (Studenmund, 1997). White's[1] test reveals that indeed errors are heteroscedastic.

---

[1] White's test detects heteroscedasticity by running a regression of the squared residuals (from the original regression, e_i) as the dependent variable on the original explanatory variables, their squares, and their cross-products. White's test statistic is computed as

$$nR^2$$

where n = sample size and R^2 is the (unadjusted) coefficient of determination of the equation that contains the original explanatory variables, their squares, and their cross-products. The test statistic has a chi-square distribution with degrees of freedom equal to the number of slope coefficients in the equation containing the original explanatory variables, their squares, and their cross-products.

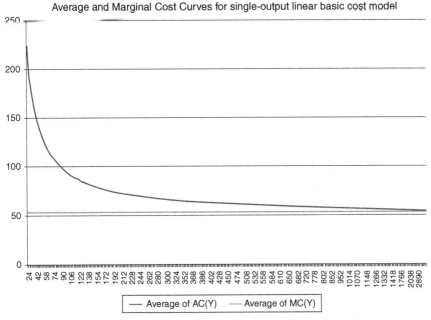

Figure 4.2 Average and marginal costs generated by basic cost model

The heteroscedasticity corrected standard errors generated the *t*-statistics displayed in parentheses under the following equation:

$$C = -17{,}635 + 53.11 \times Y + 938.80 \times p_k + 123.30 \times p_l + 351.07 \times p_p$$
$$(-4.99) \quad (10.99) \qquad (2.01) \qquad\quad (1.91) \qquad\quad (6.89)$$

$$(4.18'')$$

Evaluating equation (4.18″) at various levels of output yields the average and marginal cost curves displayed in Figure 4.2.

The average and marginal cost curves displayed are not consistent with economic theory. Due to the linear form of the basic cost equation, average cost declines with output and marginal cost is constant, unlike the appropriate U-shapes that each should have due to the law of diminishing returns in production (see Chapter 2, Figure 2.2).

Consequences of heteroscedasticity

1. Pure (as opposed to impure) heteroscedasticity does not cause bias in the parameter estimates. Note: These did not change, which indicates that there is no bias in the estimates themselves in the presence of heteroscedasticity;

2. It does, however, increase the variance of the distribution around the estimated coefficients so that they are no longer minimum variance;
3. In addition, it causes OLS to underestimate the standard errors of the coefficients, which means that the *t*-statistics of the coefficients are inflated. This, in turn, can increase the probability of committing a Type I error, which is the rejection of a true null hypothesis.

A comparison of the two equations yields the following: While the estimates themselves have not changed (again, OLS estimates are unbiased even in the presence of heteroscedasticity), the standard errors of the estimates have clearly changed; however, in some cases, we see that they have not changed in the same direction. This is an indication that a deeper, more complex issue must be addressed.

Impure heteroscedasticity

Impure heteroscedasticity results from an error in specification, such as an omitted variable or an incorrect functional form. Either can result in incorrect signs on the estimated parameters in addition to the aforementioned consequences. Since we spend much time discussing and estimating various cost specifications, this is a timely and critical discussion to pursue here.

Recall that one of the objectives in cost modeling is the testing for economies of scale and the determination of the optimal industry structure. In the case of equation (4.18), the functional form precludes any finding of anything other than increasing returns to scale, since average cost must decline with output and marginal cost is constant.

Recall from Chapter 2 that

$$SCE(y) = \text{Average cost/Marginal cost} \qquad (4.19)$$

Indeed, evaluating SCE at the sample means of the variables yields, SCE = 1.26. This confirms that there are economies of scale since SCE > 1.

Example 4.4. Specification bias (functional form, omitted variable bias)

While parsimony might be an appealing property, it is often the case that very basic regression models simply are not capable of capturing the characteristics deemed important and necessary for their intended purposes. In the preceding example, constant marginal cost and an ever-declining average cost curve do not accord with economic theory and can provide no assistance in the determination of the optimal industry structure and appropriate public policy.

The specification bias that must be addressed here is the possible omission of a relevant variable or the incorrect functional form of the equation. For the issue at hand, a fairly straightforward solution could be to allow output to enter both linearly and as a quadratic; that is, to estimate an equation of the following form:

$$C = \alpha_0 + \alpha_y Y + \frac{1}{2} \times \alpha_{yy} Y^2 + \sum_i \beta_i p_i \qquad (4.20)$$

This particular form allows for both marginal and average cost to be a function of output, which is certainly appealing and accords to economic theory. Furthermore, specifying that output enters as a quadratic "allows for the unconstrained emergence of economies or diseconomies of scale and scope as well as subadditivity" (Kwoka, 1996, p. 59).

Prior to estimating any equation, it is important to determine the expected signs of the estimated coefficients, which should accord with economic theory. In this case, a priori expectations are that the coefficients of the input price variables (β_i) are all positive (nondecreasing in factor prices) and that α_y is also positive and greater than 0 (monotonic in output). To generate a region of economies of scale, it is necessary that α_{yy}, the coefficient of output squared, be negative in sign and statistically different from 0; however, since marginal cost is a function of output, one must ensure that its magnitude does not yield a negative marginal cost, which is given by

$$\partial C(Y, \mathbf{p})/\partial Y = \alpha_y + \alpha_{yy} Y \qquad (4.21)$$

Estimation results—Quadratic cost model

Estimation results for the quadratic cost model are displayed in Equation (4.20′):

$$C = -14,417 + 73.02 \times Y - 0.017 \times Y^2 - 143.19 \times p_k + 110.12 \times p_l + 319.48 \times p_p$$
$$(-4.92) \quad (28.94) \qquad (-8.59) \qquad (-0.55) \qquad (1.86) \qquad (6.96)$$
$$(4.20′)$$

The adjusted R^2 of 0.92 indicates that the model fit has improved over the previous specification. Indeed, the signs of the estimated coefficients on the output variables are of the expected sign and statistical significance. However, a review of the other estimated coefficients gives cause for concern. In particular, that of the capital price, which is now negative (although not statistically different from 0). Furthermore,

White's test[2] indicates that heteroscedasticity is still an issue. These examples illustrate some of the issues involved in modeling costs. The exercises at the end of this chapter provide hands-on experience in dealing with some of these practical, real-world issues. In subsequent chapters, we investigate other, more sophisticated cost specifications, including the Cobb-Douglas and translogarithmic, since they have been employed throughout the economics literature to model costs for electric utilities. In addition, the quadratic form developed by Greer (2003) is explored in much more detail and employed in the case studies of Chapters 7 and 8.

4.3 A BRIEF HISTORY OF COST MODELS AND APPLICATIONS TO THE ELECTRIC INDUSTRY

The Cobb-Douglas functional form

One of the first to estimate cost models in the electric industry was Marc Nerlove (1963), who employed the dual to the Cobb-Douglas production function, which was introduced in the seminal paper by Charles Cobb and Paul Douglas in 1928. In general, a production function summarizes the relationship among inputs and output. More specifically, the production function (f) indicates the maximum possible output (y) given any combination of inputs $(x_i, i = 1, \ldots, n)$. That is,

$$y = f(x_1, x_2, \ldots, x_n; A) \qquad (4.22)$$

where A = a technical knowledge variable, which reflects improvements in technology and human capital.

Succinctly put, "the fundamental principle of duality in production: the cost function of a firm summarizes all of the economically relevant aspects of its technology" (Varian, p. 84). In other words, a production function can be recovered from a cost function, and vice versa.

---

[2] For equation (4.20), the regression that generated the White test statistic is given by

$$(e_i)^2 = \alpha_0 + \alpha_y Y + \tfrac{1}{2} \times \alpha_{yy} Y^2 + \beta_l p_l + \beta_k p_k + \beta_p p_p + \beta_{ll}(p_l)^2 + \beta_{kk}(p_k)^2 + \beta_{pp}(p_p)^2 + \beta_{lk} p_l p_k$$
$$+ \beta_{kp} p_k p_p + \beta_{pl} p_p p_l + \alpha_{yl} Y p_l + \alpha_{yk} Y p_k + \alpha_{yp} Y p_p + \tfrac{1}{2}$$
$$\times (\alpha_{yyl} Y^2 p_l + \alpha_{yyk} Y^2 p_k + \alpha_{yyp} Y^2 p_p + 2 \times \alpha_{yyy} Y^2 Y)$$

which yields a White's test statistic = nR^2 = 539.4. The null hypothesis (errors are not heteroscedastic) is rejected and the presence of heteroscedasticity is confirmed. Note: Most econometric software packages calculate the White statistic and indicate whether the null hypothesis of homoscedasticity can be rejected.

One of the most commonly used Cobb–Douglas production functions is given by:

$$Y = A \times K^{\alpha} L^{1-\alpha} \tag{4.23}$$

where

Y = value-added output.
A = technological knowledge.
K = capital (input).
L = labor (input).
α = a parameter to be estimated.

Returns to scale

In the case of this particular function, clearly, there are constant returns to scale in the production technology (since $1 - \alpha + \alpha = 1$). Mathematically, in the two-input case (such as equation (4.23)),

$$ty = tf(x_1, x_2) = f(tx_1, tx_2) \tag{4.24}$$

In general, if all inputs are scaled up by some amount t (a scalar), then output would increase by t times. Similarly, increasing (decreasing) returns to scale exist if

$$ty = tf(x_1, x_2) > (<)f(tx_1, tx_2) \tag{4.25}$$

Nerlove's Cobb-Douglas function

As the basis for his study, Nerlove employed a three-input (capital, labor, and fuel) cost model, which is the dual to the production function of the form

$$Y = Ax_1^{\alpha_1} x_2^{\alpha_2} x_3^{\alpha_3} \tag{4.26}$$

For the Cobb–Douglas production function, returns to scale (r) are equal to the sum of the exponents:

$$r = \alpha_1 + \alpha_2 + \alpha_3 \tag{4.27}$$

After much algebra, the Cobb–Douglas cost function employed by Nerlove is given by (in natural logs)[3]

$$\ln C = \ln k + (1/r) \ln y + \sum_i (\alpha_i/r) \ln p_i, \quad \text{for all } i = 1, 2, 3 \tag{4.28}$$

---

[3] See Berndt, 1991, pp. 69–71 for details.

where

ln C = natural log of cost.

ln y = the natural log of output.

ln p_i = natural log of input prices.

and

$$k = r \left[A \prod_i (\alpha_i^{\alpha_i}) \right]^{-1/r} \tag{4.29}$$

where

$$r = \sum_i \alpha_i \text{ (parameters to be estimated via regression)} \tag{4.30}$$

Substitution and arranging terms yield

$$\ln C^* = \beta_0 + \beta_y \ln Y + \beta_1 \ln p_1^* + \beta_2 \ln p_2^* \tag{4.31}$$

where

$$\ln C^* = \ln C - \ln p_3 \tag{4.32}$$

$$\ln p_1^* = \ln p_1 - \ln p_3 \tag{4.33}$$

$$\ln p_2^* = \ln p_2 - \ln p_3 \tag{4.34}$$

$$\beta_0 = \ln k \tag{4.35}$$

$$\beta_y = 1/r \tag{4.36}$$

$$\beta_1 = \alpha_1/r \tag{4.37}$$

$$\beta_2 = \alpha_2/r \tag{4.38}$$

which imply that

$$\alpha_1 = \beta_1 r \Rightarrow \alpha_1 = \beta_1/\beta_y \tag{4.39}$$

and

$$\alpha_2 = \beta_2 r \Rightarrow \alpha_2 = \beta_2/\beta_y \tag{4.40}$$

From Berndt (1991), linear homogeneity in input prices (recall that this is one of the conditions for a properly specified cost model) implies that the constraint on the underlying parameters is given by

$$(\alpha_1 + \alpha_2 + \alpha_3)/r = 1 \tag{4.41}$$

So that (Berndt, 1991, p. 71)

$$\alpha_3 = (1 - \beta_1 - \beta_2)/\beta_y \tag{4.42}$$

It is left as an exercise to check for linear homogeneity of the underlying input price parameters ($\alpha_1, \alpha_2, \alpha_3$).

Economies of scale

Analogous to the concept of returns to scale in production is that of economies of scale. You may recall from Chapter 2 that this is defined as the ratio of average cost to marginal cost. Economies of scale indicate the situation in which the cost of producing an additional unit of output (i.e., the marginal cost) of a product decreases as the volume of output increases. That is, an $x\%$ increase in all inputs yields a more than $x\%$ increase in output. For the purposes here, it is often more useful to define the degree of scale economies, which is given by

$$SCE(y) = C(y)/y \times C'(y) \qquad (4.43)$$

which is equivalent to the ratio of average cost to marginal cost. Returns to scale are said to be increasing, constant, or decreasing as SCE is greater than, equal to, or less than unity.

The degree of scale economies at y, SCE, is the elasticity of output at y with respect to the cost of producing y. Alternately, it is also the elasticity of output (at y) with respect to the magnitude of a proportionate (or any efficient) expansion in input levels (see Baumol, Panzar, and Willig, 1982, for more detail). This concept is extremely important (and relevant) in upcoming chapters.

Minimum efficient scale

Geometrically, Figure 4.3 displays the relevant regions of an average cost curve. As output is expanded, cost increases at a decreasing rate until average cost is at its minimum. Known as the *minimum efficient scale* (MES), this point indicates the optimal level of output for a firm (or firms) to produce. After this, diminishing marginal returns set in (i.e., marginal cost begins to rise, causing average cost to increase at an increasing rate). This is displayed in Figure 4.3.

This concept is extremely important, since it is an important factor in determining the optimal size and equilibrium number of firms in an industry. As such, it can have major implications for public policy, particularly where it leads to the development of natural monopolies or where monopolies that are not natural monopolies claim that they are to prevent government attempts to break them up.

Nerlove's results

Nerlove estimated the parameters of this Cobb-Douglas cost model (equation (4.31)) via ordinary least squares, which works well under certain conditions. Before reviewing his results, let us briefly discuss the a priori expectations of the estimation results.

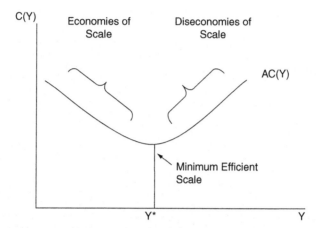

Figure 4.3 Minimum efficient scale and optimal industry output. Y^* indicates the output at which average costs are minimized, also known as the *minimum efficient scale*.

A priori expections

First and foremost, the estimated parameter (or coefficient) of the output variable, β_y, should be positive, since an increase in output should always increase total cost (i.e., monotonicity in output). Second, and also critical, is that the estimated parameters of the input price variables (β_1, β_2) should also be positive, since an increase in the price of an input should also increase total cost (i.e., nondecreasing in factor prices).

Turning now to Table 4.3, which contains the estimation results, note that the coefficient of the output variable ($\ln Y$) is indeed positive and statistically significant (given the t-statistic of 41.334). The interpretation is straightforward: A 1% increase in output yields a 0.72% increase in total cost, ceteris paribus. Similarly, the coefficient of $\ln p_1^*$ (β_1) is also positive in sign and statistically significant (keep in mind that the true parameter estimate of the price of labor variable must be recovered (it is actually α_1, which is given by equation (4.39)). Finally, the estimated coefficient

Table 4.3 Nerlove Original Data and Cost Model (Cobb-Douglas)

Variable	Parameter	Nerlove model: Estimate	Nerlove model: t-statistic
Constant	β_0	−0.6908	−5.301
$\ln Y$	β_y	0.72069	41.334
$\ln p_1^*$	β_1	0.59291	2.898
$\ln p_2^*$	β_2	−0.00738	−0.039
	Adjusted R^2	0.93	

of the "other" input price $\ln p_2^*(\beta_2)$ is negative in sign (but not statistically different from 0). Again, one must recover the actual input price coefficients to determine whether this negatively-signed coefficient is truly problematic (since it could be the case that $\alpha_2, \alpha_3 > 0$ but $\alpha_2 < \alpha_3$ so $\beta_2 < 0$). Using equations (4.39)–(4.42), this is done in Example 4.5.

Example 4.5

Table 4.3 contains the results obtained by Marc Nerlove on estimating a Cobb-Douglas cost function for 145 electric utilities in 1955. Using these results, obtain the original parameters (those of the underlying production function, assuming linear homogeneity) and estimate r, the returns to scale (equation (4.30)).

From equations (4.39)–(4.42), it is straightforward to derive $\alpha_1 - \alpha_3$:

$$\alpha_1 = 0.59291/0.72069$$
$$\Rightarrow \alpha_1 = 0.8227 \tag{4.39'}$$

And

$$\alpha_2 = -0.00738/0.72069$$
$$\Rightarrow \alpha_2 = -0.01024 \tag{4.40'}$$

From equation 4.42, linear homogeneity implies that

$$\Rightarrow \alpha_3 = (1 - 0.59291 + 0.00738)/0.72069 \tag{4.42'}$$

Or

$$\alpha_3 = 0.5751$$

Returns to scale, r, are given by equation (4.30), which is equivalent to

$$r = 1.39$$

This implies that economies of scale $= 0.39$ (since economies of scale $= r - 1$)

In Chapter 6, "Cost Models," there is an end of chapter exercise with data supplied by the Rural Utilities Service on the 711 cooperatives that distributed electricity in the United States in 1997. This is used to estimate the parameters of a Cobb-Douglas cost function and calculate the returns to scale implied by the estimation results.

Elasticities

Earlier in this chapter some of the drawbacks of the Cobb-Douglas functional form were discussed. Because input prices were omitted from that discussion, the concept of substitution elasticities among the inputs was avoided. We broach that subject now, since we include input prices into the cost specification. With this said, another concern about the Cobb-Douglas production function is that the substitution elasticities among inputs always equal unity. That is, in Nerlove's model, the substitution elasticities between capital and labor, capital and fuel, and labor and fuel always equal unity. Formally, the elasticity of substitution between inputs, which measures the degree of substitutability between inputs (x_i, x_j) is given by

$$\sigma_{ij} = \partial \ln(x_i/x_j)/\partial \ln(P_i/P_j) \tag{4.44}$$

where P_i, P_j are the marginal products of x_i, x_j.[4]

The constant elasticity of substitution functional form

To get around this limitation, an important paper by Kenneth Arrow, Hollis Chenery, Bagicha Minhas, and Robert Solow (1961) shows that solving for $\partial \ln(x_i/x_j)$ then integrating equation (4.44) yields

$$\ln(x_i/x_j) = \text{constant} + \sigma\ln(F_i/F_j) \tag{4.45}$$

where $F_i/F_j =$ the marginal rate of technical substitution (MRTS) between x_i and x_j.

The integral of the MRTS yields the implied production function, which is known as the *constant elasticity of substitution* (CES) production function. Imposing constant returns to scale, this is given by (see Berndt, 1991, p. 452, for details)

$$Y = A \times \left[\delta x_i^{-\rho}(1 - \delta)x_j^{-\rho}\right]^{-1/\rho} \tag{4.46}$$

where

$$\sigma = 1/(1 + \rho)$$

The Cobb-Douglas is a special case of the CES function in the limiting case in which $\rho \to 0$, $\sigma \to 1$.

---

[4] The marginal product (P_i) of an input is equal to the partial derivative of y with respect to that input (x_i):

$$\partial y/\partial x_i = P$$

This particular form is not well suited for empirical analyses due to its nonlinear form. I am aware of only one instance in which a CES production function was used to estimate economies of scale in the distribution of electricity. In his 1987 study, Claggett (1987) employed it to estimate economies of scale for 50 TVA electric distribution cooperatives. Specifically, he estimated a two-input equation of the form

$$Y = \tau \times [\delta K^{-\rho} + (1 - \delta)L^{-\rho}]^{-1/\rho} \qquad (4.47)$$

where τ = efficiency parameter, δ = intensity parameter, and ρ are parameters to be estimated.

As stated, this form is somewhat problematic, in that it is highly nonlinear in the parameter ρ, which must be estimated to calculate the elasticity of substitution between capital and labor. As such, it cannot be estimated via ordinary least squares.[5] Nonetheless, Claggett found increasing economies of scale in distribution and concluded that the cooperatives in his data set were too small (in terms of the quantity of electricity distributed) to be truly efficient (i.e., attain the minimum efficient scale) from a cost-minimization perspective. This conclusion has been reached by others (including Greer, 2003) and is the result obtained in the case study presented in Chapter 7.

The generalized Leontief cost function

It was not until 1971 that Erwin Diewert employed Shephard's duality theory to estimate a general Leontief cost function, a flexible cost function associated with the Leontief form of production technology. In his classic article, Diewert provided to researchers functional forms that placed no a priori restrictions on substitution elasticities but were consistent with economic theory. Among the first to implement the Generalized Leontief cost model empirically were Berndt and Wood (1975), in a study of the U.S. manufacturing industry from 1947 to 1971. In this study, a four-input, multiple-equation system was estimated, which allowed both price and substitution elasticities to vary among the inputs. The form of the cost equation is described in detail later, but first an overview of the Leontief production technology and its underlying assumptions is provided.

---

[5] However, more recently developed econometric software programs are capable of estimating such equations.

Aside: Leontief production technology[6]

The implied L-shaped isoquants[7] of the Leontief production function are shown in Figure 4.4. Such a technology is referred to alternatively as *fixed proportions, no substitution,* or *input-output* technology (or some iteration thereof). At any particular output level Y^*, there is a necessary level of capital (K^*) and labor (L^*) that cannot be substituted. Note that these levels are determined purely technologically. Increasing only labor inputs (from L^* to L'' for instance) will *not* result in any higher output. Rather, the extra labor, without the extra capital to work with, is entirely wasted. The implication is that fixed proportions technology is "no less than a formal rejection of the marginal productivity theory. The marginal productivity of any [factor] . . . is zero" (Leontief, 1941, p. 38).

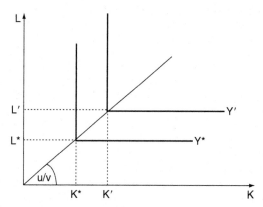

Figure 4.4 Leontief production technology, (no substitution) isoquants

---

[6] Source: http://cepa.newschool.edu/het/essays/product/technol.htm.

[7] An *isoquant* (derived from *quantity* and the Greek word *iso*, meaning equal) is a contour line drawn through the set of points at which the same quantity of output is produced while changing the quantities of two or more inputs. While an indifference curve helps answer the utility-maximizing problem of consumers, the isoquant deals with the cost minimization problem of producers. Isoquants are typically drawn on capital-labor graphs, showing the trade-off between capital and labor in the production function and the decreasing marginal returns of both inputs. Adding one input while holding the other constant eventually leads to decreasing marginal output, and this is reflected in the shape of the isoquant. A family of isoquants can be represented by an *isoquant map*, a graph combining a number of isoquants, each representing a different quantity of output.

An isoquant shows that the firm in question has the ability to substitute between the two different inputs at will to produce the same level of output. An isoquant map can also indicate decreasing or increasing returns to scale based on increasing or decreasing distances between the isoquants on the map as you increase output. If the distance between isoquants increases as output increases, the firm's production function is exhibiting decreasing returns to scale; doubling both inputs results in placement on an isoquant with less than double the output of the previous isoquant. Conversely, if the distance is decreasing as output increases, the firm is experiencing increasing returns to scale; doubling both inputs results in placement on an isoquant with more than twice the output of the original isoquant.

The production function for a no substitute case can be written as

$$Y = \min(K/v, L/u) \tag{4.48}$$

which is also referred to as a *Leontief production function*, as this form was introduced by Wassily Leontief (1941). Notice that, if K is at K^* and L is at L', then

$$K^*/v < L'/u; \text{thus}, Y = K^*/v \tag{4.49}$$

If so, then the technically efficient level of labor would, by definition, be where

$$K^*/v = L/u \quad \text{or} \quad L = (u/v)K^* \tag{4.50}$$

which, as is obvious in Figure 4.4, is at L^*. As a result, then it is the case that the following holds all along the ray that emanates from the origin:

$$Y/L = (1/v)K/L \tag{4.51}$$

The Leontief cost function

Again, via duality, the generalized Leontief (GL) cost function is given by

$$C = Y \times \left[\sum_i \sum_j \beta_{ij} (p_i p_j)^{1/2} \right] \tag{4.52}$$

where $\beta_{ij} = \beta_{ji}$ (by Young's theorem, or the symmetry of second derivatives)[8] and $i, j = 1, \ldots, n$.

Differentiating equation (4.52) with respect to p_i yields the optimal, cost minimizing input demand functions, which are given by

$$\partial C/\partial p_i = x_i = Y \times \left[\sum_j \beta_{ij} (p_j/p_i)^{1/2} \right] \tag{4.53}$$

for $i, j = 1, \ldots, n$.

For estimation purposes, it may be more convenient to divide through by output (Y), thus yielding the optimal input output demand equations, which are denoted by a_i (Berndt, 1991) and given by

$$a_i = x_i/Y = \sum_j \beta_{ij} (p_j/p_i)^{1/2} \quad \text{for } j = 1, \ldots, n \tag{4.54}$$

---

[8] Formally, Young's theorem states the following (www.economics.utoronto.ca/osborne/ MathTutorial/CLN.HTM): Let f be a differentiable function of n variables. If each of the cross partials f''_{ij} and f''_{ji} exists and is continuous at all points in some open set S of values of $(x_1, \ldots, x_n)$, then

$$f''_{ij}(x_1, \ldots, x_n) = f''_{ji}(x_1, \ldots, x_n) \text{ for all } (x_1, \ldots, x_n) \text{ in } S$$

Hicks-Allen partial elasticities of substitution

As stated previously, one of the attractive features of flexible functional forms like this one is that they place no a priori restrictions on the substitution elasticities between inputs. The Hicks-Allen partial elasticities of substitution for a general dual cost function with n inputs are computed as

$$\sigma_{ij} = C \times C_{ij} / C_i \times C_j \qquad (4.55)$$

where i and j are the first and second partial derivatives of the cost function with respect to input prices (p_i, p_j) and $i, j = 1, \ldots, n$.

We revisit substitution elasticities in more detail in Chapter 6. For now, we proceed onto one of the more popular flexible functional forms, the translogarithmic cost specification.

The translogarithmic cost function

Around the same time, Lauritis Christensen, Dale Jorgenson, and Lawrence Lau (1970) presented a paper introducing the translogarithmic (translog) specification for production and cost functions, which placed no a priori restrictions on the substitution elasticities. The translog function is a second-order Taylor's series approximation to any arbitrary cost function (in logarithms).[9] Christensen and Greene (1976) employed this cost specification in their seminal paper, "Economies of Scale in U.S. Electric Power Generation." The data in this study augmented the 1955 data set that was used by Nerlove (1963) for those same firms in 1970 to estimate economies of scale in the U.S. electricity market. This study employed a single output, three input translog cost function of the form:

$$\ln C = \alpha_0 + \alpha_y \ln y + \sum_i \beta_i \ln p_i + \left(\frac{1}{2}\right)\alpha_{yy}(\ln y)^2$$
$$+ \left(\frac{1}{2}\right)\sum_i \sum_j \phi_{ij} \ln p_i \ln p_j + \sum_i \omega_i \ln y \ln p_i \qquad (4.56)$$

where output $(\ln y)$ and input prices $(\ln p_i)$ enter linearly, as quadratics and as cross-products.

---

[9] The expansion of a function $y = f(x)$ into a Taylor series is to expand around a point x_0. This means to transform that function into a polynomial form in which the coefficients of the various terms are expressed in terms of the derivative values $f'(x_0), f''(x_0)$, etc., all evaluated at the point of expansion x_0. (Chiang, 1984, p. 254)

At the time, Nerlove recognized that the Cobb-Douglas model did not adequately account for the relationship between output and average cost (witness the negatively signed coefficient on capital price, derived in equation (4.40′). Christensen and Greene augmented the data set with cost share data to estimate the complete demand system, including the cost minimizing factor demand equations (i.e., the optimal level of inputs—capital, labor, and fuel in this case), given by Shephard's lemma:[10]

$$x_i^* = \partial C(Y, \mathbf{p})/\partial p_i \qquad (4.57)$$

where $\mathbf{p} = $ a vector of input prices.

By differentiating logarithmically, the cost minimizing factor cost share equations are obtained, given by

$$s_i = \partial \ln C(Y, \mathbf{p})/\partial \ln p_i \qquad (4.58)$$

That is,

$$s_i = \partial \ln C/\partial \ln p_i = p_i \times x_i/C$$
$$= \beta_i + \beta_{ii} p_i + \omega_i \ln Y + \left(\frac{1}{2}\right) \sum_j \beta_{ij} \ln p_j, \quad \text{for } i \neq j \qquad (4.59)$$

Defining cost shares, s_i, as the proportion of total cost allocated to each input (again fuel, capital, or labor), or

$$s_i = p_i x_i/C \qquad (4.60)$$

it follows that

$$\sum_i s_i = 1. \qquad (4.61)$$

Therefore, for the three inputs employed in Christensen and Greene's translogarithmic cost model (again fuel, labor, and capital), the respective cost share equations are given by the following. For fuel,

$$s_f = \beta_f + \beta_{ff} \ln p_f + \omega_f \ln Y + \left(\frac{1}{2}\right) \sum_j \beta_{fj} \ln p_j \qquad (4.62)$$

where $j = k$ (capital), l (labor). For labor,

$$s_l = \beta_l + \beta_{ll} \ln p_l + \omega_l \ln Y + \left(\frac{1}{2}\right) \sum_j \beta_{lj} \ln p_j \qquad (4.63)$$

[10] Shephard's lemma states that the optimal, cost-minimizing demand for an input (or factor) can be derived by differentiating the cost function with respect to the price of that input.

where $j = f$ (fuel), k (capital). For capital,

$$s_k = \beta_k + \beta_{kk} \ln p_k + \omega_k \ln Y + \left(\frac{1}{2}\right)\sum_j \beta_{kj} \ln p_j \tag{4.64}$$

where $j = l$ (labor), f (fuel).

As stated, a well-behaved cost function must be homogeneous of degree 1 in input prices, which means that, for example, doubling the price of an input doubles total cost. This implies the following restrictions can be imposed on equation (4.56):

$$\sum_i \beta_i = 1, \text{ and } \sum_i \beta_{ij} = \sum_j \beta_{ji} = \sum_i \omega_{iy} = 0 \tag{4.65}$$

Finally, symmetry, which implies that (by Young's theorem)

$$\beta_{ij} = \beta_{ji} \tag{4.66}$$

can also be imposed on the cost model, which reduces the number of parameters to be estimated and results in the (single output) final form to be estimated. This is given by

$$\ln C = \alpha_0 + \alpha_Y \ln Y + \sum_i \beta_i \ln p_i + \alpha_{YY} \ln Y^2 + \sum_i \omega_{iy} \ln p_i$$
$$+ \sum_i \sum_j \beta_{ij} \ln p_i \ln p_j \tag{4.67}$$

Once the restrictions are imposed, the system of equations (4.56) and (4.62)–(4.64) can then be estimated simultaneously by the seemingly unrelated regression (SUR) method, which is described below (Zellner, 1962).

Note: Since the cost shares (s_i) sum to unity, only $n - 1$ of the share equations are linearly independent, which implies that the covariance matrix is singular and nondiagonal (i.e., has no inverse). As such, the parameters of the equations cannot be estimated. The solution is to divide through by one of the input prices (thus deleting one of the share equations).

Dividing through by (p_k), the capital price input variable, yields the share equations for fuel and labor:

$$s_f = \beta_f + \beta_{ff} \ln (p_f/p_k) + \omega_{fy} \ln Y + \beta_{fl} \ln (p_l/p_k) \tag{4.68}$$

$$s_l = \beta_l + \beta_{ll} \ln (p_l/p_k) + \omega_{ly} \ln Y + \beta_{lf} \ln (p_f/p_k) \tag{4.69}$$

This particular form has been widely used and still remains a chosen specification for numerous studies in the electric industry, particularly those testing for scale economies and the appropriate structure of the industry. (Ramos-Real, 2004, provides a nice overview of these studies.) As such, Chapter 6, "Cost Models," contains a series of examples and exercises in which to employ data on the requisite variables to estimate various translogarithmic cost models for the rural electric cooperatives that distributed electricity in 1997. In addition, the concepts of economies of scale and scope that are described in Chapter 2, "The Theory of Natural Monopoly," are examined in much more detail. Examples and exercises are provided for hands-on experience working with cost models of this form.

Digression: Use of Zellner's Method (Seemingly Unrelated Regressions Method)

In the translog cost function estimation literature, the most popular estimation technique is that of Zellner's iterated seemingly unrelated regression (ITSUR). One nice feature of the translog specification is that, via Shephard's lemma, the optimal input demand equations can be derived and estimated simultaneously with the cost equation via this method, which yields estimates that are more efficient than equation by equation Ordinary Least Squares. This method requires an estimate of the cross equation covariance matrix, which increases the sampling variability of the estimator and yields estimates that are numerically equivalent to the maximum likelihood estimators (Berndt, 1991, p. 463). But before estimation can proceed, several precautions must be made:

1. Since the shares always sum to unity and only $n - 1$ of the share equations are linearly independent, for each observation, the sum of the disturbances across equations must always equal 0. This implies that the disturbance covariance matrix is singular and nondiagonal. Therefore, one of the equations must be deleted and its parameters inferred from the homogeneity condition. This raises the question of whether the parameter estimates are invariant to the choice of the equation to be dropped. However, as long as either maximum likelihood or Zellner's method (one-step or iterated seemingly unrelated regressions) of estimation is performed, the estimates are invariant to the choice of the equations to be estimated.

2. To preserve the linear homogeneity of the system, both of the cost share equations must be normalized by dividing each input price by

the input price that corresponds to the deleted cost share equation (in this case the price of capital, p_k). Hence, the remaining cost share equations take the form of equations (4.68) and (4.69).

Quadratic cost models

Flexibility notwithstanding, the translogarithmic functional form has its limitations. As described in the econometrics chapter (Chapter 6), the translogs' inability to deal with zero levels of outputs (or input prices) has been considered a serious flaw by many. The quadratic model specification offers a nice alternative, exhibiting the flexibility of the translog while conforming to the properties of economic theory. In fact, for multiple output markets, it is far superior to the translog. This too will be discussed in much more detail in Chapter 6. But, for now, let it suffice to introduce the general form (single output with input prices) and discuss its salient properties.

In general, the quadratic cost function is given by

$$C = \alpha_0 + \alpha_y Y + \left(\frac{1}{2}\right)\alpha_{yy}Y^2 + \sum_i \beta_i p_i \qquad (4.70)$$

where

Y = output (in this case, electricity).
Y^2 = output squared.
p_i = input prices.

Cost models often include other variables (known as *cost shift variables*). In the case of electricity, the cost of distribution often includes miles of transmission lines, miles of distribution lines, or the number of customers per mile (also known as *density*). The quadratic model specification is the subject of much detail, examples, and exercises in Chapter 6, "Cost Models." An extension to multiple outputs and two case studies are provided and discussed in Chapters 7 and 8: One on horizontal integration and the other on vertical integration.

Digression: Why the quadratic form is the "best" suited for modeling industry structure

In the econometrics literature, the quadratic form has been gaining popularity in recent years because of its favorable properties, especially where multiple outputs are concerned. Let us now examine these properties in more detail.

Multiple-output quadratic cost function

In general, a multiple output quadratic cost function is given by

$$C = \alpha_0 + \sum_i \alpha_i Y_i + \left(\frac{1}{2}\right) \sum_i \sum_j \alpha_{ij} Y_i Y_j + \sum_k \beta_k p_k \qquad (4.71)$$

where $i, j = 1, \ldots, n$.

In the case of the quadratic form, the marginal cost is given by

$$\partial C / \partial Y_i = \alpha_i + \sum_j \alpha_{ij} Y_j \qquad (4.72)$$

and the average cost by

$$C / Y_i = \left(\alpha_0 + \sum_i \alpha_i Y_i + \left(\frac{1}{2}\right) \sum_i \sum_j \alpha_{ij} Y_i Y_j + \sum_k \beta_k p_k\right) / Y_i \qquad (4.73)$$

The degree of scale economies

Recalling that the degree of scale economies, S_N, is equal to the ratio of average cost to marginal cost, in the multiple output case, we have (Baumol et al., 1982, p. 50)

$$S_N(Y) = C(Y) / Y_i C_i(Y) \qquad (4.74)$$

where $C_i(Y)$ is the marginal cost with respect to Y_i.

Substituting equations (4.72) and (4.73) into equation (4.74) and ignoring input prices yields

$$S_N(Y) = \left(\alpha_0 + \sum_i \alpha_i Y_i + \left(\frac{1}{2}\right) \sum_i \sum_j \alpha_{ij} Y_i Y_j\right) / \left(\sum_i \alpha_i Y_i + \sum_i \sum_j \alpha_{ij} Y_i Y_j\right) \qquad (4.75)$$

so that

$$S_N > 1 \text{(increasing returns to scale) as } \alpha_0 > \frac{1}{2} \sum_i \sum_j \alpha_{ij} Y_i Y_j \qquad (4.76)$$

Ray average cost

Relating this to the concept of ray average cost (RAC) allows us to envision this concept geometrically. Figure 4.5 displays the case in which the ray average cost is U-shaped for any point Y^0, which is a point along a ray emanating from the origin and is a composite commodity (i.e., in the two-output case, a function of both Y_1 and Y_2). This U-shaped ray average cost occurs when

$$\alpha_0 > 0 \text{ and } \sum_i \sum_j \alpha_{ij} Y_i^0 Y_j^0 > 0 \qquad (4.77)$$

for any point Y^0 on the ray.

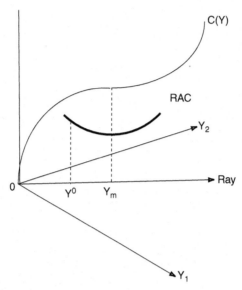

Figure 4.5 U-shaped ray average cost

The ray average cost describes the behavior of cost along a ray emanating from the origin. In this case, the minimum occurs at the point of inflection of the total cost curve, $C(Y)$.

For economies of scale to hold throughout the ray, it is necessary that

$$\sum_i \sum_j \alpha_{ij} Y_i^0 Y_j^0 < 0 \tag{4.78}$$

which, of course, implies that

$$\alpha_{ij} < 0 \tag{4.79}$$

Product-specific returns to scale

You may recall, from Chapter 2, the discussion on product-specific returns to scale and its relation to average incremental costs, which are relevant for multiple output markets. For the quadratic form given in equation (4.70), the degree of product specific returns to scale is given by

$$S_i(y) = \left[\alpha_i Y_i + \left(\frac{1}{2} \right) \alpha_{ii} Y_i^2 + \sum_{j \neq i} \alpha_{ij} Y_i Y_j \right] \Big/ \left[\alpha_i Y_i + \alpha_{ii} Y_i^2 + \sum_{j \neq i} \alpha_{ij} Y_i Y_j \right]$$

$$\tag{4.80}$$

which implies that

$$S_i > 1 \text{ as } 0 > \alpha_{ii} \tag{4.81}$$

Likewise,

$$S_i < 1 \text{ as } 0 < \alpha_{ii} \tag{4.82}$$

As such, the average incremental cost of product i is either globally declining, constant, or rising as α_{ii} is negative, zero, or positive, respectively (Baumol et al., 1982, p. 454). The interpretation is straightforward. Recalling equation (2.6) from Chapter 2,

$$S_i(y) = \text{AIC}(y_i)/(\partial C/\partial y_i) \tag{4.83}$$

When $S_i < 1$, the average incremental cost of product i is less than its marginal cost of production. Under the assumption that the price of product i is at least equal to its marginal cost, the revenue from the production of product i exceeds its average cost, which improves the financial viability of the firm.

Economies of scope

Recall from Chapter 2, "The Theory of Natural Monopoly," that economies of scope (or joint production) are integral to discussions regarding efficient industry structure (recall that economies of scope are a necessary condition for natural monopoly in a multiple-output firm). In the two-output case, the degree of economies of scope is given by

$$S_c = [C(Y_1, 0) + C(0, Y_2) - C(Y_1, Y_2)]/C(Y_1, Y_2) \tag{4.84}$$

The quadratic form is well represented in the literature in the estimation of economies of scale and scope, vertical integration, and subadditivity in the electric utility industry. Notable is a paper by John Mayo (1984), who employed multiple-output quadratic cost models to test whether there were economies of scope in the distribution of electricity and natural gas. To accomplish this, he estimated an equation of the form

$$C = \alpha_0 + \sum_i \alpha_i Y_i + \left(\frac{1}{2}\right) \sum_i \sum_j \alpha_{ij} Y_i Y_j + \sum_k \beta_k p_k \tag{4.85}$$

which is not homogeneous of degree 1 in input prices. To remedy this, Mayo multiplicatively appended input prices in the following fashion:

$$C = \left(\alpha_0 + \sum_i \alpha_i Y_i + \left(\frac{1}{2}\right) \sum_i \sum_j \alpha_{ij} Y_i Y_j\right) \Pi_k \beta_k p_k \tag{4.86}$$

Mayo imposed strict input–output separability[11] and linear homogeneity in input prices (recall that separability was rejected by Karlson). According to Baumol et al. (1982, p. 458),

> Such cost functions (with p and y multiplicatively separable) require all input demands to vary with outputs in the same fashion. In fact, input ratios and cost shares are thus assumed to be independent of output levels, and input demand elasticities with respect to each output become equal to independent of p. Consequently, multiplicatively separable cost functions are not well suited for investigation of those properties of input demand functions that relate to the effects of input prices on industry structure.
>
> Thus, we have another example of the tradeoff between tractability in empirical analysis of the functional form chosen for the cost relationship and its usefulness in testing the many properties that theory suggests are important for industry analysis.

Greer (2003) offers an improvement over Mayo's quadratic cost model, in that it is strictly concave in input prices (not equal to zero like the cost model presented by Mayo in his 1984 paper, "The Multiproduct Monopoly, Regulation, and Firm Costs"). In this cost model, input prices (and other variables) enter multiplicatively and are nonlinear in the parameters to be estimated, which allows the second derivatives with respect to input prices to take on nonzero values. (A proof is offered in the appendix to this chapter.) As such, it is a properly specified cost model in that it conforms to all properties of economic theory. Her cost model is given by

$$C = \left(\alpha_0 + \sum_i \alpha_i Y_i + \frac{1}{2} \times \sum_i \sum_j \alpha_{ij} Y_i Y_j \right) \cdot \prod p_m^{\beta_m} e^\varepsilon \quad \text{for } i,j = 1,2 \text{ and } m = 1,2,3$$

$$(4.87)$$

In this case, the input price parameters (β_m) enter nonlinearly, which allows for the concavity in input price criterion to be satisfied (as long as

---

[11] Chambers (1988) gives the necessary conditions for input–output separability for the profit maximizing producer as

$$\partial(x_i/x_j)/\partial_p = 0$$
$$\partial(y_i/y_j)/\partial_r = 0$$

The first condition implies that a change in output prices, p, does not influence the composition of inputs x_i and x_j, while the second condition implies that a change in input prices, r, does not influence the composition of outputs y_i and y_j. Rejecting input–output separability means that a change in input (output) price alters the composition of output (input) quantities.

the parameter estimates are of the expected sign. (A proof is offered in the appendix of this chapter.)

This model is monotonic (increasing) in output, increasing and concave in input prices, and capable of estimating the parameters despite a variable's taking on a value of 0 (recall the translogarithmic cost function's inability to do so). As such, it is a properly specified multiple-output cost function and unique to the literature. (Proofs are offered in the appendix to Chapter 6.) This model and its subsequent application are the focus of two case studies in upcoming sections (Chapters 7 and 8) and numerous examples and exercises throughout this book.

Cubic cost models

It is a well-established fact that total cost functions are cubic in nature; that is, there is a region of increasing returns, constant returns, and decreasing returns to scale, which yield the classic "hook shaped" marginal cost and U-shaped average cost curves as displayed in Figure 4.6.

Also displayed in Chapter 2, the cubic cost function generates the average (AC) and marginal (MC) cost curves displayed in Figure 4.6. For $Y < Y^*$, marginal cost declines and pulls average cost down with it; this is the region of the total cost curve in which cost is rising at a decreasing rate, which generates increasing returns to scale. Once diminishing returns set in, marginal costs rise and eventually cause average cost to rise as well, which occurs at Y^*, when total costs begin to increase at an increasing rate.

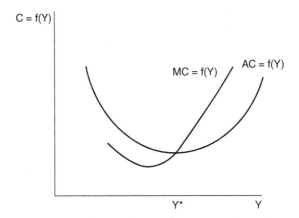

Figure 4.6 Average and marginal cost curves for cubic total cost function

That is, the total cost increases at a decreasing rate (i.e., marginal cost declines with output), then increases at an increasing rate (i.e., marginal cost increases with output), thus causing average cost to rise. This is also analogous to Figure 4.3.

These are the classic "textbook" examples that all principles of economics students are taught: Marginal cost declines in the increasing returns to scale portion of the total cost curve, which causes average cost to decline; when decreasing returns to scale set in, marginal cost begins to rise, thus causing average cost to rise (recall that marginal cost cuts the average cost curve at its minimum), which results in the classic U-shaped average cost curve.

4.4 APPENDIX

Proof that equation (4.86) allows for concavity in input prices: Nonpositive own-price effects

By Shephard's lemma, the optimal factor demand equation for the ith input price is given by

$$x_i^* = \partial C(Y, \mathbf{p}) / \partial p_i \qquad (4A.1)$$

where $i = 1, 2$.

The Hessian matrix is the matrix of second derivatives of the cost function with respect to input prices, which is equivalent to the matrix of first derivatives of the factor demand equations, x_i^*, with respect to input prices.

Since cost minimization requires that the matrix of first derivatives of the factor demand equations be negative semidefinite, which requires that the diagonal terms of the Hessian matrix be nonpositive, by equation (4.12) (in the two-input case), we define

$$C_{ii} = \partial^2 C(\mathbf{p}, Y) / \partial \mathbf{p}_i^2 \qquad (4A.2)$$

for the ith input;

$$C_{jj} = \partial^2 C(\mathbf{p}, Y) / \partial \mathbf{p}_j^2 \qquad (4A.3)$$

for the jth input; and

$$C_{ij} = \partial^2 C(\mathbf{p}, Y) / \partial \mathbf{p}_i \partial \mathbf{p}_j \qquad (4A.4)$$

where i, j represent the cross-price effects (the nondiagonal elements of the matrix).

Then the (bordered) Hessian matrix, H, is given by

$$H = \begin{vmatrix} C_{ii} & C_{ij} & H_1 \\ C_{ji} & C_{jj} & H_2 \\ H_1 & H_2 & 0 \end{vmatrix}$$

where H_1, H_2 are the constraints (on output) that result from the firm's optimization problem, which is to minimize cost subject to satisfying the demand for its output. That is,

$$\text{Minimize cost}(Y, \mathbf{p}) \tag{4A.5}$$

subject to $Y \geq$ the demand for the firm's output.

4.5 EXERCISES

1. One cause of heteroscedasticity is large changes in the explanatory variables from one observation to another, which likely contributes to the large cost differences among the coops in the sample. For example, the price of purchased power exhibits large differences, from a minimum of \$18.00/MWh to a maximum of \$90.00/MWh with a mean value of \$43.00. (Figure 4.1)

   a. Create a data set named "RUS97_low," where Cost < \$10,000 and use this data set to estimate the parameters of equation (4.20). Do the results accord with economic theory in terms of expected signs and statistical significance? Why or why not?

   b. Calculate the White test statistic. Is heteroscedasticity still an issue?

   c. In the example that used the original data set to estimate the quadratic equation (equation (4.20)), there was a potential issue with the coefficient of the price of capital, p_k. Has the new data set corrected this issue?

   d. Examine the summary statistics in this newly created data set. Could any other variables be causing the heteroscedasticity?

2. Note that that there are three types of power suppliers in the data set entitled "RUS97_Basic": generation and transmission cooperatives (G&Ts), federally owned entities (Federal), and investor-owned utilities (IOUs).

   a. Create a data set for each type of supplier and review the summary statistics. Is the same variation seen in the variables across the observations in each data set? Should one expect to see more or less variation in the price of purchased power among the three supplier types? Why or why not?

b. Create a data set from "RUS97_low" in which the supplier is G&T. Reestimate equation (4.20) and review the results.

    i. Calculate the White statistic: Is the presence of heteroscedasticity still confirmed?

    ii. What about the other coefficient estimates: Are they as expected (in terms of sign and statistical significance)? Why or why not?

3. Unlike investor-owned utilities, the rates charged by distribution cooperatives are not regulated in every state. In fact, fewer than 20 state utility commissions have jurisdiction over the rates charged to various end users by cooperatively owned entities.

a. Create two new data sets from "RUS97_low" with the supplier G&T: one for regulated entities (REG = 1) and one for non-regulated entities (REG = 0). Examine the summary statistics of the relevant variables. Are they as expected? That is, is the price of purchased power generally lower or higher for regulated entities than for non-regulated entities?

b. Again, estimate equation (4.20) using the newly created data set in which firms are regulated. What does White's test statistic indicate now about the presence or absence of heteroscedasticity?

c. What about the signs and statistical significance of the coefficients on the explanatory variables: Do they accord with a priori expectations?

CHAPTER 5

Case Study: Breaking up Bells

The breaking up of the Bell System provides an informative case study on the importance of cost modeling and, more importantly, the choice of an appropriate specification. Note: This is an updated version of a paper presented at the 1997 Southern Economic Association meetings entitled "Deregulation of 'Natural' Monopolies: A Paradox of Lessons to Be Learned From Telephony to Electricity."

5.1 INTRODUCTION

The motivation of this chapter stems from the recent surge to deregulate what were thought to be naturally monopolistic industries. In 1996, legislation was passed to promote competition in both the telecommunications industry and in electricity markets in the United States. Technological change, it had been argued, resulted in the possibility of more than one supplier; as such, competition would render each of these industries more efficient. This deregulation is discussed in some detail, since it motivates the "Lessons to be Learned" from telephony to electricity, which is the premise of this chapter. It will be shown that some very valuable lessons are to be learned from the 1984 divestiture of AT&T, which functionally separated long-distance service from local telephone service, for the deregulation of electricity.

This chapter is organized in the following manner: First, the essence of natural monopoly is discussed; more specifically, the characteristics of and the tests for a market's being a natural monopoly are examined. Next, I discuss the breaking up of the Bell System and present the results of a study that was used to determine that the Bell System was not a natural monopoly. However, this study was flawed and its results refuted, as will be shown in a brief survey of the literature surrounding the breakup. The next section posits the idea that economies of vertical integration, which are mathematically equivalent to economies of scope, could be used to establish that a market is a natural monopoly and shows the parallels between telephony and electricity, which motivates the conclusions drawn and lessons learned in the final section. It is in these lessons, for which there may exist grave implications for public policy decisions, that the value of this chapter lies; that is, in the subsequent success or failure of not only these but also future attempts to deregulate certain markets, especially those pertaining to electricity.

5.2 THE NATURAL MONOPOLY CONUNDRUM

Historically, conventional wisdom has held that certain markets were "naturally monopolistic," which means that, due to the presence of high fixed costs whose average declines with increases in output, economic efficiency is best obtained when there is only one supplier. Included herein are the markets for electricity, water, and telephone service. It has often been argued that these inefficiencies arise due to the irreversibility of the initial investment required to produce a particular good or service in a naturally monopolistic industry. More specifically, the underlying production technology of this product is such that there exists a level of output for which average cost is minimized: At levels of output below this level, average costs decline; and at levels above, they rise. This, known as *economies of scale*, is investigated further in context to its relationship with the theory of natural monopoly.

Economists have spent many years attempting to assess that level of output at which the minimum efficient scale occurs. In some industries, such as the generation of electricity, consensus has been reached that, at least in 1970, most firms were producing in and around this level, given a particular production technology (Christensen and Greene, 1976).

But things are not always so clear. In other markets, such as telephony, no one seems to have been able to determine (empirically) at what level of production the minimum efficient scale is attained, although the decision for the American Telephone and Telegraph Company (AT&T) to divest itself from its local exchange operations (the Baby Bells) was predicated on AT&T's not being a natural monopoly; that is, the thinking at the time was that the firm was so large that it must be the case that satisfying consumer demand entailed producing a level of output that went beyond the minimum efficient scale, which occurs in the diseconomies of scale (rising average cost) portion of its long-run average cost curve. Because AT&T failed to prove that telephony, which at the time comprised both local and long-distance calls, was a natural monopoly (a multiproduct natural monopoly, in fact), the 1982 Modification of Final Judgment was issued and in a consent decree AT&T agreed to divest the local operating companies, also known as the Baby Bells, so that entry, and hence competition, into the long-distance telephone market could occur. But the burning question still remains: Was the Bell System a natural monopoly?

Defining a natural monopoly

Older industrial organization literature often used the degree of *scale economies* to determine whether an industry was a natural monopoly. It is important to note that much of the *theory* of natural monopoly is concerned with the precise meaning of *increasing returns* or, equivalently, decreasing average costs.

As stated in Chapter 2, one difficulty in testing for natural monopoly is the practical application of testing for subadditivity of a firm's cost function, which is critical, since local (global) subadditivity is a necessary and sufficient condition for local (global) natural monopoly (Evans, 1983). These concepts are reviewed here.

Economies of scope

You may recall from Chapter 2 that cost savings can result from the production of several outputs at the same time; that is, in many cases and certainly in the case of electricity, fixed costs are jointly utilized in the production of the firm's outputs. These common costs, as they are also known, give rise to the concept of economies of scope (or economies of horizontal integration) and provide a basis for determining whether an industry is a multiproduct natural monopoly.

Economies of scope (also known as *economies of joint production*) are said to exist if a given quantity of each of two or more goods can be produced by one firm at a lower cost than if each good were produced separately by two different firms or even two different production processes. That is, for a two-product case, the degree of economies of scope is given by

$$S_c = [C(Y_1, 0) + C(0, Y_2) - C(Y_1, Y_2)]/C(Y_1, Y_2) \qquad (5.1)$$

As previously stated, the importance of economies of scope cannot be overstated: Economies of scope are a necessary condition for natural monopoly in a multiple-output firm.

Subadditivity of the cost function

Even if a cost function exhibits both economies of scale and economies of scope, it is not necessarily subadditive. A sufficient condition, known as *cost complementarity*, requires that the marginal or incremental costs of any output decline when that output or any other outputs increase. Mathematically, cost complementarity for a twice-differential multiproduct cost function exists if

$$\partial^2 C(Y)/\partial Y_i \partial Y_j < 0, \text{ for } i \neq j \qquad (5.2)$$

If this condition is satisfied, then the cost function exhibits cost complementarity, which is a sufficient condition for subadditivity of a multiproduct cost function. An industry is said to be a natural monopoly if, over the entire relevant *range* of outputs, the firm's cost function is subadditive.

5.3 BREAKING UP BELL: THE CASE OF AT&T

An excerpt from a paper by Celeste K. Carruthers (2008, pp. 3–5) provides a nice synopsis of the history and economics of telephony regulation.

> The roots of modern telephony regulation in the United States can be traced to the early 20th century, when American Telephone and Telegraph (AT&T) transitioned from a dominant provider of telephone services to a regulated monopoly. The company accomplished this by:
>
> (1) acquiring its independent rivals, who controlled half of the country's installed telephones in 1907; and
>
> (2) deflecting antitrust action with AT&T president Theodore Vail's campaign for "One Policy, One System, Universal Service."
>
> Universal service, at that time, referred to universally compatible telephone networks.
>
> Subscribers of one network could not always connect with subscribers of a competing network, even within the same city. AT&T pointed to this inconvenience as cause for a regulated monopoly in telephone services. Congress agreed; in 1921, the Willis-Graham Act permitted AT&T to continue acquiring independents and linking networks. The Communications Act of 1934 formalized AT&T's position as a regulated monopoly by creating the Federal Communications Commission (FCC), which has monitored and directed AT&T's operations ever since.
>
> AT&T's campaign for monopoly status relied critically on the assumption that a unified telephone network would increase the value of a telephone connection through network effects. The value of a network good like a telephone connection depends on the size of the network to which that connection belongs. AT&T argued that as a regulated monopoly, it would join rival networks and dramatically increase the value of telephone service. This would have infra- and extra-marginal benefits: existing telephone consumers would benefit from a much larger network, and potential consumers would be induced to join the network.
>
> Was a monopoly necessary to provide universal service? The disjoint systems of telephone networks were not permanently irreconcilable, and network effects could have been achieved without monopolizing the industry. Mueller (1997) notes that, "[i]t was business rivalry, not expert engineers or technology, that had brought about the geographic scope of the telephone network."
>
> An alternative solution would have been to require interconnection between competing networks. More than 70 years later, interconnection between incumbent

monopolists and entrants was one of the provisions of the 1996 Telecommunications Act.

The Bell System was thought of as a collection of natural monopolies, not because of demand-side network effects, but because of supply-side cost efficiencies.

As previously stated in Chapter 2, an industry is a natural monopoly if one firm can serve the market at lower total cost than multiple firms. This definition is consistent for single-product monopolies and multiproduct monopolies, which the Bells claimed to be. Formally, a natural monopoly has a *subadditive* cost function if, for example, given a bundle of output (say, 10 billion local phone calls and 3 billion long-distance calls), industry costs are minimized when all production is allocated to one firm, rather than split among two or more. In a market with subadditive costs, competitive pricing would lead to one firm serving the entire market. As such, that firm is thought of as a "natural" monopoly.

The breaking up of the Bell System was predicated on the finding that the markets it served were not natural monopolies. This conclusion was reached in part on work done by David Evans and James Heckman (1984) who developed a test of the subadditivity of industry cost functions and employed it to model cost data from the Bell System over the period 1947–1977. Their major finding was that the cost function was not subadditive over the period 1958–1977, which played a critical role in the breaking up of the Bell System. This study will be examined in more detail in the "Literature Review" section.

In subsequent years, a number of researchers have found issue with the study and performed their own analyses with different outcomes, which also are discussed in the "Literature Review." Some of these issues arise from the high collinearity among the variables used in the estimation procedure. In other studies, the transformation of the variables is questioned. In addition, the treatment of serial correlation has also come under scrutiny. In writing this case study, I question the choice of the functional form (a translog cost model) used to estimate the parameters of the model in a multiproduct market. Diewert and Wales (1991) went so far as to replicate the study and found something quite disturbing: The estimated cost function fails one of the basic tenets of economic theory, which is that it be nondecreasing or monotonic in output. As such they argue that: "its use in subadditivity calculations is clearly inappropriate . . . since this estimated cost function suffers from the criticism mentioned above, serious doubt is cast on the author's major finding that the Bell System was not a natural monopoly over the 1958–1977 period."

The Evans and Heckman methodology

A multiproduct translogarithmic cost function was used to estimate the Bell System data. More specifically, Evans and Heckman assumed that three inputs, namely —capital, labor, and materials—were used to produce two outputs—local and long-distance telephone service. An index of technical change was also included so that the cost model to be estimated was given by

$$
\begin{aligned}
\ln C = {} & \alpha_0 + \Sigma_i \alpha_i \ln p_i + \Sigma_i \beta_i \ln q_i + \tfrac{1}{2} \times \Sigma_i \Sigma_j \gamma_{ij} \ln p_i \ln p_j + \tfrac{1}{2} \\
& \times \Sigma_k \Sigma_j \delta_{kj} \ln q_k \ln q_j + \Sigma_i \Sigma_k \rho_{ik} \ln q_k \ln p_i + \Sigma_i \lambda_i \ln t \ln p_i \\
& + \Sigma_k \theta_k \ln q_k \ln t + \tau \ln (t)^2 + \mu \ln t
\end{aligned}
\tag{5.3}
$$

The following restrictions were imposed:

$$
\sum_i \alpha_i = 1
$$

$$
\sum_j \gamma_{ij} = 0
$$

$$
\sum_i \rho_{ik} = 0
$$

$$
\sum_i \lambda_i = 0
$$

$$
\gamma_{ij} = \gamma_{ji}
$$

and

$$
\delta_{kj} = \delta_{jk}
$$

where

L = local service.
T = long-distance, or toll service.
r = the rental rate on capital.
m = the price of materials.
w = the wage rate.
t = index of technological change.

Shephard's lemma results in the input cost share equations to be estimated (equation 3 in Diewert and Wales, 1991):

$$
S_i = \alpha_i + \sum_j \gamma_{ij} \ln p_j + \sum_k \rho_{ik} \ln q_k + \sum_i \lambda_i \ln t, \quad \text{for } i = 1, 2, 3 \tag{5.4}
$$

The equations are estimated by the method of maximum likelihood and estimation results are displayed in Table 5.1.

Evans and Heckman (1984) state that the estimated cost function is "monotonically increasing and concave with respect to all input prices in

Table 5.1 Evans and Heckman Results

Variable	Coefficient	Estimate	t-statistic
Constant	a0	9.054	1810.800
ln Y1	a1	0.462	2.044
ln Y2	a2	0.260	0.841
ln Y1sq	a11	−4.241	−3.228
ln Y2sq	a22	−8.018	−3.695
ln Y1Y2	a12	11.663	3.710
ln Y1pk	wky1	−0.359	−2.943
ln Y1pl	wly1	0.164	2.310
ln Y2pk	wky2	0.337	2.442
ln Y2pl	wly2	−0.179	−2.157
ln Pk	bk	0.535	66.875
ln Pl	bl	0.355	50.714
ln Pkk	bkk	0.219	9.125
ln Pll	bll	0.174	6.444
ln Pkl	bkl	−0.180	−9.474
ln t	ot	−0.193	−2.244
ln Y1t	oty1	1.207	0.843
ln Y2tl	oty2	−1.404	−0.938
ln tt	ott	−0.176	−0.170

Note: As reported in Table 3 of Evans and Heckman (1984).

all years" (p. 662). However, note in particular that the price of materials has been omitted from the estimation results in the table. They also state that they reject linear homogeneity in input prices (fn. 9) and the symmetry of the Hessian matrix with respect to input prices (fn. 9). Also, it is only by imposing restrictions on the cost model that they are able to determine an estimate of the price of materials and make such statements about concavity in all input prices.[1] In addition, and as pointed out in Diewert and Wales (1991), if the basic tenets of cost models are not satisfied then the cost model is not a proper cost model and should not be used to make any decisions, much less one of the landmark proportions as the breaking up of the Bell System. (Finally, recall the recurring theme of this book: That is, the translog specification is not the appropriate form to model cost in a multiproduct industry!)

All of this notwithstanding, Diewert and Wales (1991) provided to me the data used in Evans and Heckman (1983), which I used to estimate a

---

[1] Since the price of materials is not included, there is no way to determine the standard error of its estimate or its t-statistic.

Table 5.2 Marginal Costs of Toll Calls (Y_2), 1958–1977

Year	MC(Y_2) Evans and Heckman	MC(Y_2) Greer
1958	2250.42	7975.90
1959	1401.91	5870.13
1960	2036.06	5505.36
1961	—	—
1962	2010.57	4063.53
1963	1555.26	2912.15
1964	(1911.88)	(730.41)
1965	(3569.39)	(2995.69)
1966	(5861.67)	(5781.46)
1967	(6197.38)	(6532.33)
1968	(7536.01)	(8026.05)
1969	(9150.72)	(9864.45)
1970	(9795.73)	(10,556.17)
1971	(10,269.55)	(11,025.60)
1972	(12,097.87)	(12,038.51)
1973	(12,402.59)	(13,257.46)
1974	(13,362.39)	(14,075.93)
1975	(17,783.66)	(14,628.69)
1976	(21,843.28)	(14,915.25)
1977	(23,658.82)	(14,801.91)

translogarithmic cost model that includes the price of materials. Using both sets of results (those displayed in Table 5.1 and those obtained from including the price of materials), the marginal cost of toll calls (Y_2) can then be calculated. As pointed out by Diewert and Wales, it is negative in 14 of the 20 years of the period used in the test of subadditivity (1958–1977). The calculated marginal costs obtained by Evans and Heckman (which are displayed in Table 5.1) and those that result from estimation of a translog equation that includes the price of materials are displayed in Table 5.2.

Discussion of results

As displayed in Table 5.2, marginal cost is negative in the majority of the years used to determine that the Bell System was not a natural monopoly. In fact, of the total data set (years 1947–1977), the marginal cost of toll calls is negative for 21 of the 31 observations (as confirmed by Diewert and Wales). Including the material price would have helped; in doing so, the marginal cost of toll calls is negative for 16 of the 31 observations.

Aside: Quadratic cost model

Given my proclivity toward the quadratic cost form, it is only natural to estimate the parameters of such a cost model using the Bell data. Recalling that such a model is given by

$$C = \left(\alpha_0 + \sum_i \alpha_i Y_i + \tfrac{1}{2}\sum_i \sum_j \alpha_{ij} Y_i Y_j\right) p_K^{\beta k} p_L^{\beta l} p_P^{\beta p} e^{\varepsilon} \qquad (5.5)$$

(this is equation (4.87) in Chapter 4), a logarithmic transformation (as described in Chapter 6) yields

$$\begin{aligned} \ln C = \zeta \ln\left(\alpha_0 + \sum_i \alpha_i Y_i + \tfrac{1}{2}\sum_i \sum_j \alpha_{ij} Y_i Y_j\right) \\ + \beta_K \ln p_K + \beta_L \ln p_L + \beta_P \ln p_P + \varepsilon \end{aligned} \qquad (5.6)$$

The estimation results are displayed in Table 5.3.

Discussion of Table 5.3, Bell data estimated via quadratic cost model

An adjusted R^2 of 0.9998 indicates that the model fits the data well (Evans and Heckman obtained an adjusted R^2 of a similar magnitude). However, recall the earlier critique on the high collinearity among the variables: a very high adjusted R^2 along with low t-statistics (note those of Y_2, toll calls, those of the price of materials, $\ln p_m$, and the technology variable $\ln t$). As described in Chapter 4, the consequences of multicollinearity include high standard errors (hence, low t-statistics) and a very high adjusted R^2. This notwithstanding, it is informative to calculate the marginal cost of toll calls that results from the quadratic form. On doing this, I find that only the last two years (1957 and 1958) yield negative marginal

Table 5.3 Bell Data Estimated via Greer's Quadratic Cost Model

Variable	Coefficient	Estimate	t-statistic
Constant	a0	1119.82	1.98
Y1	a1	9024.18	2.76
Y2	a2	−27.70	−0.01
Y1sq	a11	−11234.40	−2.15
Y2sq	a22	−2951.34	−2.18
Y1Y2	a12	5553.04	2.15
ln pk	b1	0.515	6.80
ln pm	b2	0.099	1.06
ln pl	b3	0.386	3.30
ln t	o1	−0.127	−1.23

costs for toll calls. And this drives home a critical point: The choice of functional form can yield vastly different results and should be chosen with care. This point is further exemplified in the literature review.

Literature review: Other studies on the subadditivity of the Bell System

Given the difficulties involved in the determination of cost subadditivity, it is not surprising that the myriad of studies on the Bell System often yielded contrary results in the determination of whether telephony was a natural monopoly. Kiss and Lefebvre (1987) provide a nice survey of the fairly vast literature on this topic. Focusing on studies in which a single- or a two-output model was specified, a very brief overview is provided here only to illustrate the conflicting results and the different functional forms that have been employed.

One of the earliest is by H. Vinod (1976), who employed a statistical method known as ridge-regression technique[2] to estimate production functions with Bell System data. This technique is problematic in the sense that it makes arbitrary and unjustified adjustments to the data. Hence, parameter estimates do not equal the true value of the parameters. In other words, the estimates are biased. Not surprisingly, "The Vinod studies did not provide reliable evidence concerning the cost and production characteristics of the telephone industry. What is surprising, however, is the fact that AT&T relied heavily on these studies to support its arguments that the telephone industry is a natural monopoly" (Evans, 1983, p. 146).

Other studies attempt to estimate the cost function rather than the production function. Two major Bell Canada studies are described here. The first is by Smith and Carbo (1979), who assumed that Bell Canada produced two services, local and message toll (as monopolies), and other toll and miscellaneous (potentially competitive) toll, and private line, with three inputs: labor, capital, and materials. Using data from 1952 to 1977,

---

[2] Ridge regression has been posed as a remedy to multicollinearity, specifically to the large standard errors that tend to result. Its estimator, b_r, is given by

$$b_r = [X'X + rD]^{-1} X'Y$$

where $r =$ an arbitrarily chosen scalar and $D =$ a diagonal matrix containing the diagonal elements of $X'X$ (Greene, 1993, p. 270). This is in contrast to the typical Ordinary Least Squares estimator, which is given by

$$b = [X'X]^{-1} X'Y$$

some indication of local cost complementarity was derived from the model but no conclusion was gained concerning *global* economies of scope.

Using the same data, Kiss, Karabadjan, and Lefebvre (1981) assumed that the two outputs were local and toll calls (including message toll and private line services). After numerous specifications, they arrived at a specification in which the output variables are subject to a Box-Cox transformation[3] and the other variables transformed logarithmically. The resultant economies of scope were not statistically different from 0 nor were they realistic in magnitude. Fuss and Waverman (1981) estimated a similar cost function in which the output variable, Q^*, is equal to $(Q^\lambda - 1)/\lambda$, rather than simply log (Q). They found that λ was significantly different from 0 and, hence, rejected the cost function employed by Smith and Carbo. They found that Bell Canada had neither aggregate scale economies nor did it have a natural monopoly over local, toll, and private line services.

Yet another study by Christensen, Cummings, and Schoech (1981) used Bell data from 1947 to 1977 and various translog-cost specifications, including Box-Tidwell[4] and a modified translog function, which varied in the number of squared and cross-product terms as regressors. Under every specification, they found statistically significant economies of scale. However, there are also serious flaws in this study. Like an earlier Smith and Corbo study, they assumed that the Bell System produced a single output and simply aggregated the various outputs and measured this "single" output. Interestingly, the specification with which the data were the most consistent yielded upward-sloping demand curves for both capital and for labor. Second, the fact that the aggregate-output measure exhibited scale economies provides little evidence as to whether intercity service exhibits scale economies or even whether the telephone industry is a natural monopoly. Evans and Heckman (1984) found that by relaxing the single-output specification and estimating a multiproduct cost function using the Christensen et al. data, they obtained factor demand curves of the appropriate (negative) slope. They went on to test for the subadditivity

---

[3] A Box-Cox transformation is one in which a regressor (or independent variable, x) in an equation such as

$$Y = \alpha + \beta g(x) + \varepsilon$$

is subject to

$$g^\lambda(x) = (x^\lambda - 1)/\lambda$$

In a linear model, $\lambda = 1$, while a log–linear or semilog model results if $\lambda = 0$ (Greene, 1993, p. 239).

[4] The Box-Tidwell function uses the Box-Cox formula to transform all the explanatory variables.

of this cost function, which resulted in the rejection of the natural monopoly hypothesis as discussed earlier in this chapter. Interestingly, Charnes, Cooper, and Sueyoshi (1988) used the same data and functional form and found the opposite result by using goal-programming/constrained regression in which the objective function of the firm is to

$$\text{Minimize} \sum d_t \qquad (5.7)$$

subject to

$$f(C_t) + d_t = \log C_t \qquad (5.8)$$

where

$$d_t = C_t(\text{observed}) - C_t(\text{estimated}) \qquad (5.9)$$

The cost function, C_t, is estimated from a cost function similar to that used by Evans and Heckman (1984) using the Bell System data (Kiss and Lefebvre, 1987, p. 37). In this particular form, no standard errors or t-statistics are generated, so there is no way to tell whether the coefficients were statistically different from 0. Similar to the Evans and Heckman results, the indicators of overall economies of scale are flawed in two ways: First, toll output elasticity of cost (and marginal cost) are negative; second, scale elasticity estimates are unrealistically high. Despite this, they go on to find that the cost function is subadditive between the years 1958 and 1977, thus contradicting those results reported by Evans and Heckman (1984).

As stated, various functional forms can lead to vastly different results. Even after the breakup, studies continued to be performed in an attempt to ascertain an appropriate industry structure and seek more robust cost models for testing subadditivity. Roller (1990), using a quadratic cost model, found that the telecommunications industry prior to the Bell System breakup was a natural monopoly. More recently, Shin and Ying (1992) examined the issue of subadditivity using a pooled cross-sectional sample of actual cost data for 58 local exchange carriers (LECs) from 1976 to 1983 ($n = 384$). One problem with this study is that they calculated an overall scale elasticity by summing the output cost elasticities. These should not have been aggregated, since part of the sufficient condition for subadditivity is *product-specific* economies of scale, which are discussed in chapter 2. Shin and Ying found that the LECs did not have subadditive cost functions. (In fact, they found costs were superadditive, which means that production by one firm is more costly than by separate firms.) It is interesting to note that in their more recent paper ("Costly Gains to Breaking up: LECs and the Baby Bells"), Shin and Ying readily admit that the issues of subadditivity and economies of scope have never clearly been resolved (1993).

Gabel and Kennet (1994) offered a critique of the Shin and Ying (1992) finding of cost superadditivity. They delineated "at least five flaws with their methodology that cause us to be skeptical about their conclusions." They employed an optimization model, the results of which confirmed that, contrary to Shin and Ying, there exist economies of scope for the product access lines, toll, and exchange calls (due to the shared use of the local loop).

From all of this, two important conclusions can be reached. First, it is extremely difficult to estimate cost function subadditivity, especially for multiple-output firms. Second, the choice of the appropriate functional form is extremely important. Using the same data, radically different results can emerge, which should be considered by policy makers prior to making sweeping changes in public policy.

Note: Much of the following is an excerpt from a paper that I wrote and presented at the Southern Economic Association meetings in 1997, shortly after the deregulation of markets for telecommunications and electricity was legislated in 1996. The passage of both acts was likely precipitated by the seemingly successful deregulation of telephony in 1984, which spurred competition in the long-distance market and resulted in lower prices to consumers. The issues raised surrounding the divestiture of the long-distance service from local telephony (a vertically integrated structure, which was not considered at the time) renders this relevant and provides the reason that it is included here.

5.4 ECONOMIES OF VERTICAL INTEGRATION: AN ARGUMENT FOR NATURAL MONOPOLY?

Thus far, it has been asserted that economies of scope and subadditivity provide the basis for determining whether a market is a natural monopoly. However, given the vertical structure of certain industries, could it not be the case that economies of vertical integration and a modification of the definition of subadditivity of a cost function could also suffice in the determination of such a structure?

Economies of vertical integration

Recall from Chapter 2 that economies of vertical integration are satisfied if

$$S_v = [C(q_1, 0) + C(0, q_2) - C(q_1, q_2)] > 0 \qquad (5.10)$$

where q_1 = the first stage of production and q_1 = the second stage of production (this is equation (2.33) in Chapter 2). Mathematically, this is equivalent to economies of scope for a horizontally integrated firm, which is given by

$$S_c = \left[C(q_1, 0) + C(0, q_2) - C(q_1, q_2)\right] > 0 \qquad (5.11)$$

where q_1 = the first output and q_2 = the second output (this is equation (2.28) in Chapter 2). Given the mathematical equivalence, does this not lead to the assertion that the presence of economies of vertical integration is an argument for natural monopoly?

Discussion: Economies of vertical integration—An argument for natural monopoly?

Although mathematically equivalent, conceptually the two are different: Economies of scope are economies of *horizontal* production (products produced synchronously, e.g., local and long-distance telephony), while those of vertical integration occur sequentially (e.g., electricity is first generated, then transmitted, then it is distributed to the end user).

Even though conceptually different, some very interesting parallels can be drawn between the two industries. And from these, an examination of the effects from the deregulation of telephony can yield powerful lessons for policy makers involved in the deregulation of the electric industry.

5.5 PARALLELS BETWEEN TELEPHONY AND ELECTRICITY

Discussion: Economies of scope versus economies of vertical integration

Paradoxically, telephony and electricity have more in common than simply having shared the "natural monopoly" label. In fact, there exist additional, even more striking parallels between the two industries.

On the surface, it seems that telephony is more likely to exhibit economies of scope while electricity those of vertical integration. Consider the organization of each industry over time. For telephony, the issue yet to be resolved is that of whether joint production (i.e., economies of scope) of local and long-distance telephone service is less costly than that of separate production. For electricity, the issue is whether it is less costly for one firm to perform all three functions (generation, transmission, and distribution) than it is for each of these to be produced separately by separate firms.

To draw meaningful parallels, it should be the case that not only does telephony exhibit (potential) economies of vertical integration but also that some component of the production of electricity is characterized by economies of scope. These I examine in further detail next.

Vertical integration—The case of telephony

On the surface, it appears that economies of scope, rather than those of vertical integration, have supported telephony as a natural monopoly. This has certainly been the case in the literature. But, on careful consideration, there exist elements of both.

As previously discussed, economies of scope arise when it is less costly for one firm to produce two (or more) outputs than for two firms to produce them separately. What is critical here is the definition of *output*. For telephony, there exist many outputs. Let us concentrate on one for now: The transmission of voice, data, fax, and the like from one geographical location to another. This is one component of vertical integration, which is, like electricity, subject to network externalities, such as a bottleneck. A *bottleneck* occurs when there exists exclusive ownership of a resource that is necessary to the production of a good and is an argument for vertical integration. It approximates a natural monopoly in the sense that its cost is sunk and its duplication would be wasteful. The bottleneck itself is that which yields access to the transmission mechanism by which the product is transported from the manufacturer to its final destination, the end user.

But before anything can be transmitted, it must be *generated*. In the case of telephony, that which is generated (the output) is a voice, a thought, or even data that, in conjunction with the necessary equipment (telephone, modem, cables) is then transmitted to a local network, which is then connected to and transmitted across a long-distance network to its ultimate destination (the end user). This equipment and the output generated in this first stage constitute inputs to this network, the source of the scope economies. The vertical structures of telephony and electricity are displayed in Figure 5.1.

Given these parallels between telephony and electricity and the mathematical equivalence of the concepts of economies of scope and those of vertical integration, could it not be the case that vertical integration is also

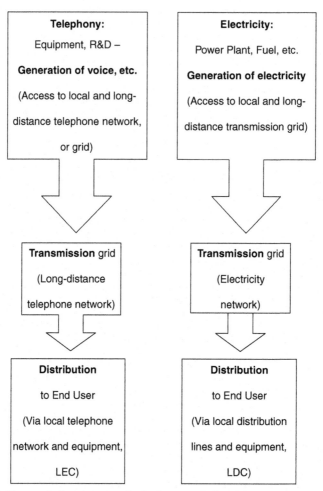

Figure 5.1 The vertical structures of telephony and electricity

a necessary condition for subadditivity of the cost function—that is, an argument for natural monopoly? According James Rosse, an economist who testified on AT&T's behalf in *U.S. v. AT&T*, it is: "The telecommunications *network* is a natural monopoly which can be 'planned, constructed, and managed most efficiently by an integrated enterprise that owns the major piece-arts of the facilities network and maintains research, development, manufacturing and systems engineering capabilities'" (Evans, 1983, p. 3).

In fact, this statement echoed the general consensus of the industry from its inception until 1974, when the Justice Department filed antitrust charges against AT&T, which subsequently led to the breakup of AT&T, one of the world's largest corporations.

The 1982 consent decree

Until the late 1950s, neither economists nor regulators questioned the conventional wisdom concerning the telecommunication industry's being a natural monopoly. In this case, the conferring of natural monopoly status was a result of "the cream-skimming argument"; that the wasteful duplication of facilities would allow a competitor to share the profitable parts of the telephone business "without assuming the burden for the unprofitable parts" (Theodore Vail, president of AT&T from 1907–1917, as quoted in Evans, 1983). However, with the licensing of private microwave in 1959, telephone service evolved into voice and data service in the 1960s (originally voice messages were transmitted in analog form), and specialized carries were authorized by the FCC in 1969. One of the first to file an application to enter was MCI, which resulted in the Justice Department's filing suit against AT&T for anticompetitive practices in 1974. Because AT&T failed to prove (nor was it disproved) its natural-monopoly status, Judge Harold Green issued the 1982 consent decree, under which AT&T "agreed" to divest itself from its local-area exchange carriers (the "Baby Bells"), a move that revolutionized the industry.

Among other things, the 1982 consent decree led to the creation of seven regional Bell holding companies (and 22 Bell operating companies), which were forbidden to offer long-distance service outside their local access and transport areas (LATAs). In addition, these operating companies were not allowed to manufacture equipment nor could they offer content-based information services.

While AT&T was allowed to keep its Long Lines division, its Western Electric equipment manufacturing division, and most of Bell Laboratories, thus remaining a *quasi*-vertically integrated firm, it no longer controlled that service for which *economies of scope* were likely. And although remaining quasi-vertically integrated, it lost probably the most substantial component of its previously integrated self: its local operating companies, which control access to and from AT&T's subscribers.

It is no secret that opening up the long-distance telephone market has been a Pareto-improving move: The subsequent entry of firms drove price almost to cost while offering more options and quality of service. But why did the local operating companies remain monopolies, including local access, thus destroying any economies of vertical integration between local and long-distance service? As prices for long-distance service plummeted, those for local service have risen steadily, due, in part, to the access fees imposed after the divestiture. In addition, prices have risen due to

1. The destruction of any scope economies that may have existed between local and long-distance service before the breakup.
2. The local operating companies formed after the divestiture were either too small or too large, either producing too little or too much output relative to the minimum efficient scale.

Technological Change

It is necessary to keep in mind that a *technological change* led to the subsequent deregulation of this industry. From the development of microwave technology in the 1950s to the use of fiber-optic cable today, advancements such as these propelled telephony from P.O.T.S. (plain old telephone service) to its current structure, now known as the telecommunications industry. This industry now embodies nine distinct, but interrelated markets.

Interexchange carriers (IXCs), of whom AT&T was the dominant firm, were among the first to employ fiber-optic technology. The use of fiber-optic cable, with its very high capacity, was the low-cost method of transport for high-traffic, high-density routes between network nodes. Once the cable is installed, the marginal cost of adding circuits is very low. The use of fiber optics gave other competitive access suppliers the ability to provide transport between IXC nodes, to bypass the local exchange carrier and supply end users with direct access to the IXCs, and to provide private lines connecting end users to each other for voice and data networks. In addition, fiber-optic cable eliminated distance as a factor in the cost of providing switched services. "Fiber-optic technology enables the new entrant to transport calls to a distant switch at very low marginal cost and thus to economize on switching facilities and associated buildings. In particular, IXCs may be able to enter local markets at low cost once they are authorized to do so" (Vogelsang and Mitchell, 1997, p. 23). Furthermore, the development and widespread use of wireless technology and digital electronics (especially high-speed switching), "allows broadband networks of cable and telephone carriers to integrate the transport of all types of services— voice, data, and video—over common broadband fiber and coaxial cable facilities" (Vogelsang and Mitchell, 1997, p. 27).

As a result of these technological advances, competition became feasible in this industry and especially so in local telephony; at this time, it was predominantly due to the presence of cable television operators, long-distance telephone service providers, and wireless services that were already in the telecommunications market.

The 1996 Telecommunications Deregulation Act—or the reintegration of the industry?

As previously stated, telephony was vertically integrated until the 1982 consent decree, after which, at least in part, this vertical structure was destroyed (as were the economies of scope that may have been inherent therein). With the Telecommunications Deregulation Act of 1996, reintegration (with competition in each component) was allowed under certain restrictions.

The premise of this act was to encourage entry into the various markets contained within the "telecommunications" industry. More specifically, it sought to encourage entry, and hence competition, into local markets, which had been operating as monopolies ever since the inception of telephone service.

One of the objectives of this act was to obfuscate the lines of distinction between markets, thus allowing all providers to compete with one another in as many markets as possible. This necessitated the removal of some of the regulatory barriers that remained in place after the 1984 divestiture, especially those concerning local telephony. As was the case of long distance telephony before the divestiture, the presence of bottlenecks necessitated the use of regulatory barriers.

Select provisions from the Telecommunications Deregulation Act

Unless a local exchange carrier was one of the Baby Bells, entry into local service was a free-for-all: cable television operators, cellular or personal communications services (PCS) providers, and long-distance service providers flocked into the local markets. One of the provisions of this act was that the regional Bell operating companies (or RBOCs) were not allowed to offer long-distance service until they proved that they opened their local markets to competition. What was interesting was that GTE (now Verizon), which operated in 28 states at the time and was every bit as large as some of the Bell operating companies, was not restricted in this fashion, since it was never a part of AT&T. In fact, GTE already offered long-distance service in some of its territory, and its bid for MCI showed it to be an aggressive player in this newly competitive environment.

Aside: First-mover disadvantage

This particular provision is quite intriguing; in economics, it is often the case that there are gains to being the first entity to supply a particular product to a market (an incumbent, if you will). That is, there exists a *first-mover advantage* in the provision of a good or service. In this case, one might presume that the Baby Bells, being the local supplier serving most of the markets in the United States at this time, would enjoy such an advantage. However, just like its former parent company AT&T, this was not the case. The reality was that there was, in fact, a *first-mover disadvantage*, similar to the one conferred on AT&T upon its divestiture, in that it was not allowed to enter the local exchange markets but other long-distance providers were.

A second provision was that the Bells were required to sell local services to their competitors on a wholesale basis. Likewise, all telecommunications carriers were obligated to interconnect with the facilities and equipment of other carriers at nondiscriminatory rates. This too created a first-mover disadvantage to the incumbents, since new entrants into these already-established markets did not have to go through the regulatory filings and proceedings, which are both costly and time consuming, that the incumbents had gone through when first establishing service and building infrastructure.[5] Given all of this, some interesting questions have emerged, which are also relevant for electricity deregulation. For example,

1. Are we (society, consumers, and producers) really better off?
2. More specifically, have the savings from deregulating the industry justified the lost gains that could have been reaped due to economies of scope and vertical integration?
3. Furthermore, was the 1996 Telecommunications Deregulation Act an attempt to finish what the 1982 decree began? Or was it an attempt to mitigate (or even reverse) some of the problematic aspects thereof? And, if so, why did it take so long to implement and what might this imply for the deregulation of electricity?

The answers to these questions are extremely relevant for the deregulation of the electric industry, which is explored next, where additional parallels between the two industries are delineated. In addition, some questions to be answered include the following: Which aspects, if any,

---

[5] The passage of PURPA (1978) also conferred a similar disadvantage to the incumbent electric utilities operating in the industry at the time in that *Qualifying Facilities* were not subject to the same rate and accounting regulations by the FERC as the incumbent utilities.

can be made competitive? Which should remain natural monopolies? And, does allowing competition in any one of the components necessarily destroy the economies of vertical integration found therein? Finally, what, if anything, can be learned from the deregulation of telephony for that of electricity? To answer some of these, we now turn to a discussion of the issues surrounding the deregulation of the electric industry.

The market for electricity

This same thinking is now being applied to the deregulation of electricity. However, unlike telephony, where there seems to have been no testing for economies of vertical integration, those in electricity have been well established. The fact that a majority of the electric utilities in the United States are vertically integrated attests to this.

Until recently, no one questioned that the production of electricity was in fact a natural monopoly, since, like telephony, what is required here is a network: a complex, interactive, interdependent connection of wires (by which end-use customers are connected to their local distribution company, which is connected to the transmission grid). This network represents an irreversible investment, which is characterized by both economies of scale and those of network planning, and as such yields a natural monopoly.

Because this network leads to externalities (one of which is the presence or creation of bottlenecks), vertical integration is the most efficient organization of the industry, especially for larger firms. But, due to the vertical nature of electricity production, questions have arisen concerning whether any aspect of the production process may not be a natural monopoly. And, if this is the case, the question then becomes: Would the market be better served by allowing competition into that component and would the gains from competition exceed the lost vertical economies that would result? This is the critical element that needs to be explored. *And this is one parallel that can be drawn, and hence lessons can be learned, from the deregulation of telecommunications.*

Vertical stage 1. Generation

In the generation component, the answer to this question has likely been answered. In their seminal paper, "Economies of Scale in Electric Power Generation" (1976), Christensen and Greene found that, by 1970, most firms were generating electricity at (and some even beyond) that point at which economies of scale had been exhausted; that is, at or even beyond the minimum efficient scale, thus rendering competition in generation not only feasible but also more efficient. Huettner and Landon (1977) have confirmed these findings; they find that scale economies are exhausted at an even lower level of output. (See Chapter 2 for more details on studies of this nature.)

Economies of scope (horizontal production) applied to electricity

As an extension to their testing for vertical economies, both Kaserman and Mayo (1991) and Gilsdorf (1994, 1995) employ a multiproduct cost function to determine whether vertical integration and economies of scale together constitute a natural monopoly. In fact, the former tests for multi-stage economies between generation and transmission/distribution. As previously stated, they too reject the separability of inputs and outputs. It is important to note that separability is not the same thing as economies of vertical integration, whereby output-output interactions matter.

The use of a multiproduct cost function implies that economies of scope and cost complementarity are relevant here. With this said, economies of scope can arise for either of two reasons:

1.   The cost function may have some *indivisible input* used in the production of both goods. For example, let F represent the cost of the indivisible input, and G and D are outputs in the production process (where G and D are, respectively, generated and distributed electricity). Then the cost of production is given by

$$C = F + G + D \tag{5.12}$$

which is characterized by economies of scope, since separate production of any $G, D > 0$ would entail duplication of F.

The cost function may exhibit cost complementarity, which means that there exists a cost interaction between the two outputs in the production process. As an example, let the cost function be given by

$$C = G + D - G \times D \tag{5.13}$$

Since $G \times D$ equals 0 for separate production of either G or $D > 0$, the negative sign implies that joint production is cheaper by the amount of the interaction term.

Hence, in the distribution of electricity, scope economies occur via the transmission/distribution grid (and the access to it), an indivisible input. You may recall that this creates a bottleneck, which is an argument for vertical integration. Economies of vertical integration are a straightforward extension of this.

Again, let $C(G, D)$ be the cost of production for a vertically integrated firm. If this is less than the sum of the cost of separate production by a pure generator and the cost of a pure distributor, or,

$$C(G, D) < C(G, 0) + C(0, D) \qquad (5.14)$$

then it is said that there exist economies of vertical integration.

This is equivalent to equation (5.10), which, as shown, is mathematically equivalent to equation (5.11). As such, this establishes that economies of vertical integration are a necessary condition for natural monopoly. [QED]

As stated earlier (in Chapter 2), a sufficient condition is also required. For this, a slight modification of the definition of cost complementarity will suffice. As defined in Chapter 2, equation (2.30), cost complementarity exists when

$$\partial^2 C(Y)/\partial Y_i \partial Y_j < 0, \quad \text{for } i \neq j \qquad (5.15)$$

However, in this case, the outputs Y_i and Y_j represent the different stages of production.

If equation (5.15) is satisfied, then the cost function exhibits cost complementarity, which is a sufficient condition for subadditivity in a multiproduct cost function. Again from Chapter 2, a market is said to be a natural monopoly if, over the entire relevant range of outputs, the firm's cost function is subadditive.

Figure 5.2 displays the source of economies of scope within the vertical structures of telephony and of electricity. For the former, it is in the "generation" of the voice, fax, or data that is an input into the subsequent stages that were displayed in Figure 5.1. In the case of the latter, economies of

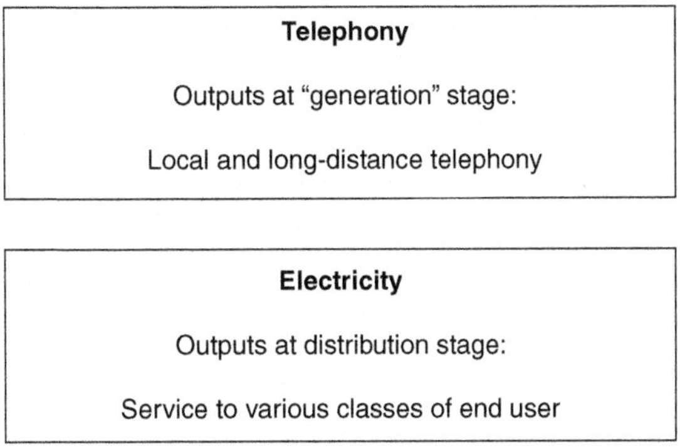

Telephony
Outputs at "generation" stage:
Local and long-distance telephony

Electricity
Outputs at distribution stage:
Service to various classes of end user

Figure 5.2 The horizontal structures of telephony (vertical stage 1) and electricity (vertical stage 3)

scope occur in stage three, the distribution of electricity to various types of end users, or customer classes, which are distinguished by voltage level, among other aspects (this is discussed in Chapter 2.)

Other parallels between telephony and electricity—and the reasons both were thought to be subject to gains from deregulation

Technological change as a parallel

The motivation behind the 1982 consent decree was not only the development of microwave technology but also AT&T's repeated attempts to prevent MCI from entering the market for long-distance telephone service. Its subsequent divestiture was solely the result of its antitrust behavior, as ruled by the U.S. Department of Justice.

While there was no such injunction of this magnitude against any electric utility (a single entity never supplied the entire U.S. market), electric utilities have also been the subject of much regulatory scrutiny. And this is the foundation of this next parallel: the amount of regulation to which each industry has been subjected. And the question then arises: Has technological change spurred deregulation or has deregulation spawned technological innovation? I think this is a very relevant, not to mention timely, question. It introduces yet another parallel concerning the vast technological innovations that have occurred in each industry over the past 20 years.

Parallels between individual components

Interestingly, the telephony industry remained quasi-vertically integrated: AT&T was allowed to keep the Bell Labs and Western Electric (both inputs to production) and its Long Lines division (transmission) but lost its local distribution companies (which can be thought of as an input to long-distance service, since it provides access to the transmission network). This, too, is what is being proposed for the deregulation of electric utilities: that the input (the generation of electricity) be separated from the transmission network.

Important parallels between the two industries can certainly be drawn concerning the transmission and distribution functions: Like telephony, the transmission grid and the distribution functions of electricity are "wires" businesses, whereby economies arise due to installation (construction and right-of-way requirements), capacity, and operation (network economies). In these cases, natural monopoly status is generally not disputed. Nonetheless, a crucial element must be kept in mind: The opening up of the transmission grid and the mandated selling of transmission capacity at cost to any generator with power to sell (assuming the capacity was available) was akin to subsidizing the non-investor-owned local exchange carriers. In essence, *FERC 888*, which mandated open access of the transmission grid created a *second-mover advantage* of its own: Not only were these generators (often exempt wholesale generators and merchant plants, which were not subject to the same regulations as the incumbents that had franchised service territories) not required to built transmission assets, but also they were not subject to the regulatory filings and related expenses that were borne by the incumbents on first establishing the infrastructure required to supply electric service. In the short run, this was likely to encourage excess entry into the market for generation (which happened, by the way). And in the intermediate run, this likely would result in what happened in telephony: mergers between the larger local exchange carriers, yielding fewer operators, which resulted in a system not palatable for competition.

Ownership parallels—non-investor-owned entities or rural versus urban service territories

As is the case in many utilities, local exchange carriers are either publicly or privately owned. And, as is the case in electricity, the many small rural providers supply only about 10% of the total demand for telephony (at this time). And, as in the case of rural electric utilities, the rural telephone cooperatives have access to lower-cost financing via the Rural Utilities Service (RUS) and are exempt from certain taxes and regulation. But unlike the case of electricity, urban providers of local telephone service (under the Universal Service Code) subsidize those in rural areas. However, as previously stated, FERC 888 was likely to yield a subsidy of its own: open access to the transmission grid at cost. And this is a double-edged sword: The incumbent owners of the grid were given no incentive to invest in upgrading or expanding the capacity of the transmission grid. Given the physical properties of electricity, and unlike telephony, wireless or microwave technologies would not provide alternatives to the transmission/distribution grid.

5.6 LESSONS TO BE LEARNED

Lesson 1. A caution to regulators regarding encouraging entry

The one success, if you will, of the 1982 divestiture was the entry of competition into, and the subsequent lowering of rates in, the long-distance telephone market. While some consumers gained (as did the entrants into the market), others lost, which is not a pareto-efficient outcome. Local rates rose, since the local exchange carriers had control over the access to the long-distance telephone network. This was especially true in the case of rural communities, the telephone companies which had to lease hardware from the still-monopoly local exchange carriers (most of whom were former Bells). In addition, a larger percentage of the calls by those residing in rural areas were long distance and subject to intra-LATA tolls charges, which were often higher than long-distance rates, since this market was not deregulated as part of the 1982 consent decree.

As previously discussed, conventional wisdom often holds that there exists a first-mover advantage in the provision of a good or service. However, in the case of AT&T, this was destroyed on the issuance of the consent decree. Almarin Phillips is correct when he states that: "The only reason the OCCs (MCI, Sprint, et al) have been profitable in recent years may be because they have not paid access fees at anything near the rates paid by AT&T" (as stated in Crew, 1985).

What message is being sent here? The message is that not only is there a second-mover advantage, but also there is, in fact, a *first-mover disadvantage* that resulted from the deregulation of the telecommunications industry, some of which likely will occur in the electric industry. This begs the question: Has the federal government not learned anything at all from the 1982 divestiture?

Unfortunately the answer to the above is, "Obviously not." Even with the passage of the 1996 Telecommunications Deregulation Act, the goal of which was, among other things, to level the playing field so that true competition could result, the Baby Bells endured another sort of first-mover disadvantage: Before they could offer long-distance service, they had to prove that they opened their local markets to competition. Neither GTE nor its other non-Bell counterparts had to abide by this restriction, even though GTE was as large as some of the Baby Bells (at the time, GTE offered local telephone service in 28 states and long distance in several). In fact, GTE's 1997 bid for MCI signaled that it was anxious to be a major player in the global marketplace.

A lesson for electricity deregulation
The 1996 deregulation of electric utilities resulted in a similar first-mover disadvantage. FERC 888 mandated the opening up of the transmission grid (owned predominantly by investor-owned utilities) and the selling of transmission capacity at cost to whomever had power to sell (assuming

the capacity is there). The fact that the generation of electricity had been deemed competitive spurred entry by nonregulated suppliers, which enjoyed a second-mover advantage in that the cost of entry was nowhere near what it cost the incumbents to establish service when no infrastructure was in place.

Given all of this, there was no incentive to transmission owners to invest in upgrading their transmission capacities, which was necessary before true competition could even begin to take place. As a case in point, California was the first state to adopt and implement the deregulation of its markets for electricity. During the summer of 1996, a series of blackouts occurred, initiated by thermal overload and sagging transmission lines in the western United States. These incited additional widespread blackouts all along the West Coast. According to a series of in depth articles on the subject, "The Principle cause of both the original outages and the ensuing blackouts was the heavy power flows that are a result of competitive pressures already at work in the industry" (*Electrical World*, October 1996, p. 26).

Lesson 2. Incentives matter

An examination of what has ensued since the 1996 act is telling for the deregulation of electricity. Witness the actions of the RBOCs (who were the predominant owners of the "transmission grid" in telephony): mergers. During 1997, mergers between Nynex and Bell Atlantic, and SBC Communications and Pacific Telesis (who then approached AT&T about merging) occurred, which resulted in fewer owners of the transmission grid, which does not bode well for competition. In this case, regulators ignored the incentives of these firms. As profit-maximizing entities, grid owners did exactly as one would expect them to do: They formed alliances with those with whom they shared complementarities (both cost and demand). An excellent example of this is the 2002 merger between American Electric Power (AEP) and Central Southwest (CSW). The merger between the two yielded the largest utility in the United States serving 4.7 million customers in 11 states.

Other lessons: From the 1982 consent decree

1. AT&T was presumed guilty until proven innocent: Although it was not disproved, AT&T failed to prove that telephony was a natural monopoly and was hence broken up. This was a far too drastic step to take when the evidence was so inconclusive, not to mention

based on erroneous results. That the 1996 Telecommunications Deregulation Act was so well received and legislation thereof so easily passed was a clear indication of an attempt to reverse or mitigate some of the damage done by the divestiture: Not only were the local exchange carriers allowed to offer long-distance service, they were also allowed to offer Internet, cable, and personal communications services.

2.   What was the thinking behind allowing the local operating exchanges to remain monopolies? At the time, no studies had been undertaken in an attempt to verify that this market was a natural monopoly. In fact, one of the first studies was that of Shin and Ying in 1992, a full 10 years after the divestiture was ordered.

Lessons on the physical structure (bottleneck)

At the heart of the electric-utility deregulation debate is whether deregulation should entail the separation of the three functional components therein: generation, transmission, and distribution. Despite several studies that rejected the separability hypothesis and numerous studies supporting the economies of vertical integration and network economies, regulators seem to be convinced that such a separation, thus allowing entry into each component, would be welfare enhancing. But, this is naïve; one need only to look at what happened in telephony as a result of such a separation. From Almarin Phillips, who spoke of the inefficiencies of the disintegration of telephony and, hence its inevitable reintegration, to Huber, Kellogg, and Thorne, whose assertion concerning what a likely market structure would be: "Each such competitor will provide transmission, both of local and long distance service, processing, storage, and switching of voice, data, and video to households, businesses, and mobile users. This rapidly evolving industry structure has been called 'the vertical reintegration that divestiture attempted to dismantle'" (quoted in Baumol & Sidak, 1994, p. 15).

And what has happened thus far, via vertical and horizontal integration, mergers, and entry confirms much of this by electric utilities. For example, shortly after passage of deregulation legislation, Baltimore Gas & Electric began offering its business customers fiber-optic access to interexchange carriers. In Oregon, Electric Lightwave gained authority to provide switched interexchange service. And, in Little Rock, Arkansas, Entergy filed applications to extend fiber-optic service to provide local exchange and video services.

A lesson for electric utility deregulation

"Electric utilities have the very properties that give rise to gains from vertical integration. Special assets with high sunk costs characterize all three stages. Scale economies at the downstream transmission/distribution stage inevitably imply small numbers. Periodic and unpredictable transmission bottlenecks further reduce the number of effective alternative competitors" (Landon, 1983; Joskow and Schmalensee, 1983, as quoted in Kwoka, 1996, p. 40)

Given the now regulatory-approved reintegration of telephony, not to mention the numerous studies that consistently reject the efficient separability in the production of electricity, why is the vertical disintegration even being discussed? The bottom line is that, like telephony, the presence of a bottleneck precludes "ordinary" economic theory from yielding optimal outcomes, since this bottleneck precludes full-fledged deregulation, thus rendering the market a natural monopoly (at least in the short and intermediate runs).

If technological advances are an argument for disintegration of the electric utility industry, then it is likely the case that such a divestiture will happen without being legislated. The 1982 divestiture may have spawned some of the technological advances in (long-distance) telephony, but it certainly did not promote those that occurred in local telephony. The advent of wireless technology resulted in a mitigation of some of the natural monopoly (bottleneck) effects, since it allows bypassing the incumbent local exchange carrier (it also yields scope economies between cellular telephone and personal communications services).

Unfortunately for electricity, wireless does not hold the same promise, unless somebody comes up with a "wireless" method to transmit electricity or a device that can store it for long periods of time.

5.7 CONCLUSION

One lesson learned from the AT&T divestiture is that the telephone industry probably was at the time of the divestiture and still is today characterized by economies of scope. If this were not the case, then why would the telecommunications industry have been deregulated in 1996, thus allowing, in essence, one firm to provide both long-distance and local telephony, cable television, and Internet service? Technological change transformed telephony into the telecommunications industry, thus creating a myriad of possibilities and services. At the time, my conjecture was that a likely scenario to emerge would be that of a vertically integrated market structure in which multiproduct firms compete with one another to provide several, if not all, of the aforementioned services. In addition, if these firms enter one another's markets, true competition could result, which was the premise of the telecommunications deregulation bill passed in 1996. At the time, what was interesting about this was that the Federal Communications Commission prevented the emergence of true competition. By restraining the Bells (from entering long-distance markets until they opened their markets to competition), they precluded these markets from becoming competitive. In essence, there was still too much regulation and propagation of second-mover advantages (or first-mover disadvantages), which likely led to the stifling of innovation and new products. Nonetheless, some valuable lessons are to be learned from this industry. Another such lesson: Just because policy makers want something to happen does not mean that it will—*incentives matter*. Profit-maximizing firms will act in a profit-maximizing fashion. Witness what else has occurred in telecommunications shortly after it was deregulated: In addition to mergers between the local exchange carriers, there have been mergers within the long-distance service market; for example, WorldCom's acquisition of MFS Communications (making it the fourth largest long-distance carrier) and the bids for MCI by British Telecom, WorldCom, and GTE.

Like telephony, the production of electricity requires specific resources, most of which tend to be sunk, thus yielding a natural monopoly. The physical properties of these resources matter, since they create *bottlenecks*, which are most efficiently remedied by vertical integration. It has been shown empirically (with consistent results, please see Chapter 2 for literature review) that *vertical integration* is best. According to Kwoka (1996, p. 21), "they [the integrated utilities] have lower overall unit costs, with substantially smaller supply and T&D expenses offsetting modestly large overhead expenses."

This chapter provides an overview of what transpired in the telecommunications industry in the latter part of the 20th century. In the next chapter, we examine some of the cost models discussed here and apply them to the electric industry.

CHAPTER 6

Cost Models

6.1 THE DETERMINATION OF AN APPROPRIATE OBJECTIVE FUNCTION: A BRIEF OVERVIEW OF THE LITERATURE

While numerous studies attempt to measure economies of scale and scope, vertical integration, and subadditivity in the electric utility industry, not all are conducted in the same manner nor do they consider the same type of firms. Some employ a production function, taking input quantities as exogenous and output as endogenous. Others estimated the dual cost function, where input prices and the level of output are exogenous. Whether to estimate a cost function or a production function typically depends on what type of data is available. Because much of the data in the electric utility industry are disaggregated, firm-level data, it is preferable to employ a cost function in which input prices are regressors, rather than a production function in which input quantities are the right-hand-side variables. Also, as Nerlove aptly noted, since electricity rates (in the United States) were set by regulators, they were exogenous so that cost, rather than production functions, were appropriate (Berndt, 1991). As such, the optimization problem is to choose inputs so that the cost of production is minimized given the input prices and the level of output, which is also exogenous, since regulated utilities have an obligation to serve the native load as part of their franchise agreement with the state regulatory commission.

Some of the earlier studies employed relatively simple functional forms, like the Cobb-Douglas function (detailed in Chapter 4) and Constant Elasticity of Substitution (CES) (also detailed in Chapter 4), to model cost or production technology. Unfortunately, these functional forms are rather limited, in that they place a priori restrictions on the elasticities of substitution among the factors of production and the returns to scale inherent within this industry. To get around such restrictions, the translog functional form was introduced circa 1961 (Heady and Dillon, 1961), which added quadratic and cross-product terms to a second-degree polynomial in logarithms and placed no a priori restrictions on substitution elasticities, a major breakthrough for empirical analysis.

Not until 1971 did W. Erwin Diewert employ Shephard's duality theory to estimate a general Leontief cost function, a flexible cost function associated with the Leontief form of production technology. Among the first to implement this was a study of the U.S. manufacturing industry from 1947 to 1971 by Berndt and Wood (1975), who were among the first to model the interrelated demands in the energy industry.

Although most of the studies thus far have concentrated on privately owned firms (i.e., investor-owned), a few examined firms that are publicly owned and attempted to quantify some of the differences between public and private ownership. Among the first were studies by Moore (1970) and Alchian and Demsetz (1972) whose property rights theory of the firm has been cited as the primary motivation in the differences between each ownership type. This theory was extended to electric utilities by both Pelzman (1971) and De Alessi (1974), who observed, on average, the price of power supplied by publicly owned utilities to be lower than power from firms that are privately owned. They concluded that price concessions are the chosen method of conferring political benefits. Meyer (1975) employed a cost function in which output enters as a cubic function to examine scale economies in production, transmission, and distribution of public versus private electric utilities. What is disconcerting about his study is that fixed costs do not seem to play much of a role in either transmission or distribution costs, even though both are capital intensive and remain the naturally monopolistic aspects of the industry (the constant is not statistically significant in either regression). This was reconciled by Neuberg (1977), who pointed out that Meyer considered only distribution operating costs—he did not include the costs that were associated with maintenance and capital (nor did he include factor prices, so the model likely suffered from omitted-variable bias); as such, it is not surprising that he found no fixed cost effects. In addition, his model is of a linear additive form, which leads to the "a priori expectation of zero values for the constant term and shift parameter" as Meyer himself concedes.

Among the first to employ a multiproduct cost model was Neuberg (1977). In his study, there were four interdependent outputs: the number of customers served, the number of megawatt-hours sold, the size of distribution territory, and the miles of overhead distribution line. He found evidence of increasing returns in distribution and that investor-owned firms were no more cost efficient that municipally owned firms; in fact, he found that the opposite occurred in most of the various regressions he specified.

The next wave of studies focused primarily on power generation; for example, studies by Pescatrice and Trapani (1980), Fare, Grosskopf, and Logan (1985), and Hayashi, Sevier, and Trapani (1987), each of which found that publicly owned systems do indeed have lower costs. Berry (1994) compared the costs of producing various three-product output bundles between cooperatives and investor-owned firms and found that investor-owned firms do so more efficiently.

As previously stated, most studies focused on investor-owned utilities. In addition to the seminal paper by Christensen and Greene (1976), Mayo (1984) specified a multiproduct cost function of a quadratic nature for firms that produce both electricity and natural gas. He found that economies of scope prevailed for smaller firms but not for larger firms. His model is revisited later in this chapter. And, more recently, Kwoka (1996), examined, among other things, the deregulation of the industry on both privately and municipally owned firms. In a comprehensive study, he estimated a fully simultaneous system of pricing, cost, and demand equations to examine such issues as public versus private ownership, economies of scale and of vertical integration, and monopoly versus competition in the distribution of electricity. He found that: "Clearly, publicly owned utilities have lower costs than comparable IOUs—5.5% lower overall. Moreover, their lower costs appear to arise in the distribution function, attesting to the 'comparative advantage' of public systems in end-user tasks."

As comprehensive as Kwoka's study is, it ignored a rather large faction of the market for electric utility distribution systems: rural electric cooperatives. In fact, very few industry studies even considered the rural electric cooperatives, which is how Greer (2003, 2008) distinguished her work from others. These studies will be the subject of the case studies provided in Chapters 7 and 8, which employ a properly specified cost model to test some of the cost concepts discussed in Chapter 2.

Rural electric cooperatives

Cooperative ownership is quite different from investor or public ownership. Some of these differences were discussed in the introductory chapter (Chapter 1) to this book but more detail is provided in the case studies presented in subsequent chapters. For now, suffice it to say that they have not been the subject of much research but provide an interesting alternative to studies performed on investor ownership. A brief review of the literature is provided in Chapter 7.

Data

The data employed to perform the exercises and examples in this manuscript come exclusively from the Rural Utility Service. The case studies are unique in that they focus exclusively on rural electric cooperatives. (However, they are also applicable to other types of firms in other industries.) Given the presence of almost 900 rural electric distribution cooperatives and 66 generation and transmission cooperatives across the United States, such studies are warranted. Cooperatives are interesting entities because, while they are privately owned and have some similarity to their investor-owned counterparts, they are not profit maximizing but rather follow a strategy of welfare maximization, which was defined in the introductory chapter.

Given the nature of the data, cost functions rather than production functions are appropriate for estimating the cost models reviewed in Chapter 4. For comparison purposes, several models have been specified and the results used to calculate efficiency measures, which were detailed in Chapter 2, "The Theory of Natural Monopoly."

Cost function estimation in the electric utility industry

Economies of scale

As was detailed in Chapter 2, in the electric utility industry, numerous studies employed single-output cost models in the determination of the efficient structure of the industry. However, they pertain mostly to the generation of electricity only. Among those studies that estimate economies of scale in generation are Nerlove (1963), who employed a Cobb-Douglas cost model (defined in Chapter 4) and found that, in 1955, all but the very largest utilities experienced increasing returns to scale. In their seminal paper, Christensen and Greene (1976), using both Nerlove's 1955 data and 1970 data, found that, by 1970, most firms were generating electricity at (and some even beyond) the point at which economies of scale had been exhausted. They were among the first to employ the translogarithmic cost function, the properties of which are discussed in an upcoming section. In a later study, Huettner and Landon (1977), using an ad hoc, semi-log quadratic cost function, confirmed the Christensen and Greene results, although they found that scale economies are exhausted at an even lower level of output. Finally, Atkinson and Halvorsen (1984) employed a shadow cost function (whereby firms base their decisions on shadow prices that reflect the effects of regulation on the effective prices of inputs). On reestimation of the Christensen and Greene model, they obtained a different result: They found that firms were not operating in the upward sloping portion of the long-run average cost curve.

While these studies focus on the generation component, a few studies focus on either transmission or distribution alone, two of the three components, and all three components. Of those that focus on some combination of the components, most do so to study the economies associated with vertical integration, which is discussed later in this chapter. In virtually all these studies, the consensus is that distributed electricity is not a homogenous good. This is discussed further in the empirical chapter (Chapter 4), but for now suffice it to say that different end users have different elasticities of demand and some users are more costly to serve than others.

Nerlove's Cobb-Douglas cost model

As previously stated, among the first to estimate a cost function for the electric utility industry was Marc Nerlove, who in 1963 employed a Cobb-Douglas cost function to assess returns to scale in the generation of electricity. The form of the equation he estimated is given by

$$\ln C = \beta_0 + \beta_y \ln Y + \beta_1 p_1^* + \beta_2 p_2^* \tag{6.1}$$

where p_i^* denotes the transformed input prices. (See Chapter 4, equations (4.26)–(4.40), for derivation.)

Using 1955 data, Nerlove found significant scale economies in the generation of electricity for nearly all firms in the sample. Years later, Christensen and Greene used a more flexible functional form to reestimate Nerlove's model, using both 1955 and 1970 data, and found that, by 1970, most of the scale economies had been exhausted. The models by Nerlove and Christensen and Greene are the subject of examples and exercises.

Example 6.1. Estimating a basic cost model

It was stated that, at the very least, a cost model is a function of output and input prices. In other words,

$$C = f(Y, \mathbf{p}) \tag{6.2}$$

The data set GT97 contains data on the 43 generation and transmission (G&Ts) cooperatives that were RUS borrowers and provided electricity in 1997. The summary statistics of the relevant variables are in Table 6.1. (The reader should verify these.)

Table 6.1 Summary Statistics for 1997 RUS Borrowers—G&T Cooperatives

Variable	Name	Mean	Std dev	Minimum	Maximum
Total cost (millions $)	TC	214,145	216,549	5791	1,073,260
Y (electricity in MWh)	GTY	4158	3823	24.00	15,250
Price of fuel ($/MWh)	gt_pf	20.26	36.12	0.00	222.32
Price of purchased power ($/MWh)	gt_pp	27.34	11.92	0.00	82.85
Average price of power (weighted average)	AvgPP_gt	28.73	8.37	0.00	44.15
Price of capital (%)	gt_pk	6.26	2.63	0.00	19.12
Price of labor ($/hour)	gt_pl	19.49	7.36	0.00	38.46

Employing the most basic model, estimate the parameters of the following equation:

$$\ln C = \beta_0 + \beta_y \ln Y + \beta_1 \ln p_1 + \beta_2 \ln p_2 + \beta_3 \ln p_3 \qquad (6.3)$$

Next, use Nerlove's specification to estimate the parameters of the log linear Cobb-Douglas specification given by

$$\ln C^* = \beta_0 + \beta_y \ln Y + \beta_1 p_1^* + \beta_2 p_2^* \qquad (6.4)$$

(Hint: You must create the variables $\ln C^*$, $\ln p_1^*$, and $\ln p_2^*$, which are derived in Chapter 4, "The Economics (and Econometrics) of Cost Modeling.") Table 6.2 displays the results.

Using the results from the basic cost model given by equation (6.3), it is straightforward to calculate r (returns to scale) and determine the degree of scale economies for the coops in the data set. Recalling from Chapter 4,

$$\beta_y = 1/r \qquad (6.5)$$

Table 6.2 Basic Cost Model versus Nerlove Cost Model Specification

Parameter (variable)	Basic cost model estimate	Basic cost model t-statistic	Nerlove model estimate	Nerlove model t-statistic
β_0	11.3498	6.92	7.58348	8.88
β_y (ln Y)	0.9575	12.85	1.00729	11.96
β_1 (ln p_l)	−0.1253	−0.4	0.53291	2.52
β_2 (ln p_k)	−0.1619	−0.65	0.2236	0.96
β_3 (ln p_f)	0.06002	0.49		
Adjusted R^2	0.918		0.94	

which implies that

$$r = 1/\beta_y = 1/0.9575$$

or

$$r = 1.044.$$

Since $r > 1$, the results of the basic cost model indicate that the firms in the sample were operating in the increasing returns to scale portion of the average cost curve.

Further considerations

It was stated previously that a proper cost model is monotonic (increasing) and homogeneous of degree 1 in input prices, which implies that, for a given level of output, a doubling of all input prices results in a doubling of total cost. What this means is that the estimated parameters of the input price variables should be positive in sign and sum to unity. Reviewing the results of the basic cost model, it is clear that neither condition holds; as such, the basic cost model does not represent an appropriately specified cost function.

At first blush, it may appear that the Cobb-Douglas specification employed by Nerlove does not conform either. However, you may recall that the estimated model is derived from the underlying production function and that the parameter estimates are actually functions of other parameters and variables, which was detailed in Chapter 4 and reviewed here. More specifically, we have

$$\beta_1 = \alpha_1/r \tag{6.6}$$

and

$$\beta_2 = \alpha_2/r \tag{6.7}$$

which imply that

$$\alpha_1 = \beta_1 \times r \Rightarrow \alpha_1 = \beta_1/\beta_y \tag{6.8}$$

and

$$\alpha_2 = \beta_2 \times r \Rightarrow \alpha_2 = \beta_2/\beta_y \tag{6.9}$$

From Berndt (1991), linear homogeneity implies that the constraint on the underlying parameters is given by

$$(\alpha_1 + \alpha_2 + \alpha_3)/r = 1 \tag{6.10}$$

so that

$$\alpha_3 = (1 - \beta_1 - \beta_2)/\beta_y \qquad (6.11)$$

(Berndt, 1991). It is left as an exercise to check for linear homogeneity of the underlying input price parameters $(\alpha_1, \alpha_2, \alpha_3)$.

End of section exercises: Basic versus Nerlove cost models

1. Refer to Table 6.2.
    a. What do you notice about the estimated parameters of the basic cost model given in equation (6.3.); in other words, do they seem reasonable? That is, do they accord to economic theory in terms of sign and statistical significance? Why or why not?
    b. What do you notice about the estimated parameters from Nerlove's log-linear Cobb-Douglas specification? Do they seem reasonable?
    c. What do the results from the Nerlove's specification (log-linear Cobb Douglas form) indicate in terms of returns to scale?
2. Table 6.3 contains the results from Nerlove's original model specification. His data set contained data on total costs, output (in kilowatt-hours), and the prices of labor (p_l), capital (p_k), and fuel (p_f) for 145 electric utility companies in 1955.
    a. What do you notice about the results?
    b. What do they imply about returns to scale?

6.2 FLEXIBLE FUNCTIONAL FORMS

In addition to the previously mentioned properties, a cost function should be flexible enough so as not to restrict the substitution elasticities between inputs. The Cobb-Douglas form restricts these substitution elasticities to

Table 6.3 Nerlove Original Data and Cost Model (Cobb-Douglas)

Variable	Parameter	Nerlove model estimate*	Nerlove model: t-statistic
Constant	β_0	−4.6908	−5.301
(ln of) Y	β_y (ln Y)	0.72069	41.334
$\ln p_l - \ln p_f$ (or $\ln(p_l/p_f)$)	β_1 ($\ln p_l p_f$)	0.59291	2.898
$\ln p_k - \ln p_f$ (or $\ln(p_k/p_f)$)	β_2 ($\ln p_k p_f$)	−0.00738	−0.039
	Adjusted R^2	0.93	

*Reestimated using Nerlove data.

equal unity, and the Constant Elasticity of Substitution function imposes that the elasticities of substitution not vary across observations. While the Leontief form provides the flexibility required, its implication that the marginal productivity of any factor is 0 is troubling. As a result, many recent studies employ the translogarithmic functional form, which is flexible enough to allow the substitution elasticities to vary across observations and easily conforms to meet many (but not all) of the qualifications of a proper cost function.

Translogarithmic cost function

The translogarithmic (translog) function is a second-order Taylor's series approximation to any arbitrary cost function. Christensen and Greene (1976) employed this cost specification when they reexamined Nerlove's cost model. In this case, they employed a single-output, three-input translog cost function, which is given by

$$
\ln C = \alpha_0 + \alpha_y \ln y + \sum_i \beta_i \ln p_i \\
+ (\tfrac{1}{2})\alpha_{yy}(\ln y)^2 + (\tfrac{1}{2})\sum_i \sum_j \phi_{ij} \ln p_i \ln p_j + \sum_i \omega_{iy} \ln y \ln p_i
$$

$$(6.12)$$

where output ($\ln y$) and input prices ($\ln p_i$) enter linearly, as quadratics, and as cross-products.

This is one of the specifications estimated later in this chapter as well as being used in the examples and exercises at the end of the chapter.

Cost-share equations

Cost-share equations allow for the assumption of cost-minimizing behavior to be imposed on the model. In general, the equation for the ith input price is given by (via Shephard's lemma, which was defined in Chapter 4)

$$s_i = \partial \ln C / \partial \ln p_i \tag{6.13}$$

That is,

$$s_i = \beta_i + \beta_{ii} \ln p_i + \omega_i \ln Y + (\tfrac{1}{2}) \sum_j \beta_{ij} \ln p_j, \quad \text{for } i \neq j \tag{6.14}$$

Therefore, for the three inputs employed here—labor (l), capital (k), and purchased power (p)—the respective cost-share equations are given by

$$s_P = \beta_p + \beta_{pp} \ln p_p + \omega_P \ln Y + (\tfrac{1}{2}) \sum_j \beta_{pj} \ln p_j \tag{6.15}$$

where $j = k, l$.

$$s_l = \beta_l + \beta_{ll} \ln p_l + \omega_l \ln Y + (\tfrac{1}{2}) \sum_j \beta_{lj} \ln p_j \qquad (6.16)$$

where $j = p, k$.

$$s_k = \beta_k + \beta_{kk} \ln p_k + \omega_k \ln Y + (\tfrac{1}{2}) \sum_j \beta_{kj} \ln p_j \qquad (6.17)$$

where $j = l, p$.

Again, linear homogeneity in input prices and symmetry are imposed by the following restrictions:

$$\sum_i \beta_i = 1, \text{ and} \sum_i \beta_{ij} = \sum_j \beta_{ji} = \sum_i \omega_{iy} = 0 \qquad (6.18)$$

So that the final form to be estimated is given by

$$\ln C = \alpha_0 + \alpha_Y \ln Y + \sum_i \beta_i \ln p_i + \tfrac{1}{2}$$
$$\times \left(\alpha_{YY} \ln Y^2 + \sum_i \sum_j \beta_{ij} \ln p_i \ln p_j \right) + \sum_i \omega_{iy} \ln Y \ln p_i \qquad (6.19)$$

Once these restrictions are imposed, the system of equations can be estimated simultaneously by Zellner's method, which is discussed in Chapter 4.

Example 6.2. Translogarithmic cost model

The data employed in this example include detailed information on the 711 distribution cooperatives that were RUS borrowers in 1997. However, only 708 were actually used in the estimation procedures due to data irregularities or missing observations. In this example, equation 6.19 was estimated. The variables are defined as:

ln C (the natural log of Total cost) = the natural log of (the Cost of purchased power + Distribution expense O&M + Customer accounts, service, and information expenses + A&G expense + Sales expense + D&A expense + Tax expense + Interest on long−term debt).

The independent variables (also known as *regressors* or *explanatory variables*) include the natural log of factor prices (capital, labor, and purchased power) and the natural log of output (electricity distributed in megawatt-hours).

Note: In exercises at the end of the chapter you will add certain cost-shift variables, such as the (natural log of) miles of transmission lines and customer density, which is defined as the number of customers per mile of distribution line.

The first set of regressors corresponds to the prices of the inputs required in the distribution of electricity: capital, labor, and purchased power, which are defined as:

P_k = the price of capital (Interest on Long − term debt/Total long − term debt)
P_l = the price of labor (Total payroll expense/Total number of hours worked)
P_p = the price of purchased power (Cost of power/Total MWh purchased)

Dividing through by the price of capital and imposing symmetry yields the cost-share equations to be estimated, which are given by

$$S_p = \beta_p + \beta_{pp} \ln (P_p/P_k) + \omega_{py} \ln Y + \sum_j \beta_{pl} \ln (P_l/P_k) \qquad (6.20)$$

and

$$s_l = \beta_L + \beta_{ll} \ln (P_l/P_k) + \omega_{ly} \ln Y + \sum_j \beta_{lp} \ln (P_p/P_k) \qquad (6.21)$$

Thus, a three-equation system characterizes this model: The translogarithmic cost function and the two cost-share equations are estimated simultaneously by Zellner's method (see Chapter 4). Estimation results are displayed in Table 6.4.

Table 6.4 Single-Output Translog Cost Model, 1997 Data

Variable	Coefficient	Estimated coefficient	t-statistic
Constant	α_0	2.6192	10.71
Output (Y) (total)	α_y	0.6653	10.23
Y^2	α_{YY}	0.0175	2.04
Input prices			
Capital	β_L	0.1641	1.69
Labor	β_K	0.2243	26.30
Purchased power	β_P	0.6117	6.25
Squares and cross–products			
Capital squared	β_{LL}	−0.1443	−7.38
Labor squared	β_{KK}	0.0324	10.24
Purchased power squared	β_{PP}	−0.0980	−4.95
Labor × Capital	β_{LK}	0.0070	1.79
Labor × Purchased power	β_{LP}	−0.0394	−12.78
Capital × Purchased power	β_{KP}	0.1373	7.01
$Y \times P_L$	ω_{ly}	−0.0171	−21.40
$Y \times P_K$	ω_{ky}	−0.0462	−2.54
$Y \times P_P$	ω_{py}	0.0632	3.48
Adjusted R^2			0.9631

A priori expectations

Before reviewing the results, it is necessary to discuss the a priori expectations concerning the signs of the coefficient estimates, which should accord to economic theory. Recalling from Chapter 4, a cost model must conform to certain characteristics: First, the total effect of a change in output (Y) should cause an increase in the total cost of distributing electricity (i.e., monotonicity in output). Next, it should be nondecreasing in input prices (i.e., share equations should be positive and sum to unity), since an increase in the price of an input should always increase total cost (but at a decreasing rate, which satisfies the concavity-in-input-prices provision). This implies that

1. Own prices must be nonpositive.
2. Cross-price effects are symmetric.

Estimation results are contained in Table 6.4.

Discussion of estimation results: Single-output translog cost equation

The estimation results of the single-output translog cost model are, for the most part, as expected in terms of the sign and magnitude of the coefficients. The adjusted R^2 of 0.96 indicates that the model is doing a very good job in explaining the variation in the total cost of distributing electricity. More specifically, the output coefficients are statistically significant and positive in sign.

Because of the inclusion of cross-product terms in this model, these too must be included in evaluating the total effect of a change in output on cost by evaluating the partial derivative of cost with respect to output (i.e., the degree of scale economies, SCE). That is,

$$SCE = C(Y)/Y \times C'(Y)(\text{or AC/MC}) \tag{6.22}$$

On doing this and evaluating the derivative at the variables' sample means, the effect is indeed positive, greater than unity, and is equal to

$$S = 1.15$$

(In an exercise, you will verify this.)

These results indicate that there were increasing returns to scale in the distribution of electricity for the firms in the 1997 sample. In other words, the average cooperative operated in the downward-sloping portion of the average cost curve in 1997, implying that marginal cost was less than average cost.

Next, we turn to the evaluation of the input-price coefficients. The input-price coefficients indicate that linear homogeneity has been preserved (since share equations sum to unity).

Note: Because each of the input-price coefficients enters both linearly and multiplicatively with the other variables in the model, an evaluation of the partial derivatives is required to obtain the appropriate interpretations. Appealing to the share equations (6.15)–(6.17), and evaluating each of the partial derivatives at the variables' sample means, all three are positive in sign (as expected) with that of the price of purchased power the largest in magnitude, which is not surprising given that the firms in the data set are distribution cooperatives. To wit,

$$s_P = \beta_p + \beta_{pp} \ln p_p + \omega_P \ln Y + (\tfrac{1}{2})\sum_j \beta_{pj} \ln p_j = 0.69$$
$$s_l = \beta_l + \beta_{ll} \ln p_l + \omega_l \ln Y + (\tfrac{1}{2})\sum_j \beta_{lj} \ln p_j = 0.09$$
$$s_k = \beta_k + \beta_{kk} \ln p_k + \omega_k \ln Y + (\tfrac{1}{2})\sum_j \beta_{kj} \ln p_j = 0.22$$

Note that share equations sum to unity as required.

Substitution elasticities among inputs: The Hicks-Allen partial elasticities of substitution

As was previously discussed in Chapter 4, one of the properties of flexible functional forms is that it places no a priori restrictions on the substitution elasticities. Appealing to the Allen partial elasticities of substitution between inputs i and j for the translog cost model, they are equal to

$$\sigma_{ij} = (\beta_{ij} + s_i s_j)/s_i s_j, \quad \text{for } i,j = 1, \ldots, n \text{ but } i \neq j \tag{6.23}$$

and

$$\sigma_{ii} = \left(\beta_{ii} + s_i^2 - s_i\right)/s_i^2, \quad \text{for } i = 1, \ldots, n \tag{6.24}$$

The results from the estimation of equations (6.23)–(6.24) are displayed in the first column of Table 6.5. As can be seen, σ_{ij}, which represent substitution among the different inputs, are all positive in sign, indicating that these are substitutes while σ_{ii} are complements.

Price elasticities

Next we turn to the price elasticities, which are equal to

$$\varepsilon_{ij} = S_j \sigma_{ij} \tag{6.25}$$

As such, this is equivalent to

$$\varepsilon_{ij} = (\beta_{ij} + s_i s_j)/s_i, \quad \text{for } i,j = 1, \ldots, n \text{ but } i \neq j \tag{6.26}$$

Table 6.5 Elasticities of Substitution and Price for Single-Output Translog Model

Inputs	Parameter	Substitution elasticities	Parameter	Price elasticities
P_p, P_p	σ_{pp}	−0.66	ε_{pp}	−0.45
P_k, P_k	σ_{kk}	−6.52	ε_{kk}	−1.44
P_l, P_l	σ_{ll}	−6.12	ε_{ll}	−0.55
P_p, P_l	σ_{pl}	0.17	ε_{pl}	0.03
P_p, P_k	σ_{pk}	0.91	ε_{pk}	1.31
P_k, P_l	σ_{kl}	0.07	ε_{kl}	0.12
P_l, P_p	σ_{lp}	0.17	ε_{lp}	0.25
P_k, P_p	σ_{kp}	0.91	ε_{kp}	0.42
P_l, P_k	σ_{lk}	0.07	ε_{lk}	0.30

and

$$\varepsilon_{ii} = \left(\beta_{ii} + s_i^2 - s_i\right)/s_i, \text{ for } i = 1, \ldots, n \qquad (6.27)$$

The second partial derivatives of a proper cost function represent the own- and cross-price effects of the inputs. More specifically, an increase in the price of an input should decrease the quantity demanded of that input. As displayed in the first three rows of Table 6.5, the own-price elasticities of demand are negative while cross-price elasticities (displayed in the remaining rows of Table 6.5) are positive (and symmetric) when evaluated at the variables' sample means. Note that the concavity-in-input-prices criterion is satisfied since the own-price elasticities are negative in sign.

Table 6.5 contains the results of equations (6.23)–(6.27) when evaluated at the sample means of the variables and the estimation results, which are displayed in Table 6.3.

Homotheticity

It is also informative to look at the relationships between output and the input prices, since the input price–output interaction terms allow for the nonhomotheticity of the underlying production function. As described in their 1976 paper, Christensen and Greene write, "A cost function corresponds to a homothetic production function if and only if it can be written as a separable function in output and factor prices."[1]

Homothetic functions are functions whose marginal technical rate of substitution (slope of the isoquant) is homogeneous of degree 0. Due to

---

[1] Homotheticity was rejected by Christensen and Greene (1976).

this, along rays coming from the origin, the slopes of the isoquants are the same. What this implies for the translogarithmic cost function is that

$$\omega_{iy} = 0, \quad \text{for all } i = 1, \ldots, n \tag{6.28}$$

The coefficients on the input price–output interaction terms measure how a change in an input's price affects its usage and how the change in its usage affects output, which then affects the total cost of distributing electricity. For example, an increase in the wage rate most likely causes less labor to be employed, thus causing a reduction in output, which in turn affects the total cost of distributing electricity (negatively since the estimated coefficient, $\omega_{ly} = -0.017$, is negative in sign). Likewise, for a positively signed coefficient; for example, in ω_{py}, the output–purchased power coefficient, the positive sign indicates that the change in output times purchased power causes a change in total cost in the same direction. That is, in this case,

$$\partial \ln C / \partial \ln Y \times P_p = 0.063 > 0$$

Again, this may seem contrary to theory, but it is probably due to the requirement that distribution entities procure enough power to serve their native loads. Anyway, because many states have a mechanism in place (known as fuel adjustment clauses), any changes in the cost of power are directly passed on to ratepayers. In effect, this mechanism renders the elasticity of supply extremely inelastic, which could support the positively signed coefficient (or it could be another problem, for example, an incorrect functional form).

End of section exercises: Translogarithmic cost function

1. Using the data set "Translog97,"
   a. Calculate the summary statistics for the variables in Table 6.3 (you need this to complete this exercise).
   b. Estimate equation (6.19) along with the relevant cost-share equations in equations (6.20)–(6.21) (recall from the discussion in Chapter 4 on Zellner's ITSUR method, you must divide $n - 1$ of the share equations by the remaining input price variable).
   c. Using the results that you obtained in part b, verify that the cost model accords to theory; that is, evaluate the following at the variables' sample means:
      i. Equation (6.22) (monotonicity in output, marginal cost should be nonnegative).
      ii. Equations (6.15)–(6.17) (share equations, should be nonnegative and sum to unity).

    iii. Equation (6.25) (concave in input prices, should be nonpositive).
    iv. Equations (6.23) and (6.24) (elasticities of substitution and prices).
    v. Verify that the restrictions in equation (6.18) hold (you must impose them prior to estimating the system of equations).
  d. Verify that the average cooperative (in terms of the amount of electricity distributed) operated in the increasing returns to scale portion of the average cost curve (i.e., evaluate equation (6.21)).

2. *Advanced.* Using the same data set,
  a. Estimate an equation that includes two cost shift variables: miles of transmission lines (O_{tr}) and customer density (O_{dm}), which is equal to the number of customers per mile of distribution line. That is, estimate the following equation:

$$
\begin{aligned}
\ln C = {}& \alpha_0 + \alpha_Y \ln Y + \sum_i \beta_i \ln p_i + \tfrac{1}{2} \\
& \times \left(\alpha_{YY} \ln Y^2 + \sum_i \sum_j \beta_{ij} \ln p_i \ln p_j \right. \\
& + \sum_m \sum_n \varphi_{mn} \ln O_m \ln O_n \left. \right) + \sum_i \omega_{iy} \ln Y \ln p_i \quad (6.19') \\
& + \sum_m \theta_m \ln O_m + \sum_m \delta_m \ln Y \ln O_m \\
& + \sum_m \rho_{mi} \ln O_m \ln p_i
\end{aligned}
$$

Along with the cost-share equations, which are of the general form

$$
\begin{aligned}
S_i = \partial \ln C / \partial \ln p_i = {}& \beta_i + \beta_{ii} \ln p_i + \omega_i \ln Y \\
& + \sum_j \beta_{ij} \ln p_j + \sum_m \rho_{mi} \ln O_m, \quad \text{for } i \neq j
\end{aligned} \quad (6.14')
$$

More specifically, for the three inputs employed here, the respective cost-share equations are given by

$$
\begin{aligned}
S_P = {}& \beta_p + \beta_{pp} \ln p_p + \omega_P \ln Y + \sum_j \beta_{pj} \ln p_j \\
& + \sum_m \rho_{mp} \ln O_m
\end{aligned} \quad (6.15')
$$

where $j = K, L$.

$$
\begin{aligned}
S_L = {}& \beta_L + \beta_{LL} \ln p_L + \omega_L \ln Y + \sum_j \beta_{Lj} \ln p_j \\
& + \sum_m \rho_{mL} \ln O_m
\end{aligned} \quad (6.16')
$$

where $j = P, K$.

$$S_K = \beta_K + \beta_{KK} \ln p_k + \omega_K \ln Y + \sum_j \beta_{Kj} \ln p_j$$
$$+ \sum_m \rho_{mK} \ln O_m \tag{6.17'}$$

where $j = L, P$.

b. Do the signs of the estimated coefficients change as a result of the inclusion of the cost-shift variables?

c. Does the inclusion of the cost-shift variables strengthen or weaken the finding of increasing returns to scale?

3. *Optional.* Another measure is the returns to density. Using the definition of Caves, Christensen, and Tretheway (1984) for the translog functional form, returns to density are given by:

$$RTD = 1/(\partial \ln C / \partial \ln Y) \tag{6.29}$$

where $RTD > 1$ indicates that there are increasing returns to density in the distribution of electricity. Evaluating equation (6.29) at the sample means of the data, do you find that returns to density are increasing, constant, or decreasing?

Aside: Translogarithmic cost model details: Calculating average and marginal cost

When calculating the marginal and average costs associated with a cost model of the translogarithmic form, it is necessary to do the following. Recall that

$$\text{Marginal cost (MC)} = \partial C / \partial Y \tag{6.30}$$

However, simply taking the derivative of equation (6.19), for example, with respect to the (natural log of) output ($\ln Y$) we obtain

$$\partial \ln C / \partial \ln Y \tag{6.31}$$

which is equivalent to

$$\partial \ln C / \partial \ln Y = \alpha_Y + \alpha_{YY} \ln Y + \sum_i \omega_{iy} \ln p_i \tag{6.32}$$

Therefore, it is necessary to multiply equation (6.32) by C/Y (the average cost, which is *not* simply equation (6.19) divided by output) to obtain

$$\partial C / \partial Y = C/Y \times \partial \ln C / \partial \ln Y \tag{6.33}$$

which is the marginal cost.

Proof

By definition,

$$\partial \ln C = \partial C / C \tag{6.34}$$

and

$$\partial \ln Y = \partial Y / Y \tag{6.35}$$

so that

$$\partial \ln C / \partial \ln Y = \partial C / C \times Y / \partial Y \tag{6.36}$$

This is equivalent to

$$\partial \ln C / \partial \ln Y = \partial C / \partial Y \times Y / C \tag{6.37}$$

or

$$\text{Marginal cost} \times (1/\text{Average cost}) \tag{6.38}$$

Thus multiplying (6.37) by C/Y (or average cost) yields the marginal cost, or $\partial C / \partial Y$.   *QED*

6.3 MULTIPRODUCT COST FUNCTIONS

Distributed electricity as a multiproduct-cost industry is well established in the literature, some of which was detailed in Chapter 2 and is expanded here.

Distributed electricity as a multiproduct industry

The motivation for multiproduct cost models is (at least) twofold:

1. First, multiproduct-cost specifications have been recently employed in the literature, particularly for distribution entities. Most studies disaggregate distributed electricity into two categories or outputs: high voltage and low voltage. Kwoka (1996) specifies a quadratic net cost equation for two outputs, generation and distribution, the latter of which is further disaggregated by voltage requirement. High-voltage customers are those that require little or no voltage reduction and thus entail smaller line losses. Kwoka finds that increasing the percentage of electricity distributed to high-voltage customers tends to lower total cost. A 1997 study for the National Rural Electric Cooperative Association (NRECA) by Christensen Associates assumes equal demand elasticities for residential and commercial customers and that both consume relatively small quantities of generation as justification in

aggregating them into the small, low-voltage category. Berry (1994) cites that, although industrial customers receive power via the distribution system, some receive power directly from the utility's high-voltage transmission lines and transform the energy down to usable levels with their own equipment. As a result, they are less costly to serve than either residential or small commercial users. In addition, industrial users tend to consume a greater percentage of power during off-peak hours (many operate around the clock), the cost of which is substantially lower than electricity consumed during peak hours, since the most expensive generating units come online to satisfy demand during peak hours. In addition, industrial loads tend to provide more stable loads. Residential and commercial customer loads tend to be more volatile often requiring power during peak hours especially on hot summer days, for example. The power sold to smaller users must go through the distribution substation and each has its own service drop, meter, and billing charges. Due to the low density that prevails in many coop territories, the costs per unit are rather high. Karlson (1986), who was quoted earlier, specified a four-output translog cost function (residential, commercial, industrial, and wholesale). He tested for and confirmed that a multiple-output specification was appropriate. Roberts (1986) found that firms that serve a large proportion of residential and small commercial customers tend to have larger demands for distribution capital, while those with large industrial loads have large demands for transmission capital. Along a similar vein, Hayashi et al. (1985) estimated a two-product translog cost function with low voltage and industrial outputs. They cite that multicollinearity resulted from separate estimation of residential and commercial users. Berry (1994) confirmed this finding;

2. The second reason for the multiple-output specification is that public utility commissions typically allocate costs in this fashion. Often, large commercial and industrial users are assigned certain charges that neither residential nor commercial users have to pay, such as demand charges. All customer classes are assigned customer charges and energy charges, both of which vary with the number of customers served. Customer charges comprise the cost of primary and secondary lines, transformers, services, and metering and are allocated by the percentage of number of customers in each class. For example, if 70% of the load is residential, then residential users equally share 70% of the total customer cost, with each paying the same amount regardless of the

cost he or she imposes on the system. Energy charges are based on actual usage, measured in cents per kilowatt-hour. Typically, residential and small commercial users pay higher energy charges than industrial users, since they tend to consume power at peak times and have more volatile loads, while industrial loads tend to be more stable. The latter tend to use a fairly constant amount of power throughout the course of the day and thus are less costly to serve. In addition, industrial customers may choose to be on interruptible contracts, further decreasing the per kilowatt-hour energy charge. Demand charges are what is left over after the customer charges have been allocated, having been determined by one of several methods, typically either the minimum investment or the minimum intercept method. Demand charges, which are a function of the capacity of the generating plant, are then allocated predominantly to industrial users, since the capacity of the plant must be built to serve its largest load. Nonetheless, this is one of the ways whereby industrial users subsidize the other rate classes. Other variables are included to capture some of the other factors that influence the cost of distributing electricity. These are known as *cost-shift variables*, and may include miles of transmission and distribution lines, the number of customers served, and the number of customers per mile of line, also known as *density*.

Multiproduct cost models

You may recall the discussion in Chapter 4 concerning model misspecification, which includes omitted-variable bias and incorrect functional form; more specifically, that in the case of distributed electricity it is more appropriate to estimate a cost function that has (at least) two outputs: electricity distributed to "small" users versus that distributed to "large" users. The distinction here being the voltage level at which the end user receives the electricity (below or above 1000 kVA). Given this, a discussion of such multiproduct specifications ensues.

Multiproduct translogarithmic cost model

Let:

$$Y_1 = \text{small users (residential and small commercial customers)}$$

and

$$Y_2 = \text{large users (large commercial or industrial customers)}$$

As such, a multiple-output translog cost function of the form (including input prices, p_i, and cost shift variables, O_m) is given by

$$\ln C = \alpha_0 + \sum_i \alpha_i \ln Y_i + \frac{1}{2} \times \left(\alpha_{ij} \ln Y_i Y_j + \sum_i \beta_i \ln p_i \right.$$

$$+ \sum_i \sum_j \beta_{ij} \ln p_i \ln p_j + \sum_m \sum_n \varphi_{mn} \ln O_m \ln O_n \bigg)$$

$$+ \sum_i \sum_g \omega_{iyg} \ln Y_g \ln p_i + \sum_m \theta_m \ln O_m \qquad (6.40)$$

$$+ \sum_g \sum_m \delta_m \ln Y_g \ln O_m$$

$$+ \sum_m \rho_{mi} \ln O_m \ln p_i, \text{ for } g, i, j = 1, \ldots, n$$

along with the cost-share equations, which are of the general form

$$S_i = \partial \ln C / \partial \ln p_i = \beta_i + \beta_{ii} \ln p_i + \sum_i \sum_j \omega_{iyg} \ln Y_g$$

$$+ \sum_j \beta_{ij} \ln p_j + \sum_m \rho_{mi} \ln O_m, \text{ for } g, i, j = 1, \ldots, n \qquad (6.41)$$

Collectively, equations (6.40) and (6.41) yield a system of equations that could be estimated jointly via Zellner's method, which is described in the appendix to Chapter 4.

More specifically, for the two–output, three–input cost model employed here, the respective cost-share equations are given by

$$S_P = \beta_p + \beta_{pp} \ln p_p + \sum_g \omega_{Pg} \ln Y_g + \sum_j \beta_{pj} \ln p_j + \sum_m \rho_{mp} \ln O_m$$
$$(6.42)$$

where $j = L, K$.

$$S_L = \beta_L + \beta_{LL} \ln p_L + \sum_g \omega_{Lg} \ln Y_g + \sum_j \beta_{Lj} \ln p_j + \sum_m \rho_{mL} \ln O_m$$
$$(6.43)$$

where $j = P, K$.

$$S_K = \beta_K + \beta_{KK} \ln p_k + \sum_g \omega_{Kg} \ln Y_g + \sum_j \beta_{Kj} \ln p_j + \sum_m \rho_{mK} \ln O_m$$
$$(6.44)$$

where $j = P, L$. (Recall, you must divide through by one of the input prices or the system of equations is singular; as such, it has no inverse, which means that the parameters of the models cannot be estimated.[2])

[2] Using matrix algebra, $\mathbf{B}$ is obtained by

$$\mathbf{B} = (\mathbf{X'X})^{-1}\mathbf{X'Y}$$

where $\mathbf{X} =$ an $N \times N$ matrix of independent variables and $\mathbf{Y} =$ (a vector of) the dependent variable.

Example 6.3. Estimation results of two-output translog with cost shift variables

Again using the data in Translog97, estimate the parameters of a multiproduct translog cost function including the cost-shift variables, miles of transmission lines and customer density. Use Zellner's method to jointly estimate the cost equation along with two of the share equations.

Table 6.6 displays the estimation results of a two-output translogarithmic cost model including cost shift variables. As before, a check of the a priori expectations of the output variables is required, namely, the two newly added cost-shift variables. In the case of the miles of transmission lines, it is expected that the total effect should be positive in sign since an increase in transmission lines should increase total cost. On the other hand, an increase in customer density, which is defined as the number of customers per mile of distribution line, should cause total cost to decrease. Note: You must calculate the partial derivatives of each of these to assess whether the coefficient estimates are of the appropriate sign.

Multiproduct cost concepts (revisited)

Ray average costs

You may recall from the Chapter 2 discussion on ray average cost, which requires that Y_1 and Y_2 move in fixed proportions, that Y, the composite product, is equal to

$$Y = Y_1 + Y_2 \tag{6.45}$$

Appealing to Baumol et al. (1982, p. 48) we can define the average cost of the composite product to be

$$RAC = C(Y)/Y \tag{6.46}$$

Again, we use the degree of scale economies to assess whether the firms in the sample that distributed electricity to both small and large users ($n = 682$) were efficient distributors of electricity according to the translog cost model. The degree of scale economies is given by equation (2.20) in Chapter 2.

The results presented in Table 6.6 are displayed as a histogram in Figure 6.1.

Histogram of ray average costs for a two-output translog cost model. As is evident, the majority of the firms in the restricted sample data set experienced scale economies greater than unity, indicating that they were operating in the increasing returns to scale portion of the average cost curve in 1997.

Table 6.6 Two-Output Translog Cost Model

Coefficient	Variable	Estimate	t-stat
A. Estimation results (output-related variables)			
a_0	Constant	3.2402	12.77
a_1	$\ln Y_1$	0.2681	3.07
a_2	$\ln Y_2$	0.3549	10.51
a_{11}	$\ln Y_1^2$	0.1422	9.28
a_{22}	$\ln Y_2^2$	0.0748	20.31
a_{21}	$\ln Y_1 Y_2$	-0.0912	-16.21
$w_p y_1$	$\ln P_p Y_1$	0.0487	1.82
$w_k y_1$	$\ln P_k Y_1$	-0.0396	-1.48
$w_l y_1$	$\ln P_l Y_1$	-0.0092	-7.45
$w_p y_2$	$\ln P_p Y_2$	0.0062	0.50
$w_k y_2$	$\ln P_k Y_2$	-0.0005	-0.04
$w_l y_2$	$\ln P_l Y_2$	-0.0057	-11.25
B. Estimation results (price-related variables)			
b_k	$\ln P_k$	0.3150	2.24
b_l	$\ln P_l$	0.1882	21.16
b_p	$\ln P_p$	0.4968	3.54
b_{pp}	$\ln P_p P_p$	-0.0404	-0.97
b_{kk}	$\ln P_k P_k$	-0.0836	-2.00
b_{ll}	$\ln P_l P_l$	0.0350	9.82
b_{pl}	$\ln P_p P_l$	-0.0391	-12.01
b_{pk}	$\ln P_p P_k$	0.0795	1.91
b_{kl}	$\ln P_l P_k$	0.0040	0.92
C. Estimation results (cost-shift variables)			
Od	lndens	0.1446	0.93
Ot	lntr	-0.0358	-0.70
oty_1	$\ln tr Y_1$	-0.0038	-0.74
oty_2	$\ln tr Y_2$	-0.0036	-1.77
Ott	lntrsq	0.0101	1.60
Odd	lndenssq	0.0442	1.05
ody_1	$\ln dens Y_1$	-0.0249	-1.31
ody_2	$\ln dens Y_2$	0.0094	1.13
Otpl	$\ln tr P_l$	0.0008	1.87
Otk	$\ln tr P_k$	0.0273	1.28
Otp	$\ln tr P_p$	0.0138	1.27
Odpl	$\ln dens P_l$	0.0019	1.04
Odk	$\ln dens P_k$	-0.0754	-1.06
Odp	$\ln dens P_p$	-0.0072	-0.17
Otd	lntrdens	-0.0163	-2.07

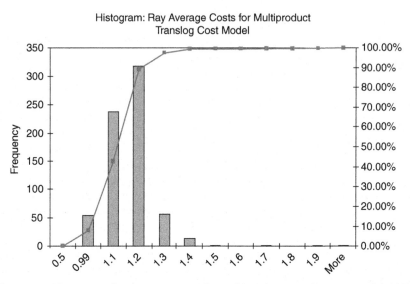

Figure 6.1 Histogram of ray average costs for multiproduct translog cost model, 1997.

Product-specific economies of scale

In the previous section, it was noted that the concept of ray average cost is relevant only for proportional changes in output. Now, we turn to a measure that allows for the variation in an output while holding other quantities of outputs constant. For this, it is necessary to define the concept of *incremental cost*, IC_i (Y), of the output to be varied. That is,

$$IC_i(Y) = C(Y) - C(\mathbf{Y}_{N-i}) \tag{6.47}$$

where $\mathbf{Y}_{N-i}$ is a vector with a zero component in the place of Y_i.

The average incremental cost, AIC_i (Y), follows from equation (6.48):

$$AIC_i(Y) = IC_i(Y)/Y_i \tag{6.48}$$

As before, it is informative to define the degree of scale economies specific to product i. Also known as *product-specific returns to scale*, this is defined as

$$S_i(Y) = IC_i(Y)/Y_i \times C_i \tag{6.49}$$

or

$$S_i(Y) = AIC_i/(\partial C/\partial Y_i) \tag{6.50}$$

Returns to scale of product i at Y are said to be increasing, decreasing, or constant as $S_i(Y)$ is greater than, less than, or equal to unity. Using equation (6.50) and the results displayed in Table 6.6, 94% of the firms in the sample data set exhibited increasing returns to scale in the distribution of electricity to small users and 70% experienced increasing returns to large users.

Economies of scope

Economies of scope (or economies of joint production) are said to exist if a given quantity of each of two or more goods can be produced by one firm at a lower cost than if each good were produced separately by two different firms or even two different production processes. That is, for a two-product case, weak economies of scope are given by

$$C(Y_1, Y_2) \leq C(Y_1, 0) + C(0, Y_2) \qquad (6.51)$$

for all Y_1, $Y_2 > 0$. If not, then there are diseconomies of scope, and separate production of outputs is more efficient.

What is useful here is a measure of the degree of economies of scope that would allow for, in the presence of economies of scope, the capturing of the relative increase in cost that would result from separate production of the two (or more) outputs. Therefore, the degree of economies of scope is given by

$$S_c = [C(Y_1, 0) + C(0, Y_2) - C(Y_1, Y_2)]/C(Y_1, Y_2) \qquad (6.52)$$

It was stated earlier that this particular form is not well suited to modeling cost for multiproduct markets. However, by restricting the sample to those firms that distributed electricity to both types of user (Y_1 and Y_2), the estimation results were used to calculate the degree of scope economies.[3]

Evaluating each of these at the sample means of the variables, the results indicate that separate production is less costly, since all but one firm in the restricted sample exhibit positive economies of scope.

Quadratic cost functions

Another functional form employed in cost estimation for electric utilities is the quadratic cost specification, which, like the translog functional form, imposes no a priori restrictions on elasticities of substitution between inputs. In general, the quadratic cost function is given by

$$C = \alpha_0 + \alpha_y Y + \tfrac{1}{2} \alpha_{yy} Y^2 + \beta_k p_k + \beta_L p_L + \beta_p p_p \qquad (6.53)$$

---

[3] Computation of equation (6.52) entails running three separate regressions: $C = f(Y_1, \mathbf{P}, \mathbf{O})$, $C = f(Y_2, \mathbf{P}, \mathbf{O})$ and $C = f(Y_1, Y_2, \mathbf{P}, \mathbf{O})$ with the last being equation (6.52).

While this is the form often employed in the electric utility cost literature, this equation is not homogeneous of degree 1 in input prices (you may recall that linear homogeneity in input prices is necessary for a properly defined cost function). Linear homogeneity implies that the total cost doubles when input prices double, which is not the case for this cost function.

One way to ensure that a function is linearly homogeneous is to impose the restriction that

$$\sum \beta_i = 1 \tag{6.54}$$

However, this restriction alone is not sufficient for this model. A proof of this is included in the appendix to this chapter.

Mayo (1984) imposes linear homogeneity by appending to the cost function the product of the input prices times their estimated coefficients. That is,

$$C = \left(\alpha_0 + \sum_i \alpha_i Y_i + \tfrac{1}{2} \sum_i \sum_j \alpha_{ij} Y_i Y_j \right) \cdot \Pi \beta_i p_i e^{\varepsilon} \tag{6.55}$$

In this form, all outputs enter the equation as both quadratic and interaction variables.

One concern may be that this model also imposes strict input-output separability, which means that the marginal rate of substitution between any two inputs is independent of the quantities of outputs and the marginal rate of transformation between any two outputs is independent of the quantities of inputs. However, studies by both Karlson (1986) and Henderson (1985) reject the separability of inputs from outputs in the distribution of electricity.

A properly specified quadratic cost function

Greer (2003) introduced a properly specified quadratic cost model in which the input price parameters enter exponentially rather than multiplicatively. Not only does this allow for individual input price parameter estimates to be obtained, it also preserves the requisite properties to which a proper cost function must conform. This equation is given by

$$C = \left(\alpha_0 + \sum_i \alpha_i Y_i + \tfrac{1}{2} \sum_i \sum_j \alpha_{ij} Y_i Y_j \right) p_K^{\beta_k} p_L^{\beta_l} p_P^{\beta_p} e^{\varepsilon} \tag{6.56}$$

This cost function is concave, nondecreasing, and homogeneous of degree 1 in input prices as well as monotonic in output and, as such, preserves the fundamental properties of a proper cost function. A proof of each is given in the appendix to this chapter.

Estimation of this particular cost function can be somewhat problematic due to the nonlinearity of the specification.[4] One solution is to transform the model so that the parameters enter linearly and the stochastic error term is additive. A logarithmic transformation, which will yield such an error term, is made possible by the creation of a variable, Z, where

$$Z = (\alpha_0 + \sum_i \alpha_i Y_i + \tfrac{1}{2} \sum_i \sum_j \alpha_{ij} Y_i Y_j) \tag{6.57}$$

so that the equation becomes

$$\ln C = \zeta \ln Z + \beta_K \ln p_K + \beta_L \ln p_L + \beta_P \ln p_P + \varepsilon \tag{6.58}$$

or

$$\ln C = \zeta \ln \left(\alpha_0 + \sum_i \alpha_i Y_i + \tfrac{1}{2} \sum_i \sum_j \alpha_{ij} Y_i Y_j\right) + \beta_K \ln p_K \\ + \beta_L \ln p_L + \beta_P \ln p_P + \varepsilon \tag{6.59}$$

where ζ has been restricted to unity.[5]

Due to the inherent complexity of the nonlinear estimation procedure, it would be informative to expound on the underlying econometric theory and technique. For this purpose, I reference Greene (1993) for assistance in this rather complex matter.

Aside: Nonlinear least squares estimation

For the reasons stated already, this model must be estimated using a nonlinear estimation procedure, namely, nonlinear least squares. In this case, the values of the parameters that minimize the sum of squared deviations are maximum likelihood estimators (as well as the nonlinear least squares estimators). Because the first-order conditions yield a set of nonlinear equations to which there will not be explicit solutions, an iterative procedure is required,[6] such as the Gauss-Newton method, which is the preferred method.

---

[4] This equation is nonlinear in parameters, which obviates the use of the ordinary least squares estimation technique.

[5] This is the true value of ζ; equation (6.56) can be written

$$C = \left(\alpha_0 + \sum_i \alpha_i Y_i + \frac{1}{2} \sum_i \sum_j \alpha_{ij} Y_i Y_j\right)^{\zeta} \times p_K^{\beta_k} p_L^{\beta_l} p_P^{\beta_P} e^{\varepsilon}$$

[6] Iterative methods include Gauss-Newton, which is the preferred method. Other methods include the Goldfeld, Quandt, and Trotter quadratic hill climbing (1966). Most other methods employ algorithms and grid searches.

Probably the greatest concern here is that the estimators produced by this nonlinear least squares procedure are not necessarily the most efficient (except in the case of normally distributed errors). An excerpt from Greene (1993) illustrates this point nicely:

*In the classical regression model, in order to obtain the requisite asymptotic results, it is assumed that the sample moment matrix, **(1/n) X'X**, converges to a positive definite matrix, **Q**. By analogy, the same condition is imposed on the regressors in the linearized model when they are computed at the true parameter values. That is, if:*

$$\text{plim} 1/n X'X = Q, \tag{6.60}$$

a positive definite matrix, then the coefficient estimates are consistent estimators. In addition, if:

$$(1/\sqrt{n})X'\varepsilon \rightarrow N[0, \sigma^2 Q] \tag{6.61}$$

then the estimators are asymptotically normal as well. Under nonlinear estimation, this is analogous to:

$$\text{plim}(1/n) \underline{X}' \underline{X} = \text{plim}(1/n)\Sigma_i[\partial h(x_i, \beta^0)/\partial \beta^0][\partial h(x_i, \beta^0)/\partial \beta^{0'}] = \underline{Q} \quad (6.62)$$

*where **Q** is a positive definite matrix. In addition, in this case the derivatives in **X** play the role of the regressors.*

The nonlinear least squares criterion function is given by:

$$S(\mathbf{b}) = \sum_i [y_i - h(x_i, \mathbf{b})]^2 = \sum_i e_i^2 \tag{6.63}$$

*where **b**, which will be the solution value, has been inserted. First-order conditions for a minimum are*

$$g(b) = -2\sum_i [y_i - h(x_i, \mathbf{b})][\partial h(x_i, \mathbf{b})/\partial b] = 0 \tag{6.64}$$

or

$$g(b) = -2\underline{X}' \mathbf{e} \tag{6.65}$$

*This is a standard problem in nonlinear estimation, which can be solved by a number of methods. One of the most often used is that of Gauss-Newton, which, at its last iteration, the estimate of **Q**$^{-1}$ will provide the correct estimate of the asymptotic covariance matrix for the parameter estimates. A consistent estimator of σ^2 can be computed using the residuals:*

$$\sigma^2 = (1/n)\sum_i [y_i - h(x_i, \mathbf{b})]^2 \tag{6.66}$$

In addition, it has been shown that (Amemiya, 1985):

$$\mathbf{b} \rightarrow N[\beta, \sigma^2/nQ^{-1}] \tag{6.67}$$

where:

$$Q = p\lim(\underline{X}' \underline{X})^{-1} \tag{6.68}$$

The sample estimate of the asymptotic covariance matrix is:

$$\text{Est. Asy. Var}[b] = \sigma_-^2 (\underline{X}' \underline{X})^{-1} \tag{6.69}$$

From these, inference and hypothesis tests can proceed accordingly.

Reasons that the quadratic form is the "best" suited for modeling industry structure

It has been stated that the quadratic is superior to the translog cost specification in estimating cost functions in multiple-output industries. In addition to its allowing for the "unconstrained emergence of economies of scope and subadditivity" (Kwoka, 1996), the Hessian matrix that results from the translogarithmic cost specification varies over input and output levels while the Hessian matrix for the quadratic form does not.[7] In this sense, the restrictions on concavity for the quadratic cost function are global—they do not change with respect to output and input prices. However, the concavity restrictions on the translog are local—fixed at a specific point, because they depend on prices and output levels. As such, in the case of the latter, the various efficiency measures described previously must be checked at every level of output and input price combination.

Given its superiority, the quadratic functional form given in equation (6.59) is the subject of the case studies presented in Chapters 7 and 8. But, first, a basic single output model is explored as an example.

Example 6.4. Basic single output quadratic cost model (equation (6.53))

Using the data contained in the data set Coops97, estimate the parameters of equation (6.53).

Table 6.7 displays the estimated equation (6.53).

Estimation results

As expected, the estimated coefficients of the output variables indicate that cost is increasing at a decreasing rate. (As an exercise you will calculate the

---

[7] An excerpt from ricardo.ifas.ufl.edu/aeb6184.production/Lecturepercent2020-2005.ppt (Lecture on Subadditivity).

Table 6.7 Basic Quadratic Cost Model Results

Variable	Coefficient	Estimate	t-statistic
Constant	a_0	−17.081	−7.07
Y	a_y	0.073	55.95
Y^2	a_{yy}	−0.0001	−17.72
Capital price	b_k	−0.092	−0.28
Purchased power	b_p	0.332	11.49
Labor price	b_l	0.344	3.67
Adjusted R^2		0.917	

degree of scale economies.) Despite a rather high adjusted R^2 (0.917), note that the results are not as expected; for example, the coefficient on the capital price variable is negative (but not statistically different from 0), which violates the nondecreasing-in-input price criteria for a proper cost model. In addition, it is clearly the case that this cost specification is not homogeneous of degree 1 in prices, since the coefficients of the input price variables do not sum to unity as required. Furthermore, one could take issue with the negatively signed constant since its t-statistic indicates that it is a significant explanatory variable in modeling the cost of distributing electricity. However, it is likely the case that these unexpected results emanate from some other problem, such as an incorrect functional form or omitted variable bias, both of which were discussed in Chapter 4. (As an exercise you will impose linear homogeneity.)

Example 6.5. Examining Mayo's specification

Next, let's examine Mayo's specification, which is the single-output version of equation (6.55). Note: To obtain convergence and unbiased estimates from Mayo's cost model it may be necessary to do the following:
1. Give starting values for the parameter estimates.
2. Impose linear homogeneity on the input price parameters.
3. Use the generalized method of moments (or similar) estimation procedure to estimate this equation.[8]

---

[8] The Generalized Method of Moments (GMM) estimation procedure is often used in the presence of heteroscedasticity to yield consistent parameter estimates. In the case of Mayo's model, it is likely that the multiplicative functional form yields difficulty in estimating the parameters on the input price variables. (It is straightforward to estimate equation (6.55) in the absence of input prices.)

Table 6.8 Mayo Single-Output Quadratic Cost Model

Variable	Coefficient	Estimate	t-statistic
Constant	a_0	0.0210	5.21
Y	a_y	0.0006	19.64
Y^2	a_{yy}	−0.0000001	−4.41
Capital price	b_k	0.357	3.71
Purchased power	b_p	0.332	4.57
Labor price	b_l	0.312	7.08
Adjusted R^2		0.915	

Table 6.8 displays the results of estimating equation (6.55). (As an exercise you will calculate the degree of scale economies.)

Discussion of Table 6.8 results

These results are certainly an improvement over the basic quadratic cost model, which is given by equation (6.53). The adjusted R^2 of 0.915 indicates that the model fits the data well, explaining over 90% of the variation in the cost of distributing electricity. However, in terms of the magnitudes of the coefficients, these results do not make sense; for a distribution entity, the cost of purchased power is by far the largest component of total cost in terms of input prices. As such, the magnitude of the coefficient should reflect this, which is not the case here. This is rectified next using the logarithmic transformation of the quadratic cost function given in equation (6.59).

Example 6.6. Estimating a properly specified quadratic cost model

Table 6.9 displays estimation results for equation (6.59). (Note: To offer a fair comparison to Mayo's estimation results, the generalized method of moments procedure was used to estimate the parameters of the cost model.)

Discussion of Table 6.9 results

The estimation results that are displayed in Table 6.9 are much improved over the previous two models. The signs of the estimates accord with a priori expectations, in that cost increases at a decreasing rate. Furthermore, the input price coefficients are of an appropriate magnitude given the type of firms in the data set. This is confirmed by the adjusted R^2, which indicates that 96% of the variation in cost is explained by the variables in the equation.

Table 6.9 Estimation Results, Equation (6.59)

Variable	Coefficient	Estimate	t-statistic
Constant	a_0	0.031229	6.66
Y	a_y	0.002602	12.63
Y^2	a_{yy}	−0.000001	−6.17
Capital price	b_k	0.070645	1.57
Purchased power	b_p	0.698658	17.50
Labor price	b_l	0.230697	6.09
Adjusted R^2		0.959	

End of section exercises

The data set Coops97 contains data on 711 distribution coops that were RUS borrowers in 1997.

1. Obtain summary statistics for the variables in the data set.
2. Estimate the equations used in Examples 6.4–6.6. Confirm the results that are displayed in Tables 6.7–6.9.
   a. Do you find that any of the models fail to converge?
   b. Concerning Mayo's model, estimate the unrestricted model (the model prior to imposing the three steps delineated previously). What do you find?
   c. Next, estimate the model using the generalized method of moments procedure. Is convergence achieved? Why or why not?
   d. Despite nonconvergence, the previous step should have yielded estimates for the parameters in the model. Using those as starting values, reestimate the equation. Is convergence attained? Why or why not?
   e. Finally, impose linear homogeneity by restricting the estimates of the input prices sum to unity. Does this achieve convergence? Note: If not, you will likely need to reset the convergence criterion or increase the number of iterations that the estimation procedure requires.
3. Assuming convergence was attained, calculate the degree of scale economies (SCE) using equation (6.22) and the estimation results from
   a. The basic cost model, equation (6.53).
   b. Mayo's cost model, equation (6.55).
   c. Greer's cost model, equation (6.59).
   What are your findings? Are they similar?

4. Add the cost shift variables, miles of transmission lines and density, then reestimate equations (6.55) and (6.59).

   a. Do the parameter estimates accord with a priori expectations in terms of sign and statistical significance?

   b. Calculate the degree of scale economies using the results obtained. Are they different than what was obtained in Exercise 6.3? If so, how are they different?

6.4 MEASURES OF EFFICIENCY FOR MULTIPLE-OUTPUT MODELS

You may recall the discussion from Chapter 2 concerning economies of scale. For a multiple-output model, it is no longer the case that scale economies may be obtained by dividing average cost by marginal cost. Now, not one but several concepts are relevant for the analysis. A brief review of the concepts is in order.

Ray cost output elasticity

The first measure to be computed is that of the ray cost output elasticity. Ray average costs describe the behavior of the cost function as output is expanded proportionally along a ray emanating from the origin. Ray average cost is defined as

$$RAC(y) = C(y)/\sum y_i \tag{6.70}$$

Ray cost output elasticity describes how responsive cost is to a change in output along a ray emanating from the origin. In general, ray cost output elasticities depend on not only the level of output but also on the output mix between Y_1 and Y_2.

Product-specific economies of scale

Because output is not always expanded proportionally for a multiproduct firm, the concept of incremental cost must be examined. This is defined as

$$AIC_i(Y) \equiv IC_i(Y)/Y \tag{6.48}$$

This allows for the identification of returns to scale that are specific to a particular output, known as *product-specific returns to scale*, which are expressed as

$$S_i(Y) = IC_i(Y)/Y_i C_i \tag{6.49}$$

which is equivalent to

$$S_i(Y) = \text{AIC}(Y_i)/(\partial C/\partial Y_i) \tag{6.50}$$

According to Baumol et al. (1982), $S_i(Y)$ has a natural interpretation in that the revenues collected from the sale of a product i (Y_iC_i) when its price equals marginal cost exceed, equal, or fall short of the incremental cost (IC_i) incurred by offering that product, as $S_i(Y)$ is less than, equal to, or greater than unity, respectively. Thus, returns to the scale of product i are said to be increasing, decreasing, or constant as $S_i(Y)$ is greater than, less than, or equal to unity. Since $S_i(Y)$ is the increment in the firm's total cost that results from the addition of an entire product to the firm's set of products, and if the marginal cost is less than the average incremental cost, the latter has a negative derivative and will decline as Y_i increases (Baumol et al., 1982).

Furthermore, the degree of product-specific returns to scale, which measures the economies or diseconomies uniquely associated with the production of a single output given that the firm may produce positive amounts of other products for the former, is given by

$$S_i = \left(\alpha_i Y_i + \tfrac{1}{2} \alpha_{ii} Y_i^2 + \tfrac{1}{2} \sum_{i \neq j} \alpha_{ij} Y_i Y_j \right) / \left(\alpha_i Y_i + \alpha_{ii} Y_i^2 + \sum_{i \neq j} \alpha_{ij} Y_i Y_j \right) \tag{6.71}$$

In general, for the quadratic functional form, the economies or diseconomies associated with the production of a single product (given that the firm produces positive amounts of other products) is determined by the sign of the estimated coefficient of the squared term in output. That is,

$S_i > 0$ for α_{ii}(estimated coefficient of squared $-$ output variable) < 0

$S_i < 0$ for α_{ii}(estimated coefficient of output $-$ squared variable) > 0

The concepts of ray average cost, average incremental cost, and product-specific economies of scale can all be characterized with the behavior of a cost hypersurface in a cross-section of cost and output space.

In addition, there exists a crucial cost concept that cannot be characterized in this fashion, since it involves the simultaneous production of several outputs in a single enterprise. Such economies result from the scope of a firm's operations, rather than from the scale of its operations. This is the topic of the next section.

Economies of scope

Economies of scope (or economies of joint production) are said to exist if a given quantity of each of two or more goods can be produced by one firm at a lower cost than if each good were produced separately by two different firms or even two different production processes. That is, for a two-product case, weak economies of scope are given by

$$C(Y_1, Y_2) \leq C(Y_1, 0) + C(0, Y_2) \qquad (6.51)$$

for all Y_1, $Y_2 > 0$. If not, then there are diseconomies of scope, and separate production of outputs is more efficient.

Useful here is a measure of the degree of economies of scope that would allow for, in the presence of economies of scope, the capturing of the relative increase in cost that would result from separate production of the two (or more) outputs. Therefore, the degree of economies of scope is given by

$$S_c = [C(Y_1, 0) + C(0, Y_2) - C(Y_1, Y_2)]/C(Y_1, Y_2) \qquad (6.52)$$

It is important to keep in mind that, due to the regulated nature of this industry, there exists a divergence between the *actual* economies experienced and those that could *potentially* result if the industry were not regulated. It is well documented in the literature that regulation reduces the competitiveness or efficiency of firms. First, due to the lack of entry and second via the average-cost pricing mechanism imposed on firms in the industry. Mayo mentions this in his 1984 paper, which, among others, attempts to identify the existence of scope economies in this industry. Using a sample of 200 firms (privately owned electric and natural gas utilities), he employs a modified (short-run, since incorporates fixed costs) multiproduct quadratic cost function to estimate the cost of producing both electricity and gas and confirms the presence of economies of scope for small firms using 1979 data. However, as output increases, he asserts that the absence of competitive pressure leads to cost inefficiencies and eventual diseconomies of scope.

For the multiproduct quadratic cost model given in equation (6.56), the degree of economies of scope, S_c, is given by

$$S_c = [\alpha_0 - (\tfrac{1}{2})\alpha_{12} Y_1 Y_2]/[\alpha_0 + \alpha_1 Y_1 + \alpha_2 Y_2 + (\tfrac{1}{2})$$
$$\times (\alpha_{11} Y_1^2 + \alpha_{22} Y_2^2 + \alpha_{12} Y_1 Y_2)] \qquad (6.72)$$

for $S_c > 0$, there are economies of scope in the production of both goods.

Cost complementarity

You may also recall from Chapter 2 that cost complementarity, which requires that the marginal or incremental costs of any output decline when that output or any other output is increased, is a sufficient condition for economies of scope. For a twice differential multiproduct cost function, cost complementarity exists if

$$\partial^2 C(Y)/\partial Y_i \partial Y_j < 0, \quad \text{for } i \neq j \qquad (6.73)$$

The sign of the estimated coefficient of the interaction term in output determines whether there are cost complementarities (interproduct complementarities) in the distribution of output.

Example 6.4

Using the data set Coops97, estimate the parameters of a two-output, three-input-price cost function (given in equation (6.59)). The outputs are electricity distributed to small users (Y_1) and electricity distributed to large users (Y_2) with the prices of labor, capital, and purchased power as inputs. Estimation results are displayed in Table 6.10.

Discussion of Table 6.10

The estimation results accord with a priori expectations in terms of the signs of the estimated coefficients and indicate that cost increases with output at a decreasing rate. The adjusted R^2 indicates that the model explains over 96% of the variation in the cost of distributing electricity in 1997.

Table 6.10 Estimation Results, Equation (6.59)

Coefficient	Variable	Estimate	t-statistic
a_0	Constant	0.0188620	7.30
a_1	Y_1	0.0028870	17.05
a_2	Y_2	0.0018150	12.72
a_{11}	Y_1^2	−0.0000007	−3.62
a_{22}	Y_2^2	−0.0000003	−2.22
a_{21}	$Y_1 Y_2$	−0.0000005	−1.17
b_k	$\ln p_k$	0.027516	0.80
b_p	$\ln p_p$	0.650672	23.2
b_l	$\ln p_l$	0.321813	11.68
Adjusted R^2		0.96	

6.5 CHAPTER CONCLUSION

This chapter provides a rather extensive overview of several cost models used to estimate efficiency in the distribution of electricity to end users. The exercises at the end of each section provide hands-on experience with data analysis, model estimation, and the interpretation of the results.

The next chapter (Chapter 7) provides a case study, which is an update on a paper that was published in *Energy Economics* in 2003. In this study, data from 1996 were used to examine how efficient rural electric cooperatives were in the distribution of electricity. Using some of the measures discussed in this chapter, the findings are that most coops were too small (in terms of the amount of electricity distributed to end users) and that cost savings could emerge via horizontal mergers among member systems, especially those that serve contiguous service territories.

6.6 END OF CHAPTER EXERCISES: MULTIPLE-OUTPUT COST MODELS

Again using the data set Coops97, perform the following exercises for the multiproduct cost models described in this chapter.

1. Estimate a multiple-output version of equation (6.59), in which the outputs are electricity distributed to small users (residential and small commercial customers, Y_1) and that distributed to large users (large commercial and industrial users, Y_2). Do your results accord with those in Table 6.10? If not, how are they different?
   a. Was convergence attained? Why or why not? (If not, try steps 1–3 detailed previously).
   b. Assuming that convergence was attained, calculate the degree of product-specific scale economies using equation (6.71) and the estimation results displayed in Table 6.10 at the sample means of the variables.
   c. Do you find that there are product-specific economies of scale in the distribution of electricity to small customers (Y_1)?
   d. What about to larger customers (Y_2)?
   e. What do you conclude about the firms in the sample data set?
2. Again assuming that convergence was obtained, calculate the degree of economies of scope using equation (6.72) and the estimation results that are displayed in Table 6.10. What do you conclude about the firms in the sample data set?

3. Add the cost-shift variables, miles of transmission line and density, then reestimate equation (6.59).
    a. Does the addition of these variables improve your results?
    b. Do the signs of the coefficient estimates accord with theory? Why or why not?

6.7 APPENDIX: PROOFS

Quadratic cost equation not linearly homogeneous

The quadratic cost equation of the following form is not linearly homogeneous in input prices:

$$C = \alpha_0 + \alpha_y Y + \tfrac{1}{2}\,\alpha_{yy} Y^2 + \beta_k p_k + \beta_L p_L + \beta_P p_P \tag{6A.1}$$

Proof

As an example, let $Y = 1$, $p_K = \$5$, $p_L = \$10$, and $p_P = \$5$. Furthermore, assume that the following estimates are obtained for the input price coefficients: $\beta_K = \beta_L = \beta_P = 0.333$. Therefore, the predicted cost is given by

$$C = Z + 0.33(\$5) + 0.33(\$10) + 0.33(\$5) \tag{6.A2}$$

or

$$C = Z + \$6.60$$

where

$$Z = \alpha_0 + \alpha_y + \tfrac{1}{2}\alpha_{yy} \tag{6A.3}$$

Now, let prices double. It follows that

$$C = Z + 0.33(\$10) + 0.33(\$20) + 0.33(\$10)$$

or,

$$C = Z + \$12.12$$

Clearly, the total cost has not doubled (it has increased by only $5.52). *QED*

Proper cost function

The following equation is a proper cost function, as defined in Chapter 4 and in this chapter.

$$C = \left(\alpha_0 + \alpha_Y Y + \tfrac{1}{2} \times \alpha_{YY} Y^2\right) p_K^{\beta_k} p_L^{\beta_l} p_P^{\beta_p} e^{\varepsilon} \tag{6A.4}$$

Proof: Increasing in factor prices

Let x_i (p, Y) be the firm's conditional factor demand for input i at price p_i. By Shephard's lemma,

$$\partial C(\mathbf{p}, Y)/\partial p_i = x_i(\mathbf{p}, y) \geq 0 \tag{6A.5}$$

In this case, the conditional factor demands for capital, labor, and purchased power are given by

$$\partial C(\mathbf{p}, Y)/\partial p_k = x_k(\mathbf{p}, Y) = (\beta_k)p_K^{(\beta k - 1)}\left(\alpha_0 + \alpha_Y Y + \tfrac{1}{2}\alpha_{YY} Y^2\right)p_L^{\beta l}p_P^{\beta p} \geq 0 \tag{6A.6}$$

$$\partial C(\mathbf{p}, Y)/\partial p_L = x_L(\mathbf{p}, Y) = (\beta_L)p_L^{(\beta L - 1)}\left(\alpha_0 + \alpha_Y Y + \tfrac{1}{2}\alpha_{YY} Y^2\right)p_K^{\beta K}p_P^{\beta P} \geq 0 \tag{6A.7}$$

$$\partial C(\mathbf{p}, Y)/\partial p_P = x_P(\mathbf{p}, Y) = (\beta_P)p_P^{(\beta P - 1)}\left(\alpha_0 + \alpha_Y Y + \tfrac{1}{2}\alpha_{YY} Y^2\right)p_L^{\beta L}p_K^{\beta K} \geq 0 \tag{6A.8}$$

Since nonnegative amounts of inputs (x_i) at nonnegative prices (p_i) are required to produce nonnegative quantities of output (Y) at nonnegative marginal costs (which implies that the quadratic term in parentheses is nonnegative) *and*, by linear homogeneity in input prices, that is,

$$\beta_K + \beta_L + \beta_P = 1 \tag{6A.9}$$

where $\beta_K, \beta_L, \beta_P \geq 0$, then this cost function is increasing in factor prices. QED

Proof: Concavity in input prices

This requires that the matrix of second derivatives of the cost function with respect to input prices must be a symmetric, negative semi-definite matrix. This has several implications:

1. The cross-price effects are symmetric (by Young's theorem).
2. The own-price effects are negative. That is,

$$\partial^2 C(\mathbf{p}, Y)/\partial p_i^2 \leq 0 \tag{6A.10}$$

In the case of the modified quadratic equation, the own-price effects are, for capital,

$$\partial^2 C(\mathbf{p}, Y)/\partial p_K^2 = (\beta_k - 1)(\beta_k)p_K^{(\beta k - 2)}\left(\alpha_0 + \alpha_Y Y + \tfrac{1}{2}\alpha_{YY} Y^2\right)p_L^{\beta L}p_P^{\beta P} \tag{6A.11}$$

for labor,

$$\partial^2 C(\mathbf{p}, Y)/\partial p_L^2 = (\beta_L - 1)(\beta_L)p_L^{(\beta L - 2)}\left(\alpha_0 + \alpha_Y Y + \frac{1}{2}\alpha_{YY}Y^2\right)p_K^{\beta k}p_P^{\beta P}$$

(6A.12)

for purchased power,

$$\partial^2 C(\mathbf{p}, Y)/\partial p_P^2 = (\beta_P - 1)(\beta_P)p_P^{(\beta P - 2)}\left(\alpha_0 + \alpha_Y Y + \frac{1}{2}\alpha_{YY}Y^2\right)p_K^{\beta k}p_L^{\beta L}$$

(6A.13)

Again, since $C(\mathbf{p}, Y)$ is linear homogeneous in input prices, the first term on the right-hand side is negative. The remaining terms are positive:
a. $\beta_K, \beta_L, \beta_P \geq 0$.
b.   By Shephard's lemma,

$$\partial C(\mathbf{p}, Y)/\partial p_i = x_i(\mathbf{p}, y) \geq 0 \qquad (6A.14)$$

Positive amounts of inputs (p_i) are required to produce positive quantities of output, so $p_i \geq 0$.
c.   Monotonicity in output (as well as positive marginal cost) ensures that the quadratic term in the parentheses is positive.
     Thus, own-price effects are negative as required.   QED

3.   For monotonicity in output (Y), an increase (decrease) in output always increases (decreases) total cost. That is, marginal cost must be nonnegative for the range of outputs in the sample. In this case, the marginal cost is given by

$$\partial C(\mathbf{p}, Y)/\partial Y = (\alpha_Y + \alpha_{YY}Y)p_K^{\beta k}p_L^{\beta L}p_P^{\beta P} \geq 0 \qquad (6A.15)$$

which holds as long as $Y \geq -\alpha_Y/\alpha_{YY}$. (This must be checked for every level of output.)

4.   For linear homogeneous in input prices, let

$$Z = [\alpha_0 + \alpha_y Y + (\frac{1}{2})\alpha_{yy}Y^2] \qquad (6A.16)$$

And impose that

$$\sum \beta_i = 1 \qquad (6A.17)$$

In addition, let $Y = 1$, $p_K = \$5$, $p_L = \$10$, and $p_P = \$5$. Furthermore, suppose that the following estimates are obtained for the input price coefficients: $\beta_K = \beta_L = \beta_P = 0.333$. Therefore, the predicted cost is given by

$$C = (Z)(5^{0.33}10^{0.33}5^{0.33})$$

or

$$C = Z \times (6.288)$$

Next, let input prices double, which implies that predicted cost is given by

$$C = Z \times (10^{0.33} 20^{0.33} 10^{0.33})$$

or

$$C = Z \times 12.567$$

Clearly, total cost has doubled as a result of input prices that have doubled and linear homogeneity is preserved by this modification. *QED*

Aside

While it is true that taking logs preserves all of the properties of the original function, I offer a proof of linear homogeneity of the log-linearized version of (1) simply as a check. However, in this case, I let the estimated coefficients vary in magnitude so that $\beta_K = 0.15$, $\beta_L = 0.25$, and $\beta_P = 0.60$.

Proof

In logs, the equation to be estimated is given by

$$\ln C = \ln Z + \beta_K \ln p_K + \beta_L \ln p_L + \beta_P \ln p_P + \varepsilon \qquad (6A.18)$$

Evaluating at sample means ($\ln Z$ is constant), the predicted cost is given by

$$\ln C = \text{Constant} + 0.15\,(1.6055) + 0.25\,(2.895) + 0.60\,(1.38)$$

or

$$\ln C = \text{Constant} + 0.2408 + 0.72375 + 0.828 = 1.79$$

Next, doubling each input price (and taking logs), then evaluating at sample means yields

$$\ln C = \text{Constant} + 0.15\,(2.2986) + 0.25\,(3.583) + 0.60\,(2.073)$$

or

$$\ln C = \text{Constant} + 0.3448 + 0.896 + 1.244 = 2.4846$$

Doubling input prices increases $\ln C$ by 0.6946, the exponential of which is equal to 2.003, indicating that total cost has doubled from a doubling of input prices. Thus, linear homogeneity in input prices is preserved. *QED*

CHAPTER 7

Case Study: Can Rural Electric Cooperatives Survive in a Restructured U.S. Electric Market? An Empirical Analysis

7.1 ABSTRACT

This paper examines the ability of rural electric distribution cooperatives to continue operating in their present form in a restructured electricity market. More specifically, I develop and estimate a quadratic cost model, which, unlike many of the cost functions employed in studies of this nature, conforms to all of the properties of a proper cost function. Using 1996 data, I find that these firms are not operating in a cost–minimizing fashion. This finding seems to occur because each is too small in terms of the quantity of electricity distributed. As a result, mergers between these firms could yield substantial savings and help ensure their survival in their present form in a deregulated market.

7.2 INTRODUCTION

In 1996, the Federal Energy Regulatory Commission issued Orders 888 and 889, which were designed to promote competition in wholesale markets for electricity in the United States. These orders were meant to apply predominantly to vertically integrated investor-owned utilities (IOUs); however, when competition did not emerge as was hoped, the FERC issued Order 2000, which indicated the FERC's intent to make *all* transmission owning entities, including those of cooperatively owned utilities and the federal power administrations, subject to FERC jurisdiction.

Reasons that cooperatively owned utilities are different

In the United States, electric cooperatives (coops) are organized as either generation and transmission (G&Ts) or distribution only (member coops), with long-term contracts in place to render them quasi-vertically integrated. However, unlike investor-owned utilities, not all states regulate electric cooperatives. In fact, fewer than 20 states have jurisdiction over coops, and the degree of regulation is not consistent among these states. For example, in Florida, Indiana, Maine, and Mississippi, the public regulatory commissions do not regulate the rates charged by coops. This inconsistency creates a special challenge for federal policy makers in the United States. Other differences between investor-owned utilities and coops include

- Urban vs. rural differences.
- Institutional differences.
- Regulatory differences.
- Philosophical differences.

Each of these will be discussed in turn.

Urban versus rural differences

Electric cooperatives were created in 1936 by the Rural Electrification Act to serve those areas that the profit-driven investor-owned utilities were unwilling to serve. Prior to the creation of this act, fewer than 12% of rural farm homes were electrified. By 1941, over 35% of these homes had been electrified (U.S. Bureau of the Census, 1975).

Rural areas are quite different from the urban areas that tend to be served by investor-owned utilities. As a result, the effects of electric restructuring on those customers who are served by rural electric cooperatives are different than those served in urban areas by investor-owned utilities. Given the special properties that characterize electricity (e.g., that it is essentially nonstorable and follows the path of least resistance), coupled with the yet to be discussed differences between rural and urban areas, a standard, federally mandated cookie cutter approach to deregulation of this industry will not work. These urban rural disparities are discussed later.

First, rural areas tend to be far less densely populated with a terrain that is more rugged compared to urban areas, which renders them more costly to serve. In addition, coops in rural areas serve mostly residential loads, which tend to be much smaller and more volatile in nature, often demanding power during peak times. Thus, on a per customer basis, distribution coops face far higher costs than their investor-owned counterparts.[1]

---

[1] In 1996, the average rural distribution coop served fewer than 6 customers per mile of distribution line and received about $7000 per mile, while their investor-owned counterparts in urban areas served almost 40 customers per mile and received over $60,000 per mile of line. Furthermore, according to the National Rural Electric Cooperative Association (NRECA), the average investment in distribution plant per consumer was $1975, which implies that coops invested $11,850 per mile versus $1535 for IOUs.

In addition, rural incomes tend to be lower than those in urban areas. According to the Economic Research Service, U.S. nonmetropolitan incomes were 26% below those in metropolitan areas in 1996. Not surprising, rural adults tend to have less education than their urban counterparts and often face local labor markets that offer few opportunities to advance beyond low-paying entry level jobs (Economic Research Service, Briefing Room, Rural Labor and Education).

Institutional differences

There are institutional differences between coops and IOUs in the United States. The first is the 85% rule, which applies to both G&T and distribution cooperatives. In the United States, both G&Ts and the distribution cooperatives must obtain 85% of their revenues from their members or they lose their tax-exempt status. This limitation has two significant effects. First, it effectively limits (and possibly even precludes, depending on capacity and native load sales) the G&Ts from participating in the wholesale power market, even though their generation costs tend to be lower than those of investor-owned firms (due, in part, to their access to less expensive federally produced power). Second, it severely limits the extent of retail competition that can take place, since distribution cooperatives are subject to the same restriction for tax exempt status; that is, 85% of revenues must come from their member end-use customers. As such, there is a high cost penalty to rural areas for coops to participate in retail choice. Moreover, since the increase in cost due to the tax would be passed directly through to members, on a per member basis, this could result in significant increases in rates given the low densities that tend to prevail in rural areas.

In addition to the tax implications of restructuring, a potential stranded cost issue must be examined. For G&Ts to obtain low-interest financing from the Rural Utilities Service, they are required to have long-term (30-year), full requirements contracts with their member distribution cooperatives. Because of deregulation, these contracts could become stranded as retail choice is made available to rural customers. These contracts will not be forgiven; they are a debt that must be repaid. As owners of the G&T, member cooperatives are responsible for any debt incurred by the G&T on their behalf; in other words, residential customers could end up bearing most of this burden, especially if larger users choose to leave the cooperative system and purchase power elsewhere. As they leave the cooperative system, the G&T's member load is reduced as are its revenues, and the possibility of not being able to repay this debt becomes a reality (unless the rates of the remaining customers rise enough to offset the lost revenues).

Furthermore, it is well documented that industrial users subsidize residential ones; despite contributing to the peak demand, demand charges are typically not assessed to residential customers but are imposed upon large commercial and industrial users. As retail choice is made available, these larger users may choose an alternative supplier, thus imposing the full cost of service onto those small users who may or may not have a choice of suppliers.[2] As a result, rural residential users are doubly harmed; because of the lack of density, these higher costs would be spread across even fewer customers, resulting in rather substantial increases in rural residential rates.

Regulatory differences

As previously stated, not all of the states in the United States regulate cooperatives. In some of the states that do, the state's restructuring legislation included opt-out clauses or other special protections for cooperatively owned firms specifically included (the state of Texas, for example). For states that do not regulate the coops, opt-in clauses were included in for those coops that wanted to participate in retail choice (e.g., the state of Iowa). In other cases, the cooperatives were required to participate but were on a delayed schedule (in the state of Delaware, for example, where the coops were on a six month delay from the investor-owned utilities in the offering of retail access). The state of Maine provided an interesting twist: All consumers had the right to choose their electric supplier but the coops are prohibited from selling generation service outside their service territory. Finally, several states regulate coops but offer neither opt-out clauses nor is special language written into any restructuring legislation that had been passed (for example, in the state of Michigan, the coops were required to implement retail access on the same schedule as the investor-owned utilities).

Philosophical differences

Cooperative ownership implies different incentives than those of either investor or even municipal ownership. Due to the coincidence of buyers and sellers, presumably cooperatives follow a welfare-maximizing strategy,

---

[2] According to Nancy Brockway (1997, p. 14): "in a competitive market, low volume, low income customers likely will be the last served. . . . In fact, in a deregulated environment, firms uniformly may refuse to serve all customers with low incomes." Furthermore, recent experience from the telecommunications industry tends to confirm this.

entailing both producer and consumer surplus maximization. As a result, certain principal agent problems tend to arise that cannot be mitigated as easily as those in investor-owned firms. For example, in the case of the latter, in the United States, there is often incentive pay (i.e., bonuses) or profit sharing, and the ownership of stock. On the other hand, nonperformance of the firm may lead to the transfer of property rights (i.e., the selling of one's stock), a depressed stock price, and the loss of one's job. These motivating schemes are typically not offered to the managers of coops (the agents), which are nonprofit entities operating on a one vote per member system. Hence, the "stock" of the firm confers no real property rights on the principals (the consumer owners), and while there is the possibility of accruing capital credits, these credits cannot be received on demand.

7.3 LITERATURE REVIEW

Few studies of the electric utility industry include cooperatively owned firms in their data sets. A group of authors, however, tend to focus on the coops and cooperatively owned distribution systems in the continental United States. Claggett (1987) used a constant elasticity of substitution (CES) production function to estimate economies of scale for 50 cooperative distributors of the Tennessee Valley Authority and found increasing economies of scale in distribution, concluding that the individual cooperatives in this group should be increased in size.[3]

Studies on property rights include Hollas, Stansell, and Claggett (1988) and Claggett, Hollas, and Stansell (1995), who employ a profit function to test for absolute and relative price efficiency for proprietary, cooperative, and municipal electric distributors in the United States. Not surprising, they find little evidence to support profit-maximizing behavior on the part of either cooperatives or municipals. Hollas and Stansell (1991) employed a similar methodology but limited the study group to rural electric distribution cooperatives. They included a regulatory variable to differentiate between those states that regulate coops and those that do not. As in their previous study, they found that coops are not absolutely price efficient (i.e., do not maximize profits). The effect of property rights is further examined in Claggett (1994), who estimated a translogarithmic cost function and found that TVA cooperatives distribute power at a lower cost

---

[3] His results confirm those of Gallop and Roberts (1981) and Neuberg (1977), who found that significant economies exist in both transmission and distribution.

than the municipal distributors of TVA power. Hollas, Stansell, and Claggett (1994) also limit their study to municipal and cooperative distributors of TVA power. Assuming welfare maximization, the authors reject the null hypothesis that there is no difference between the rates charged by municipals and cooperatives, finding that municipally owned firms charge lower rates to residential and commercial users but higher rates to industrial ones.

Berry's 1994 paper is a product of his dissertation, the purpose of which is to show that cooperatively owned electric utilities are far less efficient than their privately owned counterparts. However, his results are suspect since, to compare the results at various levels of output, Berry essentially adds the G&Ts' total cost to that of the distribution cooperatives, in an attempt to provide a common structure to that of the investor-owned firms in the sample. The problem herein is that the G&Ts and the distribution cooperatives in the sample are not necessarily related (in the sense that the distribution cooperatives in the sample are not necessarily member coops of the G&Ts in the sample), thus rendering this type of aggregation invalid.

7.4 COST MODELS

Modeling the cost of distributing electricity as a multiple output process is well documented in the economic literature.[4] The motivation for this is several fold: First, large industrial customers tend to have more stable demand patterns than their residential or small commercial counterparts, the latter of whom tend to increase demand during peak times when the more expensive generating units are likely to be online. Another reason is that public utility commissions tend to set rates with such a distinction; typically the large industrial customers pay demand charges, not the residential or small commercial ones. Finally, often, large users can accept electricity at higher voltages than their smaller counterparts; as such, they tend to be less costly to serve and experience lower line losses. Given this, a two-output approach is taken here.

In specifying a proper cost function, several properties must be ensured. First, it must be nonnegative, nondecreasing, concave, and linear homogeneous in input prices. Second, it should be capable of estimation

---

[4] For example, studies by Kwoka (1996), Hollas et al. (1994), Berry (1994), Karlson (1986), and Roberts (1986).

with zero values of some outputs, which means that it should allow for economies of scale and scope and subadditivity. While no single form satisfies all these conditions, the two most commonly employed in cost estimation are the translogarithmic and the quadratic, both of which are flexible enough to avoid a priori restrictions on the elasticities of substitution among the input variables.

Flexible cost models

Translogarithmic cost models
In modeling the cost function for the distribution of electricity, the translogarithmic functional form dominates the literature and is quite suitable to single-output cost specifications. Although often employed to estimate multiple-output cost specifications, "its inability to contend with zero output values effectively precludes a finding of economies of scope" (Kwoka, 1996). When employed in this analysis, the estimation results were not as expected, namely, the incorrectly signed second partial derivatives of two of the input prices cause this specification to fail to test for a proper cost function. As such, this form is discarded for the purposes of this analysis.

Quadratic cost models
Another functional form that can be used is the quadratic, which is superior to the translogarithmic for multiple-output specifications. Again quoting John Kwoka (1996), in contrast to the translog, "it allows for the unconstrained emergence of economies of scale and scope as well as subadditivity." In general, the multiple-output quadratic cost function is given by

$$C = \alpha_0 + \sum_i \alpha_i Y_i + \frac{1}{2} \sum_i \sum_j \alpha_{ij} Y_i Y_j + \sum \beta_k p_k \qquad (7.1)$$

where Y_j, Y_i are the outputs and p_k are input prices.

While this is the form often employed in the electric utility cost literature, this equation is not homogeneous of degree 1 in input prices, which ensures that doubling input prices doubles total cost.

To get around this, Mayo (1984) imposed linear homogeneity by appending to a multiple-output cost function the product of the input prices times their estimated coefficients. That is, he estimated the following equation:

$$C = \left(\alpha_0 + \sum_i \alpha_i Y_i + \frac{1}{2} \sum_i \sum_j \alpha_{ij} Y_i Y_j \right) \cdot \Pi \beta_k p_k \qquad (7.2)$$

where $i, j = 1, 2$. In this form, output (Y_i, which is the quantity of electricity distributed in megawatt-hours) enters as a quadratic.

When a multiproduct model is estimated, all outputs enter the equation both as squared and as interaction variables. Furthermore, Mayo's model imposes strict input–output separability, which means that the marginal rate of substitution between any two inputs is independent of the quantities of outputs, and the marginal rate of transformation between any two outputs is independent of the quantities of inputs. However, studies by both Karlson (1986) and Henderson (1985) reject the separability of inputs from outputs in the distribution of electricity.

Therefore, it is necessary to modify this equation so that individual input price estimates may be obtained while preserving the cost equations' underlying properties. I derived such a modification, which is detailed in the next section and referred to as the *modified quadratic cost model*.

Modified quadratic cost function

The modification I made is to allow the input price parameters to enter exponentially rather than multiplicatively, which preserves the requisite properties to which a proper cost function must conform. The modified equation to be estimated here is given by

$$C = \left(\alpha_0 + \sum_i \alpha_i Y_i + \frac{1}{2} \sum_i \sum_j \alpha_{ij} Y_i Y_j \right) \Pi p_k^{\beta k} e^{\varepsilon} \qquad (7.3)$$

This cost function is concave, nondecreasing, and homogeneous of degree 1 in input prices as well as monotonic in output, and as such, preserves the fundamental properties of a proper cost function. (A proof that this model conforms to each of these properties is given in the Appendix to Chapter 6.)

Estimation of this particular equation is somewhat problematic. Because it is highly nonlinear, the stochastic error term does not enter additively as required. Hence, the model must be transformed to allow it to be additive. A logarithmic transformation, which yields such an error term, is made possible by the creation of a variable, Z, where

$$Z = \left(\alpha_0 + \sum_i \alpha_i Y_i + \frac{1}{2} \sum_i \sum_j \alpha_{ij} Y_i Y_j \right) \qquad (7.4)$$

so that the modified quadratic cost equation

$$C = \left(\alpha_0 + \sum_i \alpha_i Y_i + \frac{1}{2} \sum_i \sum_j \alpha_{ij} Y_i Y_j \right) p_k^{\beta k} p_L^{\beta L} p_P^{\beta P} e^{\varepsilon} \qquad (7.3')$$

becomes

$$\text{In } C = \zeta \text{ In } Z + \beta_K \text{ In } p_K + \beta_L \text{ In } p_L + \beta_p \text{ In } p_P + \varepsilon \qquad (7.5)$$

where ζ has been restricted to unity.[5]

Data and variables

The National Rural Electric Cooperative Association provided the data used in this study. Contained herein is all pertinent information on the distribution cooperatives that distributed electricity in the United States over the 1997–2001 period. Given the nature of the data, cost models (rather than production functions) are appropriate here.

The distribution of electricity requires a large infrastructure investment in poles and conductors, voltage transformers, and in the transmission and distribution lines themselves. Because of the low customer density in the territory served by distribution cooperatives, the average cost of providing such service is quite high. To estimate the cost of distributing electricity, numerous variables are included and estimated, with the final specification including the following:

C = Total cost: operating deductions + interest on long-term debt.

Y_1 = Electricity distributed to residential and small commercial users in MWh.

Y_2 = Electricity distributed to large commercial and industrial users in MWh.

P_i = Input prices: capital (k), labor (l), and purchased power (p).

O_i = Other (cost shift) variables: miles of transmission line[6] and density, which is the number of customers per mile of distribution line.

A properly specified multiple-output quadratic cost equation

Including the cost-shift variables yields the final cost function to be estimated, which is given by:

$$C = \left(\alpha_0 + \sum_i \alpha_i Y_i + \frac{1}{2} \sum_i \sum_j \alpha_{ij} Y_i Y_j \right) p_k^{\beta k} p_L^{\beta L} p_P^{\beta P} O^{\theta tm} O^{\theta d} e^{\varepsilon} \qquad (7.6)$$

---

[5] This is the true value of ζ, since equation (7.3) is equivalent to

$$C = \left(\alpha_0 + \sum_i \alpha_i Y_i + \sum_i \sum_j \alpha_{ij} Y_i Y_j \right)^{\zeta} p_k^{\beta k} p_L^{\beta L} p_P^{\beta P} e^{\zeta}$$

when $\zeta = 1$.

[6] Data for estimation purposes are true; however, calculating predicted values for cost concepts use $\ln t_r = 0$, so missing the variable miles of transmission lines is equal to unity. This way predicted values for cost and measures can be calculated.

Taking the natural logarithm yields the actual equation to be estimated, which is given by

$$\ln C = \zeta \ln Z + \beta_K \ln p_K + \beta_L \ln p_L + \beta_P \ln p_p + \theta_{tm} \ln O_{tm}$$
$$+ \theta_d \ln O_d + \varepsilon \qquad (7.7)$$

Estimation results

Table 7.1 contains the results from estimating equation (7.7). These results accord with a priori expectations in terms of the signs and statistical significance of the estimates. First and foremost, total cost increases with output at a decreasing rate. Furthermore, both of the squared-output terms are negative in sign (as expected); as such, this cost model is concave in output and generates ray economies and product-specific economies of scale. Finally, the negatively signed (and statistically significant) coefficient on the interaction term between outputs indicates cost complementarity (defined in Chapter 2), which is a sufficient condition for economies of scope.

Table 7.1 Estimation Results, Quadratic Cost Model

Variable	Coefficient	Estimate	t-statistic
Constant	α_0	0.0248	16.51
Outputs (MWh)			
Y_1 = electricity distributed to small users	α_1	0.0044	35.62
Y_2 = electricity distributed to large users	α_2	0.0024	27.45
Y_1^2 = squared output (small users)	α_{11}	−0.0000005	−4.11
Y_2^2 = squared output (large users)	α_{22}	−0.00000003	−0.48
$Y_1 Y_2 (Y_2 Y_1)$ = output cross-product	α_{12}	−0.0000006	−2.66
Input prices			
Labor, p_L	β_L	0.2161	17.13
Capital price, p_K	β_K	0.2211	14.15
Purchased power, p_P	β_P	0.5629	50.35
Cost shifters			
Transmission lines (miles)	θ_{TM}	0.0326	22.67
Density	θ_D	−0.1136	−20.07

Cost concepts applicable to multiproduct cases

Ray average costs

In Chapter 2, it was explained that ray average costs (RAC) describe the behavior of the cost function as output is expanded *proportionally* along a ray emanating from the origin. In the two-product case, the behavior of costs along a cross-section of the total cost surface is considered. Defining a *composite* good, this measure allows a calculation of the average cost of this particular bundle and is given by

$$RAC = C(tY^0)/t \tag{7.8}$$

where Y^0 is the unit bundle for a particular mix of outputs and t is the number of units in the bundle such that $Y = tY^0$ (Baumol, Panzar, and Willig, 1982, p. 49). (This is also equation (2.23) and displayed in Figure 2.5.)

Degree of scale economies

You may recall from Chapter 2 that the degree of scale economies, S_N, is equal to the ratio of average cost to marginal cost in the single-output case. In the multiple-output case, we have

$$S_N(Y) = C(Y)/Y_i C_i(Y), \text{ for } i = 1, \dots, n \tag{7.9}$$

where $C_i(Y)$ is the marginal cost with respect to Y_i.

Given a two-output quadratic cost specification of the following form,

$$C = \left(\alpha_0 + \sum_i \alpha_i Y_i + \tfrac{1}{2} \sum_i \sum_j \alpha_{ij} Y_i Y_j \right) \Pi p_k^{\beta k} p_L^{\beta L} p_P^{\beta P} O^{\theta tm} O^{\theta d} e^{\varepsilon} \tag{7.10}$$

average cost is given by

$$C(Y)/Y_i = \left[\left(\alpha_0 + \sum_i \alpha_i Y_i + \tfrac{1}{2} \sum_i \sum_j \alpha_{ij} Y_i Y_j \right) p_k^{\beta k} p_L^{\beta L} p_P^{\beta P} O^{\theta tm} O^{\theta d} e^{\varepsilon} \right] / Y_i \tag{7.11}$$

and marginal cost by

$$\partial C(Y)/\partial Y_i = \left(\alpha_i + \alpha_{ii} Y_i + \tfrac{1}{2} \alpha_{ij} Y_j \right) \Pi p_k^{\beta k} p_L^{\beta L} p_P^{\beta p} O^{\theta tm} O^{\theta d} \tag{7.12}$$

Substituting the estimation results displayed in Table 7.1 along with equations (7.11) and (7.12), the degree of scale economies for the firms in the sample can be calculated. In doing so, I find that the degree of scale economies for every coop in the data set is greater than unity.

Interpretation of results, economies of scale

It was stated in Chapter 2 that S_N (the degree of scale economies) may be interpreted as a measure of the percentage rate of decline or increase in ray average cost with respect to output and that returns to scale at the output point Y_i are increasing as S_N is greater than unity. Using the results displayed in Table 7.1 and evaluating equations (7.11) and (7.12) at the variables' sample means, it is readily apparent that all firms in the data set were operating in the increasing returns to scale portion of the cost curve in each year that comprised the data set (1997–2001). However, it appears that a majority of the firms were approaching the minimum efficient scale (which is attained when average cost equals marginal cost, or $S_N = 1.0$) since 90% of the observations yield a degree of scale economies that is less than 1.10. This is displayed in Figure 7.1.

Product-specific economies of scale

The degree of product-specific returns to scale measures the economies or diseconomies uniquely associated with the production of a single product (e.g., electricity distributed to smaller users), given that the firm may

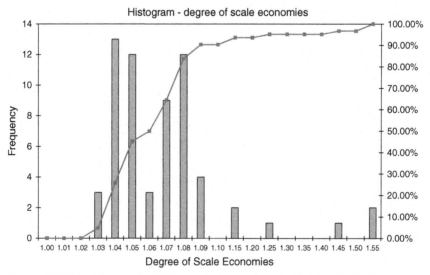

Figure 7.1 The degree of scale economies for rural electric distribution coops (1997–2001)

produce positive amounts of other products (that distributed to larger users). Since output is not always expanded proportionally for a multiproduct firm, incremental costs become relevant, the average of which is given by

$$AIC_i(Y) \equiv IC_i(Y)/Y_i \tag{7.13}$$

This allows for the identification of returns to scale that are specific to a particular output; in other words, the product-specific returns to scale, given by

$$S_i(Y) = AIC(Y_i)/(\partial C/\partial Y_i) \tag{7.14}$$

where the returns to the scale of product i are said to be increasing, decreasing, or constant as $S_i(Y)$ is greater than, less than, or equal to unity. Since $Si(Y)$ is the increment in the firm's total cost that results from the addition of an entire product to the firm's set of products, and if the marginal cost is less than the average incremental cost, the latter has a negative derivative and declines as Y_i increases.

Again using the estimation results in Table 7.1 and appealing to Baumol et al. (1982), we calculate the degree of product-specific returns to scale, which is given by

$$S_i(y) = \left(\alpha_i Y_i + \frac{1}{2}\alpha_{ii} Y_i^2 + \sum_{j \neq i} \alpha_{ij} Y_i Y_j \right) \Big/ \left(\alpha_i Y_i + \alpha_{ii} Y_i^2 + \sum_{j \neq i} \alpha_{ij} Y_i Y_j \right)$$

$$\tag{7.15}$$

(Note: You must multiply equation (7.15) by the price and cost-shift variables raised to their respective estimated coefficients.)

You may also recall from Chapter 4, "The Economics (and Econometrics) of Cost Models," that the implication of equation (7.15) is that

$$S_i > 1 \text{ as } 0 > \alpha_{ii} \tag{7.16}$$

Given the estimation results in Table 7.1, it is indeed the case that the squared-output coefficients (α_{11} and α_{22}) are negative in sign, which indicates that there are global economies in the distribution of electricity to each type of user, given that positive amounts of electricity are distributed to the other type of user. The results indicate that there are increasing returns to scale in distribution for the cooperatives in this sample, especially at higher levels of output. Thus, for 25% of the firms in the sample that distribute electricity only to smaller users (residential + commercial), gains in efficiency would result from also serving large commercial and industrial users.[7] In addition, the fact that the degree of product-specific returns is increasing (and at an increasing rate in output to large users, Y_2) indicates that those coops that serve large industrial loads quickly approach optimality from a cost-efficiency perspective.

An interesting example of this is provided by Kenergy, which was formed in 1999 by the merger between the Henderson Union and Green River, two western Kentucky distribution coops. Individually, each was among the largest distributors in the United States and collectively they formed the largest system, distributing almost three times as much electricity as the next largest distribution system (and more than 100 times the average system) in the years after they merged.

What is interesting is that they are the only entity in which the degree of product-specific returns for Y_1 (S_1 (y)) is less than unity while for Y_2, S_2 (y) is greater than unity!

Economies of scope

The final measure to be explored here is that of economies of scope. Economies of scope (or economies of joint production) are said to exist if a given quantity of each of two or more goods can be produced by one firm at a lower cost than if each good were produced separately by two different firms or even two different production processes. In other words, economies result from the scope of a firm's operations rather than from the scale of its operations. For a two-product case, weak economies of scope are given by

$$C\big(Y_1, Y_2\big) \leq C\big(Y_1, 0\big) + C(0, Y_2) \qquad (7.17)$$

for all Y_1, $Y_2 > 0$ (Baumol et al., 1982). Otherwise, separate production of outputs is more efficient.

---

[7] Unfortunately, this may prove to be a daunting task, since these large users are likely to be pursued by competitive suppliers, offering them very good deals to switch. Moreover, should these industrial users choose to leave the cooperative system, the effect on the remaining members could be devastating; it is no secret that industrial users subsidize both residential and commercial users. Because of the low density in rural areas, residential customers are especially costly to serve and pay nowhere near the true cost that they impose on the system (especially those in very remote areas who may require several miles of distribution line, a dedicated transformer, etc.). For example, residential customers typically do not pay demand charges; in addition, according to Comnes et al., "it is not uncommon for customer access charges to be priced below marginal cost" (1995, n. 49). Thus, should an industrial customer leave the system, both residential and commercial rates would have to increase substantially to cover the demand (or capacity) charges previously paid by the industrial customer. And, since rural incomes tend to be lower than those in urban areas (Economic Research Service, 1997 data), rural users could suffer an even further reduction in welfare.

Again, what is useful here is a measure of the degree of economies of scope, which would allow for, in the presence of economies of scope, the capturing of the relative increase in cost that would result from separate production of the two (or more) outputs. Thus, the degree of economies of scope is given by

$$S_c = [C(Y_1, 0) + C(0, Y_2) - C(Y_1, Y_2)]/C(Y_1, Y_2) \qquad (7.18)$$

(Baumol et al., 1982). This measure also is calculated for a two-output quadratic cost function.

It is important to keep in mind that, due to the regulated nature of this industry, there exists a divergence between the *actual* economies experienced and those that could *potentially* result if the industry were not regulated. It is well documented in the literature that regulation reduces the competitiveness or efficiency of firms. First via lack of entry and second via the average-cost pricing mechanism imposed on firms in the industry. Mayo mentions this in his 1984 paper, which, among others, attempts to identify the existence of scope economies in this industry. Using a sample of 200 firms (privately owned electric and natural gas utilities), he employs a modified (short-run, since he incorporates fixed costs) multiproduct quadratic cost function to estimate the cost of producing both electricity and gas and confirms the presence of economies of scope for small firms using 1979 data. However, as output increases, he asserts that the absence of competitive pressure leads to cost inefficiencies and eventual diseconomies of scope.

Interpretation of results, economies of scope

Referring to equation (7.16), a positive value for the degree of economies of scope indicates that there are economies of scope in the production of both goods. Using the results displayed in Table 7.1, it is straightforward to calculate the degree of economies of scope, the frequency distribution of which is displayed in Figure 7.2. As these results indicate, every firm that distributed electricity to both types of end user enjoyed economies of scope.

Figure 7.2 displays the degree of economies of scope for small users (Y_1). As is seen in the figure, at low levels of output (Y_1), higher levels of Y_2 yield lower cost savings from joint production (notice $v = 0.2$ (light line) is below $v = 0.1$ (dark line) in the leftmost portion of the figure, which is at lower levels of output). However, at higher levels of output, higher cost savings emerge as more output is distributed to large users (Y_2).

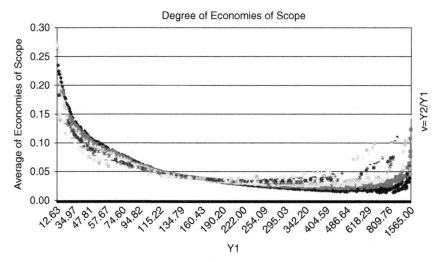

Figure 7.2 Degree of scope economies for rural electric cooperatives (1997–2001)

Since this measure is positive for all output combinations, the cost of producing each output separately is higher than joint production. In other words, cost savings are lower at lower levels of output and higher at higher levels. Since the degree of scope economies is positive for all output combinations, it makes sense for the firms in the sample to continue distributing electricity to both classes of users. The fact that it is increasing faster in Y_2 indicates that increasing the amount of electricity distributed to large commercial and industrial users enhances cost savings.

General implications of estimation results

The previous analyses indicate that the average sized coop in the United States distributes too little output relative to the optimal (i.e., cost-minimizing) quantity. Taking this one step further, these results seem to indicate that, on average, distribution territories are not large enough to capture all the economies inherent to network systems. As such, horizontal mergers between distribution systems could yield substantial cost savings and help ensure the coops' survival (in their present form) in a restructured market. Some of the sources of these potential cost savings are discussed in the next section.

In addition, the confirmation of economies of scope indicates that rather substantial cost savings would occur if these firms could increase the quantity of electricity distributed to industrial loads.

Sources of cost savings

For a distribution only utility, the bulk of the cost savings come from the significant administrative economies that can be attained. Examples include centralized call centers, employee retirements (via special early retirement programs), outsourcing and elimination of duplicate functions, and the consolidation of the boards of directors. In addition, the Rural Utilities Service offers certain incentives for the merging and consolidation of systems. For example, it will defer interest and principal payments for a period of up to five years. Finally, there are potential purchased power economies and savings in capacity costs, especially if the annual load shape is different—that is, if one coop's load is summer peaking and the other's is winter peaking. As these costs savings are passed on to ratepayers, consumer surplus is increased and society as a whole is better off. These results confirm that, under certain conditions, horizontal mergers between distribution coops could yield rather substantial benefits, thus allowing significant welfare gains along with helping ensure the survival of coops in a deregulated environment.

7.5 IMPLICATIONS FOR PUBLIC POLICY

Finally, concerning the public policy implications, some states seem to recognize the differences between coops and investor-owned utilities. In those states, such as Texas, there were specific opt-out clauses for the coops. In addition, at the time that restructuring legislation was being formulated, the Clinton administration attempted to offer a rural safety net, offering assistance grants to those who reside in rural areas. Fortunately, the Clinton plan left to each state's discretion how retail choice would be implemented.

Despite the fact that many states offered opt-out clauses and other protections for cooperatively owned entities, it was often the case that the opt-out process is costly and time consuming. Subsequently, the survival of the coops may not be a function of how efficiently they operate but of the restructuring legislation adopted by the individual state and whether the state even has jurisdiction over coops. For those states that do not have jurisdiction, some offered opt-in clauses for coops, leaving it up to the members to decide whether or not to participate in the competitive market. Thus, given the differences between investor and cooperative ownership, it is imperative that the states be allowed to decide what is best for the utilities that they regulate. And for those that do regulate coops, simple opt-out clauses and other protections must be put in place to ensure that no ratepayer is adversely affected.

One of the goals of electric restructuring is the creation of a level playing field. However, given the inconsistent treatment of coops within and among the states,[8] the question then becomes: How will this be accomplished? And how does this bode for a "level playing field" between and among the states, when some states

1. Do not regulate coops but offer an opt-in clause for coops and municipally owned utilities.
2. Regulate them but offer an opt-out clause (or other special language).
3. Regulate some coops but not others (since distribution entities that purchase power from federally owned suppliers are not subject to state jurisdiction).
4. Regulate coops but not municipally owned distribution systems.

These are just a few of the questions that need to be answered before a successful retail access program can be implemented. (Note: The original paper was written in 1999, prior to all of the issues that transpired that rendered deregulation of the industry an abject failure. Some of the text and analysis has been updated—for example, including data from 1997–2001—but for the most part the conclusions and policy implications have been left intact.)

7.6 CONCLUSION

This chapter sought to determine whether rural electric coops in the United States are efficient distributors of electricity. Employing a multiple-output quadratic cost model, I find that, during the 1997–2001 time period, they were not; the estimation results indicate that these firms were operating in the increasing-returns-to-scale portion of the average cost curve. According to the results of the various efficiency measures employed, none of these firms is distributing anywhere near the cost minimizing number of megawatt-hours. The closest any one of them comes is

---

[8] Especially when, in states like Kentucky, for example, the distribution coops served by the Tennessee Valley Authority (a federally owned power supplier) are not regulated by the Kentucky Public Service Commission but those member coops supplied by generation and transmission coops are. Given this, the question then becomes: How is a level playing field ensured under such conditions? This is difficult, given that there is no universally accepted definition. To the investor-owned utilities, it may mean the ending of certain subsidies, whereas to the rural distribution coops, which average fewer than six people per mile of line, it could mean something entirely different.

Kenergy, which was formed in 1999 by a merger between the Henderson Union and Green River systems in the state of Kentucky. Between them, they served over 50,000 customers and distributed 927 and 9200 GWh of electricity to small users and large users, respectively, in 2001. Over the 10 year study period, the savings from this merger were expected to be $23.6 million dollars and, within 1 year, Kenergy filed for a $2.5 million dollar rate reduction. Thus, horizontal mergers between coops could yield significant cost savings and help ensure the survival of coops in their present form in a deregulated environment.

CHAPTER 8

A Test of Vertical Economies for Non-Vertically Integrated Firms: The Case of Rural Electric Cooperatives[1]

8.1 ABSTRACT

This paper seeks to evaluate the lost economies of vertical integration for rural electric cooperatives in 1997. Given the well-established network economies that are inherent in the generation, transmission, and distribution of electricity, the coops' long-standing choice of market structure is questionable (especially given their chosen strategy of welfare maximization). Organized as either generation-and-transmission or distribution-only, the traditional measures of vertical economies will not work. Thus, I have devised an alternative method by which to measure such economies and find that, on average, cost savings in excess of 39% could have been realized had the coops adopted a vertically integrated structure.

8.2 INTRODUCTION

This paper is a follow up to my previous study on cooperatively owned firms. In that study, I examined the economies of scope and product-specific economies of scale in an attempt to determine whether they were operating at the optimal scale to ensure their viability in a deregulated environment. I found that the average distribution coop was too small (in terms of the amount of electricity distributed) to enjoy the economies of scale and scope, thus ensuring its survival, in a deregulated environment. In this study, I employ 1997 data (one year later than my previous study) to determine whether the choice of organizational structure is optimal given the objective of welfare maximization.

---

[1] This paper was published in *Energy Economics* in May 2008. Do not reprint without permission.

Electricity Cost Modeling Calculations
DOI: 10.1016/B978-1-85617-726-9.00008-X

8.3 BACKGROUND: RURAL ELECTRIC COOPERATIVES

In the United States, rural electric cooperatives (RECs) are organized as either generation and transmission (G&Ts) or distribution-only (member coops), the majority of which having long-term, full-requirements contracts in place; as such, they can be considered *quasi*–vertically integrated. Born from the Rural Electrification Act of 1936, rural electric distribution cooperatives were charged with providing electric service to areas in which there was no electric service due to the simple fact that these areas were rural in nature and hence costly to serve. Because of their profit incentive, investor-owned utilities had no interest in serving these areas, and as a result the act was signed into legislation.

Until the mid-1950s, distribution cooperatives purchased power from both privately and federally owned power suppliers. However, as their supply needs increased, they decided that they needed reliable, inexpensive sources of power—hence, the birth of generation and transmission cooperatives (G&T). While not truly vertically integrated, the member distribution cooperatives are typically contractually bound to a G&T via long-term full-requirement purchased power agreements. In addition to ensuring adequate supply these contracts also intrinsically obligate the member coops to the obligations of the G&T itself; as owners of the G&T, they are not only responsible for debts undertaken to serve end users but also are responsible for the debt obligations of the G&T (hence the phrase *quasi-vertically integrated*). This is the foundation of the term *cooperatively owned*.

8.4 REASONS THAT COOPERATIVELY OWNED UTILITIES ARE DIFFERENT

Unlike investor-owned utilities (IOUs), not all states regulate electric cooperatives. In fact, fewer than 20 states have jurisdiction over coops, and the degree of regulation is not consistent among these states. For example, in some states, the Public Regulatory Commissions do not regulate the rates charged by coops, but rather the terms of their service obligations. This inconsistency creates a special challenge for federal policy makers in the United States, whose intention is to require that all transmission-owning entities join a region transmission organization (RTO) to facilitate competition in the industry.

There are other differences as well:

- **Urban versus rural differences.** Unlike the urban areas that IOUs serve, the rural areas served by coops tend to be far less populated (7 vs. 35 customers per mile of distribution line) with terrain that is rugged in nature and difficult to serve; as such, they are more costly to serve.
- **Institutional differences.** Coops are subject to the 85% rule, which means that they must receive 85% of their revenues from their members or lose their tax-exempt status, which effectively precludes the coops participation in both wholesale and retail markets.
- **Customer differences.** The loads served by cooperatives tend to be mostly residential (83%), which tend to be smaller, more volatile, and demand power during peak times. As such, they are more costly to serve.
- **Philosophical differences: Welfare vs. profit maximization.** While both objective functions suggest some level of cost minimization, the coops' emphasis is on the maximization of consumer (as opposed to producer) surplus. As a result, the focus is on reliability, rather than return, which implies a higher cost of service. Furthermore, the choice of welfare rather than profit maximization can lead to certain inefficiencies that are not as easily mitigated as they would be in a profit-maximizing firm, for example, certain principal-agent problems. Unlike for-profit firms, coops do not tend to offer bonuses, profit sharing, or stock options. Furthermore, nonperformance is likely more tolerated (it would be difficult to fire someone who is an owner of the firm).
- **Organizational differences.** Coops are considered to be vertically integrated only to the extent that there are long-term full-requirements contracts in place with a G&T cooperative. However, it is often the case that contracts do not fully mitigate all of the transactions costs and other inefficiencies that tend to arise with long-term agreements (see Williamson, 1971; Landon, 1983).

A more detailed description of each of the above is detailed in Greer (2003).

8.5 LITERATURE REVIEW

Economies of vertical integration have been well established in the generation, transmission, and distribution of electricity. Studies include, but are not limited to, the work of Landon (1983), Henderson (1985), Roberts

(1986), and Hayashi, Yeoung-Jia Goo, and Chamberlain (1997), which have tested for and determined that, indeed, the downstream costs of transmission and distribution are dependent upon input usage at the generation stage. Multiproduct cost functions are employed by Kaserman and Mayo (1991) and Gilsdorf (1994, 1995), who test for cost complementarities between the stages of production. What is interesting is that, while Kaserman and Mayo found that such economies prevailed throughout the relevant range of outputs, Gilsdorf's results were inconsistent with the cost complementarity hypothesis. However, it is entirely possible that the latter's results had something to do with his choice of the translogarithmic cost specification: As Kwoka (1996) aptly states about the quadratic cost specification, "in contrast to the translog, it (the quadratic) allows for the unconstrained emergence of economies of scope or scale as well as subadditivity."

This study takes a different approach entirely. Operating on the premise that, if the G&T and distribution cooperative were truly vertically integrated, the distribution coops' purchased power cost would be exactly that: what it costs the G&T to procure the power that it in turn sells to its member distribution cooperatives.[2]

8.6 DATA

In order to assess the potential lost cost savings due to the lack of vertical integration, it was first necessary to truncate the data set to only those distribution coops that purchase power from a G&T; otherwise, I had no information on the supplier's cost of power, which is necessary to complete this analysis. Using 1997 data on RUS borrowers, an attempt can be made to quantify (at least) two sources of inefficiency. First, the fact that the power supplied to the distribution cooperative is not necessarily at cost but rather is set in long-term purchased power agreements that reflect the cost of power at the time of the contract, may in and of itself give rise to other inefficiencies. As Landon (1983) states: "The existence of technological interdependence and idiosyncratic capital, the requirement for long-term contracting, the informational and transactions requirements, and the difficulties of appropriate pricing between vertical levels all would tend

---

[2] In actuality, many generation and transmission coops do not generate any power at all; often, it is purchased from other suppliers, typically federally owned or investor-owned. In fact, only 25 of the 45 G&Ts that operated in the 1997 data owned any generating capacity.

to increase the costs of contracting versus ownership. Transactions and information costs would increase, perhaps substantially."

This statement is exemplified by the fact that the price paid by member coops over the G&T's cost of electric service is in excess of 10% for 40% of the member coops (mode = 5%), which seems to be evidence of double marginalization. (The difference from the G&T power supply cost is even greater.) Second, it is also often the case that the distribution coop purchases more power than it actually sells to its customers (7.7% on average, which effectively raises the price to member coops even further).[3] Table 8.1 displays the relevant summary statistics for this group of coops.[4]

Table 8.1 Descriptive Statistics of Rural Cooperatives in 1997

Summary statistics	Mean	Std dev	Min	Max
G&T GWh (Generated + Purchased)	4158	3823	24.00	15,250
G&T cost of electric service ($/MWh)	38.18	6.45	27.35	48.87
G&T cost of power ($/MWh)	27.71	13.02	8.47	66.60
G&T cost of capital	6.41	2.47	1.52	19.12
G&T cost of labor	20.95	5.20	7.53	38.46
Member coops				
GWh purchased from G&T	320	403	14	4606
GWh sold to end users	300	391	13	4575
Cost of purchased power ($/MWh)	40.82	8.28	24.61	82.58
Cost of power − Sold to end users ($/MWh)	43.78	9.65	18.40	77.60
Cost of capital	4.94	0.78	1.92	7.19
Cost of labor	15.58	3.20	5.46	58.60
Miles of transmission line	82.24	76.91	0.39	319
Density	5.28	3.15	1.00	23.60

[3] Granted, these could be line losses. Typically, line losses account for around 6%. However, for the coops in this sample, the average between the quantity of electricity purchased or generated and that sold is well over 11% (G&T and distribution coop) with some experiencing differences of 20%. For the coops in this study, over 300 exhibited a difference that is greater than 14%.

[4] It is interesting to note that 17% of the coops in this study are not served by a G&T. Over half are served by federally owned suppliers with the remainder served by IOUs (or other).

8.7 METHODOLOGY

Several methodologies were employed in this study. Each involved the estimation of a two-output quadratic cost model, which is the same as that employed in my previous paper and is given by:

$$C = \left(\alpha_0 + \sum \alpha_i Y_i + \tfrac{1}{2} \times \sum_i \sum_j \alpha_{ij} Y_i Y_j \right) \cdot \prod p_m^{\beta_m} \cdot \prod O_n^{\theta_n} e^{\varepsilon}, \text{ for } i,j = 1,2$$

(8.1)

where

C = total cost: operating deductions + interest on long-term debt.

Y_1 = electricity distributed to residential and small commercial users in GWh.

Y_2 = electricity distributed to large commercial and industrial users in GWh.

P_m = input prices: capital (k), labor (l), and purchased power (p).

O_n = other (cost-shift) variables: miles of transmission line and customer density.

Unlike previously estimated quadratic models in the literature, this cost function is concave, nondecreasing, and homogeneous of degree 1 in input prices as well as monotonic in output, and as such preserves the fundamental properties of a proper cost function. (A proof that this model conforms to each of these properties is given in Greer, 2003.)

Estimation of this particular equation is somewhat problematic. Because it is nonlinear, the stochastic error term does not enter additively as required. Hence, the model must be transformed so as to allow it to be additive. A logarithmic transformation, which will yield such an error term, is made possible by the creation of a variable, Z, where:

$$Z = \alpha_0 + \sum \alpha_i Y_i + \tfrac{1}{2} \sum \sum \alpha_{ij} Y_i Y_j, \text{ for } i = 1, 2, i \neq j \qquad (8.2)$$

so that the modified multiproduct quadratic cost equation becomes:

$$\ln C = \zeta \ln Z + \beta_K \ln p_K + \beta_L \ln p_L + \beta_P \ln p_P + \theta_{tm} \ln O_{tm} + \theta_d \ln O_d + \varepsilon \quad (8.3)$$

8.8 PRELIMINARY RESULTS—ALL COOPS

The first cost model includes all distribution coops that were RUS borrowers in 1997. Estimation results are displayed in Table 8.2. An adjusted R^2 of 0.9694 indicates that the model fits the data well. Estimated

Table 8.2 Estimation Results—1997 Distribution Cooperatives (Generalized Method of Moments)

Parameter (variable)	Parameter estimates	t-statistics
α_0 (constant)	22.28156	5.59
α_1 (Y_1)	2.878406	11.81
α_2 (Y_2)	1.82474	12.56
$\alpha_{11}\left(Y_1^2\right)$	−0.00036	−3.22
$\alpha_{22}\left(Y_2^2\right)$	−0.00013	−1.65
α_{12} ($Y_1\ Y_2$)	−0.00045	−2.68
β_1 (price of capital)	0.113364	3.12
β_2 (price of purchase power)	0.716718	17.62
β_3 (price of labor)	0.169918	5.12
σ_1 (miles transmission lines)	0.018082	4.26
σ_2 (density)	−0.06803	−4.46
Adjusted R^2	**0.9694**	

coefficients are of the expected sign and statistical significance, indicating both product-specific economies of scale as well as economies of scope in the distribution of electricity. These are similar to the results obtained in my previous study (Greer, 2003), which used data from 1996.

8.9 ECONOMIES OF VERTICAL INTEGRATION

The contribution of this paper is a test for vertical integration for firms that are not vertically integrated in the truest sense of the term. While the results in Table 8.2 confirm the findings in my previous study, what is important here is the development and confirmation of the claim that cooperatively owned firms have not necessarily adopted the most efficient (i.e., welfare-maximizing) organizational structure to help ensure their success in the type of market that the FERC envisions (which seemingly ignores the well-established presence of economies of vertical integration in this industry). Unlike the telecommunications industry, whereby data are storable and information can be transmitted wirelessly, electricity must be consumed when it is produced and requires physical infrastructure to generate, transmit, and distribute it to end users.

Appealing to Kaserman and Mayo (1991), weak vertical economies between successive stages of production, i and j, are said to exist if:

$$S_{ij}(\gamma) = [C(Yi, 0) + C(0, Y_j, p_i) - p_i Y_i(Y_j \mathbf{p}) - C(Y_i, Y_j)]/C(Y_i, Y_j) \geq 0$$

$$(8.4)$$

This equation is modified so that it is possible to estimate the lost savings due to the coops' choice of organizational structure. That is, to quantify the "wedge of inefficiency" due to the separation of the generation and distribution functions, requires the estimation of three separate cost models $[(C(Y_{i,}\ 0),\ C(0,\ Y_{j},\ p_{i}),\ \text{and}\ C(Y_{i,},\ Y_{j}))]$.

Let:
1. $C(Y_{i,}\ 0) = \ln C_GT = $ estimated G&T cost.
2. $C(0,\ Y_{j},\ p_{i}) = \ln C_PP = $ member coop's cost of electric service.
3. $C(Y_{i},\ Y_{j}) = \ln C_PPs = $ cost if vertically integrated.

Note: $p_{i}Y_{i}(Y_{j},\ \mathbf{p})$, the cost of power purchased from the G&T and sold by the member coop, must also be computed.

Substituting into (8.4) yields:

$$S_{ij}(\gamma) = [\ln C\_GT + \ln C\_PP) - p_{i}Y_{i}(Y_{j}\ \mathbf{p}) - \ln C\_PPs)]/\ln C\_PPs \geq 0 \quad (8.5)$$

8.10 ESTIMATION RESULTS

Estimation results of the three cost models are displayed in Table 8.3.

The results of the first model $[C(Y_{i,}\ 0)]$, which estimates the G&T's cost, are not as strong as those that estimate the costs for the member coops. Estimated as a single-output model (with input prices), no scale economies emerge and the adjusted R^2 is 0.6431, which is not a surprising result given that the deregulation of the wholesale market was predicated on the lack of

Table 8.3 Estimation Results: Economies of Vertical Integration—Comparison of Estimates for Cost Models Employed in Vertical Economies Study

Parameter (variable)	Model: $C(Y_{i,}\ 0)$	t-stats	Model: $C(0,\ Y_{j},\ p_{i})$	t-stats	Model: $C(Y_{i},\ Y_{j})$	t-stats
α_0 (constant)	3007	1.83	14.0705	4.12	40.7821	5.25
α_1 (Y_1)	2.244	1.32	2.27687	10.50	4.1499	15.42
α_2 (Y_2)			1.44718	10.44	2.1656	11.04
α_{11} $\left(Y_1^2\right)$	0.0002	0.63	−0.00063	−3.85	−0.0010	−2.49
α_{22} $\left(Y_1^2\right)$			−0.00012	−2.60	−0.0003	−2.38
α_{12} $(Y_1\ Y_2)$			0.00005	0.40	0.0001	0.19
β_1 (price of capital)	0.4497	2.27	0.03810	0.77	0.2952	7.70
β_2 (price of power)	0.2460	1.20	0.85815	19.76	0.5475	23.84
β_3 (price of labor)	0.3043	2.02	0.10375	3.77	0.1572	4.46
σ_1 (trans lines)			0.02078	4.02	0.0249	4.41
σ_2 (density)			−0.05797	−3.37	−0.0707	−3.16
Adjusted R^2	**0.6431**		**0.9759**		**0.9659**	

scale economies at the generation stage. The models that estimate the distribution coops' costs $[C(0, Y_j, p_i), C(Y_i, Y_j)]$ are more robust, although neither indicates economies of scope in the distribution of electricity, which seems odd given that the first model estimated (includes all coops) indicates the presence of such economies. Both do, however, indicate product-specific economies of scale in the distribution of electricity to both small and large end users. Both models fit the data well with each having an adjusted R^2 above 0.965.

Given that the model that included all coops yielded economies of scope, I also estimated a model that included only those coops not served by a G&T ($n = 120$). As expected, this model indicated strong economies of scope in the distribution of electricity to both types of end users. Further examination revealed that the coops in this group, although smaller in terms of electricity distributed, tended to serve a higher percentage of large users, which tends to drive both scale and scope economies. (This is confirmed in Greer, 2003.)

8.11 TESTS FOR VERTICAL INTEGRATION

Using equation (8.4), the predicted values of each of the cost models were used to construct the measure of the lost cost savings from the coop's being quasi-vertically integrated. For all but one coop[5] the degree of vertical economies, $S_{ij}(Y)$ is greater than 0, with the value itself indicating the cost savings that could emerge were these firms truly vertically integrated. For the group of coops in the sample, the average cost savings is slightly above 40% when evaluated at the sample means of the data. Further examination reveals that, in general, lower purchased power costs coupled with high levels of output tended to reduce the gains from vertical integration, which makes perfect sense. Figure 8.1 and Table 8.4 display the degree of vertical economies for a subset of the coops in the sample (those whose output ratio, $Y_2/Y_1 = 0.3$, which is the sample average). As the table indicates, for a given level of generation (Y_g), increasing distributed output (Y_d), tends to reduce the cost savings from vertical integration; however, as generation is expanded, for a given level of distributed output, the cost savings from vertical integration tend to increase, which is confirmed in the literature. Furthermore, as the output ratio increases (i.e., more

---

[5] Green River Electric Coop, which is served by Big Rivers G&T, distributed the highest quantity of electricity to large users in both 1996 and 1997.

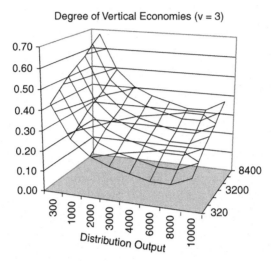

Figure 8.1 Degree of vertical economies for 1997 rural electric coops

Table 8.4 Degree of Vertical Economies: 1997 Rural Electric Cooperatives

$v = 3$	320	1100	2134	3200	4268	6350	8400	10,500
300	**0.44**	0.48	0.53	0.56	0.59	0.64	0.68	0.71
1000	0.28	**0.32**	0.36	0.39	0.42	0.46	0.49	0.52
2000	0.20	0.24	**0.28**	0.31	0.33	0.37	0.41	0.43
3000	0.17	0.20	0.24	**0.27**	0.29	0.33	0.36	0.39
4000	0.14	0.18	0.22	0.24	**0.27**	0.31	0.34	0.36
6000	0.12	0.15	0.19	0.22	0.24	**0.28**	0.31	0.34
8000	0.12	0.15	0.19	0.22	0.24	0.28	**0.31**	0.34
10,000	0.16	0.20	0.24	0.27	0.29	0.33	0.37	**0.39**

Note: Increasing output to large customers allows for the emergence of economies of scope, and vertical economies begin to rise (note values on the diagonal).

electricity distributed to large users, for example, $Y_2/Y_1 = 3.0$), increasing distributed output (again, for a given level of generation output) eventually causes the savings from vertical integration to rise (see Table 8.4 and Figure 8.1).[6] This particular phenomenon is likely the result of the economies of scope that exist in the distribution of electricity between large and small users (see Greer, 2003).

---

[6] It is important to keep in mind that there would be other cost savings as well: administrative, labor, not to mention any network economies that would emerge.

8.12 CONCLUSION

This paper seeks to derive a measure of the lost cost savings due to the coop's choice of organizational structure. Although the existence of long-term full-requirements contracts with a G&T coop renders them vertically integrated to some degree, it is these contracts themselves that may be the problem, often resulting in unforeseen transactions costs and other inefficiencies, including purchasing more power than they actually need. To wit: A comparison between what the G&T pays for power, its cost of electric service, and what the member coop effectively pays for the power it sells is telling. In a number of cases, this return exceeded 20% over the G&T's cost of electric service in 1997.

In order to quantify the lost cost savings, I devised a method to measure the degree of vertical economies for the quasi-vertically integrated coops in the sample. In all but one instance, the coops in this sample could benefit from vertical integration (in the strict sense of the term) with possible cost savings of around 40% (on average). These results confirm the results of previous studies involving investor-owned firms; it is unique in its focus on cooperatively owned firms and the adaptation of the measure of the degree of vertical economies to firms whose generation and transmission functions are only contractually related to its distribution function. Given this, not only would horizontal mergers help ensure their survival in a deregulated market (Greer, 2003) but also vertically integrating would as well. Granted, the latter may prove to be a difficult task given the Federal Energy Regulatory Commission's desire that all utilities join regional transmission organizations, but given the differences between cooperatively owned and investor-owned utilities, a more cautious approach to the deregulation of the industry is in order; More specifically, in the crafting of the policies related to the *mandated* joining of RTOs and, among other things, to the possible implications of pricing mechanisms employed in the name of economic efficiency.

CHAPTER 9

Load Forecasting—The "Demand" for Electricity

9.1 WHAT IS FORECASTING?

In general, econometric forecasting means using independent variables to predict the expected value of a dependent variable, in this case the amount of electricity that will be consumed over a given period of time (hourly, daily, monthly, and annually) for a given number of years into the future. All firms forecast sales for various reasons; for planning purposes, regulated utilities are required to forecast future values of the quantity demanded of electricity demand (or sales) and provide a long-term plan to public regulatory commissions to ensure that customers needs are satisfied as part of satisfying the requirements attached to their having been granted a monopoly franchise in servicing their predefined service territory.

Forecast time horizons: Short-term versus long-term forecasts

Forecasts of electricity sales are generally characterized into three time periods: hourly (or day ahead), short-term (1–3 years), and long-term (20–30 years). The focus here is on the latter two, which tend to be of more relevance for budgeting and planning purposes. Each will be described in detail.

Short-term load forecasts

For an electric utility, the importance of short-term sales and demand forecasts cannot be understated: They are essential in the establishment of rates and fuel purchases (i.e., for budgeting purposes), the scheduling of outages for maintenance and other operational purposes, and for establishing the level sales that can be sold off-system, or into the wholesale market.

Several factors affect sales in the short-term, which are typically forecasted on a monthly basis, thus giving rise to the seasonality factor (or weather) that is a large determinant of sales for weather-sensitive rate classes, namely, residential and commercial customers. However, economic factors such as incomes and prices play an important role. Furthermore, the saturation of electricity-using appliances and equipment and the efficiency levels thereof play a critical role, which has given rise to and

Electricity Cost Modeling Calculations
DOI: 10.1016/B978-1-85617-726-9.00009-1

increasing importance of end-use modeling for forecasting monthly electricity sales. Finally, there is also a random component to electricity sales that may be due to changes in customer tastes or preferences (e.g., conservation) or other unanticipated events.

Long-term forecasts

As said, the importance of short-term forecasting plays a critical role in the budgeting process and the timing of rate cases. However, in terms of capacity and expansion planning, long-term forecasts are critical. In fact, many state utility commissions require the utilities under their jurisdiction to file an integrated resource plan (IRP) every three (or so) years to ensure that the utility's capacity expansion plan enables it to reliably (and at least cost) serve its native load customers (i.e., the customers that reside in its franchised service territory). The IRP typically includes detailed explanations of its load forecasting methodology and the results from various runs of its generation simulation software (Prosym, other), which are inputs into the expansion planning process. The IRP also contains the utilities' expectations in terms of the timing of new generating capacity (or purchased power requirements) and the type of capacity (base load or peaking) that might be required over the next 20–30 years. (Note: Given the amount of time it takes to site and build new generating capacity, it is necessary to forecast this far in advance.)

9.2 DATA SOURCES: THE ENERGY INFORMATION ADMINISTRATION

At the national level, one of the objectives of the U.S. Energy Information Administration (EIA), which is part of the U.S. Department of Energy (DOE), is to perform annual projections of the consumption of various fuels in the United States and internationally. Both in total and at the sector level, the analyses performed by the EIA often incorporate legislation that has either been passed or is being proposed by Congress. One of their products is the Annual Energy Outlook (AEO), which projects consumption for various energy (or fuel) sources, including natural gas, renewables, and electricity via 12 modules, which is the National Energy Modeling System (NEMS) (see Appendix 9.2 for details).

In addition to forecasting on a national basis, the EIA also produces regional forecasts by census division both in total and by end-use sector. Figures 9.1 and 9.2 provide examples of each. The former provides the EIA's most recent projections of electricity consumption by sector

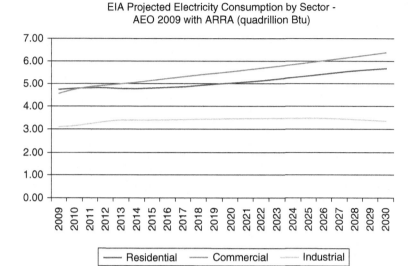

Figure 9.1 AEO 2009—Projection of electricity consumption by sector

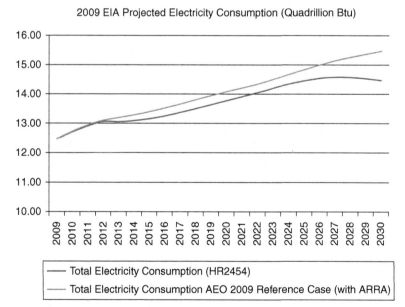

Figure 9.2 Total projected electricity consumption in the United States: AEO 2009 reference case vs. H.R. 2454—Cap and Trade (Waxman and Markey, 2009), expected impacts

(residential, commercial, and industrial) on a national scale. It incorporates the provisions of the American Recovery and Reinvestment Act of 2009 (ARRA), the intent of which is to save and create 3–4 million jobs, (90% of which are in the private sector), provide more than $150 billion to low-income and vulnerable households, modernize health care and the aging infrastructure, improve schools and accessibility to higher education, and invest in the clean energy technologies of the future (see www .recovery.gov/?q=content/act).

You may notice that, in 2012–2013, Figure 9.1 indicates that sales to residential customers are projected to decline. This is due, at least in part, to the legislation on lighting that was included in the Energy Independence and Security Act of 2007 (EISA). More specifically, the forecast of electricity sales to the residential sector, which is based on the residential demand module of NEMS, uses a discrete choice model and is discussed in more detail in a later section. A model such as this is based on certain economic and demographic variables and incorporates changing efficiency standards and the stock of electricity-using appliances to forecast the quantity demanded of electricity through 2030. What is evident in Figure 9.1 is the impact of legislation on incandescent light bulbs, which is phased in over 2012–2014 with more restrictive standards in 2020. One of the provisions of EISA, the lighting standard, specifically requires that light bulbs use 29% less wattage per bulb in the first phase-in, increasing to 67% in 2020. Other provisions are updates to the dehumidifier standard that was specified in the Energy Policy Act of 2005 (EPACT), which results in a 7% increase in electricity savings, relative to the EPACT requirement. Standards are also set for boilers (September 2012) and dishwashers (January 2010).

Projected electricity consumption by residential and commercial customers relative to AEO 2009 is lower due to weatherization and efficiency improvements in both homes and buildings that yielded significant savings in the energy used for heating and cooling. Industrial sales were relatively flat, reflecting a slower projected growth in exports and investment.

H.R. 2454: The American Clean Energy and Security Act of 2009

In June 2009, the U.S. House of Representatives passed an energy bill that was aimed at reducing the amount of carbon emissions emitted into the atmosphere. Proposed by Representatives Henry Waxman and Edward Markey, known as the American Clean Energy and Security Act of 2009 (ACESA), this legislation would establish a cap and trade system to reduce greenhouse gases, an approach favored by most economists over conventional regulatory approaches because it provides a great deal of flexibility in how emissions targets are met.

Figure 9.2 shows the EIA's outlook for total electricity consumption in the United States compared to that which might occur under the Waxman-Markey Cap and Trade Program (H.R. 2454), which is an attempt to reduce greenhouse gas emissions into the atmosphere. (This is discussed in far more detail in the chapter on regulation.)

Title III of H.R. 2454 focuses on reducing greenhouse gas emissions by establishing a cap on emissions beginning in 2012 that covers electricity generators, liquid fuel refiners and importers, and fluorinated gas manufacturers. In 2014, the cap is expanded to include industrial sources that emit greater than 25,000 tons of carbon dioxide (CO_2) equivalent emissions, and in 2016, it is further expanded to include retail natural gas distribution companies. Relative to their emissions in 2005, covered sources must reduce their emissions 3% by 2012, 17% by 2020, 58% by 2030, and 83% by 2050. It provides for unlimited banking of allowances, while borrowing future allowances to meet current compliance obligations is allowed with some restrictions (www.eia.doe.gov/oiaf/servicerpt/hr2454/background.html).

Needless to say, H.R. 2454 is expected to lead to higher prices and lower electricity demand, especially in states that rely on coal for much of their generation. As displayed in Figure 9.3, most of the price impacts

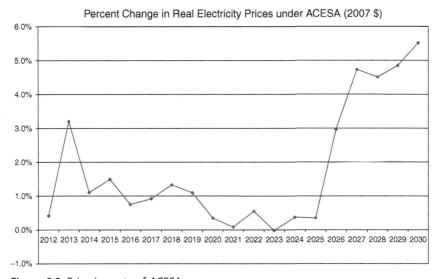

Figure 9.3 Price impacts of ACESA

are expected to occur after 2025, when the emissions allowances that have been allocated to retail electricity providers have been phased out. And there is clearly an impact: From 2025 to 2030, real electricity prices are expected to increase by 25%, substantially higher than the price increases over the years leading up to 2025.

In the EIA base case, emission allowances are free and given to regulated electric and natural gas distribution companies. Such allowances, which represent the right to emit some amount of carbon dioxide annually, can be used to offset fossil-fuel-fired production.[1] The allocation of free allowances ceases after 2025, resulting in significant price increases.

EIA historical projections

Also of interest is that since 2002, the EIA has successively lowered its outlook for energy consumption. As is displayed in Figure 9.4, the Annual Energy Outlook of U.S. energy consumption has been lowered every year.

Beginning with the 2003 AEO, the impact of the recession in 2002–2003 resulted in that year's projected energy consumption to be notably below that of 2002. After this, the lowering of subsequent forecasts was influenced not only by increasing efficiency standards and increasing fuel prices but also by the globalization of the economy, in which numerous

---

[1] According to the Executive Summary to the EIA Service Report "Energy Market and Economic Impacts of H.R. 2454, the American Clean Energy and Security Act of 2009":

The role of offsets is a large area of uncertainty in any analysis of ACESA. The 2-BMT annual limit on total offsets in ACESA is equivalent to one-third of total energy-related GHG emissions in 2008 and represents nearly six times the projected growth in energy-related emissions through 2030 in the Reference Case used in this analysis.

While the ceiling on offset use is clear, their actual use is an open question. Beyond the usual uncertainties related to the technical, economic, and market supply of offsets, the future use of offsets for ACESA compliance also depends both on regulatory decisions that are yet to be made by the EPA, on the timing and scope of negotiations on international agreements or arrangements between the United States and countries where offset opportunities may exist, and on emissions reduction commitments made by other countries. Also, limits on offset use in ACESA apply individually to each covered entity, so that offset "capacity" that goes unused by one or more covered entities cannot be used by other covered entities. For some major entities covered by the cap-and-trade program, decisions regarding the use of offsets could potentially be affected by regulation at the State level. Given the many technical factors and implementation decisions involved, it is hardly surprising that analysts' estimates of international offset use span an extremely wide range. One recent analysis doubts that even 150 MMT of international offsets will be used by 2020, while another posits that 1 BMT of international offsets will be used almost immediately from the start of the program in 2012, followed by a quick rise towards an expanded 1.5-BMT ceiling shortly thereafter.

(See www.eia.doe.gov/oiaf/servicerpt/hr2454/execsummary.html for more detail.)

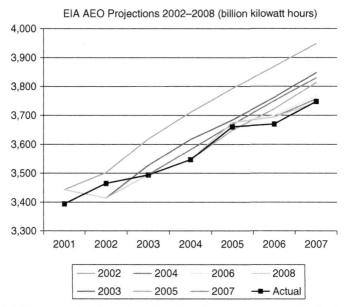

Figure 9.4 The successive lowering of projected energy consumption in the United States

manufacturing industries (and jobs) were exported to other countries. Figure 9.4 displays actual sales against the forecasts that were generated by the EIA in years 2002–2008. (It is important to keep in mind that these data are not weather normalized, so that seeming increases may be the result of weather alone; for example, the summer of 2007 was much warmer than normal in various parts of the United States, which led to significantly higher electricity demand for cooling in those parts of the country. This is clearly seen in Figure 9.4, where the slope of the Actual line increases precipitously from 2006 to 2007 (after having been relatively flat from 2005 to 2006). A similar situation existed in 2005, which is also clearly indicated in Figure 9.4. In both 2005 and 2007, the number of cooling degree days (CDDs) was 12% and 13% above normal for the entire United States, respectively. Note: In this case, normal, or average number of, cooling degree days are based on data from 1971 to 2000 (see www.eia. doe.gov/emeu/aer/txt/ptb0110.html).

The successive lowering of the EIA Annual Energy Outlook reflects the fact that expected sales have not materialized (see the *Actual* line). Were one to draw a line from 2001 to 2007, sales would have increased by far less than forecasted. And, in the years that sales seemingly increased, it was more than likely due to abnormally warm weather, since the sales figures produced by the EIA are not weather normalized, which could easily lead one to erroneous conclusions. Again, this exemplifies the difficulties, and complexities, of load forecasting when, in the period of a few years, the picture changes so dramatically.

A historical perspective

Historically, the growth in sales of electricity to end users has slowed significantly. Figure 9.5 shows the year-over-year change in electricity usage by customer class from 1951 to 2008. With the exception of the industrial sector, year-over-year growth to residential and commercial customers has been robust, averaging between 7% and 10% per year. During the remaining years the effects of high inflation (the 1970s and early 1980s) and recessionary periods are evident. Despite increased population, there has been a downward trend in the growth of electricity sales throughout this period that is due to a myriad of factors, such as increasing fuel prices and energy efficiency.

Note: In preparing the Annual Energy Outlook, the Energy Information Administration evaluates a wide range of trends and issues that could have major implications for U.S. energy markets. This overview focuses primarily on one case, the AEO reference case, which takes a macroeconomic view of the economy.

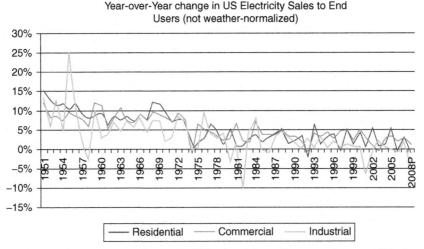

Figure 9.5 Year-over-year change in U.S. electricity sales to end users. With few exceptions sales to end-use sectors have generally increased at a decreasing rate.

On a more regional or service territory level, microeconomic variables tend to also come into play, which will be explored in the next sections and the remainder of this chapter.

9.3 AN OVERVIEW OF ELECTRICITY FORECASTING MODELS

Now, let us turn to a general overview of load forecasting models used by individual utilities that incorporate a more microeconomic view, predominantly the service territory served.

In general, a forecast of electricity demand is comprised of two components:

1. **Usage.** The amount (or quantity) of electricity (in kWh or MWh) that will be demanded by customers in various customer classes over a specific period (typically monthly). Since rates are allocated in this fashion, this allows the utility to forecast its future revenues for *budgeting purposes*;

2. **Peak demand.** The maximum demand (or quantity demanded) in a particular hour of the month, which is used for *capacity planning purposes*.

The focus here is monthly forecasts (which, of course, can be translated into annual forecasts) of the amount of electricity demanded by customer class of ratepayer. Various methodologies are discussed and econometric issues associated with them (some of which were discussed in Chapter 4) are detailed, along with the requisite independent variables (or regressors) that are typically employed to forecast the quantity demanded of electricity (which of course determines the maximum (i.e., peak) demand in any given month (and year), also required for capacity planning purposes (i.e., timing and type of additions to be made to the utilities' generating assets).

Figure 9.6 contains another perspective on historical sales of electricity by class of end user. In this case, it is the actual sales, which have in general been increasing for residential and commercial end users but relatively flat or declining for industrial customers.

In the case of the former, since commercial establishments tend to locate where residential customers are present and population increases imply more residential customers, this tends to bode well for commercial customers and sales. In addition, increased usage by residential customers due to larger homes, the increased use (and penetration) of air conditioning, and electricity-using appliances as well as the proliferation of

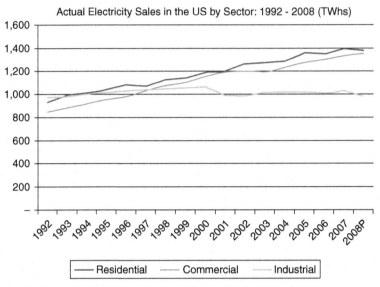

Figure 9.6 Historical electricity sales to end users in the United States

computers, large-screen televisions, cell phones, and other gadgets have all contributed to the increased usage by residential customers.

In stark contrast to the increased electricity usage in the residential and commercial sectors is the pronounced decline in electricity usage in the industrial sector, which clearly never recovered from the economic downturn in 2000, when the trend toward moving operations to other countries, especially overseas, began to take hold. This has proven to be a challenge for forecasting usage and in how much history should be included in forecasting models.

Despite some bumps along the way, electricity sales to residential and commercial customers have been increasing since 1992, experiencing compound average growth rates (CAGR)[2] of 2.5% and 2.9%, respectively. Industrial sales, however, have remained virtually flat (CAGR = 0.1%).

Given all of this, forecasting residential- and commercial-sector models requires more sophisticated methodologies and forecasting electricity sales on an end-use basis requires forecasts of the requisite independent variables to estimate such models. This is discussed in more detail in a subsequent section.

[2] The compound average growth rate is calculated as

$$CAGR = (\text{Ending value}/\text{Beginning value})^{(1/\text{number of years})} - 1$$

9.4 LOAD FORECASTING METHODOLOGIES

Prior to 1970, the forecasting of electricity demand was rather simple: Since the annual growth in sales of electricity had been averaging about 6% since the Second World War, many utilities simply forecasted sales to grow at this level indefinitely. However, with the sharp rise in energy prices in the 1970s along with a slowdown in economic activity, newer, more sophisticated techniques were sought.

It was in this period that econometric forecasting gained much popularity. The ability to use relevant variables (economics, weather, etc.) to determine expected sales volumes was a major breakthrough and forecasting models became more sophisticated and seemingly more accurate. End-use models, which according to the theory that the quantity demanded of electricity is a function of the stock of electricity-using appliances and equipment as well as other economic and demographic variables, became very popular in the early 1990s. This is discussed in more detail later.

Electricity as a derived demand

The demand for electricity is a derived demand; that is, it is a function of the types of electricity-using appliances that exist in a particular type of dwelling (or building). For example, residential customers have numerous appliances that require electricity to operate, in terms of heating, ventilation, and air conditioning systems (HVAC systems); in addition, homes have refrigerators, stoves, microwaves, and other miscellaneous kitchen appliances as well as water heaters for dishwashing, bathing, and washing clothes. Clothes dryers and lighting constitute yet another derived demand along with multiple computers (and equipment), large-screen televisions, cell phones, and other peripheral equipment, which have created "phantom usage" in recent years. Larger homes with "great rooms" expanded the amount of space to be heated (and cooled) and created the need for an increased demand of electricity.

Another consideration is that the *equipment stock* in a particular dwelling is durable, so that only a change in its utilization has an impact on the amount of electricity required for its operation in the *shorter* run. For example, many HVAC systems are designed to last for 15–20 years, while refrigerators and other appliances tend to vary in terms of usable life.

Given this, the demand for electricity in the short run will likely differ from that in the longer run, as the equipment stock is retired and replaced with newer, more efficient models. But an increase in population and dwelling size also has an impact, as has the increased proliferation of gadgets that use electricity (large-screen televisions, computers, and cell phones, to name a few).

Prices

The price of electricity (and the appropriate modeling thereof) is an important and complex component in the forecasting process. As described in the chapter on pricing, utility price schedules (or tariffs) often comprise both fixed (or customer) charges and variable (energy) charges. (For larger customers, demand charges also apply.) Often, the energy charges are in block rates (either increasing or decreasing) with seasonal variations. As such, there is a divergence between the average and marginal price of electricity.

As stated throughout this text, economic theory dictates that the marginal price should be used in the determination of the quantity of electricity demanded by end users. With such multipart tariffs, there could exist different marginal prices, depending upon the level of consumption. As such, the modeling of electricity demand is typically based on the average usage (in kilowatt-hours) per customer. With multipart tariffs, this introduces a bias due to simultaneity, which may be exacerbated when the average price is used as a regressor in ordinary least squares estimation (Berndt, 1991, p. 309). That is, not only is price a function of the quantity demanded but the quantity demanded also is a function of price.

According to Berndt (1991), two other comments should be made. First, since it typically costs more to provide electricity to meet peak demands (discussed in Chapter 10) utilities often charge premium rates during such times (months or time of day), which clearly affects the marginal price and adds an additional complication in modeling (forecasting) the quantity demanded of electricity. Second, it is often more cost effective to meter the consumption of larger users (industrial and large commercial) on a continuous basis and bill them not only on the basis of usage but also on their peak kilowatt demand over a short time interval, often a 15-minute or one-hour time span (known as a *demand charge*), which further complicates the measure of the marginal price. This has been largely ignored, which again raises the simultaneity issue and results in biased parameter estimates when ordinary least squares is used as an estimation technique.

Given the importance of electricity demand forecasts and their implications, forecast models have become end use in nature; that is, they are approached in a bottoms-up fashion, incorporating the demands of the various components (or end uses) of the appliances and electricity-using equipment in the dwelling (or building).

9.5 END-USE MODELS

As stated, the demand for electricity is a derived demand. Given this and the importance of accuracy in forecasting the demand for electricity (Note: *Demand* and *quantity demanded* are used interchangeably), not only is it imperative to include an appropriate measure of price in forecast models but also to include the stocks of equipment (i.e., electricity-using appliances and equipment) in such models.

Houthakker (1951) was among the first to recognize the importance of distinguishing between short- and long-run responses to not only price but also from the stock of equipment. This differs radically from what is typical of industry practitioners, who for many years merely used extrapolation techniques. As stated, such techniques worked well until the 1970s, when energy prices increased dramatically and actual sales fell far short of those forecasted in this fashion. The implications of this were grave: New generating assets (i.e., power plants) built based on forecasted demand that never materialized were (at least some portion) disallowed in the rate base, so that regulated utilities were not able to recover all of the costs of these investments in rates; as such, the utilities themselves or shareholders (in the case of investor-owned firms) bore the financial consequences of these inaccurate forecasts. Subsequently, it was determined that more sophisticated techniques were required to accurately forecast electricity sales. In the case of residential and commercial sales, the realization that a bottoms-up approach that explicitly included appliance and equipment stocks, weather, and other economic variables was needed spurred econometricians to pursue the development of such models, which is discussed here in some detail.

Residential end-use models

One of the first models that explicitly included the equipment stock is that of Franklin Fisher and Carl Kaysen (1962). Their model of the short-run demand for electricity of residential customers used engineering information on kilowatts used per hour of normal consumption by each appliance in a typical household, which was then aggregated to form a composite variable, W_{it}, for the ith household in time t. That is, the model they specified was given by

$$Q_{it} = P_{it}^{\alpha} Y_{it}^{\beta} W_{it} \tag{9.1}$$

where
   $P =$ price.
   $Y =$ income.
   $\alpha, \beta =$ parameters to be estimated.
Nonlinear in parameters, a logarithmic transformation yields

$$\ln Q_{it} = \alpha \ln P_{it} + \beta \ln Y_{it} + W_{it} \tag{9.2}$$

Attempting to estimate W_{it} by states and years with "any kind of reliability is simply out of the question" (Berndt, 1991).

Rather, they assumed that the stock of appliances in a given household in the ith state grew at a constant rate of γ percent per year:

$$W_{it}/W_{it-1} = \exp(\gamma_i) \tag{9.3}$$

or

$$\ln W_{it} - \ln W_{it-1} = \gamma_i \tag{9.4}$$

Lagging equation (9.2) by one time period and subtracting it from equation (9.2) yields (substituting in equation (9.4))

$$\ln Q_{it} - \ln Q_{it-1} = \gamma_i + \alpha_i(\ln P_{it} - \ln P_{it-1}) + \beta_i(\ln Y_{it} - \ln Y_{it-1}) \tag{9.5}$$

A random disturbance term (assumed to be independently and identically normally distributed (i.i.d.)) was then added to reflect the effects of stochastic elements and omitted variables, which were assumed to be uncorrelated with the regressors. Using data from 1946 to 1957, Fisher and Kaysen estimated the parameters α_i, β_i, and γ_i for each state in the United States using ordinary least squares.

Given the logarithmic specification of their model, the estimates of α_i and β_i are the estimated short-run price and income elasticities of demand for electricity, conditional on the stock of equipment in the household. In most cases, they found that these elasticities were close to 0 except in states whose economies were less developed; in these cases, the elasticities were much larger but less than unity.

At this juncture, it is important to reiterate how important the underlying data are in obtaining results. As is often the case and as was conceded by Fisher and Kaysen in the estimation of a long-run model, the poor quality of the data yielded positive estimates of the coefficient of the price variable and often those of the income variable were not statistically differ ent from zero in many instances.

This issue (the data) was also emphasized by Taylor, Blattenberger, and Rennhack (1984) who concluded that: "The results . . . are better than might have been realistically expected, but they are clearly much poorer than might have been hoped for. In general, the utilization equations are very good, whereas the capital stock equations leave much to be desired."

This notwithstanding, Taylor, Blattenberger, and Verleger (TBV, 1977) developed a model for the Electric Power Research Institute (EPRI) under a contract with Data Resources, Inc. (Electric Power Research Institute, 1984). More specifically, this model estimated the average use per customer as a function of electricity prices, per capita income, the availability of natural gas, and the ratio of actual to normal heating and cooling degree days weighted by the saturations of electric space heating and air conditioning, respectively. This allowed for the response to weather on appliances that were affected by weather. The original model used panel data comprising 15 annual observations (1960–1975) for each state. Some of the attributes include

1. The separation of the electric price into fixed versus marginal components.
2. The availability of natural gas, which allows for the possibility of fuel substitution and price elasticities.

A similar model was developed for the U.S. Department of Energy by Carney and Hirst at Oak Ridge National Laboratory (ORNL) for Residential and Commercial customers. The ORNL Residential Energy Demand Model (REDM) calculates annual energy use for four fuels (electricity, natural gas, oil, and other) by eight end uses (space heating, air conditioning, water heating, refrigeration, freezing, cooking, lighting, and other) in each of three types of dwelling (single family, multifamily, and mobile homes) for each year from 1970 to 2000. The REDM was composed of four major modules, each of which is a complex model on its own (EPRI, 1984):

1. **Housing module.** Calculates the housing stock by type of dwelling and keeps track of the vintage of the housing stock.
2. **Economics module.** Calculates fuel market shares and appliance utilization rates based on price and income elasticities for the ownership and use of appliances.
3. **Technologies module.** Analyzes equipment efficiency versus capital and operating costs to determine optimal efficiency levels for appliances and buildings.
4. **Energy-use simulation module.** Uses modules 1–3 to determine energy use by housing type, end use, and fuel.

This model had the capability to distinguish explicit fuel substitution and the ability to separate price elasticities into three components: ownership (i.e., market share), efficiency, and usage. Like the TBV model, this model allows for explicit fuel substitution and the separation of price elasticities into three components: market share, efficiency, and usage.

The EPRI Residential Sector End-Use Electricity Planning Model (REEPS)

A paper produced by Koomey, Brown, Richey, Johnson, Sanstad and Shown (1995) entitled, "Residential Sector End-Use Forecasting with EPRIREEPS 2.1. Summary Input Assumptions and Results" provides a nice synopsis of this model, which is discussed in some detail since it is still used by many utilities in the United States:

1. Introduction

Energy end-use forecasting models characterize the long-term structure of energy consumption in homes under differing assumptions, scenarios, and policies. At the national level, end-use forecasting models facilitate the analysis of energy conservation programs and policy initiatives that are broad in scope, such as residential standards and national energy policy initiatives. In addition, utilities rely on end-use forecasting models to do long-term forecasting, assess market trends for new technologies, and to develop demand-side management (DSM) programs.

The Residential End-Use Energy Planning System (REEPS 2.1)1, developed by the Electric. Power Research Institute (EPRI), is a forecasting model that allows users to define customized models for various energy end-uses in the residential sector, including appliances and heating, ventilation, and air conditioning (HVAC) equipment. The model for each end-use can be configured with its own structure, data, and functional relationships. Using the modeling framework provided by the Appliance and HVAC modules in REEPS, researchers at the Ernest Orlando Lawrence Berkeley National Laboratory (LBNL) have developed individual forecasting models for refrigerators, freezers, clothes dryers, water heaters, clothes washers, dishwashers, lighting, cooking, and HVAC equipment.

2. Overview of the REEPS Model

The REEPS model incorporates the basic features of residential end-use forecasting into a generalized modeling framework in which the user has considerable control over the algorithms and model structure. All users of the REEPS forecasting system use a common software framework that allows them to focus on the substantive aspects of analysis and avoid potential programming errors introduced by changes in the software source code. The REEPS framework allows for greater flexibility than traditional forecasting models, which are "hardwired" for particular formulations of residential-sector energy use. Rather than relying on a fixed set of equations and/or parameters, the user can customize the equations used to forecast future appliance, HVAC equipment, and housing char-acteristics. Both the functional form and the parameters included in these equa-tions can be modified by the user. This allows the user to model a wide range of scenarios and policies, at varying levels of disaggregation, without ever changing the computer program's source code (McMenamin et al., 1992).

REEPS uses a state-based approach to forecasting in which consumer pur-chase decisions are modeled based on the "state" of the decision maker (e.g., household characteristics and household ownership of appliances and HVAC equipment). Base-year (1990) data are used to characterize the existing stock of appliances and HVAC equipment and the homes in which they are used.

Empirical values of unit energy consumption (UEC), ownership, efficiency, and size/capacity in the control year (1991) are used to calibrate decision models within the end-use models. Based on this control-year data, the model creates a set of calibration factors that remain in place for the duration of the forecast.

As described in the REEPS manual (McMenamin et al., 1992), the three primary steps of forecast execution for each forecasted year are:

1. Accounting for changes in stock, based on equipment decay;
2. Execution of equipment purchase models; and
3. Updating of equipment stock and computation of energy sales.

In the first step, equipment decay is used to account for changes in the aver-age stock efficiency due to retirements and replacements of equipment. In the second step, ownership, efficiency, and equipment size/capacity are calculated for replacement purchases, equipment conversion purchases, and purchases for installation in newly constructed houses. In the third step, the characteristics of the equipment stock are updated based on the results of the purchase decisions identified in the second step.

Special issues for the HVAC equipment module

As mentioned above, HVAC equipment is treated differently from appliances in REEPS because of the complex physical and economic interactions that charac-terize HVAC systems. HVAC equipment is therefore modeled as a combination of heating, cooling, and distribution system components, so that an HVAC system is chosen by the model. In addition, the energy use of an HVAC system is largely dependent on the thermal shell of the house in which it is installed.

Consequently, engineering data on building thermal shells are incorporated into the HVAC equipment module.

In the HVAC module, there are ten primary heating technologies and two primary cooling technologies. Secondary sources (such as Room AC and wood stoves) are considered to be supplements to primary sources and are modeled in less detail in the REEPS modeling framework. The three distribution systems in the model are hydronic, forced-air, and "none". The combination of a heating technology, cooling technology, and distribution system defines a discrete HVAC system in REEPS. Sixteen unique systems of heating and cooling equipment are modeled; these systems are tracked independently throughout the model.

Estimating the shares of the various options for HVAC equipment is accomplished via a discrete choice modeling (see later, "Digression: Discrete choice models for determining HVAC appliance shares") methodology, which specifically accounts for multiple factors such as

- The influence of space cooling preferences on heating equipment choice.
- The impact of capital and operating costs on HVAC system choice.
- The impact of changing efficiency standards.

The REEPS model contains discrete choice equations for each end use that incorporate numerous factors, including those mentioned previously. Choice equations are maintained for 18 HVAC systems and eight household appliances. The choice equations are used to construct a "multinomial" share system for all end uses. Each equation relates the market share of an end use to its economic attractiveness relative to that of alternative technologies. This reflects the notion that customer choice is dependent on the available alternatives. These equations incorporate projected changes in energy prices, efficiency standards, equipment capital costs, structure characteristics, household income, natural gas availability, household decay rates, and other household demographics to derive the relative attractiveness of the competing end-use technologies. The equations are calibrated to known market shares for a base year and the first forecast year, which typically come from customer surveys that utilities perform on a regular basis. A calibration term is estimated in the calibration process and represents an estimate of all the noneconomic factors affecting market share of an appliance. The market share of each end use for different dwelling types (single family, multifamily, and mobile home) may then be calculated by the discrete choice equations.

In the first iteration, the REEPS model predicts the percentage of residential customers that would select electric space heating. HVAC system conversions are part of this electric space heating saturation forecast. Then the forecasted percentage of electric space heating customers would be multiplied by the customer forecast for each housing type. The resulting customer forecast is used as an input to a second REEPS model. This model incorporates a database of households with electric space heating and could be used to predict the percentage of customers with electric space heating that will also select electric water heating. The forecasted electric water heating saturations from the second model are multiplied by the electric space heating customer forecast.

Digression: Discrete choice models for determining HVAC appliance shares

End-use models begin with the simple assumption that consumers seek to maximize utility (or comfort) by choosing that combination of heating and cooling technology that provides the most comfort for a given cost, which typically involves a trade-off between purchase price and operating cost. More specifically, the consumer's objective function is given by

$$\text{Max } U_{ij} = \beta_1 PP_{ij} + \beta_2 OC_{ij} + \varepsilon_{ij}, \text{ for all } i, j \in n \text{ and for all } n \in N \quad (9.6)$$

where

PP = the purchase price of the appliance (including installation).

OC = the operating cost of the appliance, which is a function of fuel price, efficiency, capacity, and dwelling size; In addition, weather and personal preferences come into play.

One relevant feature that must be considered in choosing a specification is the interrelationships among various appliances. For example, if a dwelling is heated with natural gas, then it is likely that it also has a gas water heater, dryer, and uses natural gas for cooking. In this case, the likely choice of cooling is either central air or room air conditioners, since a heat pump would be redundant in terms of heating. Given this, one of the most commonly used specifications is the sequential logit model, which was developed by Daniel McFadden, who has done extensive work in the area of travel demand. Since the cost of the cooling system chosen (*i*) depends highly on the type of heating system installed (*j*), the two choices are modeled jointly via a sequential logit model (also known as a *nested-logit specification*), in which there are two levels: the lower-level heating choice and the upper-level cooling choice. More specifically, the utility function specified in (9.6) is of the general form

$$U_{ij} = V_i + W_{ij} + \varepsilon_{ij}, \text{ for all } i, j \in n \text{ and for all } n \in N \quad (9.7)$$

where

i = index of cooling alternatives.

j = index of space heating alternatives.

U_{ij} = total utility from a given HVAC system, n.

V_i = utility from central air alternative i, which is a function of capital and operating cost.

W_{ij} = utility from the heating choice j given the choice of cooling i (also a function of costs).

ε_{ij} = random components of utility; assumed to be GEV distributed (see Appendix 9.1 for details).

n = one of the choices.

N = all of the choices.

Collecting the appropriate data enables estimation of this model, which then becomes an input to another equation that enables the utility to forecast the share (or probability) of a household's choice of HVAC system. Such an equation is given by

$$\text{share}_n = \exp{(U_n)}/\sum\nolimits_N \exp{(U_N)}, \text{ for all } n \in N \qquad (9.8)$$

(These are discussed in more detail in the section "Nested-logit models.")

To estimate these equations, it is necessary to collect cost data on HVAC systems, which is the next step. Because of the interdependency among heating and cooling systems, the nested-logit specification is appropriate to calculate the shares. The next section provides a description of this methodology.

Nested-logit models

Due to the high correlation between the choice of space heating fuel and the presence of central air conditioning, the decision regarding the purchase of each is most appropriately made jointly. As such, a multinomial logit model to represent the joint choice requires two levels, each requiring the specification of a utility function: one for the "upper-level" cooling choice and the other for the "lower-level" heating choice. This is known as a *nested-logit model*. Such a structure is displayed by the decision tree in Figure 9.7 for a very simple model that has two level cooling choices:

1. Central air for cooling and a forced air furnace with two fuel choices for heating.
2. A heat pump (air or ground source) for cooling and for heating.

(Actual steps and mathematics are detailed in Appendix 9.1 of this chapter.)

Kenneth Train's Web site[3] contains data on 250 new homes in California, which can be used to calculate the expected shares of heating and cooling appliances. An example in which these are calculated is included in Appendix 9.1 and the results are displayed in Table 9.1.

---

[3] See http://elsa.berkeley.edu/~train/ps.html.

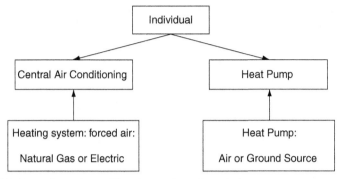

Figure 9.7 Nested structure of heating and cooling choice

Table 9.1 Estimated Shares of HVAC Systems, California Data on 250 New Homes

Alternative	Description	Share
1	CAC—gas furnace	0.745
2	CAC—electric furnace	0.0158
3	CAC—electric room	0.0045
4	HPMP—HPMP	0.104
5	No CAC—gas furnace	0.096
6	No CAC—electric furnace	0.0036
7	No CAC—electric room	0.0309

Discussion of results

As Table 9.1 shows, the most likely choice is the first one: central air conditioning (CAC) with a gas furnace, which is present in 74.5% of households. The next most likely choice is CAC with an electric furnace (expected to be chosen by 15.8% of households) followed by a heat pump (10.4% of households), and so forth.

Needless to say, such models are extremely data intensive; often, the data required for these models are not only expensive (in terms of cost and time) but also the models themselves are quite cumbersome (in terms of complexity). The REEPS model is characterized by both. However, when end-use models came into vogue, much work was done in the data collection and the writing of documentation explaining how such models were constructed, and several papers were written in explanation of the REEPS model and each of its modules. For example, share equations were estimated from data gathered in the late 1980s; as such, the parameters in REEPs are exogenous rather than estimated via the model itself. (One of the selling points of the model was that the users could change the parameters to fit the characteristics of their service territory, which would in itself take extensive knowledge of discrete choice models, the appropriate software that is capable of estimating such models, and of course, the required data.)

As a simpler step, RER (now Itron) developed the Statistically Adjusted End-Use Model (SAE) which uses data provided by the Energy Information Administration for the shares and efficiencies required to estimate end-use models and accord to a particular region in the United States. (The EIA uses these data along with other economic and demographic variables in, at least, two of the modules of the National Energy Modeling System, NEMS, to produce the Annual Energy Outlook discussed previously in this chapter.) The SAE model is discussed in the next section.

The Statistically Adjusted End-Use Model

The SAE model uses economic and demographic variables along with weather, dwelling size, and the stock and efficiency of electricity-using appliances and equipment to forecast the per customer usage of electricity for both residential and commercial customers. The focus here is on the residential end-use model.

Model design

More specifically, the equation to be estimated is given by

$$\text{Use per customer}_t = \alpha_1 \, \text{Xheat}_t + \alpha_2 \, \text{Xcool}_t + \alpha_3 \, \text{Xother}_t + \varepsilon_t \quad (9.9)$$

where

$\text{Xheat}_t = $ the component of usage due to heating in time t.

$\text{Xcool}_t = $ the component of usage due to cooling in time t.

$\text{Xother}_t = $ the usage associated with "other" electricity-using appliances and equipment in time t.

These are known as the X variables and are discussed in more detail later.

Often, it is the case that a first-order correction for serial correlation is included (an AR(1) term), which is defined as:

$$\varepsilon_t = \rho \, v_{t-1} + v_t \quad (9.10)$$

where $v_t \sim N(0, 1)$.

X variables

In general, the X variables in the preceding equation are functions of weather, economic and demographic factors, and structural and technological characteristics of homes and appliances. More specifically, each of

them is a function of two components: an index, which captures the struc
tural and technological aspects of a particular appliance; and a use variable,
which encompasses the economic and demographic aspects of that variable. The form of the X variable is given by

$$X = \text{Index}_y \times \text{Use} \tag{9.11}$$

where

X = estimated energy use for the year (kWh).

Index_y = annual index of equipment (a weighted average across equipment type of equipment saturation levels normalized by operating efficiency levels).

Use = annual usage multiplier.

That is, the index variable is defined as

$$\text{Index}_y = \sum_{\text{Type}} \text{Wgt}^{\text{Type}} \times \text{SI} \times \left(\text{Share}_y^{\text{Type}}/\text{Eff}_y^{\text{Type}}\right) \Big/ \left(\text{Share}_{by}^{\text{Type}}/\text{Eff}_{by}^{\text{Type}}\right)$$

$$\tag{9.12}$$

where

$\text{Share}_y^{\text{Type}}$ = share of appliance for each year.

$\text{Share}_{by}^{\text{Type}}$ = share of appliance in the base year.

$\text{Eff}_y^{\text{Type}}$ = efficiency of appliance for each year.

$\text{Eff}_{by}^{\text{Type}}$ = efficiency of appliance in the base year.

Wgt^{Type} = unit energy consumption of appliance in the base year.

SI = structural index (volume of space to be heated or cooled).[4]

As stated, economic and demographic data are captured via the use variable, which is defined as

$$\text{Use}_y = (\text{BD, DD}_y)/\text{NormDD} \times (\text{HHSize}_y/\text{HHSize}_{by})^\gamma$$
$$\times (\text{Income}_y/\text{Income}_{by})^\eta \times (\text{Price}_y/\text{Price}_{by})^\varepsilon \tag{9.13}$$

where

BD, DD_y = annual billing, degree days.

NormDD = normal value of annual billing, degree days.

HHSize_y = average household size in a year.

HHSize_{by} = average household size in the base year.

Income_y = average real income per household in a year.

[4] $\text{SI}_y = \text{SA}_y \times$ Shell efficiency$_y/\text{SA}_{by} \times$ Shell efficiency$_{by}$ where SA_y = Surface area = $892 + 1.44 \times$
Dwelling size (square feet)

Income$_{by}$ = average real price of electricity in the base year.

Price$_y$ = average real price of electricity.

γ, η, and ε = elasticities of demand.

Data sources and so forth

As stated, the U.S. EIA provides much of the information required to estimate this model. However, some series are particular to a particular utility, such as prices, which tend to be proprietary in nature.

Commercial end-use models

The commercial sector also has certain characteristics that are well suited for end-use modeling. One of the first models developed to estimate electricity consumption in this sector was created by DRI for EPRI. Similar to the TBV model, the EPRI Commercial Model estimated consumption by electricity price (also broken down between fixed and marginal components), per capita income, population, and the ratio of actual to normal cooling degree days weighted by the stock of commercial floor space. This model was estimated using the variance-components by Balestra and Nerlove on a panel data set consisting of eleven annual observations (1965–1975) for each of the lower 48 states (Electric Power Research Institute, 1984).

The Oak Ridge National Laboratory also developed an end-use model for the commercial sector. The ORNL Disaggregated Commercial End Use Model (CEUM) calculated the annual consumption of four fuels (electricity, natural gas, oil, other) for each of five end uses (space heating, cooling, water heating, lighting, and other) in each of 10 building types. Like the residential model, there are several components to this model, including

1. **Building stock** calculates new additions, removals (or demolitions), and the total stock of floor space in each year.
2. **Energy use indices** specify the amount of energy required per square foot of floor space served by a particular end use and fuel.
3. **Utilization rates are** relative to a base year and are calculated for each fuel and use on the basis of short-run, own-price elasticities.

Like the residential end-use model, this model had the capability to incorporate explicit fuel substitution and separate price effects into fuel choice, efficiency, and usage components. In addition, it also provided the capability to separate price-induced conservation from mandated conservation and incorporate building and appliance efficiency standards.

The Commercial Statistically Adjusted End-Use Model

Like the residential SAE model, the commercial model estimates per customer usage as a function of heating, cooling, and other end-use equipment. That is,

$$\text{Use per customer}_t = \alpha_1 \, X\text{heat}_t + \alpha_2 \, X\text{cool}_t + \alpha_3 \, X\text{other}_t + \varepsilon_t \quad (9.14)$$

Both models are similar in structure; however, in the case of the commercial model, *output* (or real gross state product) is substituted for *income* in the use variables. Also, like the residential models, regions are divided into nine census divisions and the requisite data can be obtained from the EIA, which is used in the Commercial Demand Module of NEMS.

Industrial models

Both EPRI and ORNL also produced industrial end-use models. However, given that many industrial customers export their products, service territory characteristics have not proven to be the best explanatory variables and end-use models have not worked well. Given this and that some industries are more energy intensive than others, macroeconomic variables tend to be better in forecasting industrial sales. For example, the Industrial Production Index (IPI) for a particular industry (steel, for example) will likely prove to be an important regressor in the forecast of electricity sales to a steel mill or industries that utilize steel in the production process of the ultimate output being produced (autos, for example). However, with this said, certainly, microeconomic variables also come into play. Clearly, the price (or rate) paid for electricity is an important factor. In many cases, it can mean staying in business, closing a plant, or relocating facilities (and jobs) elsewhere.

This chapter provides a brief history and overview of electricity demand forecasting models, including data sources and some other issues of interest. It is in no way meant to be complete nor comprehensive since there are many fine textbooks on the subject.

APPENDIX 9.1 A NESTED-LOGIT MODEL FOR DETERMINING HEATING AND COOLING CHOICE: EXAMPLE

An (advanced) example can be used to illustrate a nested-logit model for heating and cooling choice in new homes. At his Web site, Kenneth Train provides an example that uses the following choices:
1. Central cooling with a gas furnace.
2. Central cooling with an electric furnace.

3. Central cooling with electric room heating (resistance heating).
4. Heat pump (central heating and cooling).
5. No central cooling, gas furnace.
6. No central cooling, electric furnace.
7. No central cooling, electric room heating.

The state of California provides excellent data sources on installed costs as well as operating costs for these choices so that the shares can be calculated (via equation (9.8))

Recalling that the individual consumer's utility function is given by equation (9.7):

$$U_{ij} = V_i + W_{ij} + \varepsilon_{ij}$$

where

V_i = utility from cooling choice i.

W_{ij} = utility from heating choice j given cooling choice i.

Specifically, Figure 9.8 displays the nested-logit structure of the consumer's utility maximization problem.

That is, from equation (9.7),

$$W_{ij} = \alpha_1 \text{Alt1} + \alpha_2 \text{Alt2} + \alpha_3 \text{Alt3} + \beta_{\text{HIC}}\text{HIC}_i \\ + \beta_{\text{HOC}}\text{HOC}_i + \delta_{\text{incr}}\text{Incr}_i + \varepsilon_i \tag{9A.1}$$

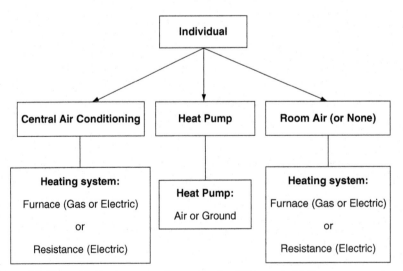

Figure 9.8 Nested-logit structure of consumer's utility maximization

and

$$V_i = \beta_{CIC}CIC_i + \beta_{COC}COC_i + \delta_{incc}Incc_i + \varepsilon_i \qquad (9A.2)$$

where

Alt1–Alt3 = binary variables for alternatives 1–3 (central air, heat pump, no air).

HIC, CIC = installation costs of heating (HIC) and cooling (CIC).

HOC, COC = operating costs of heating (HOC) and cooling (COC).

Incr, Incc = binary variables for income × room heating and income × central cooling options.

These equations, (9A.1) and (9A.2), are estimated via the following steps:

1. Estimate heating equipment choice parameters (conditioned on AC choice i), β_{HIC} and β_{HOC}:

$$W_{ij} = \beta_{HIC}HIC_{ij} + \beta_{HOC}HOC_{ij} + \varepsilon_{ij} \qquad (9A.1')$$

The conditional probability of choosing heating option j given the choice of cooling option i can be expressed as:

$$P_{ij} = \exp\left[W_{ij}/(1 - \theta)\right]/\sum_{\jmath} \exp[W_{i\jmath}/(1 - \theta)], \text{ for all } j \in \mathcal{J} \qquad (9A.3)$$

where θ is the parameter for the generalized extreme value (GEV) distribution. It measures the correlation between the error terms of the heating technologies and cooling equipment choices. In this case, $\theta = 0.6526$.[5] Estimation allows one to calculate the index of aggregate characteristics at the lower level, which is known as the inclusive value. This is given by

$$I_i = \ln\left(\sum_{\jmath} e^{W_{i\jmath}}\right) \qquad (9A.4)$$

2. Estimate the cooling equipment choice parameters, β_{CIC} and β_{COC}:

$$V_i = \beta_{CIC}CIC_i + \beta_{COC}COC_i + \varepsilon_i \qquad (9A.2')$$

where the marginal probability of choosing cooling option i is given by

$$P_i = \exp(V_i + \theta IV)/\sum_I \exp(V_i + \theta IV), \text{ for all } i \in I \qquad (9A.5)$$

---

[5]

$$\mathbf{F}(\varepsilon_{11} \ldots \varepsilon_{ij}) = \exp\left\{-\sum_i\left[\sum_j \exp(\varepsilon_{ij}/(1 - \theta)\right]^{(1-\theta)}\right\}$$

For consistency with utility maximization, $0 < \theta < 1$.

Table 9A.1 Nested-Logit Model Results

Parameter	Estimate	t-statistic
α_1	2.82	5.92
α_2	2.69	2.53
α_3	12.04	5.01
β_{HIC}	−0.0069	−5.80
β_{HOC}	−0.0270	−5.50
β_{CIC}	−0.0035	−3.84
β_{COC}	−0.0231	−2.85
δ_{Incr}	−0.3590	−4.05
δ_{Incc}	0.2499	4.84
θ	0.6526	3.27

Estimation results are provided in Table 9A.1.

As indicated in Table 9A.1, all estimated coefficients are statistically different from 0.

McFadden's likelihood ratio test is analogous to R^2 in linear regression models. In this case,

$$R_M^2 = 1 - \ln L/\ln L_0 = 0.8641$$

Given the results obtained in Table 9A1, the share (i.e., probability of choosing) of heating when cooling is given by the conditional probability, P_{ji}, which is expressed as

$$P_{ji} = \exp\left(2.82 \times \text{Alt1} + 2.69 \times \text{Alt2} + 12.04 \times \text{Alt3} - 0.0069 \times \text{HIC} - 0.027 \times \text{HOC}_i - 0.3590 \times \text{Incr}\right)/\sum_{\mathcal{J}}\exp(2.82 \times \text{Alt1} + 2.69 \times \text{Alt2} + 12.04\text{Alt3} - 0.0069 \times \text{HIC} - 0.027 \times \text{HOC}_i\, 0.3590 \times \text{Incr})$$

and the marginal probability, P_i, is given by

$$P_i = \exp(-0.0035 \times \text{CIC}i - 0.023 \times \text{COC}i + 0.25 \times \text{Incc}_i + 0.6526 \times IV)/\sum_I\exp(-0.0035 \times \text{CIC}_i - 0.023 \times \text{COC}_i + 0.25 \times \text{Incc}_i + 0.6526 \times IV)$$

where $IV = \ln\sum_{\mathcal{J}}\exp(W_{ij})$, the natural log of the denominator of P_{ji}.

Note: P_{ji} and P_i are analogous to

$$\text{share}_n = \exp(U_n)/\sum_N\exp(U_N) \qquad (9A.6)$$

The results from these calculations are displayed in Table 9.1.

APPENDIX 9.2 THE COMPONENTS OF THE EIA'S AEO 2009 MODEL

1. Macroeconomic Activity Module
2. International Energy Module
3. Residential Demand Module
4. Commercial Demand Module
5. Industrial Demand Module
6. Transportation Demand Module
7. Electricity Market Module
8. Oil and Gas Supply Module
9. Natural Gas Transmission and Distribution Module
10. Petroleum Market Module
11. Coal Market Module
12. Renewable Fuels Module

Appendix. Handling of Federal and Selected State Legislation and Regulation in the Annual Energy Outlook: The Energy Independence and Security Act of 2007 (EISA07)

From the Commercial Demand Module: EISA 2007

The EISA07 legislation passed in December 2007 provides standards for the following explicitly modeled commercial equipment. The EISA07 requires specific energy efficiency measures in commercial walk-in coolers and walk-in freezers effective January 1, 2009. Incandescent and halogen lamps must meet standards for maximum allowable wattage based on lumen output starting in 2012 and metal halide lamp fixtures using lamps between 150 and 500 watts are required to have a minimum ballast efficiency ranging from 88 to 94%, depending on ballast type, effective January 1, 2009.

The EISA07 requirement for Federal buildings to use energy efficient lighting fixtures and bulbs to the maximum extent possible is represented by adjusting the proportion of the commercial sector assumed to use the 10-year Treasury Bill rate as an implicit discount or hurdle rate for lighting.

Efficient Pricing of Electricity

In this chapter, we examine the various methodologies by which rates are set under regulation and the reasons that these rarely lead to a Pareto efficient outcome, which occurs when no one is made better off if someone else is made worse off. In fact, only by pricing at marginal cost, which is both allocatively and productively efficient (and maximizes welfare), does such an outcome result, and this is the theme of this chapter.

10.1 THE DEBATE ON THE OPTIMAL PRICING OF ELECTRICITY: A BRIEF HISTORY

The idea of marginal cost pricing is not new; for centuries, economists have espoused that pricing goods and services at marginal cost is both allocatively and productively efficient. In the case of electricity, it was actually two engineers who, in the late 19th century, argued for marginal cost pricing, also known as *time-of-use* or *real-time* pricing. The following excerpt contains a nice synopsis of the history of the debate on the optimal pricing of electricity, which requires an accurate estimation of the marginal cost of providing service to various types of end users (residential, commercial, industrial, etc.).

In the introduction to his treatise on demand response and efficient pricing, "Renewed Interest in Demand Response, but 'Whither the Economic Rationale for Efficient Pricing?'" which appeared in the *USAEE Dialogue* in August 2007, John Kelly (president of the American Public Power Association), wrote: "The time for implementing practical marginal cost pricing programs is long overdue, and almost anything that encourages marginal cost pricing is beneficial, whether under the guise of demand response or otherwise. However, it is appropriate to ask whether current analyses and discussions of demand response—which have become a cottage industry—are producing more heat than light on the subject because they stray from basic notions about economic costs."

This is an excellent point and in the next two sections he provides a brief history of the concept of marginal cost pricing applied to electricity, which I reprint here with Mr. Kelly's consent.

Electricity Cost Modeling Calculations
DOI: 10.1016/B978-1-85617-726-9.00010-8

II. Demand Response Proposal More than a Century Old

Professors John Neufeld and William Hausman tell us that in 1894 engineer Alfred Gibbings made the case for time-of-use rates in terms that "came quite close to holding that prices should equal marginal costs." He criticized rates based on demand charges on grounds that are essentially the same as those modern economists use to criticize such charges. Neufeld and Hausman go on to note that W. S. Barstow, an engineer like Gibbings, was another early advocate of time-of-use rates and argued for the principle of marginal cost pricing. In 1895 at a meeting of the Association of Edison Illuminating Companies (AEIC), he argued that a utility should charge "customers a low rate during the light load" periods. Particularly interesting is Barstow's rationale for adopting time-of-day rate structures: The two-rate system seems to produce two desired results:

1. *The broadening of the maximum peak, and*
2. *An equally important result, the increasing of minimum peaks; that is it encourages the forming of peaks during the minimum period of the load curve.*

This justification is especially important because it states a central rationale for the principle of marginal cost pricing. It recognizes the implications of such pricing for economic efficiency of electricity production and lowering costs, specifically by designing rate structures to improve the utilization of electricity plants and to lower average costs. It seems that engineers, like Gibbings and Barstow, were the first to recognize the important connection between time differentiated rates, capacity utilization, and costs. Hausman and Neufeld "found no evidence that professional economists had any input into the electric power industry's discussion about rate structures" during the very early years of the industry. But when economists eventually enter discussions about rate structures "they immediately embraced time-of-day rates on the basis of marginal cost considerations, even though they did not use the term 'marginal cost.'" For example, in a 1911 paper titled "Rates for Public Utilities," John Maurice Clark advocated prices based on marginal cost: If consumers can make extra demands on the utility without paying as much as the extra expense they are causing, they are likely to make wastefully large demands on it . . . But any consumers who cannot make extra use of the utility without paying many times more than the extra expense they would be causing, will skimp on their use, and the tendency will be to keep the plant in wasteful idleness."

About ten years later, economist George Watkins wrote one of the first books, Electric Rates, devoted solely to the pricing of electricity. Hausman and Neufeld found that "the justification for differential rates was clear" to Watkins; it "was to improve the efficiency of resource allocation. Differential rates existed solely to improve the utility load factor and Watkins emphasized rates reflecting marginal costs as the way to achieve this greater efficiency and enhance social welfare." The main reason customers should be charged more during peak periods than nonpeak periods, Watkins said, was to encourage consumption during nonpeak hours, thereby making better use of utility plants and lowering the average cost of electricity.

The emphasis on the importance of marginal cost as a guide to efficient pricing and the efficient use of existing resources was continued in the 1930s with Harold Hotelling's classic paper "The General Welfare in Relation to Taxation and of Railway and Utility Rates." James Bonbright at the time considered Hotelling's "one of the most distinguished contributions to ratemaking theory in the entire literature of economics."

From the late 1940s to the end of the 20th century, Professor William Vickrey was among the leading proponents of efficient pricing of utility services. He urged that electric rate structures should "be developed by careful weighing of the relevant factors with a view of guiding consumers to make efficient use of facilities that are available." He argued that electricity should be priced based on short-run marginal cost, and although the principle need "not in practice to be followed absolutely, it must play a major and even dominant role in the elaboration of any scheme of rates or prices that seriously pretends to have a major motive of the efficient utilization of available resources and facilities." More broadly, marginal cost principles are recognized as the starting point for the proper pricing of goods and services.

Thomas Nagle and Ronald Holden tell managers in other industries that "not all costs are relevant for every pricing decision." Relevant costs are "costs that are incremental (not average), avoidable (not sunk)." They go on to note that relevant costs are "those that actually determine the profit impact of the pricing decision."

Unfortunately, most discussions of demand response obscure the compelling economic logic that prices should reflect the time-varying cost – the marginal cost – of electricity service so that existing facilities are used more efficiently and rates are lower than under existing ratemaking practices based on fully allocated cost accounting practices.

III. A Renewed Interest in Demand Response, But "Whither the Economic Rationale for Efficient Pricing?"

The last time there was such high interest in demand response as there is today was in the late 1970s after the Public Utility Regulatory Policies Act was enacted. A large part of the recent interest is due to the disconnect between the time-varying prices of electricity in spot markets and the essentially nonvarying prices charged in retail markets.

In 2004, the Government Accountability Office issued a report that concluded that increased use of demand response would improve efficiency in the electric utility industry and recommended that state utility commissions do more to promote demand response programs. The Energy Policy Act of 2005 directed the Secretary of Energy to provide "Congress with a report that identifies and quantifies the national benefits of demand response and make a recommendation on achieving specific levels of such benefits." The U.S. Department of Energy (DOE) early the following year issued a report titled "Benefits of Demand Response in Electricity Markets and Recommendations for Achieving Them." The act also instructed the Federal Energy Regulatory Commission to assess the use of demand response programs and related metering technologies in the nation, and in August 2006 the FERC released the results of an industrywide survey. In addition, states have showed renewed interest in demand response. For example, the state of California *commissioned a study to evaluate the benefits of so-called "critical peak pricing" that would allow sharply higher prices during critical peak times.*

But what does the term "demand response" mean? The term is variously defined, but DOE's definition is representative: Changes in electricity usage by end-use customers from their normal consumption patterns in response to changes in the price of electricity over time, or to incentive payments to induce lower electricity use at times of high wholesale market prices or when system reliability is jeopardized.

The DOE report says that states should consider aggressive implementation of price-based demand response a "high priority." They should do this because "flat, average-cost retail rates that do not reflect the actual cost to supply power lead to inefficient capital investment in new generation, transmission, and distribution infrastructure and higher electric bills for consumers."

More specifically, it states that:

> " [The] disconnect between short-term marginal electricity production costs and retail rates paid by consumers leads to an inefficient use of resources. Because customers don't see the underlying short-term cost of supplying electricity, they have little or no incentive to adjust their demand or supply-side conditions. Thus, flat electricity prices encourage customers to over-consume relative to an optimally efficient system in hours when electricity prices are higher than average rates, and under-consume in hours when the cost of producing electricity is lower than average rates. As a result electricity costs may be higher than they would otherwise be because high-cost generators must sometimes run to meet the non-price responsive demands of consumers."

These are cogent words, but how do we put them into practice? That is where the topic of rate design comes into play.

10.2 RATE DESIGN

In the introductory chapter, the utility's *revenue requirement* is introduced; that is, the amount of dollars that must be collected from ratepayers to recover the utility's expenses (and required return, in the case of investor-owned utilities) for the period during which such rates would be in effect. However, until now, no discussion has examined how the revenue requirement would be allocated among different customer classes nor the various methodologies by which said revenue requirement would be recovered. And this is the objective of this chapter: to present the various methodologies employed in the process of rate recovery and some of the consequences that could emerge as the result of nonoptimal rate-making mechanisms. In essence, what we are once again talking about is how to design rates to motivate both producers and consumers to make appropriate choices and behave in an optimal manner in terms of consumption, investment, and conservation.

Formally, the *rate design* process is that which determines how the revenue requirement will be allocated among the various customer classes. At best (and at the highest level), it is presumably determined according to the cost that each class imposes on the system, which is also known as cost-of-service regulation. However, politics often enter into the mix and certain customer classes do not necessarily pay the full cost that servicing them imposes on the system (i.e., their cost of service). As such, the issue of *cross-subsidy* is pervasive and an important consideration. Residential customers are voters and are well represented at utility rate proceedings (by the states' Attorneys General office); as such they are often subsidized by the larger classes, which is discussed later in this chapter.

More about rate design: In theory

As said, the rate design process determines the portion of the revenue requirement to be recovered by each customer class and the methodology by which it will be recovered; that is, fixed versus usage charges.

In most cases, the process begins with a cost-of-service study performed by the utility. It attempts to classify the costs of generation, transmission, and distribution among the components of such costs (i.e., customer, energy, and demand charges) by the various customer classes (residential, commercial, industrial, and other). In some cases, these costs are further delineated by season (winter or summer) and even by-time-of use (peak vs. off-peak, or more frequent).

More formally, the rate design process consists of the following steps:
- Determination of total costs and revenue requirements.
- Functionalization of costs.
- Classification of costs.
- Identification of rate classes.
- Design of end-user rates.

Each will be discussed in turn.

An overview of the rate design process
Total revenue requirements

Total revenue requirements are the total costs incurred by the utility in the provision of service. It is the amount to be recovered from ratepayers as authorized by the state's public regulatory commission. In the determination of this amount, costs are grouped into capital, operations and maintenance (O&M), administrative, and taxes. The revenue requirement (or total cost of service) is the sum of the return on undepreciated capital investment and all other expenses. The standard equations for revenue requirements are[1]

$$RR = (RB) \times r + E + D + T + O \tag{10.1}$$

and

$$RB = (PV - CD) \tag{10.2}$$

where RR = revenue requirements; r = allowed rate of return; RB = rate base; E = operating expenses; D = annual depreciation; T = taxes; O = other expenses; PV = plant value (investment in plant); CD = cumulative depreciation.

Functionalization and classification of costs

Utilities are required to keep a detailed accounting of their costs, which can be grouped by major category, such as utility plant, operating expenditures, and taxes. Under each of these a number of subaccounts exist; for example, utility plant may include land and right of way, plant equipment, and other structures and improvements. For the purpose of rate design, costs from the different categories are grouped by operating function: generation, transmission, and distribution. This is the process of functionalization.

Once functionalized, these costs are further broken down by their consumption or cost causation characteristics, which includes demand (or capacity), energy related (the cost of fuel), customer related (metering and billing), and revenue related (tax receipts and some overhead costs) (Harunuzzaman and Koundinya, 2000).

Determination of rate classes

The next step is to separate customers into rate classes so that the costs of servicing each can be determined. Rate classes are defined by certain characteristics that are common among the members, such as size (or usage

---

[1] See Harunuzzaman and Koundiny. "Cost Allocation and Rate Design for Unbundled Gas Services," 2000, for more details.

level), load factor,[2] and customer type (i.e., residential, commercial, industrial).

Once this is done, costs are allocated to each rate class. In some cases, the causation is clear-cut: Installing a meter in a residence is a customer-related cost to the residential rate class. However, often, the delineation is not so evident. Joint or common costs characterize public utilities; in fact, these attributes give rise to their being natural monopolies. In the case of electricity, the transmission lines provide service to all customer rate classes. Clearly, the allocation of transmission and related costs is a difficult undertaking.

Joint (or common) cost allocation

The most common method of allocating joint costs is the fully distributed cost (FDC), which assigns costs on the basis of the relative demand of each rate class. Based on embedded costs, this method uses various techniques to allocate costs to each classification of service (Harunuzzaman and Koundinya, 2000). The classifications of embedded costs are

- **Demand or capacity costs.** Including coincident and noncoincident peak, and average and excess (again see Harunuzzaman and Koundinya, 2000).
- **Commodity or energy costs.** Typically based on the share of total energy consumed by each customer class.
- **Customer costs.** Generally tied to the number of customers in a given class.

Allocation of fixed costs

While seemingly simple, the allocation of fixed costs among customer classes can be difficult. In the case of electricity, often, the fixed costs (i.e., customer charges or entry fees) paid by residential customers is different from those paid by commercial and industrial consumers. In addition,

---

[2] Load factor is an index of a customer's consumption pattern, defined as the ratio of average consumption to peak consumption. Low load factor customers, such as residential and small commercial customers, tend to have a spiked consumption pattern, characterized by high peak consumption relative to their average consumption. High load factor customers, on the other hand, tend to have a flatter consumption pattern, with their peak consumption closer to their average consumption. Load factor is an important determinant of cost allocation. It generally costs more to deliver a unit of energy to a low load factor customer than to a high load factor customer since the former imposes a relatively high capacity cost on the system, which needs to be recovered from fewer units of energy (Harunuzzaman and Koundinya, 2000).

the latter tend to pay demand charges based on the maximum demand (monthly) that serving them imposes on the system.

Later, it will be demonstrated that two-part tariffs can be beneficial and increase total surplus (although not necessary to increase consumer and producer surplus equally, which is a different matter; rates are not designed for equality but for fairness—the distinction is important). Seemingly, it is straightforward to calculate an appropriate entry fee (and in the Exercises at the end of the chapter you will). In the real world, demand functions are not necessarily known (nor are supply or cost functions) so other methodologies must be employed.

As stated, one methodology of allocating common costs, such as the costs of generation, transmission, and distribution, is known as fully distributed cost pricing. Under this method, the regulator

1.   Allocates the costs to serve a particular customer to that customer.
2.   Divides common costs among customers.

For many years utilities have been using cost, output, and revenue data from the most recent 12 months (the test period) to be used in the allocation of costs by function and by customer class. In some cases, price elasticities have been used, but these are often difficult to ascertain, especially under the conditions that prevailed in the 1980s and early 1990s; declining (or flat) energy costs yield little in the measurement of customer response to price changes. According to Brown and Sibley (1986, p. 49), "price elasticities of demand have no place in setting FDC rates, except perhaps in forecasting revenue, so FDC prices will generally be much different from Ramsey prices."

Although the most widely used, the FDC pricing methodology provides no incentive to increase efficiency, since it is an average cost rather than setting prices based on marginal cost. And then there is the issue of cross subsidization, which is discussed in an upcoming section

Design of end-user rates

Rates (or tariffs) typically comprise fixed charges (customer access/entry fee) and variable charges (those that apply on a per unit consumed basis), which are generally called *energy charges*. However, often, the energy charges include some demand-related costs. This is especially true in the residential and smaller commercial rate classes.

The energy charge can be constructed in a variety of ways:

- Block rates (uniform or linear, increasing or declining), which may vary by season, day of the week, or time of day.

- Marginal cost pricing.
- Average cost pricing.

As said, these often vary by class of customer. But which of these yield prices (i.e., rates) that result in the most efficient allocation of resources and sends the appropriate signal to end users to give them the incentive to use electricity wisely? In other words, which represents an optimal rate design?

10.3 THE THEORY OF EFFICIENT PRICES

The introductory chapter (and the common theme of this book) purports that pricing at marginal cost is both productively and allocatively efficient. But what, exactly, does this mean? Let us start with a basic definition and build on it. First, what is economic efficiency? And, how is it attained? Simply put, economic efficiency means maximizing the level of output while minimizing the amount of (and cost of) inputs, the latter also are known as the *factors of production* (e.g., labor and capital). But, is this all? Is it really this simple? Or, is there some deeper, more complex underlying issue here? Actually, the answers to these questions are yes and no.

Figure 10.1 displays a market in equilibrium, which yields price $= P^*$ and output level Y^*. In this situation, both producer (PS) and consumer surplus (CS) are maximized; as such, a Pareto efficient outcome emerges, which means that no one can be made better off without anyone else's being made worse off.

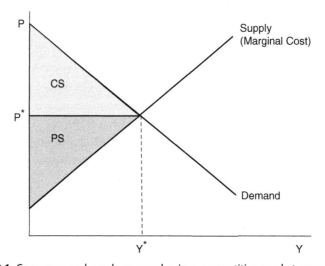

Figure 10.1 Consumer and producer surplus in a competitive market paradigm

In Figure 10.1, marginal-cost pricing (the supply curve above average variable cost, not shown) maximizes total welfare, which is equal to the consumer surplus (CS) plus producer surplus (PS). Thus, a Pareto efficient outcome is attained.

But is it really this simple? In the case of regulated utility industries, the answer is clearly no; such entities are regulated because they are "natural monopolies," requiring investments that are highly sunk so that duplication would be wasteful and competition infeasible. As such, both fixed and variable costs must be incurred (and recovered) to provide service to end users, which is the reason that regulated firms often charge both fixed and variable charges to end-use customers.[3] The next section provides a review and overview of methodologies employed in pricing such services.

Efficient public utility pricing

In the adoption of efficient pricing for the regulated firm, three concepts are worth noting:
1. Efficient prices are those that maximize total welfare.
2. Changes in prices can create "winners" and "losers." However, it is possible that the "winners" can compensate the "losers" in some fashion so as to render them better off than before the change.
3. Since the firm typically must break even out of its own sales revenues (i.e., no government subsidy or taxes), it is likely that total welfare is reduced.

Regarding the first point, the absence of competition creates the ability for producers to gain at the expense of consumers. Figure 10.2 illustrates this point nicely. (Note: Marginal cost is constant for simplicity.)

In the absence of regulation, the monopolist maximizes profit by producing a level of output, Y^M, which equates marginal revenue (MR) and marginal cost (MC). Because the demand curve (D) slopes downward, the price charged in the market is P^M, which is well above the price that would result in a competitive market (P^*). In addition, market output is below that which would occur were competition present (Y^*).

What has occurred is a transfer of surplus from the consumer to the producer, which is equal to the area of the rectangle above P^* below the demand curve. That is,

$$\Delta PS = (P^M - P^*) \times Y^M \qquad (10.3)$$

---

[3] This is not the quarrel here but rather the fact that, often, the variable charges do not necessarily reflect the true marginal cost of supplying electricity.

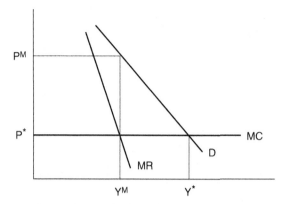

Figure 10.2 Monopoly supplier in absence of regulation

In addition, the consumer (and society) has lost the surplus associated with the area of the triangle, which is given by

$$\Delta CS = \frac{1}{2} \times (Y^* - Y^M) \times (P^M - P^*) \qquad (10.4)$$

The latter, known as the *deadweight loss*, represents the lost output that has value to society. To the point expressed in the second concept, even if it were feasible for some type of tax or subsidy to be created to compensate consumers the initial loss in surplus (given by equation (10.3) or that lost to the producer), the deadweight loss is not able to be compensated and is truly a loss to society.

Example 10.1

A monopolist has the following cost structure:

$$TC = 500 + 20Q \qquad (10.5)$$

Market demand for its product is given by

$$P = 100 - Q \qquad (10.6)$$

What profit-maximizing output and price will prevail in the market? Setting $MR = MC$ and solving for Q^* and P^* yield

$$Q^* = 40$$

and

$$P^* = 60$$

which yields

$$\text{Profit} = \text{total revenue} - \text{total cost, or}$$
$$\text{Profit, or producer surplus,} = \$1100$$

In this case, consumer surplus has been reduced and transferred to the producer in the form of profit (i.e., producer surplus). In addition, there is a deadweight loss, which is entirely absorbed by the consumer.

Ramsey prices: A second-best option[4]

The discussion thus far illustrates the reason(s) that price regulation is necessary in the case of public utilities, which also motivates a discussion on the third concept introduced previously. The first-best option of marginal cost pricing does not work; the presence of fixed costs means that a regulatory structure that sets price equal to marginal costs implies that all costs will not be recovered in rates. One solution (in the case of other countries) is that the government imposes a tax (or a subsidy) so that fixed costs are recovered. However, in the United States, the absence of taxes or government subsidies implies that utilities must at least break even from their sales revenues. In addition, in the case of investor-owned firms, they must earn a "fair return" to shareholders (this is typically determined by the public utility regulatory commission in each state).

And this is where reality also sets in: Marginal costs are not constant, and over the relevant range of output, it is likely that average costs (embedded or fixed costs) are above marginal costs so that marginal cost pricing does not allow the firm to break even. Furthermore, neither marginal nor average cost is constant (or even linear, for that matter), which adds an additional element of complexity. This situation is illustrated in Figure 10.3.

In Figure 10.3, average costs exceed marginal costs over the relevant range of output, so that marginal-cost pricing does not allow the firm to break even. One option is the two-part tariff, which charges a fixed charge that approximates the differential between average and marginal cost. In reality, this is far more complex an undertaking.

A breakeven constraint implies the presence of fixed costs that must be recovered in some fashion. The fact that such costs are common to all

---

[4] Formally, Ramsey pricing is a linear pricing scheme designed for the multiproduct natural monopolist (see Frank Ramsey. "A Contribution to the Theory of Taxation," *Economic Journal*, March 1927).

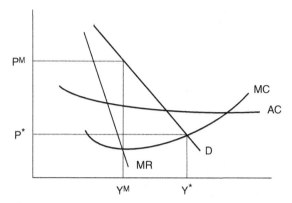

Figure 10.3 Profit-maximizing price and output for a natural monopoly

classes of customers necessitates the ability to allocate these costs among these classes (e.g., residential, commercial, industrial). For now, let us focus on one solution to this problem. An example from Brown and Sibley (1986) illustrates this point nicely.

Example 10.2. A two-period electricity pricing example

Suppose there are two periods, off-peak and on-peak, and the quantity demanded (Q_i) in each period is given by

$$Q_1 = 720 - 4000\, P_1 \qquad (10.7)$$

and

$$Q_2 = 180 - 1000\, P_2 \qquad (10.8)$$

Note: That there are two equations implies that there are two different prices (and levels of output).

Fixed costs are $2.00 and marginal costs (c_i) are equal to

$$c_1 = \$0.09$$

and

$$c_2 = \$0.02$$

Also note that the marginal cost of electricity is much less expensive in the off-peak period, which is not surprising, (Why?)

The firm's objective then is to earn total revenue (TR) so that total costs (TC) are covered, which implies that

$$TR = TC$$

More specifically,

$$\text{TR} = P_1(720 - 4000\,P_1) + P_2(180 - 1000\,P_2) \qquad (10.9)$$

and

$$\text{TC} = \$0.09 \times (720 - 4000\,P_1) + \$0.02 \times (180 - 1000\,P_2) + 2.00$$
$$(10.10)$$

In this example, several pairs of prices satisfy the firm's breakeven constraint and the objective then becomes to find that pair that yields the lowest deadweight loss, which according to Brown and Sibley (1986), is that $P_1 = \$0.09$ (*equivalent to marginal cost*) and $P_2 = \$0.034$ (*above marginal cost*); *in essence, the off-peak users absorb the entire fixed cost.* Does this appear to be an efficient outcome? Why or why not? (As an exercise, you will show that this minimizes the deadweight loss and, as such, is the most efficient outcome.)

Ramsey pricing: The "second-best" option

Since the first-best option (i.e., marginal-cost pricing) is not necessarily feasible in the presence of fixed costs, a "second-best" option is now presented. In the most basic form, the most efficient uniform[5] second-best prices are those that

Maximize total surplus with respect to price $(P_1, P_2, \ldots, P_n)$

subject to $\text{PS} = F$, where $F =$ fixed costs of the firm.

What this entails is, in essence, finding the markup over marginal cost in each market (or customer class) that reduces total surplus by the least amount. This amounts to increasing the price more in markets (i.e., customer classes) that are less sensitive to changes in price, which is equivalent to a lower price elasticity of demand.[6] That is,

$$\text{Markup} = (P_i - c_i)/P_i = \lambda/\varepsilon_i \qquad (10.11)$$

where

$P_i =$ price in market i.

$c_i =$ marginal cost.

---

[5] Uniform (or linear) prices are those that do not vary with output.
[6] Formally, price elasticity of demand is given by

$$\varepsilon = \partial Q/\partial P \times P/Q$$

This measures the percentage change in quantity demanded that results from a change in price. When ε is less than unity, the quantity demanded is inelastic (insensitive) to changes in price. When greater than unity, the quantity demanded is said to be elastic.

λ = a proportionality constant.

ε_i = price elasticity of demand in market i (or customer class i).

Also known as the *inverse elasticity rule* (IER), this pricing rule is a well-known result in the literature on efficient public utility pricing. Formally, this rule states that the price that maximizes social welfare (TS) subject to a profit constraint exceeds marginal cost by an amount that is inversely proportional to elasticity of demand.

Another way of expressing equation (10.10) is that (for a two-output market)

$$\lambda = [(P_i - c_i)/P_i] \times \varepsilon_i = [(P_j - c_j)/P_j] \times \varepsilon_j, \text{ for } j \neq i \qquad (10.12)$$

What this implies is that for any pair of markets (or customer classes), the percentage increase over marginal cost, weighted by the price elasticities of demand, should be equal to λ, which is known as the *Ramsey number* (Brown and Sibley, 1986).

Example 10.1 (continued). Marginal cost pricing in the presence of fixed costs

(This example is reprinted with consent from Rothwell and Gomez, 2003, p. 94.) An electric utility has the following cost structure:

$$TC = 500 + 20 \, Q \qquad (10.13)$$

Market demand for its electricity is

$$P = 100 - Q \qquad (10.14)$$

If price is set at marginal cost, what is the electric utility's profit?

Solution: Setting price equal to marginal cost implies that

$$P = 20 \text{ and } Q = 80.$$

As such,

$$\text{Profit} = \text{Total Revenue} - \text{Total Cost, or}$$

$$\text{Profit} = (100 - Q) \times Q - 500 - 20 \, Q$$

At $Q = 80$,

$$\text{Profit} = -\$500$$

(As an exercise you will verify this.)

Not surprising (due to the presence of fixed costs), the first-best optimal pricing (i.e., price equal to marginal cost) strategy does not allow

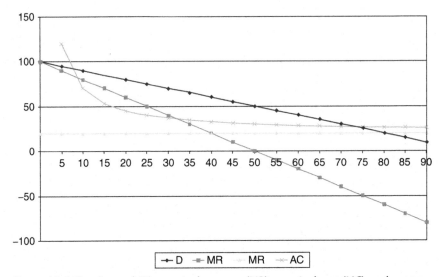

Figure 10.4 The demand (D), marginal revenue (MR), marginal cost (MC), and average cost (AC) for the regulated firm depicted in Example 10.1

the firm to recover all of its costs and a loss of $500 occurs. This situation is displayed in Figure 10.4.

Another option: Average-cost pricing

At first blush, one might think that a feasible solution is to set the price at the average cost; after all, this seems to address the utility's need to recover all costs associated with providing service. And, given the situation depicted in Figure 10.4, the price charged (and the quantity delivered) does not seem to diverge much from the optimum, which occurs when price equals marginal cost. But appearances can be deceiving, as we will see in the continuation of this example. (Nonetheless, average-cost pricing is one of the most popular rate-making mechanisms employed by utilities (and accepted by regulators in the United States).

Example 10.1 (continued)

Next, if the price is set at the average cost, what are the equilibrium price and output? Setting price equal to average cost yields

$$100 - Q = 20 + 500/Q \tag{10.15}$$

Solving for the equilibrium output, Q^*, requires the use of the quadratic formula, which implies that

$$-Q^2 + 80Q - 500 = 0 \qquad (10.16)$$

Solving for Q^* yields two solutions: $Q^* = 6.8$ and $Q^* = 73.2$, but only the former is feasible. (Why?) This yields a price $= \$93$, which is significantly higher than the first-best solution (which sets price equal to marginal cost).

What deadweight loss is associated with this pricing scheme? In this case, the deadweight loss can be approximated by

$$DWL = \tfrac{1}{2} \times (\$93 - \$20) \times (80 - 6.8) \qquad (10.17)$$

or

$$DWL = \$2672$$

In this example, the differential between the average-cost pricing scheme (or mechanism, which is often employed in the United States) and that which represents the first-best solution (or even marginal cost pricing with fixed charges to recover fixed costs) is substantial; not only does a significant deadweight loss occur, but the price paid by consumers is significantly higher that it would have been under an optimally designed pricing scheme.

10.4 TWO-PART TARIFFS

Example 10.1 shows that, even though average-cost pricing allows the firm to recover all of its costs, allocating fixed costs to a variable charge results in a deadweight loss to society. Another option, and one that is used throughout the industry, is the *two-part tariff*, which allows that fixed costs be recovered via fixed charges while variable costs are recovered by marginal-cost pricing. Originally suggested by R.H. Coase (1946), the structure of this tariff is that the usage charge is set equal to marginal cost and the entry charge (or fixed component) is set equal to the regulated firm's total fixed costs, which are divided by the number of users, so that each customer pays the firm's average fixed cost. As such, the firm's total costs are covered and, since the price paid for each unit (the usage charge) is equal to marginal cost, the deadweight loss is eliminated. Total surplus is unaffected (there is, however, a transfer of surplus from the consumer to the producer). This is often called an *optimal* two-part tariff. (Note: It is

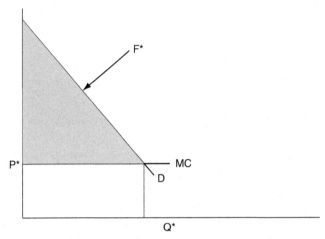

Figure 10.5 "Optimal" two-part tariff in which perfect price discrimination allows the producer to extract the entire consumer surplus as a fixed (or entry) fee; clearly, it is optimal for the producer but not for the consumer

optimal for the producer, who extracts the entire consumer surplus.) This is displayed in Figure 10.5.

Example 10.1 (continued). A two-part tariff

The firm depicted in this example requests that the state public regulatory commission allows it to recover its costs via a two-part tariff, which, it argues, is more efficient than average-cost pricing. (Why?) Given this, what fixed charge (or entry fee) will appear on the customer's bill?

Recalling that the consumer surplus is the shaded area in Figure 10.5, we have

$$CS = \frac{1}{2} \times (100 - 20) \times 80$$

This yields

$$CS = \$3200$$

Under this pricing mechanism, the consumer is sent the appropriate price signal, there is no deadweight loss, and the producer recovers all of its costs.

Two-part tariff with different customer classes

An interesting twist occurs when a second class of customer is distinguished. In this case, the optimal two-part tariff would dictate that the entry fee (*F*) be allocated between the two classes and that each could pay a usage fee (P) that equals a common marginal cost (c) so that the firm recovers its total costs. That is,

$$TC = F + (Q_1 + Q_2) \times c \qquad (10.18)$$

where $Q_2 < Q_1$. In other words, the customers in the second group are much smaller users (consuming Q_2) than those in group 1 (consuming Q_1).

In addition, suppose that the consumers in group 2 are not willing to pay the same entry fee as those in the first group; after all, they are not consuming as much output and it could be that the fixed fee more than offsets the gains from marginal-cost pricing (compared to average-cost pricing), so that a negative consumer surplus would be earned by the customers in group 1. That is, they could elect to drop out of the market and consume nothing, whereby they would earn zero consumer surplus, which is clearly better than a negative surplus. In this case, how would a two-part tariff be constructed, especially if the customers in group 2 are clearly better off with group 1 in the market? (Why?) They might even be willing to pay a higher entry fee, thus subsidizing the customers in group 1, which is not an uncommon occurrence (see "Aside: The issue of cross-subsidization in utility rate making," later in this chapter).

Alternately, one of the groups may be willing to pay a usage fee that is above the marginal cost but below what would be charged under average-cost pricing, such as P^* in Figure 10.6.

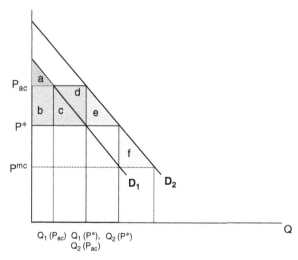

Figure 10.6 Two-part tariff with different customer classes: Group 1 customers are characterized by the demand curve labeled D_1; as smaller users, their willingness to pay is lower than that of the customers in group 2; whose demand curve is D_2

It has been stated that the two-part tariff is better than the average-cost pricing methodology for rate-making purposes. But, given a choice, not all customers would choose the former. At P_{ac}, Group 1 customers would consume $Q_1(P_{ac})$ and gain the triangle a in surplus. Should they opt for the two-part tariff, they would pay a lower usage charge (P^*) and consume more $(Q_1(P^*))$. However, they would also have to pay the entry fee, which is equal to the shaded area bcd, which appears to render a negative consumer surplus. This group is better off under the average-cost pricing scheme.

The customers in group 2, however, represent a different view. Under the two-part tariff, they pay P^* and consume $Q_2(P^*)$. However, unlike group 1, the larger users maintain a positive surplus (area e) even after paying the entry fee (area bcd). As such, this group of customers would select the two-part tariff.

And what about the firm? Clearly the firm is better off with the two-part tariff, which we have seen before. In particular, the firm is able to charge P^*, which is above the marginal cost. This translates into a profit equivalent to the area f in Figure 10.6. A seemingly Pareto optimal situation has occurred.

Note: It is often not the case that consumers have such a choice. Many utilities file two-part tariffs (or more than two parts). In the case of two such groups, what typically occurs is that the fixed fee is equivalent to the entire consumer surplus of the smaller users, so they experience no gain at all while larger consumers (and the producer) gain.

Example 10.3. The case of distinct customer demands

(This example is from Rothwell and Gomez, 2003, Chapter 4, exercise 4.2.4.) The demands of two distinct sets of 10 customers are given by the following. For group 2 (four customers),

$$P_2 = 100 - 80Q_2 \qquad (10.19)$$

or group 1 (six customers),

$$P_1 = 100 - 6.3Q_1 \qquad (10.20)$$

The utility's cost is given by

$$TC = 500 + 20Q \qquad (10.21)$$

where

$$Q = Q_1 + Q_2$$

Given these conditions, what choice would each group of customers make?

The largest charge that group 2 consumers would pay is equal to their consumer surplus. In this case,

$$CS_2 = 0.5 \times (100 - 20) \times 1 = 40$$

If the 10 customers equally divide the $500 fixed entry fee, each would have to pay $50. However, each customer earns a surplus of only $40, so the group 2 customers would not be interested in the two-part tariff but would instead pay the higher average cost of $21.5 per kilowatt-hour. The derivation of this is provided later.

What about group 1?

$$CS_1 = 0.5 \times (100 - 20) \times 12.7 = 508$$

This group would be willing to pay up to $508 to connect to electric system if the regulator would allow different access charges so that each customer pays at or below his or her consumer surplus. However, only one solution is optimal.

Optimal two-part tariff: The solution
As stated, the optimal two-part tariff minimizes deadweight loss by charging a connection fee equal to the consumer surplus of the smaller customer (group 2) and charges all customers the same usage fee (P^*). In this case,

$$CS_2 = 0.5 \times (100 - P^*) \times [(100 - P^*)/80]$$

but a determination of P^* is required. Since total revenue is equal to 10 times the connection charge (in this case, the consumer surplus of group 2) multiplied by the price times output, which is equal to the quantity demanded of group 1 plus the quantity demanded by group 2, we have

$$TR = 10 \times CS_2 + P \times (Q_1 + Q_2)$$

or

$$TR = 10 \times CS_2 + P \times [(100 - P^*)/6.3] + P^*[(100 - P^*)/80]$$

and total cost is given by

$$TC = 500 + 20[(100 - P^*)/6.3] + 20[(100 - P^*)/80]$$

Since profit is equal to total revenue minus total cost, the solution (P^*) can be obtained by maximizing profit with respect to price; that is, by setting the derivative of profit with respect to P^* equal to 0 and solving for P^*. That is,

$$\partial\pi/\partial P^* = 0 \tag{10.22}$$

which yields $P^* = 21.5$.

This implies that the access charge, which is equal to the consumer surplus of group 2, is given by

$$CS_2 = 0.5 \times (100 - P^*) \times Q_2(P^*)$$

or

$$CS_2 = 38.5$$

Aside: The issue of cross-subsidization in utility rate making

An excerpt from a 2004 article in *Public Utilities Fortnightly* (Casten and Meyer, 2004) makes this point well: "Indeed, the cross-subsidization concept is found throughout utility rates: From discounted rates to low income families to systems benefits charges, there are huge swathes of customers who pay less than their full cost of service, thus being subsidized by other customers who pay more to make up the difference. We tolerate and encourage such rate setting out of the belief that the social benefits created by such subsidization outweigh the resulting economic inefficiency."

The authors go on to cite the various forms that cross-subsidization is put in place to achieve certain economic, social, and political objectives, including

1. **Geographic diversity within the same rate class.** It is well known that urban customers subsidize those residing in rural cost areas. The latter, which are clearly more costly to serve due to lower density and more rugged terrain, typically pay the same rates as those in more populated areas within each customer class.

2. **No price signal.** Rather than pay the actual cost of the power they consume at any given time, prices are based on the average cost over the year (or during the time between rate cases). (This is obviated to some degree if the utility has some type of time-varying rates, but unless pricing is on a real-time basis, cross-subsidization still occurs).

3. **DSM or other energy efficiency recovery charges.** These "below-the-line" items are charged to all customers in a particular class to fund a variety of energy-efficiency and renewable-power projects. However, not all ratepayers within the class benefit from these programs. (Note: Other below-the-line items include fuel adjustment clauses and cost recovery for environmental expenditures.)

4. **Interclass subsidization.** Representation at rate case proceedings on behalf of residential and industrial customers often means that the

commercial customers are the most profitable to utilities. In the case of the former, the state's attorney general is the advocate on the consumer side, whose status as voters confers upon them certain benefits, which take the form of minimal changes in usage rates and customer charges. And in the case of large industrial customers, the ability to leave the utility service territory (and even the state or country) confers similar benefits; in fact, often, the industrial customers are represented by legal counsel who argue on their behalf at rate proceedings. (See the article for more details.)

10.5 MULTIPART TARIFFS

What we have seen thus far is a variation of a *multipart* tariff, which differentiates customers based on the quantity of usage. (This is also known as *nonuniform pricing*.) However, more often, the utility's tariff itself distinguishes usage levels by not only the usage charge but also the customer (or entry) charge and, in many cases, a demand (or capacity) charge. These are typically based on the class of customer (e.g., residential, commercial, industrial) and quite often a cross-subsidization among such classes exists. That is, there are different customer charges, energy charges, and demand charges, the last of which apply only to industrial users (even though both residential and commercial users contribute to the utility's peak demand and hence its capacity requirements).

Nonuniform pricing: Block rates

And now we are starting to embark upon a path toward more efficient pricing of electricity; that is, by allowing the (variable) usage charges to reflect the true marginal cost of providing service at the time (or level) that it is required. In the simplest case, we recall the example provided earlier (Example 10.2, on-peak vs. off-peak electricity consumption), which exemplified the fact that the price of electricity in on-peak hours can differ quite vastly from the prices that prevail in off-peak hours.[7]

It is often the case that utilities charge a different rate for different levels of usage, which may also vary depending on the season. For example, the first 1000 kWh of usage may be priced at one rate while all kilowatt hours above 1000 are charged a different rate. This is an example of a three-part

---

[7] On-peak hours are typically defined as the weekday hours between 10:00 A.M. and 6:00 P.M. (EST).

tariff in that there is a fixed charge (or entry fee), and a breakpoint at a particular level of usage, or

$$P(Q_1) = P_1, 0 < Q \leq 1000$$

and

$$P(Q_2) = P_2, 1000 < Q$$

Such a pricing mechanism results in a "kinked" supply curve, such as that displayed in Figure 10.7.

Note: As displayed in Figure 10.7, block rates can be increasing or decreasing but only the former is a step toward pricing at marginal cost, since higher levels of output require more expensive generating units to come online to supply load. Not only do declining and flat block rates fail to yield a price signal to consumers, the former actually provides an incentive to over consume, which is totally anathema to the ideas of conservation and efficiency that are currently being espoused.

In Mr. Kelly's (2007) article, quoted at the beginning of this chapter, there is a quote from the U.S. Department of Energy that specifically denigrates flat-block rate pricing, since it provides no price signal whatsoever. However, in some states, this is the standard methodology for setting usage charges. For example, in the state of Kentucky, the Kentucky Public Service Commission (KPSC) allows the utilities under its jurisdiction to offer flat rates to its customers. In fact, in a rate case filed in 2004, one of the largest utilities in the state went from offering seasonal rates for its weather sensitive customer classes to a flat energy rate, which does not vary with usage. This is shown as R_1 in Figure 10.7.

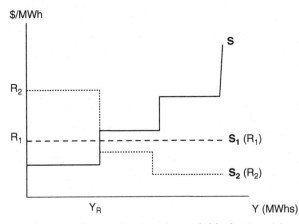

Figure 10.7 Supply curves for an electric utility with block-rate pricing

Yet another type of block rate is the declining block rate in which the per kilowatt-hour price of electricity actually declines with increased usage. The epitome of a perverse incentive (especially today, when we are talking about conservation and energy efficiency as a means to reduce greenhouse gas emissions), numerous utilities in the United States use rates fashioned in this respect. Duke Energy, Indiana, is an example of this, as are the Indianapolis Power and Light (IPL) Company and the Northern Indiana Public Service Company (NIPSCo). This rate structure is represented by R_2 in Figure 10.7.

$S_1(R_1)$ represents the supply curve of a producer charging a flat-block (R_1), and $S_2(R_2)$ represents a supply curve that is a function of the declining block rate R_2. The marginal cost curve is given by $\mathbf{S}$, which increases with output, since higher-cost generation must come online to serve load. For $Y < Y_R$, the utility is overcharging (i.e., it "overearns") for electricity, but for $Y > Y_R$ it does not charge enough to recover its costs and hence underearns, which typically triggers the filing of a rate case. Had the utility adopted a more reasonable approach to setting rates (i.e., an inclining block rate schedule), it could have recovered most of its incremental costs and not have to go through the time and the expense of a rate case. (Note: Overearning will *never* cause an investor-owned utility to file a rate case.)

In Figure 10.7, generating units are dispatched according to marginal cost, which is predominantly based on the cost of fuel. This is represented by $\mathbf{S}$, the supply function. In the region of the supply curve where $Y < Y_R$, baseload capacity is the first generation to be dispatched, which is typically pulverized coal, hydro (if in the northwestern part of the United States or if one of the power administrations is the supplier), or nuclear generation. The next units to come online may be natural gas fired, which are typically used for peaking capacity. Given the cost, renewable resources such as wind or solar may be the last to be dispatched *if there is no renewable portfolio standard*. Again, it depends upon the marginal cost of the fuel at the time, which can affect the stacking order of the generation dispatched and whether market purchases supplement the utilities' own generation.

Example 10. 4. Block rate pricing

An electric utility offers the tariff to its residential customers shown in Table 10.1. The pricing scheme in Table 10.1 yields the demand (and supply or marginal cost) curves in the summer season displayed in Figure 10.8.

Table 10.1 Pricing Scheme of Example 10.4

	Summer	Winter
Customer charge (monthly)	5.00	5.00
First 1000 kWh (cents/kWh)	0.08	0.04
Over 1000 kWh (cents/kWh)	0.05	0.01

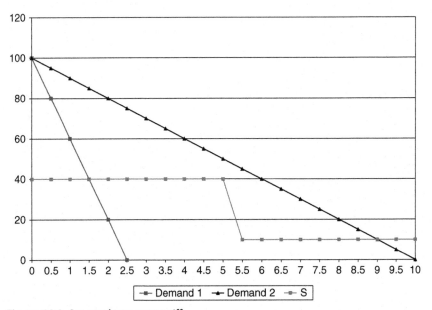

Figure 10.8 Seasonal two-part tariff

Consider the firm whose tariff is displayed in Table 10.1. What is the entry fee under an optimal tariff design?

Solution. The optimal entry fee is equal to the consumer surplus of the smaller consumer (Group 1), which in this case is given by

$$CS = 0.5 \times (100 - 40) \times 1.5$$

The entry fee is equal to $45 divided by the number of customers in Group 1.

10.6 TIME-OF-USE RATES

A further extension of a multipart tariff is that of time-of-use rates, which includes a critical peak price in addition to a peak and off-peak price, the objective being to shift consumption to the off-peak period, when the cost of generating (or procuring) electricity is relatively low. In addition, extreme weather conditions may call for a critical peak price (CPP), which would reflect the cost of procuring power when demand is highest. For example, an electric utility may offer a tariff that distinguishes between different time periods throughout the weekday (which may be different on weekends), which likely depends on the season (but this may vary depending on the climate).

A brief history of time-of-use pricing

Until the 1970s, there was little interest in pricing electricity efficiently. It was not until the twin energy crises of 1973–1974 and the late 1970s that there was a desire to set prices according to marginal cost, thus encouraging a more efficient use of energy and reducing the need for new generating capacity. During this time, numerous studies were funded by the Federal Energy Administration (the predecessor of the U.S. Department of Energy) to assess how customers would respond to time-varying rates, and in 1978, the Public Utility Regulatory Policies Act (PURPA) was passed by Congress. In addition to other objectives (see Chapter 3 for more details) PURPA required state regulatory commissions to consider rates that varied by time, by type of customer, and by season.

A study authored by Dennis Aigner ("The Residential Electricity Time-of-Use Experiments: What Have We Learned?" Aigner, 1985) focused on a group of time-of-use pricing experiments for a group of utilities over a six-year period beginning in 1975. The main objective of these experiments was to determine whether time-of-use pricing would yield a change in the load shapes of residential customers and the impact of such pricing on utility revenues and consumer welfare. Depending on the results, important policy decisions could be made, which could influence the rate-making process and obviate the need for additional investments in utility infrastructure. One outcome of the study was the estimation of own- and cross-price elasticities, which directly affect both the utilities revenues and the surplus of the consumer. The outcome is summarized as: "All studies showed some reduction in usage during the peak period under TOU [time-of-use] rates. However, reduction in usage during the peak period was not accompanied by statistically significant increases in baseperiod usage. Total usage seemed either to decline or remain the same in all projects.... Peak-day usage shifts and average-day usage shifts appeared to be about the same" (Miedema and White 1980, 4).[8]

Given the renewed interest in efficient pricing, time-of-use rates are clearly a step toward marginal cost pricing, in that end-use customers are charged the cost of power during the time in which it is being consumed. For example, during peak usage times, more expensive peaking capacity (typically natural-gas-fired combustion turbines (refer to Figure 10.7)) is being employed to generate electricity to meet demand. From an economic efficiency perspective, it is a necessary step in providing proper incentives to consumers to use energy wisely, and which may also save them money by reducing their total bill. Numerous utilities in various states have adopted such a pricing structure, which varies by the time of day, the day of the week, and the month of the year (summer or winter, known as seasonal pricing). An excerpt from the Hydro Ottawa Web site makes this point nicely: "Shifting electricity use to off peak periods reduces the need for investment in new electricity supply projects, which will help to moderate future rate increases. It also benefits the environment by reducing our reliance on additional power generation brought on-line or imported from other jurisdictions. Many create additional pollution and are more expensive to operate."

This tariff went into effect on May 1, 2008, in various Ottawa neighborhoods and has four distinct periods on weekdays during summer months, five in winter months, and one on the weekend. Some companies, like Arizona Power Service (APS), have a super critical peak price from 3:00 P.M.–6 P.M. With 40% customer enrollment, APS leads the nation in time-of-use customer participation.[9] But the key is that there must be enough of a differential between the peak and off-peak prices. Nevada Power's time-of-use rate, which went into effect on July 1, 2008, offers a nice example here whereby the residential on-peak rate, which is from 1:00 P.M. to 7:00 P.M., is almost three times the off-peak rate (23.08 vs. 7.097 cents/kWh).[10]

---

[8] It was duly noted that "A number of design considerations have an impact on the ultimate usefulness of the experimental data that have been forthcoming, not the least of which is the amount of variation available in peak, midpeak and off-peak prices. Many of the DOE experiments have but one set of TOU prices, and therefore the inferences available are limited to a single statistical comparison of control-group and experimental households" (Aigner, 1985).

[9] (www.reuters.com/article/pressRelease/idUS155472+24-Mar-2008+BW20080324).

[10] (www.nevadapower.com/conservation/home/home_rebates/time_of_use.cfm).

10.7 REAL-TIME PRICING

Taking this one step further still is the concept of real-time pricing, which has actually been around for some time. California was one of the first states to offer real-time prices in the mid 1980s. The price, which varied hourly, was quoted a day in advance, for all energy consumed. As such, participants' entire load was exposed to the volatility that characterized the real-time prices they faced. These tariffs were designed to be revenue neutral over average climatic conditions, for the class of customers deemed likely to participate. However, because such a large portion of the revenues generated from these tariffs was related to actual hourly supply and weather conditions, revenue recovery could not be guaranteed.

Niagara Mohawk's Hourly Integrated Pricing Pilot (HIPP), launched in 1988, introduced a new real-time tariff design: a two-part rate with a customer-specific access charge. A unique customer baseline load (CBL) profile, comprising a kilowatt-hour value for each hour of the year, was established for each participant from his or her historical interval billing data. The customer-specific access charge was calculated by applying the energy and billing demand rates from the customer's otherwise applicable tariff to his or her CBL load profile. Deviations between the customer's actual load and its CBL in each hour were settled at the prevailing real-time price. Because only marginal changes in usage were subject to real-time prices, participants' had less exposure to price volatility, and the utility had greater revenue stability, compared to earlier real-time tariff designs.[11]

Not until the mid- to late-1990s did real-time pricing become popular in states with retail choice. The real-time tariffs introduced in these states were generally based on a rate structure composed of hourly energy prices for the commodity component and unbundled transmission and distribution charges assessed on the customer's billing demand or energy consumption. However, in most cases, the predominantly larger commercial and industrial customers participated.

In recent years, participation rates declined significantly, but that is now changing. With a renewed focus on energy efficiency and conservation, programs such as this are making a comeback, even offering residential customers the opportunity to participate. According to a recent article "ComEd Pioneers Real-Time Pricing Program (RRTP) for Residential

---

[11] An excerpt from *A Survey of Utility Experience with Real Time Pricing*, LBNL-54238 (www.osti.gov/ energycitations/servlets/purl/836966-SZe2FO/native/836966.PDF).

Customers,"[12] participants for all 12 months in 2007 experienced an annual savings of between 7% and 12% compared to the fixed rate other residential customers received. RRTP participants are billed for the electricity they consume based on hourly wholesale market prices. They have access to hourly pricing information via the Internet and pricing alerts via text messaging and email. Participants may choose to make adjustments in their electricity usage based on the hourly prices. For instance, if pricing alerts indicate that electricity prices could reach or exceed 13 cents/kWh, about 2.5 cents higher than Commonwealth Edison's fixed rate, customers can save money by shifting their electricity usage to lower-priced hours later in the day.

10.8 CONCLUSION

But, with all of this said, the need to price electricity efficiently is still at the forefront, especially given that emissions of greenhouse gases from (60%) coal-fired power plants are the worst offenders (emissions from a coal-fired generating plant are almost twice that from natural gas to fuel the generation of electricity). Given this, should not the customers of utilities with coal-fired generation pay more for their electricity (and not just via below-the-line items, such as cost-recovery mechanisms for environmental or automatic adjustments for fuel costs) than ratepayers in the service territories of lower-emitting utilities? In other words, should not consumers pay more for electricity generated from "dirty sources" than that generated from "clean resources"? And, in the case of investor-owned utilities, should there not be a higher return to the shareholders of firms that have made investments in renewable resources and other efficiency-improving investments?

It is often said that energy efficiency is the lowest-cost option; however, energy efficiency requires investment in more energy-efficient appliances and equipment, which tends to command a relatively higher cost.[13] My opinion is that conservation is clearly the lowest-cost option; however, for this to occur there must be a price signal to which end users can respond. At the very least, this means that energy charges reflect

---

[12] (www.reuters.com/article/pressRelease/idUS274507+31-Jan-2008+PRN20080131).

[13] If you perform a life-cycle cost analysis you may be surprised; you may want to review Chapter 9, "Load Forecasting—The 'Demand' for Electricity," for a discussion of discrete choice models and the theory underlying the trade-off between installation and operating costs in terms of appliance choices.

marginal costs in that they increase with usage, since higher usage implies higher costs of generating (or procuring) electricity. (In other words, *at the very least*, there must be an increasing-block tariff; flat rates and declining-block rates have no place in the pricing of energy, especially electricity!)

And, while time-of-use and real-time pricing are attempts to emulate the marginal costs of supplying electric service, they also require a significant investment in infrastructure (smart meters, etc.) on the part of utilities (and hence, consumers), which may be prohibitive.

To date, little work has been done in the estimation of the marginal costs of providing electricity for rate-setting purposes. As described in Chapter 4 (and elsewhere in this book), estimation of marginal costs would require an appropriately specified cubic cost model, which is not without its challenges.

10.9 EXERCISES

1. In Example 10.2, it was stated that the pair or prices that yield the lowest deadweight loss is that $P_1 = \$0.09$ and $P_2 = \$0.034$.
   a. Why is this the most efficient outcome? Prove that this pair of prices minimizes the deadweight loss.
   b. Does it make sense that the off-peak price is lower than the on-peak price? Why or why not?
2. Verify that the firm depicted in Example 10.1 (continued), marginal cost pricing in the presence of fixed costs, suffers a loss of $500.
3. An electric utility faces the following:

$$\text{Total cost} = 50 + 20Q \qquad (10.23)$$

Individual customer demand (inverse demand function) is

$$P = 100 - 6.25Q \qquad (10.24)$$

   a. In the absence of price regulation,
      i. What price and output would prevail?
      ii. What profit is earned by the firm?
   b. If the state regulatory commission were to impose average-cost pricing,
      i. What price and output would prevail?
      ii. What is the firm's profit?
      iii. Is there a deadweight loss? If so, calculate.

    c. Instead, assume the state regulatory commission requires marginal cost pricing,

      i. What price and output will prevail?

      ii. What is the firm's profit (loss)?

      iii. How can this be rectified?

      iv. Does a deadweight loss result?

4. The firm depicted in Exercise 2 has convinced the state regulatory commission that a two-part tariff would be better than any other pricing mechanism.

    a. What arguments might it have used to support its contention?

    b. What is the gain to the producer from adopting this pricing scheme?

5. A second type of customer is recognized by the state regulatory commission. This class of customer has a demand function given by

$$P = 100 - 8.0Q \qquad (10.25)$$

    a. If price is equal to marginal cost, what level of output will be consumed by this class of customer?

    b. What will the firm's profit be?

    c. What entry fee will be paid by each type of customer so that the firm covers all its costs?

6. The public regulatory commission requires all classes of customers to be treated the same, so that the customers described in Exercises 3 and 4 must pay according to a two-part tariff.

    a. What usage fee will be charged (P^*)?

    b. What will the access (or entry) charge be?

    c. Is this an optimally designed tariff? Why or why not?

7. What type of tariff is represented in Table 10.1? Is it optimal? Why or why not?

8. (This exercise is reprinted from Rothwell and Gomez with permission.) Assume that a cogeneration heating distribution system can be constructed for $14,600/kW and operated at a variable cost of $0 (heat is supplied by an industrial facility that operates 24 hours every day). Assume that, during eight hours of the day, the on-peak demand for heat is given by

$$P = 16 - 0.08Q$$

Further assume that during the other 16 hours of the day is one half of the on-peak demand, or

$$P = 16 - 0.16Q$$

a. If the existing capacity (Q) were 120 units, what would be the socially optimal prices during the on-peak hours and during the off-peak hours?

b. What would be the optimal capacity?

c. What would prices be at the optimal capacity?

CHAPTER 11

Case Study: The California Debacle (or What Not to Do)

11.1 INTRODUCTION

In 1996, FERC Orders 888 and 889 were passed to facilitate wholesale competition in the bulk power supply market. More specifically, Order 888 addresses the issues of open access to the transmission network, giving FERC jurisdiction over all transmission issues, especially pricing. Order 889 requires utilities to establish electronic systems to share information about available transmission capacity. In addition, as of June 30, 1996, 44 states and the District of Columbia (more than 88% of the nation's regulatory commissions) had started activities related to retail competition in one form or another.

California was the first state to pass restructuring legislation that allowed retail choice among consumers beginning in 1998. Prior to the passage of deregulation legislation, the electric industry in California comprised both publicly and investor-owned vertically integrated utilities (IOUs), the latter of which supplied 75% of California's retail load (Rothwell and Gomez, 2003). The remainder was served by a mix of publicly and cooperatively owned entities, and two of the largest cities in California were served by the former. In Los Angeles, the Los Angeles Department of Water and Power (LADWP) provided electricity to 9.6% of California's total native load customers. And in Sacramento, the Sacramento Municipal Utility District (SMUD) provided electric service to 4.0% of the total load in California.

At this time, the rates paid by ultimate consumers were among the highest in the nation and, like most states, distinguished by the type of customer (i.e., residential, commercial, industrial, or other). Figure 11.1 displays the average rates paid by California native load customers by customer class from 1990 to 2007. Note the rather precipitous increase after 1999, which is due to several factors that will be discussed in this case study.

Prior to passing restructuring legislation, the utilities were regulated by three separate and distinct entities: the California Public Utilities Commission

Electricity Cost Modeling Calculations
DOI: 10.1016/B978-1-85617-726-9.00011-X

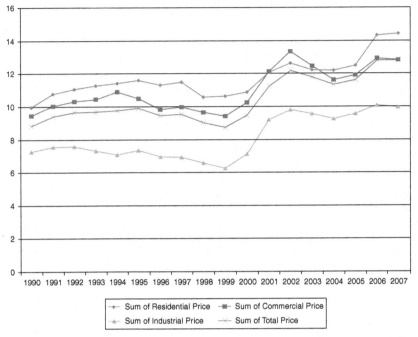

Figure 11.1

(CPUC), which had jurisdiction over the rates and operations of the utilities; the California Energy Commission (CEC), which oversees new plant siting and construction activities; and the Federal Energy Regulatory Commission (FERC), which regulates wholesale electricity trading and interstate transmission for all energy suppliers in every state.

Rates paid by end users in California were among the highest in the nation averaging 9 cents/kWh in 1998. By 2001, the confluence of events that transpired to lead to the California debacle resulted in even higher rates (a 24% increase over 1998 rates; by 2002, the increase was over 40%). Not surprising, the state of California has subsequently rescinded restructuring legislation.

11.2 THE ELECTRICITY CRISIS: SUMMER 2000

Factors precipitating the crisis

A confluence of events and poor decisions ultimately led to what is known as the *California Debacle*, including

1. No new generation in years.
2. Utilities were forced to divest generating assets and buy power back from a newly created power exchange at spot prices.
3. No bilateral trading.
4. Retail rates were frozen (even reduced by 10%).
5. Reliability was compromised—blackouts ensued.
6. Ability to game system (Cal ISO problems)—EnronOnline.

Each will be discussed in turn.

11.3 CHRONOLOGY OF THE CALIFORNIA ELECTRICITY CRISIS: LESSONS LEARNED (OR WHAT NOT TO DO)

Rather than building new generating assets in the years leading up to the restructuring of California's electric market to keep up with double-digit population growth (13% throughout the 1990s), the state relied on imported power from the north; the Bonneville Power Administration had been producing ample hydroelectric generation to supply much of the load in Washington and Oregon and had enough electricity to export power to California to supply the load that was not being met by California's own utilities. Despite this, California had among the highest rates in the country, which precipitated the passage of California Assembly Bill 1890 (AB 1890), which introduced competition into California's electricity market. Key features of AB 1890 included the establishment of the California independent system operator (CAISO) to operate the transmission facilities of California's investor-owned utilities, which encouraged (read: mandated) the investor-owned utilities to sell off their generation assets, requiring them to buy all their power in a newly created "spot" market run by the California Power Exchange (PX). In addition, the investor-owned utilities in the state were forbidden from entering into long-term, "bilateral" contracts, which can serve as a hedge against future price volatility. Furthermore, AB 1890 capped retail rates that the utilities could charge customers below the then current cost of electricity. From April 1998, when the California market commenced, until late May of 2000, the plan worked relatively well. But, in May 2000, spot prices began to rise notably: From 1999 to 2000, the total wholesale cost of supplying electricity to meet load in California nearly quadrupled, rising from $7.4 billion to $28 billion. Average wholesale electricity prices typically exceeded $100/MWh and, in some cases, exceeded $300/MWh. Unusually warm temperatures

CRISIS PRICES:

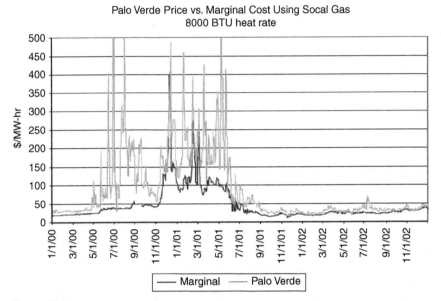

Figure 11.2

in the summer of 2000 coupled with the other factors delineated already resulted in prices reaching $500/MWh (Palo Verde, summer 2000), which was the imposed price cap at the time. This is displayed in Figure 11.2.

The drought conditions in the northwestern United States in 2000 resulted in a lower-than-anticipated water runoff to fuel the hydroelectric power generation on which California had become dependent. In addition, disruptions in the supply of natural gas (California utilities were predominantly gas fired, due to environmental standards) and transmission constraints further exacerbated the imbalance between supply and demand. Finally, the rules that accompanied California's restructuring legislation led to a situation that was ripe for market manipulation, which is exactly what transpired.

Unable to pass on the higher costs of purchasing electricity (due to the rate freezes that accompanied AB 1890), the utilities' financial well-being was severely jeopardized. And, in June 2000, rolling blackouts occurred in the San Francisco area. Two months later, San Diego Gas & Electric filed a complaint against the utilities that were selling into the California ISO and to the PX markets, requesting that the price cap that had been imposed at $500/MWh be lowered to $250/MWh. A formal investigation was launched, and in November, the FERC issued its report on the bulk power market in California:

the electric market structure and market rules for wholesale sales of electric energy in California are seriously flawed and that these structures and rules, in conjunction with an imbalance of supply and demand in California, have caused, and continue to have the potential to cause, unjust and unreasonable rates for short-term energy (Day-Ahead, Day-of, Ancillary Services and real-time energy sales) under certain conditions. While this record does not support findings of specific exercises of market power, and while we are not able to reach definite conclusions about the actions of individual sellers, there is clear evidence that the California market structure and rules provide the opportunity for sellers to exercise market power when supply is tight and can result in unjust and unreasonable rates under the FPA.

(See www.ferc.gov/industries/electric/indus–act/wec/chron/chronology.pdf for more detail)

A number of remedies were proposed, and on December 15, 2000, many were adopted.

Mistakes

The mistakes that were made in the adoption of restructuring legislation are enumerated here.

Mistake 1

As part of the restructuring process, AB 1890 required that the IOUs divest themselves of their generating assets, then required them to purchase the power required to serve native load (or load, since very few retail customers chose a different supplier) from the Power Exchange (this was to reduce the possibility of horizontal market power). (Note: The IOUs served 75% of California's native load in 1998.) In addition, no buyback provisions (or long-term power contracts, also known as *bilateral trades*) left utilities at the mercy of skyrocketing wholesale power prices (which reached $500/MWh in Palo Verde in the summer of 2000, see Figure 11.2).

Mistake 2

Under the guise of protecting ratepayers, not only were rates frozen but also a mandatory rate reduction was imposed—rates were reduced by 10% for residential and small commercial customers from 1996 levels in 1998 with the intention of reaching 20% by 2002. However, the crisis that ensued put an end to retail access in 2001. (Again, no price signal to consumers!) This coupled with Mistake 1 eventually led to huge losses for the IOUs and the almost financial ruin and subsequent bankruptcy of Pacific Gas & Electric, one of California's largest electric suppliers, which supplied 33.5% of the total native load in 1998.

Mistake 3

Reliance on imported power (20% in 1999) to serve native load left Californians even more exposed to the vagrancies of the wholesale power market and manipulation by the players in the game (see next section).

Mistake 4. The inability to game the system

Enron (and others) proved to be masterminds in figuring out ways to game the California market. Enron was instrumental in the development of a proprietary trading platform, EnronOnline, which became an industry trading platform that was used by many of the players in the industry to view bid and ask prices for electricity (and natural gas), to make trades, and to value portfolios, which were done via the Mark-to-Market accounting methodology.[1] Despite the fact that Enron traders spoke in codes (using the gaming nomenclature, described later, the FERC

---

[1] According to Wikipedia: (http://en.wikipedia.org/wiki/Mark-to-market_accounting), mark-to-market or fair value accounting refers to the accounting standards of assigning a value to a position held in a financial instrument based on the current fair market price for the instrument or similar instruments. Fair value accounting has been a part of US Generally Accepted Accounting Principles (GAAP) since the early 1990s, and investor demand for the use of fair value when estimating the value of assets and liabilities has increased steadily since then as investors desire a more realistic appraisal of an institution's or company's current financial situation. Mark-to-market is a measure of the fair value of accounts that can change over time, such as assets and liabilities. It is the act of recording the price or value of a security, portfolio or account to reflect its current market value rather than its book value.

The practice of *mark to market* as an accounting device first developed among traders on futures exchanges in the 20th century. It was not until the 1980s that the practice spread to big banks and corporations far from the traditional exchange trading pits, and beginning in the 1990s, mark-to-market accounting began to give rise to scandals.

To understand the original practice, consider that a futures trader, when taking a position, deposits money with the exchange, called a "margin." This is intended to protect the exchange against loss. At the end of every trading day, the contract is marked to its present market value. If the trader is on the winning side of a deal, his contract has increased in value that day, and the exchange pays this profit into his account. On the other hand, if the market price of his contract has declined, the exchange charges his account that holds the deposited margin. If the balance of this account falls below the deposit required to maintain the position, the trader must immediately pay additional margin into the account to maintain his position (a "margin call"). As an example, the Chicago Mercantile Exchange, taking the process one step further, marks positions to market *twice* a day, at 10:00 am and 2:00 pm.

As the practice of marking to market caught on in corporations and banks, some of them seem to have discovered that this was a tempting way to commit accounting fraud, especially when the market price could not be objectively determined (because there was no real day-to-day market available or the asset value was derived from other traded commodities, such as crude oil futures), so assets were being "marked to model" in a hypothetical or synthetic manner using estimated valuations derived from financial modeling, and sometimes marked in a manipulative way to achieve spurious valuations.

eventually caught on and Enron (and several others, including El Paso Natural Gas Trading Company, Williams Energy Marketing & Trading Company, and AES Southland, Inc.) were eventually brought down. Unfortunately, in the interim, the havoc wreaked on ratepayers, shareholders, and taxpayers was in the billions of dollars.

One such scheme, called *Fat Boy*, involved scheduling power to the California ISO to nonexistent or exacerbated loads. (The computer systems at the California ISO were apparently unable to recognize a systematic pattern of abuse.) A number of market participants engaged in this practice until the PX eventually caught on. In the meantime, it has been estimated that this scheme alone cost consumers over $3.5 billion (McCullough, 2003).

Another scheme was known as *wash trades*. According to the Federal Energy Regulatory Commission's *Final Report on Price Manipulation in Western Markets Fact-Finding Investigation of Potential Manipulation of Electric and Natural Gas Prices* (2003), the term *wash trade* is generally defined as a *prearranged* pair of trades of the same good between the same parties, involving no economic risk and no net change in beneficial ownership. These trades expose the parties to no monetary risk and serve no legitimate business purpose. Potential motives for wash trading are numerous. Wash trades might be used to create the illusion that a market is liquid and active or to increase reported trading revenue figures. Wash trades might be arranged at prices that diverge from the prevailing market in an attempt to send false signals to other market participants. Alternatively, the intent might be to affect the average or index price reported for a market, which in turn could benefit a derivatives position or affect the magnitude of payments on a contract linked to the index price.

The subsequent FERC findings were that: "In general, wash trading is viewed as damaging to the integrity of a market and has the potential to mislead a host of market stakeholders (including competitors, regulators, analysts, and investors) through the various forms of manipulation outlined above. Although the Commission has no regulations on wash trading, wash trades are prohibited in markets regulated by the Commodity Futures Trading Commission. This chapter provides statistical evidence indicating that wash trading in energy products was more common than previously recognized."

And, concerning EnronOnline, "Staff concludes that EnronOnline (EOL), which gave Enron proprietary knowledge of market conditions not available to other market participants, was a key enabler of wash trading" (FERC, 2003).

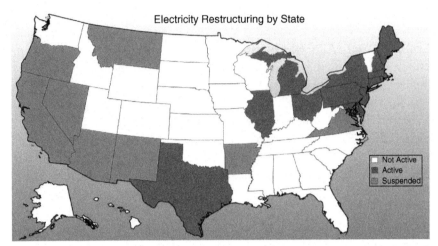

Figure 11.3 Status of electric restructuring, May 2009 *(Source: www.eia.doe.gov/cneaf/ electricity/page/restructuring/restructure_elect.html)*

This confluence of mistakes proved to be the fatal flaws in the dereg-ulation of the industry and eventually led to the subsequent reregulation in not only California but also seven other states, which are indicated in Figure 11.3.

11.4 CONCLUSION

So where do we go from here? That is an excellent question. Needless to say, there is no conclusion to be written, as the future of this industry is still unfolding (see Chapter 3 for details). There is still much to transpire (and to be learned and written) about in this industry.

Aigner, D., 1985. The Residential Electricity Time-of-Use Pricing Experiments: What Have We Learned? In: Hausman, J.A., Wise, D.A. (Eds.), Social Experimentation. University of Chicago Press, Chicago, pp. 11–54.

Alchian, A., Demsetz, H., 1972. Production, Information Costs, and Economic Organization. Am. Econ. Rev.

Arrow, K., Chenery, H., Minhas, B., Solow, R., 1961. Capital-Labor Substitution and Economic Efficiency. Rev. Econ. Stat. 43 (5), 225–254.

Atkinson, S.E., Halvorsen, R., 1984. Parametric Efficiency Tests, Economies of Scale, and Input Demand in the U.S. Electric Power Generation. International Economic Review 25 (3), 647–662.

Averch, H., Johnson, L., 1962. Behavior of the Firm under Regulatory Constraint. Am. Econ. Rev. 52 (5), 1052–1069.

Bailey, E., Friedlaender, A., 1982. Market Structure and Multiproduct Industries. Journal of Economic Literature 20, 1024–1048.

Barbose, G., Goldman, C., 2004. A Survey of Utility Experience with Real Time Pricing. Ernest Lawrence Berkeley National Laboratory, LBNL-54238.

Baumol, W., Panzar, J., Willig, R., 1982. Contestable Markets and the Theory of Industrial Structure. Harcourt, Brace, and Jovanovich, New York.

Baumol, W., Sidak, J.G., 1994. Toward Competition in Local Telephony. The MIT Press, Cambridge, MA.

Berndt, E., 1991. The Practice of Econometrics, Classic and Contemporary. Addison Wesley Publishing Co., Reading, MA.

Berndt, E., Wood, D., 1975. Technology, Prices, and the Derived Demand for Energy. Rev. Econ. Stat.

Berry, D., 1992. Rural Electric Cooperatives and the Cost Structure of the Electric Power Industry: A Multiproduct Analysis, dissertation.

Berry, D., 1994. Private Ownership Form and Productive Efficiency: Electric Cooperatives versus Investor-Owned Utilities. J. Regul. Econ. 6, 399–420.

Berry, W.W., 1983. The Deregulated Electric Utility Industry. In: Plummer, J., Ferrar, T., Hughes, W. (Eds.), Electric Power Strategic Issues. Public Utilities Reports, Inc., Arlington, VA, p. 3.

Bonbright, J.C., 1961. Principles of Public Utility Rates. Columbia University Press, New York.

Braithwait, S., Hansen, D., O'Sheasy, M., 2007. Retail Electricity Pricing and Rate Design in Evolving Markets. Christensen Associates Energy Consulting, LLC. Prepared for: Edison Electric Institute.

Brockway, N., 1997. Electric Deregulation May Leave Poor in Dark. Forum for Applied Research and Public Policy 11, 13–17.

Brown, S.J., Sibley, D.S., 1986. The Theory of Public Utility Pricing. Cambridge University Press, New York, NY.

Bullis, K., 2009. Pricing Carbon Emissions. Technol. Rev.

Lee, B.-J., 1995. Separability Test for the Electricity Supply Industry. Journal of Applied Econometrics 10, 49–60.

California Energy Commission, 2007. Integrated Energy Policy Report. see www.energy.ca.gov/2007_energypolicy/.

Charnes, A., Cooper, W., Sueyoshi, T., 1988. A Goal Programming/Constrained Regression Review of the Bell System Breakup. Manag. Sci. 34 (1), 1–26.

Carruthers, C., 2008. Twombly and the Evolution of Telecom Regulation. The Antitrust Bulletin 53 (1), 95–116.

Casten, S., Meyer, J., 2004. Cross Subsidies: Getting the Signals Right: Should Regulators Care about the Inefficiencies? Public Utilities Fortnightly December.

Caves, D.W., Christensen, L.R., Tretheway, M.W., 1984. Economies of Density versus Economies of Scale: Why Trunk and Local Service Airline Costs Differ. Rand J. Econ. 15, 471–489.

Chiang, A., 1984. Fundamental Methods of Mathematical Economics. McGraw-Hill, New York.

Christensen, L., Cummings, D., Schoech, P., 1981. Econometric Estimation of Scale Economies in Telecommunications. Working Paper No. 8124, SSRI, University of Wisconsin—Madison.

Christensen, L., Greene, W., 1976. Economies of Scale in U.S. Electric Power Generation. Journal of Political Economy 84, 655–676.

Christensen, L., Jorgenson, D., Lau, L., 1970. Conjugate Duality and the Transcendental Logarithmic Production Function. Econometrica 225–256.

Claggett Jr., E.T., 1987. Cooperative Distributors of Electrical Power: Operations and Scale Economies. Quarterly Journal of Business and Economics 26 (3), 3.

Claggett Jr., E.T., 1994. A Cost Function Study of the Providers of TVA Power. Managerial and Decision Economics 15, 63–72.

Claggett, E., Hollas, D., Stansell, S., 1995. The Effects of Ownership Form on Profit Maximization and Cost Minimization Behavior within Municipal and Cooperative Electric Distribution Utilities. Q. Rev. Econ. Finance 35 (Special Issue), 533–550.

Clinton Administration, 1999. The Comprehensive Electricity Competition Act, March 1999.

Coase, R.H., 1946. The Marginal Cost Controversy. Economica 13, 169–182.

Comnes, G.A., Stoft, S., Greene, N., Hill, L., 1995. Performance—Based Regulation for Electric Utilities: Review of Plans and Analysis of Economic and Resource Planning Issues, vol. 1. Lawrence Berkeley National Laboratory.

Conkling, R.L., 1999. Marginal Cost Pricing for Utilities: A Digest of the California Experience. Contemporary Economic Policy 17.

Costello, K., 2006. Revenue Decoupling for Natural Gas Utilities. NRRI Briefing, Paper (06–06).

Crandall, R., 1991. After the Breakup. The Brookings Institute, Washington DC.

Crew, M.A., 1985. Analyzing the Impact of Regulatory Change in Public Utilities. D. C. Heath and Company, Lexington, MA.

Crew, M.A., 1992. Economic Innovations in Public Utility Regulation. Kluwer Academic Publishers, Boston.

De Alessi, T., 1974. An Economic Analysis of Government Ownership and Regulation: Theory and the Evidence from the Electric Power Industry. Public Choice 19 (1), 1–42.

Demsetz, H., 1968. Why Regulate Utilities? Journal of Law and Economics.

Diewert, E., 1971. An Application of the Shepard Duality Theorem: A Generalized Linear Production Function. Journal of Political Economy 79 (3), 482–507.

Diewert, W.E., Wales, T.J., 1991. Multiproduct Cost Functions and Subadditivity Tests: A Critique of the Evans and Heckman Research on the U.S. Bell Systems. Discussion Paper No. 91–21, University of British Columbia, Victoria.

Edison Electric Institute, 1998. Electric Utility Restructuring/Competition Issues. Edison Electric Institute, Washington, DC.

Edison Electric Institute, 2007. Retail Electricity Pricing and Rate Design in Evolving Markets. Edison Electric Institute, Washington, D.C.

Electric Power Research Institute, 1984. Adapting State and National Electricity Consumption Forecasting Methods to Utility Service Territories. EPRI EA-3622.

Evans, D.S. (Ed.), 1983. Breaking up Bell: Essays on Industrial Organization and Regulation. North Holland, New York.

Evans, D.S., Heckman, J.J., 1984. A Test for Subadditivity of the Cost Function with an Application to the Bell System. Am. Econ. Rev. 74 (4), 615–623.

Fare, R., Grosskopf, S., Logan, J., 1985. The Relative Performance of Publicly-Owned and Privately-Owned Electric Utilities. Journal of Public Economics 26 (1), 89–106.

Fisher, F., Kaysen, C., 1962. A Study in Econometrics: The Demand for Electricity in the United States. North-Holland, Amsterdam.

Fraquaelli, G., Piancenza, M., Vannoni, D., 2004. Scope and Scale Economies in Multi-Utilities: Evidence from Gas, Water and Electricity Combinations. Appl. Econ. 36 (18), 2045–2057.

Fraquaelli, G., Piancenza, M., Vannoni, D., 2005. Cost Savings from Generation and Distribution with an Application to Italian Electric Utilities. J. Regul. Econ. 28 (3), 289–308.

Freshwater, D., 1999. Testimony before the U.S. House of Representatives Committee on Agriculture, Hearing on Electricity Deregulation.

Freshwater, D., Goetz, S., Samson, S., Stone, J., Johansson, T., Greer, M., 1997. The Consequences of Changing Electricity Regulations for Rural Communities in Kentucky. National Rural Electric Cooperative Association, Lexington, KY.

Fuss, M., Waverman, L., 1981. The Regulation of Telecommunications in Canada. Economic Council of Canada, Ontario.

Gabel, D., Kennet, D., 1994. Economies of Scope in the Local Telephone Exchange Market. J. Regul. Econ. 6, 381–398n.

Gallop, F., Roberts, M., 1981. The Source of Economic Growth in the U.S. Electric Power Industry. In: Cowing, T., Stevenson, R. (Eds.), Productivity Measurement in Regulated Industries. Academic Press, New York.

Giles, D., Wyatt, N., 1989. Economies of Scale in the New Zealand Electricity Distribution Industry. In: Performance Measures and Economies of Scale in the New Zealand Electricity Distribution System. Ministry of Energy, Wellington, New Zealand.

Gilsdorf, K., 1994. Vertical Integration Efficiencies and Electric Utilities: A Cost Complementarity Perspective. Q. Rev. Econ. Finance.

Gilsdorf, K., 1995. Testing for Subadditivity of Vertically Integrated Electric Utilities. Southern Economics Journal 62 (14), 126–138.

Glyer, D., Herrara, C., 1997. The Effects of Retail Access on Rural Electric Cooperatives: A Study of Distribution Co-op Customers in Wisconsin. National Rural Electric Cooperative Association.

Goldfeld, S.M., Quandt, R.E., Trotter, H.F., 1966. Maximization by Quadratic Hill Climbing. Econometrica 34, .

Goto, M., Nemoto, J., 2004. Technological Externalities and Economies of Vertical Integration in the Electric Utility Industry. International Journal of Industrial Organization 22, 676–681.

Grace, R.C., Rickerson, W., Corfee, K., 2008. California Feed-in Tariff Design and Policy Options. Prepared for the California Energy Commission. Publication number: CEC-300-2008-009D. Accessed at www.energy.ca.gov/2008publications/CEC-300-2008-009/CEC-300-2008-009-D.PDF.

Greene, W., 1983. Simultaneous Estimation of Factor Substitution, Economies of Scale, Productivity, and Non-Neutral Technical Change. In: Dogramaci, A. (Ed.), Econometric Analysis of Productivity. Kluwer-Nijoff, Boston.

Greene, W., 1993. Econometric Analysis, second ed. Macmillan Publishing Co, New York.

Greer, M.L., 2003. Can Rural Electric Cooperatives Survive in a Restructured US Electric Market? An Empirical Analysis. Energy Economics 25 (3), 487–508.

Greer, M.L., 2008. A Test of Vertical Economies for Non-Vertically Integrated Firms: The Case of Rural Electric Cooperatives. Energy Economics 30 (5), 679–687.

Harunuzzaman, M., Koundinya, S., 2000. Cost Allocation and Rate Design for Unbundled Gas Services. The National Regulatory Research Institute (NRRI 00-08).

Hayashi, P., Sevier, M., Trapani, J., 1987. An Analysis of Pricing and Production Efficiency of Electric Utilities by Mode of Ownership. In: Crew, M.A. (Ed.), Regulating Utilities in an Era of Deregulation. St. Martin's Press, New York.

Hayashi, P., Sevier, M., Trapani, J., 1985. Pricing Efficiency Under Rate-of-Return Regulation: Some Empirical Evidence for the Electric Utility Industry. Southern Economic Journal 51.

Hayashi, P.M., Yeoung-Jia Goo, J., Chamberlain, W.C., 1997. Vertical Economies: The Case of U.S. Electric Utility Industry, 1983–1987. Southern Economics Journal 710–725.

Heady, E., Dillon, J., 1961. Agricultural Production Functions. Iowa State University Press, Ames.

Henderson, J.S., 1985. Cost Estimation for Vertically Integrated Firms. In: Crew, M. (Ed.), Analyzing the Impact of Regulatory Change in Public Utilities. D. C. Heath, Lexington, MA.

Hiebert, L.D., 2002. The Determinants of the Cost Efficiency of Electric Generating Plants: A Stochastic Frontier Approach. Southern Economic Journal 68 (4), 935–946.

Hirst, E., Carney, J., 1978. The ORNL Engineering-Economic Model of Residential Energy Use. Ridge National Laboratory, Oak. ORNL/CON-24.

Hollas, D., Stansell, S., 1991. Regulation, Ownership Form, and the Economic Efficiency of Rural Electric Distribution Cooperatives. Review of Regional Studies 21, 201–220.

Hollas, D.R., Stansell, S.R., Claggett, E.T., 1994. Ownership Form and Rate Structure: An Examination of Cooperative and Municipal Electric Distribution Utilities. Southern Economic Journal 61 (2), 519–529.

Hollas, D.R., Stansell, S.R., Claggett, E.T., 1988. An Examination of the Effect of Ownership Form on Price Efficiency: Proprietary, Cooperative, and Municipal Electric Utilities. Southern Economic Journal 336–350.

Hotelling, H., 1938. The General Welfare in Relation to Taxation and of Railway and Utility Rates. Econometrica 6 (3), 242–269.

Houthakker, H.S., 1951. Electricity Tariffs in Theory and Practice. Economics Journal 61, 1–25.

Huettner, D.A., Landon, J.H., 1977. Electric Utilities: Scale Economies and Diseconomies. Southern Economic Journal 44, 892–912.

Hyman, L.S., 1994. America's Electric Utilities: Past, Present and Future, fifth ed. Public Utilities Reports, Inc., Arlington, VA, p. 102.

Jacobsson, S., Lauber, V., 2005. Germany: From a Modest Feed-in Law to a Framework for Transition. In: Lauber, V. (Ed.), Switching to Renewable Power: A Framework for the 21st Century. Earthscan, London, pp. 122–158.

Joskow, P.L., 1997. Restructuring, Competition and Regulatory Reform in the U.S. Electricity Sector. J. Econ. Perspect. 11 (3), 119–138.

Joskow, P.L., Schamalensee, R., 1983. Markets for Power: An Analysis of Electricity Utility Deregulation. MIT Press, Cambridge, MA.

Kahn, A.E., 1970 and 1971. The Economics of Regulation: Principles and Institutions (volume I: Economic Principles, 1970; volume II: Institutional Issues, 1971). John Wiley & Sons Inc., New York.

Kahn, A., 1990. Thoughts on the Past, Present, and Future of Telecommunications Regulation. In: Allison, J., Thomas, D. (Eds.), Telecommunications Deregulation: Market Power and Cost Allocation Issues. Quorum Books, New York.

Kamerschen, D.R., Thompson, J.R., 1993. Nuclear and Fossil-Fuel Steam Generation of Electricity: Differences and Similarities. Southern Economic Journal 60, 14–27.

Karlson, S.H., 1986. Multiple-Output Production and Pricing in Electric Utilities. Southern Economics Journal 73–86.

Kaserman, D., Mayo, J., 1991. The Measurement of Vertical Economies and the Efficient Structure of the Electric Utility Industry. Southern Economics Journal 39 (5), 483–502.

Keeler, A.G., 2008. State Commission Electricity Regulation under a Federal GHG Cap-and-Trade. NRRI Publication, John Glenn School of Public Affairs, Ohio State University.

Kelly, J., 2007. Renewed Interest in Demand Response, but "Wither the Economic Rationale for Efficient Pricing?" USAEE Dialogue August.

Kiss, F.S., Karabadjan, Lefebvre, B., 1981. Economics of Scale and Scope in Bell Canada. In: Courville, L., et al., (Ed.), Economic Analysis of Telecommunications: Theory and Applications. North-Holland, New York, 1981.

Kiss, F., Lefebvre, B., 1987. Econometric Models of Telecommunications Firms: A Survey. Revue economique 38 (2), 307–374.

Klein, A., Pfluger, B., Held, A., Ragwitz, M., Resch, G., Faber, T., 2008. Evaluation of Different Feed-in Tariff Design Options. In: Best Practice Paper for the International Feed-in Cooperation. Second ed., funded by the Ministry for the Environment, Nature Conservation and Nuclear Safety (BMU). Available at www.feed-in-cooperation.org/images/files/best_practice_paper_2nd_edition_final.pdf.

Kleit, A.N., Terrell, D., 2001. Measuring Potential Efficiency Gains from Deregulation of Electricity Generation: A Bayesian Approach. Rev. Econ. Stat. 83 (3), 523–530.

Koomey, J., Brown, R., Richey, R., Johnson, F., Sanstad, A., Hanford, J., 1994. Residential HVAC Data, Assumptions and Methodology for End-Use Forecasting with EPRI-REEPS 2.1. LBL-34045. Ernest Orlando Lawrence Berkeley National Laboratory, University of California, Berkeley.

Koomey, J., Brown, R., Richey, R., Johnson, F., Sanstad, A., Shown, L., 1995. Residential Sector End-Use Forecasting with EPRIREEPS 2.1: Summary Input Assumptions and Results. LBL-34044, Ernest Orlando Lawrence Berkeley National Laboratory, University of California, Berkeley.

Kwoka, J., 1996. Power Structure: Ownership, Integration, and Competition in the U.S. Electricity Industry. Kluwer Academic Publishers, Boston.

Landon, J., 1983. Theories of Vertical Integration and Their Application to the Electric Utility Industry. Antitrust Bulletin 101–130.

Leontief, W., 1941. The Structure of the American Economy, 1919–1939: An Empirical Application of Equilibrium Analysis. Oxford University Press, New York.

Lee, B., 1995. Separability Test for the Electricity Supply Industry. Journal of Applied Econometrics John Wiley & Sons, Ltd., 10 (1), 49–60.

Maloney, M., 2001. Economies and Diseconomies: Estimating Electricity Cost Functions. Rev. Ind. Organ. 19 (2), 165–180.

Marshall, A., 1927. Principles of Economics. Macmillan, London.

Mayo, J.W., 1984. The Multiproduct Monopoly, Regulation, and Firm Costs. Southern Economics Journal (51), 208–218.

Mayo, J.W., Kaserman, D.L., 1991. The Measurement of Vertical Economies and the Efficient Structure of the Electric Utility Industry. Journal of Industrial Economics 39 (5), 483–505.

McMenamin, S., Rohmund, I., Pritchard, J., Fabiszak, D., 1992. REEPS 2.1: Residential End-Use Energy Planning System User's Guide. Prepared by Regional Economic Research, Inc. for the Electric Power Research Institute. EPRI Research Project 2863–01.

McCullough, R., 2003. Regional Economic Losses from Enron's Fat Boy Scheme, memorandum, May.

Meyer, R.A., 1975. Publicly Owned versus Privately Owned Utilities: A Policy Choice. Rev. Econ. Stat. (4), 391–399.

Mitchell, B.M., Vogelsang, I., 1991. Telecommunications Pricing: Theory and Practice. Cambridge University Press, Cambridge, England.

Moore, T., 1970. The Effectiveness of Regulation of Electric Utility Prices. Southern Economics Journal 36, 365–375.

Moss, C., Production Economics AEB6184, Lecture 20: "Subadditivity of Cost Functions." Available at ricardo.ifas.ufl.edu/aeb6184.production/Lectureper cent2020-2005.ppt.

Mueller, M.L., 1997. Universal Service: Competition, Interconnection, and Monopoly in the Making of the American Telephone System. MIT Press., Cambridge, MA.

National Action Plan for Energy Efficiency, 2007. Aligning Utility Incentives with Investment in Energy Efficiency, prepared by Val R. Jensen, ICF International.

National Rural Electric Cooperative Association, 1997. Facts about Electric Cooperatives (accessed via Web site at www.nreca.org/coops/elecoop3.html).

Nerlove, M., 1963. Returns to Scale in Electricity Supply. In: Christ, C. (Ed.), Measurement in Economics: Studies in Mathematical Economics and Econometrics in Memory of Yehuda Grunfeld. Stanford University Press, Stanford, CA, pp. 167–198.

Network for New Energy Choices, 2008. Freeing the Grid: Best and Worst Practices in State Net Metering Policies and Interconnection Standards. Network for New Energy Choices, New York.

Neuberg, L.G., 1977. Two Issues in the Municipal Ownership of Electric Power Distribution Systems. Bell Journal of Economics 303–323.

Osborne, M., 2007. Mathematical Methods for Economic Theory: A Tutorial. University of Toronto, Toronto.

Panzar, J., Willig, R., 1997. Economies of Scale in Multi-Output Production. The Quarterly Journal of Economics MIT Press 91 (3), 481–493.

Pelzman, S., 1971. Pricing in Public and Private Enterprises: Electric Utilities in the United States. Journal of Law and Economics.

Pescatrice, D., Trapani, J., 1980. The Performance and Objectives of Public and Private Utilities Operating in the United States. Journal of Public Economics 13 (2), 259–276.

Phillips, A., 1984. The Reintegration of Telecommunications: An Interim View. In: Crew, M.A. (Ed.), Analyzing the Impact of Regulatory Change in Public Utilities. D.C. Heath and Company, Lexington, MA.

Pollitt, M., 1995. Ownership and Performance in Electric Utilities. Oxford University Press, Oxford, New York.

Primeaux, W.J., 1986. Direct Electric Utility Competition. Praeger, New York.

Ramos-Real, F.J., 2004. Cost Functions and the Electric Utility Industry. A Contribution to the Debate on Deregulation. www.grjm.net/documents/Divers-WP/ramos-real-2004.pdf.

Ramsey, F., 1927. A Contribution to the Theory of Taxation. Economic Journal 37, (145), 47–61.

Roberts, M., 1986. Economies of Density and Size in the Production and Delivery of Electric Power. Land Economics November.

Roller, L., 1990. Proper Quadratic Cost Functions with an Application to the Bell System. Rev. Econ. Stat. 72 (2), 202–210.

Rothwell, G., Gomez, T., 2003. Electricity Economics: Regulation and Deregulation. IEEE Press, New York.

Salvanes, K., Tjotta, S., 1994. Productivity Differences in Multiple Output Industries: An Empirical Application to Electricity Distribution. J. Prod. Anal. 5, 23–43.

Salvanes, K., Tijotta, S., 1998. A Test for Natural Monopoly with Application to Norwegian Electricity Distribution. Rev. Ind. Organ. 13, 669–685.

Schmalensee, R., 1978. A Note on Economies of Scale and Natural Monopoly in the Distribution of Public Utility Services. Bell Journal of Economics 9, 270–276.

Sharkey, W., 1982. The Theory of Natural Monopoly. Cambridge University Press, Cambridge U.K.

Shin, R., Ying, J., 1992. Unnatural Monopoly in Local Telephone. Rand J. Econ. 23, 171–183.

Shin, R., Ying, J., 1993. Costly Gains to Breaking up: LECS and the Baby Bells. Rev. Econ. Stat. 75 (2), 357–361.

Sing, M., 1987. Are Combination Gas and Electric Utilities Multiproduct Natural Monopolies? Rev. Econ. Stat. 392–398.

Smith, J., Carbo, J., 1979. Economies of Scale and Economies of Scope in Bell Canada. Working Paper, Department of Economics, Concordia University, Montreal.

Sovacool, B.K., Brown, M.A., 2010. Is Bigger Always Better? The Importance of Sorting out Scale in Addressing Climate Change. In: Generating Electricity in a Carbon Constrained World. Elsevier, Burlington, MA.

Stigler, G.J., Friedlander, C., 1962. What Can Regulators Regulate? The Case of Electricity. Journal of Law and Economics October 1–17.

Studenmund, A.H., 1997. Using Econometrics: A Practical Guide. Addison-Wesley.

Taylor, L., Blattenberger, G., Rennhack, R., 1984. Residential Energy Demand in the United States: Empirical Results for Electricity. In: Moroney, J.R. (Ed.), Advances in the Economics of Energy and Resources, vol. 5. JAI Press, Greenwich, CN, pp. 103–127.

Taylor, L., Blattenberger, G., Verleger, P., 1977. The Residential Demand for Energy. EPRI EA-235.

Thompson, H.G., 1995. Economies of Scale and Vertical Integration in the Investor-Owned Electric Utility Industry. NRRI Publication.

Thompson, H.G., 1997. Cost Efficiency in Power Procurement and Delivery Service in the Electric Utility Industry. Land Economics 73 (3), 287–296.

Thompson Jr., H.G., Rose, K., 1996. Merge, Consolidate, Grow, or Spin Off? The Costs and Synergies of Vertical Integration. Public Utilities Fortnightly September.

Thompson Jr., H.G., Rose, K., 1996. Is the U.S. Rushing into the Dark? A Special Report. Electrical World October.

Thompson, H.G., Wolf, L., 1993. Regional Differences in Nuclear and Fossil-Fuel Generation of Electricity. Land Economics 69 (3), 234–248.

U.S. Bureau of the Census, 1975. Historical Statistics of the United States, Colonial Times to 1970, Bicentennial Edition, Part 2. U.S. Department of Commerce, Washington, DC.

U.S. Committee on Energy and Natural Resources of the United States Senate, The American Clean Energy Leadership Act of 2009. Available at http://energy.senate .gov/public/_files/TheAmericanCleanEnergyLeadershipActof2009.pdf.

U.S. Congressional Budget Office, Congressional Budget Office Cost Estimate of H.R, 2454, The American Clean Energy and Security Act of 2009. Available at www .cbo.gov/ftpdocs/102xx/doc10262/hr2454.pdf.

U.S. Department of Agriculture, Economic Research Service, U.S. Fact Sheet: Population, Employment, and Income, 1997 Data. Government Printing Office, Washington, DC.

U.S. Department of Agriculture, 2000, Economic Research Service, Briefing Room— Rural Labor and Education (accessed via Web site at www.ers.usda.gov).

U.S. Department of Agriculture, Rural Utilities Service, 1997a. 1996 Statistical Report Rural Electric Borrowers. Government Printing Office, Washington, DC.

U.S. Department of Agriculture, Rural Utilities Service, 1997b. 1997 Statistical Report Rural Electric Borrowers. Government Printing Office, Washington, DC.

U.S. Department of Energy, Energy Information Administration, 1996a. Annual Outlook for U.S. Electric Power.

U.S. Department of Energy, Energy Information Administration, 1996b. Factors Underlying the Restructuring of the Electric Power Industry.

U.S. Department of Energy, Energy Information Administration, 1997. The Changing Structure of the Electric Power Industry. pp. 1–7.

U.S. Department of Energy, Energy Information Administration, Status of State Electric Industry Activity as of January, 2002. www.eia.doe.gov/cneaf/electricity/chg_str/regmap.html.

U.S. Department of Energy, Energy Information Administration, 2007. "Emissions of Greenhouse Gases Report" and "Electric Power Annual."

U.S. Department of Energy, Energy Information Administration, 2008. Annual Energy Outlook Retrospective Review: Evaluation of Projections in Past Editions (1982–2008). http://www.eia.doe.gov/oiaf/analysispaper/retrospective/pdf/0640(2008).pdf.

U.S. Department of Energy, Energy Information Administration, 2009a. Electric Power Industry 2007: Year in Review. www.eia.doe.gov/cneaf/electricity/epa/epa_sum.html.

U.S. Department of Energy, Energy Information Administration, 2009b. Electric Sales, Revenues and Price. www.eia.doe.gov/cneaf/electricity/esr/esr_sum.html.

U.S. Department of Energy, Energy Information Administration, 2009c. An Updated Annual Energy Outlook 2009 Reference Case Reflecting Provisions of the American Recovery and Reinvestment Act and Recent Changes in the Economic Outlook. Report SR-OIAF/2009–03. www.eia.doe.gov/oiaf/servicerpt/stimulus/summary.html.

U.S. Department of Energy, Energy Information Administration, 2009d. Energy Market and Economic Impacts of H.R. 2454, the American Clean Energy and Security Act of 2009. Report SR-OIAF/2009–05. www.eia.doe.gov/oiaf/servicerpt/hr2454/background.html.

U.S. Department of Energy, Energy Information Administration, 2009. Emissions of Green House Gases in the United States in 2008. DOE/EIA-0573(2008).

U.S. Department of Energy, Energy Information Administration, 2010. Electric Power Monthly with Data for December 2009. www.eia.doe.gov/cneaf/electricity/epm/table5_6_b.html.

U.S. Environmental Protection Agency, 2007. National Action Plan for Energy Efficiency.

U.S. Federal Energy Regulatory Commission, 1993. Policy Statement Regarding Regional Transmission Groups. RM93-3-000, July 30.

U.S. Federal Energy Regulatory Commission, 1994. Transmission Policy Statement. RM93-19-001.

U.S. Federal Energy Regulatory Commission, 1995. Final Rule Order on Reconsideration and Clarifying the Policy Statement, May 22.

U.S. Federal Energy Regulatory Commission, 1996. Orders 888 and 889, Final Rule. RM95-8-000, and RM94-7-001, April 24.

U.S. Federal Energy Regulatory Commission, 1999. Order Number 2000. RTO—Final Rule Issued on December 20.

U.S. Federal Energy Regulatory Commission, 2000a. Order 2000 United States of America 90 FERC 61. 201 Federal Energy Regulatory Commission. 18 CFR Part 35[Docket NoRM99–2-001; Order No. 2000A] Regional Transmission Organizations (issued February 25, 2000b).

U.S. Federal Energy Regulatory Commission, 2005. The Western Energy Crisis, the Enron Bankruptcy, and FERC's Response. Available at www.ferc.gov/industries/electric/indus-act/wec/chron/chronology.pdf.

U.S. Federal Energy Regulatory Commission, 2003. Final Report on Price Manipulation in Western Markets Fact-Finding Investigation of Potential Manipulation of Electric and Natural Gas Prices. Docket No. PA02-2-000. Staff of the Federal Energy Regulatory Commission, March.

U.S. Office of Management and Budget, 2007. Budget of the United States Government. Fiscal Year 2008—Appendix. Department of Agriculture, Washington, DC, p. 146. Available at http://www.whitehouse.gov/omb/budget/fy2008/appendix.html.

Varian, H., 1984. Microeconomic Analysis, second ed. W. W. Norton, New York.

Vinod, H., 1976. Application of New Ridge Regression Methods to a Study of Bell System Scale Economies. Journal of the American Statistical Association 71 (356), 835–841.

Vogelsang, I., Mitchell, B., 1997. Local Telephone Competition: The Last Ten Miles. MIT Press and AEI Press, Cambridge, MA.

White, H., 1980. A Heteroskedasticity-Consistent Covariance Matrix Estimator and a Direct Test for Heteroskedasticity. Econometrics 48, 817–838.

Williamson, O.E., 1971. The Vertical Integration of Production: Market Failure Consideration. Am. Econ. Rev. 114–118.

Yatchew, A., 2000. Scale Economies in Electricity Distribution: A Semiparametric Analysis. Journal of Applied Econometrics 15 (2), 187–210.

Zellner, A., 1962. An Efficient Method of Estimating Seemingly Unrelated Regression Equations and Tests for Aggregation Bias. Journal of the American Statistical Association 57, 348–368.

Note: Page numbers followed by *f* indicate figures, *t* indicate tables.

Printed in the United States
By Bookmasters